# ENGAGING TERROR

THE HUMAN CONDITION SERIES

# ENGAGING TERROR
## A CRITICAL AND INTERDISCIPLINARY APPROACH

THE HUMAN CONDITION SERIES EDITORIAL BOARD

BrownWalker Press
Boca Raton

*Engaging Terror: A Critical and Interdisciplinary Approach*

The Human Condition Series Editorial Board:
Jane Haig
Anas Karzai
Guy Kirby Letts
Hermínio Meireles Teixeira
Marianne Vardalos

Copyright © 2009 Jane Haig, Anas Karzai, Guy Kirby Letts,
Hermínio Meireles Teixeira, and Marianne Vardalos
All rights reserved.
No part of this book may be reproduced or transmitted in any form or by any means, electronic or mechanical, including photocopying, recording, or by any information storage and retrieval system, without written permission from the publisher.

BrownWalker Press
Boca Raton, Florida • USA
2009

ISBN-10: 1-59942-453-3 *(paper)*
ISBN-13: 978-1-59942-453-8 *(paper)*

ISBN-10: 1-59942-497-5 *(ebook)*
ISBN-13: 978-1-59942-497-2 *(ebook)*

www.brownwalker.com

Library of Congress Cataloging-in-Publication Data

Engaging terror : a critical and interdisciplinary approach / [edited by] Marianne Vardalos ... [et al.].
      p. cm.
   Includes bibliographical references.
   ISBN-13: 978-1-59942-453-8 (pbk. : alk. paper)
   ISBN-10: 1-59942-453-3 (pbk. : alk. paper)
   1. Terrorism. 2. Terrorism and mass media. 3. Terrorism--Psychological aspects. I. Vardalos, Marianne, 1966- II. Title.

HV6431.E547 2009
363.325--dc22

2009030133

This book is dedicated to the potential of humanity
and those committed to it.

*"Terror becomes total when it becomes independent of all opposition: it rules supreme when nobody any longer stands in its way."* —Hannah Arendt

# Table of Contents

Foreword ............................................................................................. XIII
Preface and Acknowledgments ........................................................... XV
List of Contributors ........................................................................... XVII

Introduction
*Guy Kirby Letts* ................................................................................. 19

The Rhythm of Terror
*Nandan Choksi* ................................................................................. 23

Who is the Terrorist?: Analyzing the Discourse and Practices Surrounding the Confrontation Between Governments and Insurgent Organizations
*Maritza Felices-Luna* ........................................................................ 31

Media as an Anti-Peace Making Tool in the Context of Globalization: Analyzing News Coverage in a Time of Terror and War
*Narges Valibeigi* ................................................................................ 43

The Media in the Service of Terrorism
*Dario Kuntić* ..................................................................................... 67

Liberalism and Governmentality in the War on Terror
*Matthew Morgan* ............................................................................... 75

Combating Terror of Law in Colonial India: The Law of Sedition and the Nationalist Response
*Aravind Ganachari* ............................................................................ 93

Terror, Outlawry, and the Experience of the Impossible
*Mary Bunch* ...................................................................................... 111

What's in a Name? Interpreting Terrorism from the Perspective of Personal Construct Theory
*James Horley and Ian McPhail* .......................................................... 119

On Terror Considered As One of the Fine Arts
*Milo Sweedler* ................................................................................... 129

IX

Some Thoughts on Political Terrorism and Film Music
*Panayiotis Demopoulos* .................................................................................. 141

Re(con)figuring the Spectacle: State Flexibility in Response
to Imaged Terror
*Rebecca A. Adelman* ..................................................................................... 149

"Don't Say the Zed Word!": Toward a Linguistic Construction
of Social Class in the Contemporary *Living Dead* Film
*Leslie Russell Ashby* ...................................................................................... 159

Fate and Terror in Don DeLillo's *Falling Man*
*Christine Muller* ............................................................................................ 167

Terror as Text: DeLillo's *Falling Man* and the Representation
of Poker as Terror
*Charly Norton* ............................................................................................... 175

Creative Action: Language and Gender Beyond Terror
*Stephanie Barann* .......................................................................................... 185

Cosmopolitan Hospitality in Post-9/11 Popular Fiction:
Asad's *The Reluctant Fundamentalist*
*Amy Hildreth* ................................................................................................ 195

Stereotyping Islam: A Critical Study of Terror in John
Updike's *Terrorist*
*Amal Al-Leithy* .............................................................................................. 203

The Tyrannizing Order of Mental Health Promotion
*Cindy Vander Meulen* ................................................................................... 209

Terror of AIDS: Risky Sexual Behavior of Migrants
in Two Cities of India
*Parveen Nangia* ............................................................................................. 229

Addressing Terror Through Group Psyche
*Sophia C. Hughes* .......................................................................................... 245

Curing and Educating Through Terror: (A Comparative Case Study)
*Razvan Amironesei* ........................................................................................ 255

# Table of Contents

The Possibility of Terror Through the Story of Anxiety
*Melissa Abbey Strowger* ............................................................................ 269

Constructing the Aboriginal Terrorist: Depictions of Aboriginal
Protestors, the Caledonia Reclamation, and Canadian Neoliberalization
*Jennifer Adese* ........................................................................................... 275

Unresolved Issues: The Roots of the 1970 FLQ Crisis in the
Rebellions of 1837-1838 in Lower Canada
*Marty Wood* .............................................................................................. 287

Technologies of Resistance: The Role of Public and Collective Memory
in Responding to Past and Present State-Violence in Argentina
*Ana Laura Pauchulo* .................................................................................. 301

Terrorizing (Un)citizens: A Genealogy of Security Certificates
*Sarah Hamilton* ......................................................................................... 309

CTOs: A New Order of Terror?
*Katie Aubrecht* .......................................................................................... 323

Taking Back Projections:
The Despair and Hope in Projective Identification
*Karyne Messina* ........................................................................................ 331

Learning Rules And Roles
*Dianne D. Bergsma* ................................................................................... 345

Narrative Interlude: The Rules and the Game
*Beatrix Prinsen* ......................................................................................... 351

The Rules Do Not Make a Game
*Maureen Connolly* ..................................................................................... 357

Youth Terror or Terrorized Youth? Youth Violence in Nigeria:
Redefining Spaces of Politics and Belonging
*Andrea Kirschner* ...................................................................................... 369

Humanist Terrorism in the Political Thought of Robespierre and Sartre
*Timothy Johnson* ...................................................................................... 387

The Importance of Propaganda for Germany's Fascist Regime:
A Comparison of Two Academic Accounts
*Beatrice Marry* ................................................................................................ 399

The Man with the Hissing Bomb: Anarchism and Terror in the
North American Imagination
*Richard JF Day* ............................................................................................... 405


Endorsements for *Engaging Terror* ................................................................ 415

# Foreword

It seems right to say that since 9/11, all western societies have been forced to accept the significance of international and non-nation-state forms of terrorism. As these forms of terrorism have only spread and worsened globally, a conference on terror would be very timely. But if 9/11 changed anything with respect to this timeline, it was not in forcing the sudden realization that there is a terrorist threat against which we must mobilize. It was in awakening us to the critical realization that the significance of the threat can reside in other spaces and forms. Today, in witnessing the intense tactics of social mobilization throughout the western world, it becomes clear that the truly significant phenomena are those diverse forms of terror used in these very tactics of mobilization. One witnesses governed uses of fear, insecurity, states of emergency and pathologies. One experiences them in our communities, schools, public institutions, consumption patterns and societal relations. These tactics and forms have precise histories that have been extended beyond the western world and long pre-date 9/11. Herein lays the timeliness of these significant forms of terror which are never reducible to the forms of terrorism. The former reveal a historical and social backdrop intimate with terrorized and terrorizing activities, for which the new international terrorism is only a recent and partial player (though clearly a pressing one). In our view it was highly appropriate to stage a conference on terror if one multiplies the fields of critical research beyond the priority that is too often accorded, quite uncritically at times, the new forms of international terrorism (especially by the mainstream western media).

The concept of terror is often found safely hidden and un-thought in diverse cultural, philosophical, and religious traditions and ways of life. One can see these safe havens extending from the divine mythologies of religious experience to the seemingly opposed rationalized life of contemporary hi-tech societies. With respect to religious experience, it is clear that we have to seriously reconsider the dynamics of organized religion in the face of rising religious fundamentalisms and terrorist activity. But terror in the highly rationalized world of technological societies can also impose its existing logic as a way of maintaining the order of things. We give it various positive names that conceal its potency and negative effects—at precise moments in history terror's potency has appeared in benign terms such as "child welfare", "residential schools", the "founding nation", the "developed world", the "hysterical woman", the "mentally ill", the "social and sexual deviant", the "immigrant problem", the "disposable income" and the "democratic liberation of other peoples". It is essentially the absurd rationalizations of these terms in the face of concrete realities that covers over terror's effects and keeps it intact.

Most importantly, the conference was interested in investigating what role terror has in maintaining the contemporary condition of humanity and what hope there is of envisioning a condition in which terror is natural and organic rather than strategic and imposed.

The Human Condition Series Editorial Board

# PREFACE

In May of 2008 The Human Condition Series (THCS) held its second annual interdisciplinary conference on the timely theme of Terror. Over 100 presenters from around the world descended on Barrie, Ontario in Canada to present their research and engage in genuine and meaningful dialogue.

The Human Condition Series, founded in 2006, is an ongoing series of international, interdisciplinary conferences that seek to address the current state of the human condition. Unlike the diversity and eclecticism of multi-disciplinary approaches, an interdisciplinary approach seeks out the creative antagonisms and tensions existing between the diversity of disciplines and emphasizes the complements and unifying elements among them. The series brings together people from a variety of disciplines to assess a singular topic from artistic, cinematic, literary, ethical, social, political, philosophical, psychological and religious perspectives. Presenters come from around the world to share innovative ideas and new ways of thinking and acting. These original theorizations transcend traditional boundaries and contest the very foundations upon which whole fields of ideas are divided, disciplined and sanctioned as true forms of knowledge. In 2007, the theme was Empire.

# ACKNOWLEDGEMENTS

Our sincerest thanks to our international presenters representing scholarship from Australia to Mumbai, from Singapore to Zimbabwe. It would not be an international conference were it not for those willing to make the journey to Barrie, Ontario, Canada. We especially acknowledge the courage of those international scholars who tried to attend but were prevented, faced with adversity in the forms of being denied a visitor's visa, institutional funding or permission from other authorities to travel and share their ideas. We gratefully acknowledge the generosity of Sunera Thobani, Henry Giroux and Sut Jhally for sharing their most recent scholastic forays into terror and for making themselves accessible to the many participants who traveled so far to hear them.

Sincere appreciation to founding student organizers whose voluntary fundraising efforts continue to bear fruit because of their personal commitment to the series: Deborah Clyne, Jana Carpenter, Katrina Dobson, Derek Fleur, Susan Mills, and Andrew Preston. Welcome to incoming organizers Melissa Aceto, Ashley McNaughton, Kyle Patterson, and Mark Welsh. Thank you to the many, many more who assisted behind the scenes.

A special thank you to the artists who donated their talents to make the conference extraordinary: Teena Aujla for her artistic vision and graphic designs, Valerie Selnyk and Callam Rodya for their performance of spoken word poetry to original music, and Arturo Escobar of Theatre of the Oppressed for his moving one-man show.

At Laurentian University, Sudbury, we gratefully acknowledge the financial support of the Office of the Vice-President Academic (Anglophone Affairs), the Office of the Dean of Social Sciences and Humanities, and the departments of Sociology and English. We continue to be grateful to The University Partnership Centre at Georgian College, for financial, physical and administrative support. We thank Christine Redfern and Andrea MacGregor for so competently taking care of business and gratefully acknowledge the hard work of Liane Chesire, Darlene Forrester and Linda Taylor-Eddington.

Thanks to the Library Commons of Georgian College, specifically, Vicki Macmillan for both intellectual and financial contributions to the conference with the establishment of the THCS Screening Room. Thank you also to the Library of Social Sciences in New York for showcasing the publications of our keynote speakers and presenters.

Thanks to Jeff Young of Brown Walker Press for bringing the deserving proceedings of these annual meetings to a readership. Last but not least, we thank Brandy Foster for the preparation of the manuscript, no small feat that it was.

# LIST OF CONTRIBUTORS

*Rebecca A. Adelman*
Department of Comparative Studies, Ohio State University, U.S.A.

*Jennifer Adese*
Department of Indigenous Studies, Trent University, Canada

*Amal Al-Leithy*
Department of English, Alsun Ain Shams University, Egypt

*Razvan Amironesei*
Laval University, Canada

*Leslie Russell Ashby*
Department of English, Illinois State University, U.S.A.

*Katie Aubrecht*,
Department of Sociology, York University, Canada

*Stephanie Barann*
New York University, U.S.A.

*Dianne D. Bergsma*
Department of Philosophy, Brock University, Canada

*Mary Bunch*
Centre for the Study of Theory & Criticism, University of Western Ontario, Canada

*Nandan Choksi*
American Intercontinental University, U.S.A.

*Maureen Connolly*
Department of Education, Brock University, Canada

*Richard JF Day*
Queens University, Canada

*Panayiotis Demopoulos*
University of Athens, Greece

*Maritza Felices-Luna*
Department of Criminology, University of Ottawa, Canada

*Aravind Ganachari*
University of Mumbai, India

*Sarah Hamilton*
Department of Theory, Culture and Politics, Trent University, Canada

*Amy Hildreth*
Department of English, Emory University, U.S.A.

*James Horley*
Department of Psychology, University of Alberta, Canada

*Sophia C. Hughes*
The Union Institute & University, U.S.A.

ENGAGING TERROR

**Timothy Johnson**
Twinsberg, U.S.A.

**Andrea Kirschner**
Centre for Interdisciplinary Research, Bielefeld University, Germany

**Dario Kuntić**
Department of Comparative Politics, University of Zagreb, Croatia

**Guy Kirby Letts**
Departments of Anthropology and Sociology, Laurentian University, Canada

**Beatrice Marry**
Department of Political Science, McGill University, Canada

**Ian McPhail**
Department of Psychology, University of Alberta, Canada

**Karyne Messina**
Washington Center for Psychoanalysis, U.S.A.

**Matthew Morgan**
Institute of Political Economy, Carelton University, Canada

**Christine Muller**
American Studies, University of Maryland, U.S.A.

**Parveen Nangia**
Department of Sociology, Laurentian University, Canada

**Charly Norton**
University of Winchester, U.S.A.

**Ana Laura Pauchulo**
Sociology & Equity Studies, University of Toronto, Canada

**Beatrix Prinsen**
Department of Education, Brock University, Canada

**Melissa Abbey Strowger**
Department of Sociology & Equity Studies, University of Toronto, Canada

**Milo Sweedler**
Cultural Analysis & Social Theory, Wilfrid Laurier University, Canada

**Narges Valibeigi**
Institute on Globalization & the Human Condition, McMaster University, Canada

**Cindy Vander Meulen**
Cultural & Policy Studies, Queens University, Canada

**Marty Wood**
Department of History, Georgian College, Canada

# INTRODUCTION

*Guy Kirby Letts*

Terror (terrorem): to be frightened or filled with great fear and dread. While the term 'terrorism' and 'terrorist' are a part of our collective lexicon within contemporary popular culture, the concept of terror as a psychosocial phenomenon is accorded little if any attention. As both a phenomenological and sociological aspect of the human condition, what is terror, how does it function, what are the conditions that facilitate it, and how is it situated within the social body? These are a few of the questions that will be addressed in *Engaging Terror: A Critical and Interdisciplinary Approach*.

*Engaging Terror* is a collection of select, extended papers drawn from The Human Condition Series (THCS). THCS is part of The Centre for the Study of the Human Condition (CSHC) which provides research, analysis, publications, and international forums on aspects of the human condition. The thirty-five essays presented here are a representative sample of the 115 papers presented as part of The Human Condition Series Conference on Terror that took place in 2008. The international scope of the conference drew participants from twenty-three countries including Brazil, Columbia, Cuba, France, Israel, Lebanon, Lithuania, New Zealand, Nigeria, Pakistan, Philippines, Scotland, Singapore, South Africa, Turkey, and United Kingdom.

In this volume, scholars from Croatia, Egypt, Greece, Germany, India, and from across Canada and the U.S. share their insights from a variety of perspectives on the representation and production of terror. Terror is examined not only from a contemporary western perspective, but also as a historical and global phenomenon, including analysis and case studies from Argentina, Germany, India, and Nigeria. Ana Laura Pauchulo's essay, "Technologies of Resistance: The Role of Public and Collective Memory in Responding to Past and Present State-Violence in Argentina," for instance, examines collective memory in relation to state violence, trama and resistance, and its impact on constructing democracy in Argentina, while Aravind Ganachari's piece entitled, "Combating Terror of Law in Colonial India: The Law of Sedition and the Nationalist Response," traces the Indo-British Law of Sedition through the diverse phases of India's struggle for freedom.

Several thematic topics are evident throughout the book. For example, terror is analysed in the context of the state, mass media, fiction, film, health practices, and education, to name a few. The book begins with Nandan Choksi's provocative essay, "The Rhythm of Terror," which asserts that terror is an inevitable and immutable aspect of existence and an integral element in the forces of disintegration and destruction, as well as integration and reconstruction. Choksi goes on to argue that while terror is a subset of fear, it is neither good nor evil, but simply a rhythm. While Choksi addresses the ontological aspects of terror as a natural and organic phenomenon, the essays by Maritza Felices-Luna and Matthew Morgan confront the strategic and imposed notion of terror as a decidedly socio-political construct within relations of power. Felices-Luna's grounded case study, "Who is the Terrorist?: Analyzing the Discourse and Practices Surrounding the Confrontation Between Governments and Insurgent Organizations," traces the Bush administration's legal and political construction of 'torture culture' which was used as a tool in the 'war on terror'. Morgan's more structural treatment, "Liberalism and Governmentality in the War on Terror," on the other hand, examines the changes in technologies of self and government within liberal democracies under the rubric of the 'war on terror'. According to Morgan, the development of new surviellance techniques are designed to socially sort members of the liberal polity into categories based on their precieved threat to the social order.

Within the topic of power and socio-political constructs, Jennifer Adese's, "Constructing the Aboriginal Terrorist: Depictions of Aboriginal Protestors, the Caledonia Reclamation, and Canadian Neoliberalization," and Richard JF Day's, "The Man with the Hissing Bomb: Anarchism and Terror in the North American Imagination," look at the imaginary construction and representation of Aboriginal protestors and anarchists as both social deviants and terrorists. Like Aboriginal peoples, anarchists are being singled out not for what they have done, but for who they are. In this sense, not only are those deemed a threat to the social order targeted, but also marginalized groups, in the case of Aboriginal peoples, as part of an ongoing effort to maintain structures of repression and hierarical supremacy. As Adese puts it, such 'representations conceal the institutionalized racism of the Canadian state and citizens'.

The role of the state in the construction of 'terrorist groups' is often facilitated through the media. Much of what we know about the world is mediated through the press and news coverage. While Adese's essay focuses on an analysis of newspaper articles in constructing Aboriginal protestors as terrorists, Narges Valibeigi's, "Media as an Anti-Peace Making Tool in the Context of Globalization: Analyzing News Coverage in a Time of Terror and War," examines the characterization of Islam in news reports from CNN and the BBC which ultimately reinforces otherness and stereotypes about Muslims. While mass media is often the voice of the state and reflects dominant cultural values, Dario Kuntić's essay, "The Media in the Service of Terrorism," illustrates the ways in which non-state terrorist organizations utilize the media and mass communications, such as the internet, both to support their cause and to spread fear.

The media, then, is a fundamental element in the modern construction of terror, terrorism and terrorists. Beyond the immediacy of news coverage, however, other forms of media and communications—such as fiction, film and music—also figure prominently in the production, configuration, and reproduction of terror. The culture industry, for instance, reifies terror within the field of popular culture, tacitly informing the popular imaginary. Milo Sweedler's, "On Terror Considered As One of the Fine Arts," and Rebecca A. Adelman's, "Re(con)figuring the Spectacle: State Flexibility in Response to Imaged Terror," look at how non-state terrorism and terrorist acts are turned into spectacles as part of the spectacular within mediated culture. Sweedler notes that while Jean Baudrillard is right to insist that 9/11 was symboliclly important, the success of the attack was irreducible to the destruction of the symbol and the spectacular aspect of the destruction itself. Adelman too sees the importance of the spectacle in the discourse of terrorism and outlines the strategies used by the U.S. to reconfigure spectacular defeat into small victories in the global war on terror, though no spectacular triumphs were ever present.

Mass communication and popular culture are significant factors in both informing and expressing collective experience. While state and non-state terrorism are part of a global narrative, the stories we tell can shape the kinds of questions that might be asked in the face of catastrophe and fear. Here, the relationship between fiction and terrror is explored from Amal Al-Leithy's, "Stereotyping Islam: A Critical Study of Terror in John Updike's *Terrorist*," and Amy Hildreth's, "Cosmopolitan Hospitality in Post-9/11 Popular Fiction: Asad's *The Reluctant Fundamentalist*," to Christine Muller and Charly Norton's essays on Don DeLillo's novel *The Falling Man*. The events of 9/11 usured in a new poetics of terror in the west, bringing with it a new language and perspective. As part of the new poetics of terror, literary works are being used as a means of exploring catastrophe and its residue. Film too, as in Leslie Russell Ashby's paper, "'Don't Say the Zed Word!': Toward a Linguistic Construction of Social Class in the Contemporary *Living Dead* Film," also plays with the social meanings of terror. Ashby's essay, for instance, looks at the relationship between terror and language in the construction of social class. According to Ashby, 'the living dead are a class subjected to the definitions and limits placed upon them by the living survivors who always deem themselves to be more human'. In this sense, certain truths are revealed about our social interactions as we come to terms with our own 'living dead'.

Circumventing the obvious impact of the media and popular culture on constructing and defining terror is the more subtle role that social institutions and institutional practices play in the formation of terror. The terror of institutional discourses, for instance, is reflected in medical and educational practices. Cindy Vander Meulen's, "The Tyrannizing Order of Mental Health Promotion," demonstrates how psychological illness transformed mental health into a medical problem by treating it according to a disease model of human development. As a result, mental health professionals work from a standpoint that re-enfolds individuals into a social norm of deviance, psychological evaluation, and treatment. The three inter-related papers by Dianne D. Bergsma, Beatrix Prinsen, and Maureen Connolly examine the rules and regularities that produce power, fear and dread within education. Drawing on the works of L. Bain's hidden curriculum and Paulo Freire's archaeology of consciousness, the authors look at the dynamics of power and normative logics that produce the familarization of fear and deter the politics and pedagogy of liberation.

Henry Giroux reminds us that,

> Democracy begins to fail and political life becomes impoverished when society can no longer translate private problems into social issues… In the post-911 world, the space of shared responsibility [in the west] has given way to the space of private fears… and the social obligations of citizenship are now reduced to the highly individualized imperatives of consumerism. (2006:1)

For Giroux, the terror of neoliberalism, domestically, is predicated on undermining the social contract which emphasizes the public good through expanding social provisions such as adequate access to health care, housing, employment, education and public transit whereby the conditions of democracy could be experienced and critical citizenship could be engaged. However, the social contract "has been replaced with a notion of national security based on fear, surveillance, and control rather than on a culture of shared responsibility" (2004:xv). Many of the concerns raised by Giroux are also addressed in *Engaging Terror* from Sarah Hamilton's, "Terrorizing (Un)citizens: A Genealogy of Security Certificates" and Katie Aubrecht's, "CTOs: A New Order of Terror?," to Andrea Kirschner's, "Youth Terror or Terrorized Youth? Youth Violence in Nigeria—Redefining Spaces of Politics and Belonging" and Karyne Messina's essay, "Taking Back Projections: The Despair and Hope in Projective Identification." These essays, as well as those mentioned earlier, not only resist state definitions of terror and defy the notion of fear as a defining and totalizing experience, but represent the reclaiming of both the social and political spheres as a place of promise in which the human condition can flourish, in all its complexity, beyond the confines of commercialism and institutional domination.

## References

Giroux, Henry A. (2006). *Beyond the Spectacle of Terrorism: Global Uncertainty and the Challenge of the New Media*. Boulder, Colorado: Paradigm Publishers.

Giroux, Henry A. (2004). *The Terror of Neoliberalism: Authoritarianism and the Eclipse of Democracy*. Aurora, Ontario, Garamond Press.

# The Rhythm of Terror

*Nandan Choksi*

Terror is fun! The Tower of Terror, at Disney World, is a source of immense pleasure to millions. But terror can also cause immense pain. In order to create either pain or pleasure, however, terror must be learned. Terror is only a subset of fear—it is extreme fear. And psychologists have long ago demonstrated that fear is itself learned rather than innate. Professor R. L. Gregory explains in *The Oxford Companion to the Mind* that "The impact of early behaviorism with its massive emphasis on the importance of acquired behavior led to the demise of the notion that some fears may be innately determined" (257).

Those of us who subscribe to the Jungian school of thought believe in archetypes, the notion that everyone is born with some inherent qualities and capacities. Even so, however, it is not necessary to believe that one is born with the knowledge of fear of any type. Certainly, one is born with the capacity to learn from anything one experiences. Exactly what each person learns from his or her unique experiences, however, is infinitely variable. But, even assuming that a person can and does learn to fear, the capacity to learn something implies, equally, the capacity to unlearn it and/or to learn something else that may help us manage what we have learned already.

Extreme fear, like anything else, becomes unpleasant when the circumstances causing it are perceived as being, not simply uncontrolled, but uncontrollable. Mere knowledge of possible death or disaster creates no terror. Usually, it fails to create even mild fear. Extreme terror is caused, then, not so much by the fear of any actual consequences, but by the feeling of total loss of control. But it is possible to learn to deal with any emotion, including the feeling of total loss of control.

## Role of Government and Society
There is no such thing as social terror. An entire society can never be terrorized. It is always the individual who feels terror. But society can and does play a very significant role in causing the individual to feel terror. Society amplifies the feeling of terror associated with certain types of acts or events. Political and business leaders use the various media as tools to perpetuate fear throughout society. In their essay, *The Strategy of Terror and the Psychology of Mass-Mediated Fear*, the analysis of professors Breckenridge and Zimbardo is that, "Social amplification is especially common when there is ambiguity, doubt, or misinformation, which provoke fear and instigate rumor" (123).

Social amplification, however, is a technique that can be used with equal effectiveness by governments and criminals alike. In their analysis of Professors Scott Gerwehr and Kirk Hubbard's essay, "What is Terrorism? Key Elements and History," professors Pratchett, Brown and Bongar point out, "Gerwehr and Hubbard posit that the success or failure of a terrorist campaign depends on the ability to achieve each of the six stages outlined in the Yale model of social influence: exposure, attention, comprehension, acceptance, retention and translation" (454).

But why does terrorism exist? What purpose does it serve? From a purely business perspective, terrorism is counter-productive. To train a suicide bomber, for instance, the terrorist needs a trainer. Then the terrorist needs someone who can make a bomb that the bomber can operate. Someone must fund the entire project. And, in the end, nothing is left—the money, the trainer, the bomb, and the bomber are all gone. The organizer often takes no credit for the deed, fearing for his or her own life. To continue being a terrorist for an extended period of time, the terrorist must, inevitably, have access to practically unlimited resources—financial and social.

The government and media can do what nobody else can—they can decide what stories to tell and they can disseminate those stories freely and openly. When the government runs out of money, it can raise more by the simple expedient of legally raising taxes. But why would people agree to pay higher taxes to fund terrorist activities? Nobody would—unless, of course, they feel that the government needs the money to fund anti-terrorist programs.

But why should people believe that there are so many terrorists committing so many crimes that an anti-terrorist fund is necessary? According to Loretta Napoleoni, in her book, *Modern Jihad: Tracing the Dollars Behind the Terror Networks*, government-backed counter-insurgency has been a staple of US foreign policy since the 1960s when then-President John F. Kennedy, "presented the National Security Council with an immediate budget allocation of $19 million (equivalent today to $100 million) as part of an ambitious counter-insurgency program including an expansion of the US Army's Special Forces from a few hundred to 4,000 men" (13). It is Dr. Napoleoni's contention that Kennedy, however, is not the first or only political leader to espouse counter-insurgency. Dr. Napoleoni asserts that, "A new concept in political warfare, counter-insurgency effectively legitimized state-sponsored terrorism" (12). Whether or not one agrees with Dr. Napoleoni's views, it is certain that every major government in the world today is popularizing the idea of a terrorist threat to its people.

And it is not only the Al-Qaedas and the IRAs and other religious extremists of the world, who engage in acts of terror, and it is not only religious extremists that various governments target as terrorists. The problem, as Dr. Philip Cole says, in a chapter aptly entitled "Communities of Fear," in his book, *The Myth of Evil*, the politics of terrorism is much deeper and more complex than that:

Rather than political communities forming themselves around shared identities, they are formed through the exploitation by political authorities of social fears and insecurities, by focusing those fears upon one threatening 'evil' figure—the vampire, the witch, the Jew, the migrant, the asylum seeker, the Gypsy, the 'Islamicist' terrorist—and claiming to protect the 'genuine' members from those deviant and dangerous threats. (81)

According to Dr. Cole, Dr. Napoleoni and others, then, governments not only fund counter-insurgency programs, but use the media and other resources at their command to isolate and demonize specific minority groups. The purpose, of course, is to show that governments and politicians are not only useful, but indispensable. The effect, however, is quite often just the opposite. By isolating, alienating, and disenfranchising specific groups and individuals for reasons that have more to do with political expediency rather than national security, all governments create a seething, powerless minority in every country in the world. Inevitably, some members of such minorities express their displeasure at being marginalized through angry words and rather literally explosive actions. Up to a certain point, it is in the government's interest to ensure the existence of such groups. And therefore, either directly or indirectly, every government in the world funds such groups and individuals.

But such a strategy will ultimately fail. Loneliness and impotence are powerful weapons in the arsenal of any government, when used sparingly and directed against groups and individuals that do, truly, threaten national security. Hannah Arendt is quite correct when she says, in the chapter entitled "Ideology and Terror" in her famous book-length analysis of governmental excess, *The Origins of Totalitarianism*, "Nevertheless, organized loneliness is considerably more dangerous than the unorganized impotence of all those who are ruled by the tyrannical and arbitrary will of a single man" (478).

## Terror as Image and Symbol

Medusa, the Gorgon, she of the venomous blood and deadly gaze, for instance, is as much terrified as terrifying. Although, as a Gorgon she has fearsome powers, as compared to a mortal, she is powerless before the gods of Olympus, such as Athena and Poseidon. It is Poseidon's rape of Medusa in Athena's temple that causes Athena to curse Medusa, turning the once-beautiful and gentle Medusa into a hateful and terrifying creature. And even so, she terrorizes nobody. She continues her pregnancy until the great hero, Perseus, sneaks into her home, and kills her while she sleeps, without even looking at her. And, despite everything, Medusa gives birth. And her children are neither monsters nor monstrous. Chrysaor goes on to become a great king while Pegasus the winged horse becomes the mount of the great hero, Bellerophon. It is not, therefore, Medusa's actions, nor her associations, that make her terrifying, but the mere image of her—a woman with snakes for hair, a woman whose every drop of blood turned into giant, poisonous scorpions, a woman whose looks alone could kill.

There is, similarly, in Arabic folk literature, the ghoul. The ghoul is a terrifying woman with supernatural powers. According to various legends, a ghoul can be the daughter of a demon or one who chooses to become a demon by some act. One act typically considered demonic enough to turn a woman into a ghoul is the act of mourning for a dead child, particularly a newborn one, until the mother herself dies. The angry, vengeful spirit of the mother supposedly returns as a ghoul, seducing men with the purpose of murdering them to eat them. A ghoul, according to legend, can eat only human flesh, not ordinary food, and she remains young and beautiful for as long as she has access to that type of food. Upon absence of that diet, a ghoul eventually dies by consuming parts of her own body, from the toes up, until there is nothing left to consume. Here, too, then, the terrifying female is as much victim as predator. The fear comes from not knowing whether a woman is human or a ghoul. Supposedly, the simple act of watching her not eat for several days is proof positive. However, a ghoul can eat only at night. And she will kill and eat anyone close enough to watch her at night. Proof, therefore, is somewhat difficult to procure, though not entirely impossible. Various tales tell us that not only is it possible to identify a ghoul but also to destroy her without any significant deleterious effect being visited upon the one who kills the ghoul.

There are, of course, many such creatures and an even larger number of stories about such creatures in countries and cultures around the world. But the bottom line is always the same—both the creatures as well as the stories are created to inspire fear in the heart of the listener. As the world has changed, however, so have the creatures and the stories. Although many of the folktales are taken from religious sources, a new source of folktales has sprung up in the twentieth and the twenty-first centuries. In an age where religion has lost much of its power, and technology has taken over, a new type of folktale has emerged—the urban myth.

The, ghouls, vampires and Gorgons of ancient folklore have been replaced by terrorists, serial killers, and black-marketers who deal in body parts. Fear of crime and criminals is not always or even mostly irrational. Such fears, however, given time and therapy, can be unlearned or at least easily managed. The kinds of terror that can never be unlearned or managed, however, are the terrors sponsored by the government and the media. The partnership between these two entities is well-nigh impossible to defeat. In fact, the average person cannot even shield himself or herself from the effects of this partnership.

## The Power of Media
Even while the world debates the effect of media-depicted violence, the real issue is often over-looked. It is not important, really, whether watching or

reading or hearing about violence drives individuals to be violent. More and more, the violence depicted in newspapers, on television, and in movies, is fantastic in the extreme. The ordinary person cannot even dream of imitating such violence. David Trend makes a very astute observation, in regard to media violence, in his book, *The Myth of Media Violence*:

> The assertion is often made that violence in the media is becoming increasingly graphic and "real." In fact, the opposite is taking place. Part of what makes media violence appealing to viewers is the extent to which it is anesthetized and transformed by production technologies. (55)

Mr. Trend's assertion is supported by an expert on cinema, Dr. James Iaccino, who writes in his book, *Psychological Reflections on Cinematic Terror*, while referring to the *Nightmare on Elm Street* movie franchise, that, "the strength of the original *Nightmare* lies in the ability of the victims to discriminate between dreaming and wakefulness so that they never know when terror might intrude upon their reality" (174). What Mr. Trend says about the characters in the movie now applies equally to those of us who are starring in the movie of life itself—it has become impossible for most of us to distinguish between the images presented in the media and the actual truth. And we do not know when—or if—terror might intrude into our reality. And the worst of it is that government—any government—is not really interested in resolving the issues that lead to the creation of terror and terrorists. The response of government to violence is simple—tighter security, leading to loss of civil rights, and, of course, violence even more deadly than that of the terrorists. More civilians lose their lives and their liberty when attacked by government forces than when attacked even by the most powerful of terrorist groups.

**Rhythms of Terror**
Terry Eagleton's wisdom is indisputable when he says that, "If you greet the violence of others simply with red-necked repression, you are likely to have your buildings blown up" (*Holy Terror* 7) Dr. Eagleton is absolutely correct when he says that, "Justice is the only prophylactic for terror" (*Holy Terror* 15). But how shall we end the repression? And how will we ensure that justice is done?

The world is on the cusp of a new type of folklore—a folklore created and disseminated by the government and media. And as the folklore spreads throughout the world, terror among the populace will grow. Whenever the tide of terror begins to ebb, it will be made to rise again—and again and again. It is up to every individual in the world to resist the stultifying rhythms of the media and to re-invigorate the vibrant rhythms of folklore, the knowledge of the people. It is not, after all, the media and the governments who truly know or understand what is going on in the world—it is the people. The government of the people, by the people and for the people will, one day, perish from the face of the earth if the people do not speak for themselves, if the people do not write their own stories, if the people do not play their own music but dance, instead, to the tune of the government and of the media.

Terror is a rhythm. It is a rhythm of loneliness and hopelessness and the dreariness of imaginative anesthesia. It will never be muted. But let us rise and dance to a tune of our own making—a timeless melody of joy and harmony that we play with our minds upon the unbreakable strings of the heart. And the heart, we know, despite Pandora, or because of her, holds the wings of hope. Even terror and despair cannot, for all their strength and power, rise to the heights and the ecstasies to which we can fly with the rhythm and the energy of hope.

# References

Arendt, Hannah. 1958. *The origins of totalitarianism.* 2nd Extended Edition. New York: Meridian Books.

Breckenridge, James N. and Philip G. Zimbardo. 2006. "The strategy of terror and the psychology of mass-mediated fear." *Psychology of terrorism*, ed Bruce Bongar, et al. New York: Oxford Univ. Press (UK).

Cole, Philip. 2006. *The myth of evil.* Edinburgh: Edinburgh Univ. Press.

Eagleton, Terry. 2005. *Holy terror.* Oxford, NY: Oxford Univ. Press (UK).

Gregory, R.L. 1987. *The Oxford companion to the mind.* New York: Oxford Univ. Press (UK).

Iaccino, James. 1994. *Psychological reflections on cinematic terror.* Connecticut: Praeger.

Napoleoni, Loretta. 2003. *Modern jihad: Tracing the dollars behind the terror network.* Sterling, VA: Pluto Press.

Pratchett, Laura et al. 2006 "Reflections of the psychology of terrorism," in *Psychology of Terrorism*, ed Bruce Bongar, et al. New York: Oxford Univ. Press (UK).

Trend, David. 2006. *The myth of media violence.* New Jersey: Wiley-Blackwell.

# WHO IS THE TERRORIST? ANALYZING THE DISCOURSE AND PRACTICES SURROUNDING THE CONFRONTATION BETWEEN GOVERNMENTS AND INSURGENT ORGANIZATIONS

*Maritza Felices-Luna*

**Introduction**

Since the events of September 11, there has been a renewed scientific interest on issues regarding political violence and armed conflict. However, the political environment has had an impact in the way we approach the subject. Academic freedom, freedom of the press, and freedom of expression have been restricted under the notion of national security. Inevitably, the current rhetoric "with us or against us" has infiltrated the scientific realm limiting debate through the emotional imperative to protect western[1] society from its destruction. Criticism of policies, legislations, practices of law enforcement, justice, immigration, etc. is considered unpatriotic and in support of "terrorism."

In such a climate, analyzing the current situations in terms of dynamics of conflicts is considered as legitimizing "terrorist organizations." Thus, scientific research has to explicitly follow the analysis conducted by western governments and the terminology used by them. Otherwise, their contributions are discredited as being irrelevant, irresponsible, even dangerous, or are simply discarded for working under the wrong premise given that the insurgents[2] or terrorists are not considered evil. Furthermore, the idea that past contributions to the field could be helpful in understanding the phenomena has been rejected as the standpoint of western States is that we are dealing with a new phenomenon. The "war on terror" is said to be warranted by a "new breed" of "terrorists" presenting a uniquely flexible and malleable structure, supported by a particular strain of an apocalyptic ideology that leaves no room for a political compromise as it elicits a never before seen fervor and determination from its members[3]. However, these characteristics have already been attributed to other organizations in different regions and

---

1. The term *western* is used to refer to a kind of private club in which a limited number of countries mutually acknowledge each other as being part of the club.
2. I prefer to use the term *anti-establishment armed group*. I considered it to be a less biased term that clearly indicates the type of organization relevant to the study without implying a moralistic or political judgment. However, for rhetorical purposes, the terms *insurgent* and *terrorist* will be used.
3. Ashby, Richard, "Human Rights in the War on Terror," in *Human Rights in the War of Terror* ed. Richard Ashby (Cambridge: Cambridge University Press, 2005).

through different time periods. The same ideological fervor, determination, and impasse to finding a peaceful political solution had been previously attributed to other organizations such as the Shining Path of Peru or the Japanese Red Army. Moreover, the use of a flexible structure as proof that it is in fact a "new breed" of terrorists results not from a change in nature but, on the contrary, the capacity organizations have to learn, adapt, and develop new strategies in response to those of the enemy. For example, during the Irish conflict, the IRA changed from a battalion structure to a cell structure in order to counter the strategies deployed by the British armed forces and law enforcement agencies. Thus, despite the existence of a rhetoric asserting that the world is facing a new and global "threat," it is in fact the same phenomenon: an organization with limited means and members confronting a more powerful enemy as a means to ensure the survival, continuation, and expansion of a community perceived to be threatened by the identified enemy. The enemy usually takes the form of a state, and the organization confronting it is seeking to reconfigure the geographical boundaries, take control of the government, or destroy the state in order to build it a new. Hence, the "terrorist" organization represents a threat not only to the government, but to the continuity of the state in its current form.

This paper aims to contribute to the understanding of the dynamics of armed conflicts between so called terrorist organizations and a State. This will be done by disregarding the aforementioned premises stipulated by Western States. The cases of Ireland and Peru will be used as examples of western and non-western conflicts that took place between the 1970s and the 1990s before the "new breed of terrorists" emerged. In fact, we will use material collected during a fieldwork in Peru and Belfast, where I interviewed women who were involved or had been involved in insurgent organizations[4]. The conflicts of Peru and Ireland will serve to demonstrate that the nature of insurgency or terrorism is the confrontation between two States: one that already exists and one that is in formation. Through this presentation we will see how terrorist or insurgent organizations construe themselves to be the legitimate State of a reconfigured or previously existing territory occupied by an illegitimate State that has usurped power and is oppressing the indigenous or righteous community. The organization portrays itself in this manner not only to the community it claims to represent but also to the other parties involved in the conflict: the general population and the international community. Whenever any of these actors publicly recognizes it as a State in formation, the organization will present it as a sign of its legitimacy. However, any refusal to be recognized as such is used as proof that those actors are themselves illegitimate.

---

4. Felices-Luna, Maritza, *L'implication des femmes au sein des groupes armés contestataires: les cas du Pérou et de l'Irlande* (Montréal: Université de Montréal, 2005).

Through a weberian conceptualisation of the State, we can see insurgent organizations embarking on three courses of action that allows them not only to construe themselves as the legitimate State, but to become one in reality. This means:

1. using military strategies to defeat their opponent and consolidate the monopoly of legitimate violence;
2. drawing on rhetorical and discursive strategies to legitimize their own actions and projects while at the same time discrediting and de-legitimising the opposition;
3. undertaking the distribution, maintenance, and/or transfer of power either as means to other aims or for its own sake. In other words, the implementation of the actual function of governing.

If we look at each one of these strategies more in detail we can see that these three strategies are not autonomous, but interplay in the consolidation of the organization as a State. It is important to mention that even if the means at their disposal are different, the official State needs to use the same strategies in order to guarantee its survival. However, for the purpose of this presentation I will primarily demonstrate these strategies as deployed by insurgent or terrorist organizations.

## Military Actions

Military actions aim to:

*Gain a military advantage over the adversary:* This means for the insurgent organization to gain control over a particular territory, to deplete material resources and personnel, as well as lower the moral of the adversary. This is quite straightforward and is the best-known use of military strategies in an armed conflict. A Peruvian interviewee described being part of the taking over of certain towns under the control of the military as well as attacking military patrols in order to expand the Shining Path's control over a geographical area.

*Obtain and/or protect the necessary material resources to continue the military confrontation* (money, armament, sustenance, medical supplies, clothing, and equipment, etc.). Insurgent or terrorist organizations usually need to steal resources, whereas the State actually has funds and the infrastructure required to obtain them. A Peruvian interviewee described how the Shining Path would organize raids in small towns in order to procure themselves with medicine, clothes, food, and other basic necessities. The MRTA was particularly known for kidnapping businessmen in order to exchange them for money. Both organizations forcibly collected "revolutionary taxes" and were also involved in robberies of mines and factories in order to obtain explosives and other materials used for combat purposes. Despite this strategy being used particularly by insurgent organizations, some law enforcement and military personnel have also been known to be involved in this type of activities in order to secure the material resources needed to do their job. For example, up to the mid 1980s, Peruvian police officers had to pay for their own bullets, which they could not afford to do with their salary. Furthermore, the State might also need for economic reasons to obtain these resources through other means or to make sure they maintain control over the exploitation of natural resources in order to have a continuous income allowing them to maintain the "war effort."

*Create and/or confirm a general image of the organization that is coherent with their official discourse.* In other words, with the way they present themselves (anti-capitalist: destruction of factories, franchises, banks, etc.; nationalist or fascist: attacks on immigrant organizations, businesses, places of worship, etc.). The MRTA was inspired by the Cuban revolution and tried to differentiate itself from the Shining Path, which followed a Maoist perspective. Therefore when it first appeared, they tried to show that difference through military actions by, for example, getting the people out of a building before blowing it up. This was the case in the attack of a KFC franchise in the early 1980s. By doing this they showed that they were an anti-capitalist organization fighting the imperialist expansion of the US without hurting innocent civilians. The IRA also used a similar strategy by calling in before an explosion so that the building could be evacuated without hurting civilians. When civilians were actually hurt, there was a reciprocal denunciation where the State condemned the killing of innocent civilians by the IRA while the IRA blamed the State for not taking the necessary action and allowing civilians to die for their own publicity. Furthermore, some organizations will actually openly apologize when they make mistakes, as was the case with the IRA in the 1990s when they attacked the headquarters of a loyalist organization, but in the process killed people that were in a fish-shop. Other organizations, on the contrary, directly target civilians in order to show that there are no bystanders or innocents in an armed conflict because if they are not joining the organization they are allies of the enemy, thus becoming legitimate targets. For example, the Shining Path attacked in the early 1990s a residential building in an upscale district at night when most people would actually be home.

*Communicate with the opposition.* Aside from official and unofficial talks between representatives of the State and insurgent organizations, these organizations use military actions to send clear messages about their intentions. For example in 1989, there was an attack by the Shining Path on the presidential guard as it was coming off duty, one block off from the presidential palace. The message was quite straightforward and aimed to show the President that they had the means to get to him. In retaliation, in 1992 there was a death squad formed by the new President who killed 14 people that were members of the Shining Path and that were hiding in the same house as those responsible for the attack in 1989. The same year, 9 students and 1 university professor were disappeared by the same death squad sending the message that the universities were no longer a safe haven for members of the Shining Path)[5].

*Finally, military strategies also serve to send a specific message to the population.* In Peru there were numerous cases of public extrajudicial executions by both the armed forces and the insurgent organizations. The purpose was to show they were in control of that particular area; to explain to the locals what was expected from them and to demonstrate the consequences of collaborating with the enemy (the armed forces or the insurgent organizations accordingly).

## With Regards to Discursive Strategies

Given that the different organizations directly involved in the armed conflict conceptualize themselves as the legitimate State, they are not only fighting over the control of the monopoly of legitimate violence but also over the control over legitimate discourse. Thus, each party attempts to legitimize its own actions and projects while at the same time discrediting and de-legitimizing the opposition. In other words, both the terrorist and the official State claim that the other is the terrorist as it is an illegitimate, violent, and apolitical organization that represents a threat to the well being of the community. This means that the State needs to create a conceptual difference between its own acts of violence, which are presented as legitimate, and those of the population or the opposition, which are qualified as illegitimate. In order to do so, it uses differently the terms *force* and *violence*[6]. Force becomes the use of legitimate violence by the State or its agents, and violence refers to illegitimate acts from those who are not in power or do not benefit from the authorization of those in power to use those means. Through this differentiation in the labelling of the same acts, the agents of the State are portrayed as following norms and acting under the law whereas the opposition is portrayed as being disruptive, violent, illegal, and therefore criminal. Force is conceptualised as being regrettable but necessary whereas violence is unnecessary and evil.

The State does not only attribute itself the monopoly of legitimate violence but also it attributes itself the power to define it[7]. In other words, it has the right to define what violence is and when an act is due to violence or force. It is important to remember that the State uses the law as a tool to back up this definition and categorization. Through this differentiation, the State's rhetoric presents politics as being disassociated from violence. So, the State presents itself as being political and therefore not violent allowing it to

---

5. Jara, Umberto, *Ojo por Ojo: La verdadera historia del Grupo Colina* (Lima: Norma, 2003).
6. Tilly, Charles, The Politics of Collective Violence (Cambridge: Cambridge University Press, 2003).
7. Balibar, Étienne, "Violence: idéalité et cruauté," in *De la Violence*, ed. Françoise Héritier, (Paris: Odile Jacob, 1996), 55-88.

hide its own violence by representing it as something else, as force. Those who use violence (as it has not been sanctioned by the State) are seen as a-political, according to the State rhetoric the use of violence is incompatible with politics. This renders them illegitimate actors in the political realm and criminals according to the law[8]. In terms of the rhetorical strategies used, this means that:

*Both terrorist organizations and the State present themselves as using necessary "force" to fight off the "violence" of* the other who is actually responsible of the first aggression that gave place to the initiation of the conflict When I interviewed women from different republican movements, they went in an in-depth description of the discriminatory policies previous to the troubles, the sectarian attacks by loyalists during the troubles and the verbal and physical abuse they were subjected to from law enforcement agencies and from the military in order to explain their decision to join an organization involved in an armed struggle.

*Both the State and the insurgent organization opt for an ethics of responsibility rather than an ethics of the final goal and this is translated in their discourse.* The use of force is usually justified by stating they are acting according to what Weber[9] calls an ethics of responsibility over an ethics of the final goal. The ethics of responsibility means that the State is willing to pay the price of using morally dubious means or at least dangerous ones and facing the possibility or even the probability of evil ramifications. On the other hand, the ethics of the final goal means that the State is opting to protect a higher principle such as morality, rule of law, or human rights even if that implies negative consequences and suffering in the short term. The protection of the higher goals is more important than the protection of the immediacy.

By opting to use military strategies to obtain their political goal, insurgent organizations are clearly opting to protect the community they claim to represent from an illegitimate State. It is therefore necessary for these organizations to explain that the use of violence is the last resort and that in fact they are using force to protect the community from the violence of the opposition. To this effect, a leader of a republican organization explained to me very candidly that she would love for the conflict to be solved peacefully so that there would be no more loss of life on either side, but that it is impossible because Britain never left a colony willingly; it had to be bombed out of it. She believes the Good Friday Agreement won't last because the Irish people will realize at some point that it is a farce concocted by the British and some

---

8. The labeling of an organization as legitimate or illegitimate by the State is an important political battle in itself. Hall, Stuart, "Deviance, Politics and the Media," in *Deviance and Social Control*, ed. Paul Rock and Mary McIntosh, (London: Tavistock, 1974), 261-306.

9. Weber, Max, *Politics as a Vocation* (Oxford: Oxford University Press, 1958).

republicans that are more interested in themselves and having a career in politics rather than in the community.

*Finally, they present their combatants as being responsible and active citizens willing to die in order to protect their community*[10]. As a member of another Republican organization states, joining is a massive decision because you're either going to end up on the run, in prison, or dead, but it is something that needs to be done and she is proud of doing it for her community. A Peruvian interviewee expressed the same sentiment when declaring that she joined because she truly believed it was the right thing to do to create a more just and equal society and that she considered she had done her part to contribute to that goal and actually felt guilty of not continuing in the struggle.

The discursive strategy is important in the dialogue between the "terrorist" organization and the State and in terms of gaining support both from the international community and from the community they claim to represent. But most importantly, it is important for the recruitment of new combatants and the ideological consolidation or reaffirmation of more experienced combatants. Many of the interviewees both in Peru and Ireland explained how they were exposed to the discourse of the insurgent organization and became profoundly convinced on the legitimacy of the struggle and the illegitimacy of the State. They also described how it was important throughout their involvement to have political discussions, further their political education, and have the opportunity to share the camaraderie of people fighting together for their community.

## With Regards to Government

Whoever is in control over a certain territory needs to actually take responsibility over it. In other words, if the different sides are claiming to be the legitimate State, they actually need to assume the responsibilities that come with it. Those responsibilities are encompassed in what is called governing. This means that whoever is in control of a particular territory needs to:

*Guarantee that issues of health, education, the economy, road infrastructure, etc., are dealt with in an appropriate way.* For example in the territories under the Shining Path, the education curricula were changed in order to follow the ideology of the organization and its version of history, geography, religion, etc.

*Ensure the monopoly of legitimate violence.* Combating the opposition is the most direct way of ensuring the monopoly of legitimate violence. These confrontations not only take place outside from areas under their control but also within their own territory. They need to defeat any local attempts of in-

---

10. Felices-Luna, Maritza, « L'implication des femmes au sein des groupes armés contestataires: la déviance au service d'une entreprise citoyenne, » *Champ Pénal* [online] (Vol 4, 2007), 25p. Available from:
http://champpenal.revues.org/document3173.html

surrection and they also need to disarm members of the community that are not part of the organization.

*Protecting the population under its control of attacks from the enemy:* For example during the troubles, there were neighborhoods that were under the control of the IRA. Those neighborhoods thus needed to be protected from sectarian attacks as well as from attempts by the British Army to regain control over the territory. This task of protecting the community actually is still in place even after the peace agreement. While conducting the fieldwork, I was invited to observe this type of activity on July 11th when bonfires celebrate the arrival of the Orangemen parade. Members of a Republican organization actually patrolled nationalist neighborhoods in order to protect them from loyalist attacks. The people I was with explained that the police would not mobilize to protect those neighborhoods and that in previous years there had been pipe bomb attacks. They considered that by actually physically guarding the borders of the neighborhood they were protecting their community so that they could sleep peacefully. This was an challenging task as those patrolling actually worked during the day and stood guard overnight for a couple of days facing harassment from loyalist and sometimes direct attacks.

*Creating a moral and behavioral code that has to be respected by members of the organization.* Republican organizations as well as the Shining Path and the MRTA are known for punishing members of the organization who have disobeyed orders, tarnished the organization through their actions, or broken the moral code of behavior they are expected to adhere to.

This normative and moral code of behavior does not only apply to members of the organization, but also to all members of the community they claim to represent or that live under their control. In fact the organization attributes itself a police role to control antisocial behaviors (such as alcohol consumption by minors, vandalism, etc.), immoral behaviors (such as laziness, homosexuality, or adultery) or criminal behavior (drug trafficking, rape, and conjugal violence).

Interviewees in both the Irish and the Peruvian conflict describe the organizations' attempts with these regards. A Peruvian interviewee explained that drug addicts, alcoholics, adulterers, homosexuals, and people that did not do their job properly (for example, teachers that would not go to school because there was no control from the official State), would receive a warning to mend their ways. If there was a second complaint from members of the community, they would be punished and in some cases executed. This was also the case with people involved in criminal activity. The same interviewee used an anecdote to show the extent to which her organization was respected. She told me about a time in which she was walking late at night through a dangerous area and was approached by a man attempting to rob her. She confronted him by stating she was a member of the organization working in that area; the robber ended up apologizing, giving her money for transportation and told her to give his name to anyone who bugged her in the area. On the same token, the IRA has acknowledged punishing members of the community involved in drug trafficking or antisocial behavior. One of the interviewees told me that they had to take appropriate measures in order to deal with members of the community who had raped a nurse on her way back to work.

These policing activities have continued in Belfast even after the peace accord with more or less support from the community. While I was conducting the fieldwork I was invited to join members of the republican movement in two policing activities. One of the activities was to patrol an area for about three hours because there was going to be a march of Orangemen passing near a nationalist neighborhood. The idea was to make sure that neither kids nor adults interfere with the march in order to avoid police intervention and a violent confrontation with unionists and loyalists. The other activity was on July 11$^{th}$ to patrol nationalist neighborhoods in order to take away alcohol beverages of under age drinkers in order to avoid problems emanating from the nationalist community during a particularly tense period. Both activities were not welcomed by those who were targeted by it. They openly expressed their disagreement, stating that they had no right to do it but nonetheless did as they were told. Those who complained expressed the belief that now that the peace agreement had been signed the republican movement no longer had the right to police the community as there were other instances designated to do so. Those who participated in the activities declared their frustration at trying to do what was best for the community and trying to protect them from themselves and being challenged and criticized for it.

What we can see here is that contrary to the State who has a bureaucratic, institutional, and administrative apparatus that allows it to govern; a separate military who protects the integrity of the State; and a police and judicial power who deals with the creation and enforcement of a normative behavior or law and order, insurgent organizations have limited resources to accomplish these three tasks. Thus, even when they have different sections that take control over those different roles, the infrastructure is small and usually members play more than one role at the same time or at different stages of their involvement in the organization creating a certain level of confusion or even incoherence in their actions as the different bodies are not clearly recognizable to the community. However difficult and problematic, this normative role is important because it actually shows the existence of a political project as well as its role as protector of the community from its own misguided, antisocial, or criminal members.

## Conclusion

An armed conflict between an insurgent organization and the State takes place between two entities that claim to represent the legitimate State in a particular territory. Therefore they both attribute themselves the monopoly of legitimate violence and of legitimate discourse and claim to be using the necessary force in order to face the violence of those who threaten the community and the State. The State uses law enforcement as well as the military to assert its monopoly of legitimate violence at the same time as it continues its task of governing the political community. Likewise, insurgent organizations are not only involved in a military confrontation with the State, given that they claim that they represent the legitimate State, they are also conducting activities assumed to be the responsibility of a legitimate State: governing the territories under their control, protecting their community from organized violence, creating and enforcing a moral and normative code of behavior by policing antisocial, immoral and criminal acts.

When a State is confronted with an internal armed conflict, its survival is put at risk in terms of the State's actual physical existence through issues regarding geographical boundaries and the physical territory it occupies. More importantly, by symbolically questioning the legitimacy of the existing State, the insurgents put its continuation at risk as they call for its physical, and not only symbolic, destruction in order to be able to build a legitimate State. This particular type of armed conflict needs to be understood as a complex process involving, on the part of the terrorist or the insurgency the creation of a State or the consolidation of an embryonic State and on part of the official State the survival and continuation of an already existing State. Thus, for both parties, the other, the opponent, is the terrorist because they represent a real threat to their existence and to the fulfillment of their political project.

## References

Ashby, Richard. 2005. "Human rights in the war on terror," in *Human rights in the war of terror*, ed. Richard Ashby, Cambridge: Cambridge Univ. Press.

Balibar, Étienne. 1996. "Violence: idéalité et cruauté," in *De la violence*, ed. Françoise Héritier, 55-88. Paris: Odile Jacob.

Felices-Luna, Maritza. 2005. *L'implication des femmes au sein des groupes armés contestataires: les cas du Pérou et de l'Irlande*, Montréal: Université de Montréal.

―――― "L'implication des femmes au sein des groupes armés contestataires: La déviance au service d'une entreprise citoyenne," *Champ Pénal* [online] Vol 4, (2007), 25p. Available from: http://champpenal.revues.org/document3173.html.

Hall, Stuart.1974. "Deviance, politics and the media," in *Deviance and social control*. ed. Paul Rock and Mary McIntosh, 261-306. London: Tavistock.

Jara, Umberto. 2003. *Ojo por Ojo: La verdadera historia del Grupo Colina*. Lima: Norma.

Tilly, Charles. 2003. The politics of collective violence. Cambridge: Cambridge Univ. Press.

Weber, Max. 1958. *Politics as a vocation*. Oxford: Oxford Univ. Press.

# MEDIA AS AN ANTI-PEACE MAKING TOOL IN THE CONTEXT OF GLOBALIZATION: ANALYZING NEWS COVERAGE IN A TIME OF TERROR AND WAR

*Narges Valibeigi*

**Preface**

How the media introduces a set of beliefs, like a religion through the coverage of a terrorist action and in the wartime, is the major schemes of this research. In particular, this paper has focused on the ways Western news media represent Muslims, using the example of a case study of news reportage from the CNN during the Israeli Defense Force (IDF)—Hezbollah war (33 days' war: July 12th to August 14th, 2006). To effectively undertake the study of how Western media represent Muslims based on Western ideologies, we will need to answer what are the major characteristics by which Western media introduce Muslim identity, do the Western media bring equivalent sources for their news to avoid any bias or discrimination, and do Western media state enough evidence and definition for their news? Or, is some of the information missed in these reports?

As Vaughan pointed out, "The distrust and hatred that begets violence and war between people does not spring suddenly and wholly formed from a culture" (as cited in Schaffner 1995, 61). Culture is based on the ideologies that a group of people believes in and upon which they operate. One of the ways we can analyze the ideologies of a society is to look at the every-day life discussions and explanations of political and social events considered newsworthy by its culture. In contemporary societies, the interpretations and explanations expressed in the media have an influence on opinions about every aspect of society, especially during times of conflict and war (Schaffner 1995).

This research shows the way in which Western media represent Easterners as "Others" (Said 1979) and how stereotypes[1] define the Middle East—directly or indirectly—as a threat for the global peace. Edward W. Said (1979) in *Orientalism* analyzed the historical background of the relationship between the West and the East. As Said (1979) argues, there are many stereotypes that the Western media always play with and repeat as the basis for their news or reports; these stereotypes determine what non-Muslims "know" about Islam and the Muslim world. Therefore, we can find characteristics like "extremist," "backward," and "dangerous," for Islam in Western media (Said 1979). Also Karim

---

[1] In sociology, stereotype is defined as "the prejudicial views or descriptions of some categories of people" (Macionis 2005, 623).

(2003) discusses the concept of globalization and how the growth of communication has paralleled rising misperceptions between Northern and Muslim societies. Such misperceptions are fed by historical stereotypes and the ongoing manipulation of information on both sides. According to Karim (2003), because of the domination of the Western powers, the concepts that Western media transfer to public opinion appear to be the only available form of rational and universally valid information about the East. In this sense, media portrayals of Islamic violence are influenced by the dominant cultural meanings attached to both Islam and violence (Karim, 2003).

Edward Said (1997) contributed another study of the relationship between the Western media and the Muslim world in *Covering Islam*. He tried to show how the modern Western media ultimately work to control and manipulate public perception of Islam and the Muslim world through techniques and preferences in journalistic practice, as well as through their representation of social problems and key political events. In this book, Said considered how the Middle East is largely unknown to Americans, except as it is related to newsworthy issues such as oil or terrorism also how newsworthy issues are determined largely by very particularistic groups and interests. He also addressed how easily Western science can be employed to misrepresent a distant and alien society such as Islam (Said 1997). But what is missing in Said's work is an analysis of the new definition of terrorism that appeared after September 11. Since Al-Qaeda's attack on September 11, the Western media have not reported on different kinds of terrorism happening in the world, rather all the detached violent events have been defined as a terrorism that is threatening the whole world. This is the difference between what the threat of communism *was* and what the threat of Islam *is* for the West (Thussu 2003). I accept Stuart Hall's argument (cited in Karim 2000, 5) that:

> There is, not a deliberate plan by the mass media to portray certain issues in particular ways, but a 'naturalized' hegemonic process through which they adhere to a common field of meanings. Nor is it valid to speak of capitalist, liberal, or Zionist control over media content.

Nevertheless, I cannot ignore the consequences of Western media representations of Muslims as a threatening 'Other,' which ultimately serve to undermine prospects for global peace.

The CNN and BBC, as the primary mainstream news corporations have been chosen as the focus of this paper because they tend to dominate the global flow of audio-visual news material, and thus have the greatest influence on world's public opinion (Thussu 2000)[2]. Because of their global

---

[2] "The Atlanta-based cable news network (CNN) is undoubtedly the world leader. CNN, 'the world's only global, 24-hour news network,' best symbolizes American

dominance, they play a hegemonic role in shaping Western stereotypes about the "threats" posed by Muslims and by Islam in general. In addition, their representation of events involving Muslims remain consistent throughout the various media forms these corporations produce, including television and radio programming, and also new media such as websites. Therefore, the restriction of the analysis to the websites of these news corporations is sufficiently representative of the CNN and BBC's overall strategies.

The matter of repeating and reinforcing stereotypes[3] in the news media reports directs our attention to another point that relates to the meaning of globalization. Based on what is defined as the process of globalization, one can realize that one of the most important themes in this process is the concept of peace, which is seen as necessary for shaping global connectivity and security. The media, as one of the most important tools in the flow of information, can direct public opinion and political trends to worsen a critical situation and destroy any hope for making peace in the globalization process. This research does not aim to show that the news media directly and consciously support their powerful governments in creating war; but that the media can help war-makers achieve a positive atmosphere to reach their political goals, even if this is not the media's intent.

## Methodology

In this study three main methods are applied to collect and analyze the data:

1. Case study: to explore the meanings and ideas mentioned about war, media, and Muslim society, including the case of the war between IDF and Hezbollah in 2006.

2. Content analysis: to analyze data from the CNN and BBC's online sources related to this topic to test my hypotheses.

3. Discourse analyses: to identify the major discourse(s)[4] Western media rely upon in their representation of Muslims during times of military conflict.

## Theoretical Arguments

Defining globalization is an important step in order to identify the major connecting points between globalization and the meaning of peace. Globalization in general has been defined as the democratization of finance, technology, and information with the goal of reaching a better life for human be-

---

television journalism, influencing news agenda across the world and indeed shaping international communication."

3 See, For example, Said (1979, 26) as said: "one aspects of the electronic, post modern world is that there has been a reinforcing of stereotypes by which the orient is viewed. Television, the films, and all the media's resources have forced information into more and more standardized molds."

4 Fairclough (2003, 133) says: "we have seen that discourses are ways of representing the world which can be identified and differentiated at levels of abstraction."

ings (Marquardt 2005). Globalization has several dimensions that should be developed all around the world if we expect to achieve global prosperity, peace and freedom, which are just a few of the goals of globalization. Connectivity and cooperation in those dimensions is also needed, such that every single country can take part in the improvement of global society. Globalization is a process that includes some major flows that give it meaning. It is the flow of information that increases the quality and quantity of knowledge that individuals have of the situations and beliefs of others, so this is the most important flow as it shapes the ideology and awareness of global civil society. The information revolution transforms and shrinks the world, and even more importantly, creates virtual communities and networks that cut across national borders (Nye 2004). In the information age, which is the other name for the globalization era, news-making and publishing have become for a source of power for countries that have developed the right technology. News media in the globalization era have become political institutions that have all the dimensions of global institutions (Schudson 2002) and have a component of the governmental process.

Having equal access to different kinds of resources, such as economic, informational, and technological resources, is the most important goal for globalization; this goal would not exist without making and keeping a peaceful atmosphere. There is a global tendency to make peace for a better life as Scholte (2005) mentioned: "the OECD states [organization for economic cooperation and development] have not gone to war against each other since 1945. Military conflict between states of East Asia, Europe and North America also seems unlikely in the foreseeable future. To this extent there is some cause to applaud a correlation between globalization and greater peace" (282). Therefore, by expanding the globalization process, peace is also spread through the increased access to financial, informational, and knowledge-based resources. In a time of war, it is obvious that resources will be divided unequally; because each side of the conflict wants to win, each will use what resources exist to benefit only themselves. What is interesting here is that through the U.N., and many other international and supranational organizations, there exist various agreements and contracts limiting or banning the use of specific weapons during wartime[5]. Although this demonstrates a global tendency towards peace-making, we can see that very little peace actually exists as there are several wars going on in the world. However, we can hope that globalization and the rise of supraterritoriality may reduce militarization and warfare in the world.

Globalization is intended to make and keep peace in order to develop its goals, but how can we define peace in this context when powerful states have tried few other conflict management approaches than war? Who are the main

---

5. For instance, see Price (1998) and Mekata (2000) for the agreement about prohibition of using chemical weapons and discouraging the spread of the nuclear energy.

actors making and keeping peace, and why do not some states—mainly the more powerful ones—use all their means to spread peace around the world? According to Adler (1998), the conditions which encourage peace and oppose war are: civic culture; commitment to the peaceful resolution of disputes; strong institutions; mutual legitimization; peacemakers; social communicative process; material and normative resources; social learning; shared trust; and a collective purpose and social identity (Adler 1998). All of these characteristics are also desirable in global society. But what is important for this study is that these characteristics are also defined by who starts a war in order to make peace. Through this definition peace becomes a practice that needs agencies. There should be some people and physical groups/resources such as the U.N. and other international and regional organizations and institutes that work as peace makers/keepers to practice, teach and learn it; because peace owes its existence to the attachment of meaning to physical reality in particular historical, cultural and political contexts, so "peace is socially constructed" (Adler 1998, 4). Peace, as with many other social concepts such as language, has to be defined and taught in society. This way, people can think and operate based on the theories that deal with peace, not war. Also, on a large scale, suprastate governments and international organizations have to teach and explain the conditions of peace to their members so that they can find peaceful ways for dealing with global issues.

On the one hand, one of the most important agencies for improving knowledge about peace and its essential conditions is the media, which can promote and teach peace to people around the world. As Scholte declared, informal public education is raised through the mass media from which citizens obtain their information and perspectives regarding social life: "thus the mass media significantly affect the amount and type of knowledge that people gain about global issues" (Sholte 2005, 356). In fact, through different media, concepts and news are published which affect common peoples' every day life and shape most of the ideologies and viewpoints regarding others. This means that "the world that we have to deal with politically is out of reach, out of sight, out of mind . . . nearly all of the concerns on the public agenda, citizens deal with a second-hand reality, a reality that is structured by journalists' reports" (McCombs 2004, 1). Therefore, as a tool for transformation, the media can form reality in a specific way by its representation of issues, and can motivate people to reflect in a specific way about what happens in the world. Thus, the media can help the process of cooperation and connectivity or it can destroy this process by representing other peoples and countries as bad, irregular, or unreasonable, and thereby further interrupting global security.

The media, as an important tool in the context of globalization, can create a new meaning of domination and emphasize the gap between powerful and weaker countries. According to Scholte (2005, 345) "the free flow of information principle in global communications has flavored dominant social circles." Thus, one can say that the discourses published in that mainstream news media dominate the public's opinions. These discourses shape both ideology and people's reflection regarding that news. By this, Scholte (2005) also referred to the concept of stratification which exists between Northern and Southern countries in the global society, especially regarding the flows of information and the media; therefore, the more power and access to information a country has, the more influence it can have on public opinion. The monopoly of particular news corporations and media conglomerates on the flows of information is a critical issue in the context of globalization that should be studied for this paper. Like many other flows in globalization, flows of information have the problem of stratification wherein the powerful countries can direct both the quality and quantity of the media's content. In this sense, the weaker and minority groups in global society have little chance to represent themselves in an appropriate way in the news. Because the main (Northern) news conglomerates cover the news for the whole globe, the news is usually portrayed through their eyes and those of their political leaders, although the news media may claim that this is not the case. Consequently, if the dominant news media decide to represent a group of people or a country in a way that motivates other people to boycott or support the war against them, the survival of said country or group will be more limited as compared to other nations.

According to Scholte (2005), the concentration of global communication is on –and from— the North, men, urban dwellers, and a younger generation. Thus, when news agencies like the CNN and BBC want to cover a war and report on it, they choose the specific events and ideas that are more beneficial to them, in the interest of political leadership in the North. Many points and events, those which are in contradiction to their goals, are left out of their news reports. Therefore, in the context of globalization, the media play the role of a tool that expands the powerful countries' hegemony (particularly that of the U.S.).

Based on the points mentioned above, an important concept of "soft power" (Nye 2004) emerges. "Soft power" refers to "the ability to get what you want through attraction rather than coercion or payments. It arises from attractiveness of a country's culture, political ideas, and policies. When our policies are seen as legitimate in the eyes of others, our soft power is enhanced" (Nye 2004, p. x), which has contrast with the "hard power." Soft power is always more effective than coercion, and many meanings and concepts are emphasized through soft power throughout the whole world. Based on Nye's definition (2004), there are three main sources for soft power: culture, which is the most attractive element for people; political values, which are used inside and outside of a country; and finally, the foreign policies of a state that has established legitimacy and authority. "Culture is the set of values and practices that create meaning for a given society and has many manifestations" (Nye 2004, p. 11), and it is usually transferred by selling cultural commodities to other countries. But trade is only one of the ways in which culture is transmitted. It also occurs through personal contacts, visits, exchanges (Nye 2004) and more importantly, through flows of information, especially news and information publishing in the world.

The news is an influential soft power, which has developed an important role in attracting a nation's attention. Information and news deeply affect the whole world and the countries that have access to this soft power can influence the whole global system. Power in both forms—soft and hard—makes social stratification. Social stratification leads to the hegemony of powerful countries over global society. Based on Gramsci's ideas, many scholars define hegemony as "a social control theory, which argues that social and cultural intuitions, including everything from public schools to holiday festivals, function primarily to control people's behavior, usually in the interest of powerful elites" (Rydell and Kroes 2005, p. 4). Who plays the role of the elites in this globalized world depends on who has the power to influence others' lives. Who defines who is an enemy and who is not? Who defines who is with us and who is against us? The media's role here is obvious: the media can define and represent all these things in a single shot through their audio-visual reports for people all around the world. In this sense, the media's and politicians' goal to improve their power and lead public opinion is in harmony with each other.

In fact, there are many overlapping issues and goals confronting governments and the media. Through the news, which is constantly being aired by many different kinds of media, peace negotiations have a critical role in shaping the global atmosphere toward the anti-peace making tendency in public opinion. But political leaders try to keep the media out of these peace negotiations in global or regional political systems because they know that "the greater the level of media involvement, it is claimed, the more likely the talks will fail" according to Wolfsfeld (as cited in Darby 2003, p. 87). This means that governments believe that the media will at least interrupt the peace process, if not destroy it entirely. On the other hand, the news media wants to find newsworthy information to publish. The media, especially the news agencies, are the most important resources in global society that can inform people about what is going on around the world. Because of this role, the news media try to reach the hottest and the most exclusive news from the sites of conflict, including peace negotiations themselves.

It is true that one of the goals in every society is for the government to take control over events and the flow of information; "when governments are in a position to initiate events it provides them with important advantages in their relations with the news media. It allows them to carefully orchestrate what happens in the field and to prepare the accompany spin" according to Wolfsfeld (as cited in Darby 2003, p. 90). The most important points that connect the government to the news media is that the government produces newsworthy information for the news media. When, on the other hand, journalists are in a position to cultivate alternative sources of information it increases their ability to play an independent role, the government loses its power to dedicate storylines (Darby 2003). This is why political leaders usually try not to let news agencies use alternative sources that may be in contrast with their goals. Governments do not completely succeed at that; however, they can make a political atmosphere in which the news media only cover what the politicians want and in a way that they agree with.

Moreover, the most powerful states try to control the news media in order to legitimize in the public opinion the war making they have done in order to make peace. News agencies usually try to convince audiences that the main reason for the war is to make peace. Not all news agencies rely exclusively on what their politicians have said about a war, neither do all of them accept their politicians' ideologies regarding the war. However, by representing war through politicians' perspectives—for instance, identifying the instigator of the war or defining who is the enemy and who is not—the media become tools of war-making because they are only repeating their political leaders' thoughts about the war and peace-making. Also, politicians realize that they should try to control the content of the news media because the news media can shape public opinion and set the public agenda. In situations where governments are unable to mobilize a wide level of support for their efforts, the news media can lend important assistance to political leaders in shaping public agenda to match politicians' goals. Moreover, it is difficult for political leaders to carry out long-range policies in the peace negotiations during war time if the political environment becomes increasingly hostile over time (Wolfsfeld 2002); if the media are unsuccessful in changing public opinion regarding the war, politicians may find themselves in a difficult position for defending their goals. In this sense, one may argue whether or not the media can still have an informative function in the context of globalization when governments have power over media content. More importantly, one can ask what is the role of the news media in the process of peace making in the global society?

The news media are extremely sensitive to the political environment, and they depend on whoever has the power to set the agenda strongly and quickly. These kinds of media tend to be sensationalist, negative, and portray a horrible world. The more sensationalist the media environment, the more likely the news media will serve to escalate conflict and to obstruct attempts at peace making. If news coverage is sensationalized, the world becomes a terrifying place filled with threats and violence, one in which political leaders and citizens must be always concerned with security. This is the desire that the peace-making process should mention in the context of globalization. But when the news media represent a world in which enemies appear to be powerful and unwilling to compromise, as they usually do in reporting on

"Eastern"[6] people who are defined as the enemy, there is no way other than war for making peace in the world. Given this atmosphere, those promoting peace and reconciliation appear to be naïve (Wolsfeld 2002).

A peace process is also a rather boring affair because it involves negotiations happening over a long period of time. There may be some interesting news during the peace negotiations themselves, but political leaders have little to provide journalists throughout the long periods in between. Those opposed to peace, on the other hand, are often in a better position to provide exciting news to the media. Political violence and war is always more newsworthy than the peace negotiations and it has a major impact on both the amount and quality of news stories (Wolsfeld 2002). Therefore, it is better for the media to represent the interesting news that a conflict situation offers.

One of the most important characteristics of the media which relates to this subject is that the media always want to simplify the situation and define which side of the war is the enemy and which one is not. Many media reports regarding the terrorist actions and wars taking place in the Middle East or by Middle Easterners have been oversimplified and sensationalized, particularly in terms of exaggerating the global threats these wars pose to global security. For instance, in the study of the online news coverage of the IDF-Hezbollah war, one can find that the CNN and BBC often made the distinction for their audiences that the IDF was not the instigator of the war, but that Hezbollah was the one that provoked the IDF by arresting/capturing two Israeli soldiers. Therefore, Israel was portrayed as the victim and Hezbollah as the enemy, who should be removed from that region in order to create peace in the Middle East. They make the situation a black and white one, and define who the guilty party is and who the victim is without referring to the historical context in which the war has happened.

The news plays a critical role in introducing a group like Hezbollah to the people who are unfamiliar with it. Because most people around the world were not inside the war and may not have heard anything about the Hezbollah and its reasons for fighting with Israel, the newsmakers were able to hide the historic basis for the conflict in the Middle East. As the study of the news coverage for IDF-Hezbollah war shows, the news media like the CNN and BBC continued to repeat old stereotypes about Arabs, Muslims, and the Middle East in their reports on the war. Therefore, many of the people for whom the most reliable source of information are these major news media, identified the minority group –like Hezbollah—as an obvious force behind fundamentalism and insecurity in the world. In this sense, the media become an anti-peacemaking actor who does not desire actual peace in the world. What the media do in these kinds of situations is just increase the feeling of

---

6. This refers to the division that Edward Said (1979) talked about in his pioneering work, *Orientals*. I have talked about this term in the background section of this paper.

hatred among people in the world against a specific group[7]. However, it should be noted that by studying the content of news coverage, one can find the politicians' footprints in these reports. In fact, there are many subjects hidden in news reports that may affect the audience differently from what politicians want; reporters may consider these hidden subjects as those that influence public opinion most significantly. By hiding some pieces of information and emphasizing others in their reports, the media exaggerate and sensationalize the war situation. "In general, a sensationalist news media serves to intensify political conflicts and to make peace more difficult . . . [political] leaders' attempts to mobilize citizens for war however will find the sensationalist press to be eager allies"(Wolfsfeld 2002, 151-2).

The news media also have an important impact on political conflict and the peace process when they provide broad publicity for the weaker side of the conflict, even if this side is not as strong or threatening as the media claim. When the weaker side achieves coverage, it becomes an important player in the conflict. However, it may be represented as one of the most dangerous threats for global society and as decreasing the overall level of security around the world. It is in these situations that the news media become participants in the conflict and make it more difficult for political leaders to take control. On the other hand, when the news media allow the stronger side of the conflict to dominate media coverage, existing gaps in power are reinforced; because the powerful side has the benefit of introducing the weaker side in a way that it want to legitimize the war and attacks on the weaker. The media often choose to report on shocking stories or attractive names and events to the general public. This manner of being tremendously contentious, loud or attention grabbing is called sensationalism. "The more the media in a particular context move toward a sensationalist format the more dangerous they become. The world portrayed by tabloid journalism is a frightening place" (Wolfsfeld 2002, 152-3) in which every argument becomes a crisis and every danger a serious threat.

A terrorist action, which is defined as unlawful violence or threat of unlawful violence to inculcate fear, in this sense, is a situation that makes a sensational atmosphere for the politicians as well as the news media; especially when the terror takes place in the Middle East or by Easterners. As mentioned before, Said emphasized the role that stereotypes play in shaping the meaning of "other" regarding Easterners. In Western media, such as the CNN and BBC, a group like Hezbollah is defined as "other" who deals with terrorist action regardless of its non-violence and social missions in its society. The "terrorist" term in Western media is a label attached to military groups in the Middle East who fight against Israel; because the Western political leaders have financial and political profits in

---

7. Refer to Table 1 to see how a group is described in the Western news media.

supporting Israel. Meanwhile, the news media cannot escape from this political atmosphere.

Terror is a meaning that is –more or less—attached to the Muslim community because of the specific way the news media define it. There is a network of terror shown in the media through the coverage of different wars and terrorist actions that connects all the unlawful violence actions together against the West and Israel. After 9/11 all the operations defined as terrorist actions are believed to be linked to each other. This new concept of terrorism, which is a matter of publicity, only reminds the media audiences of only one group: Muslims. A group like Hezbollah is characterized as terrorist because it doesn't accept the Western and Israeli agreements about Lebanese land which is still occupied by Israel and Muslims who are in the Israeli jail. Although Hezbollah accepted the capture of Israeli soldiers in July 2006 – which became Israel's pretext to attack Lebanon—, the media rarely mentioned why Hezbollah did this violence/terrorist action.

If we want to briefly summarize the relationship between Hezbollah and Israel, we should point out that Hezbollah emerged in the wake of Israel's all-out invasion of Lebanon in 1982. From that time, the IDF moved freely back and force across the border (Norton 1999). Also, "there is a little doubt that Iran and Syria were deeply involved in the creation of Hezbollah" (Norton 1999, 24). With Israel showing no intention of withdrawing from Lebanon, and a central government in Beirut whose actions belied its claim to represent all Lebanese, Hezbollah soon began attracting a large number of followers and became a strong party that could provide some seats in Lebanon parliament and government membership. After a long struggle with the IDF, in 2000 Hezbollah liberated most of southern Lebanon from the long occupation by Israel but not completely. In July 2006, Hezbollah captured two Israeli soldiers; in reply, Israel began to attack southern Lebanon, then Beirut and other Lebanese cites to put pressure on Hezbollah to release those soldiers. Consequently, Hezbollah attacked Israel and tried to force Israel to liberate Lebanese and Palestinian prisoners in Israeli jails whose faults are not proved in any formal court yet. Whether or not the media can operate as an unbiased and unprejudiced tool, and can represent these stories while avoiding the use of existing stereotypes and political traps is a matter that is studied in this paper.

**The Quantitative Data: The Frequencies in the News Reports**
According to Riffe et al. (1998) content is the central point of each message. Therefore, if we want to measure the level of influence the message has on the receivers, we should measure how many times a specific variant is repeated in the text and what the systematic process of forming that message is (Riffe et al. 1998, 9). Content analysis offers a foundation for a multidimensional look at news coverage during a global crisis. Holsti (1969) said that quantitative content analysis gives the research reliability based on its three

main characteristics: objectivity, systematic, and generality. By *objectivity* Holsti (1969) meant that "each step of the research process must be carried out on the basis of explicitly formulated rules and procedures" (Holsti 1969, 3). Systematic refers to when the inclusion and exclusion of content is shaped based on applied rules; and generality occurs when the findings have theoretical relevance (Holsti 1969). The main reason why content analysis has been applied in this paper is that by analyzing the content of the news the research can be shaped based on objectivity, systematic and generality by which it would become reliable for the readers.

In this section, three main subjects are measured under the main question: How is Hezbollah characterized by the CNN and BBC: 1) how often did these two news agencies define Hezbollah as a violent group directly? 2), how often did the CNN and BBC characterize it as a terrorist and violent group indirectly, and 3) how often did they mention non-violent features for Hezbollah? As with other quantitative research, a specific time period has been chosen for this research. Fifty reports from the CNN and BBC website have been studied. All the reports are directly about the IDF-Hezbollah's war between July 12th and August 14th 2006.

Table 1: Characterizing Hezbollah as a violence group directly[8]

| Character [9] | BBC | CNN |
|---|---|---|
| Muslim Militia | 24 | 32 |
| Militia/ Guerrilla/ Fighter/ Gunman | 33 | 59 |
| Terrorist/ Deadly org./ Bloodstained | 7 | 10 |
| Suicide bomber/ Taking Hostages | 7 | 4 |

The first table contains characteristics that directly define Hezbollah as a violent group: Muslim Militia with the frequency of 24 in the BBC and 32 in the CNN among 50 reports is a high frequency. Three different characteristics categories: "Terrorists/deadly org/bloodstained," "Guerrilla/ gunman," "Suicide bomber/hostage taking," all remind the audiences of Hez-

---

8. As mentioned above, 50 reports from the CNN have been read for this study.
9. The number associated with each characteristic includes the number of times that characteristic was repeated within a single report as well as within all 50 reports.

bollah being a violent/terrorist group. Based on the media coverage, all the operations and activities of Hezbollah are unlawful and against the international agreements. Therefore, when the CNN and BBC described Hezbollah members as "fighters," most of the audiences think that Hezbollah fights against Israel—the most important ally of the US—illegitimately. The news media based on the political rules give legitimization to one side of the war and the other side –in this case Hezbollah—is defined as ruthless and terrorist group/party.

Table 2: Characterizing Hezbollah as a violence group indirectly[10]

| Character[11] | BBC | CNN |
|---|---|---|
| Supported by Iran and Syria | 35 | 21 |
| Fundamental/Extremist | 3 | 2 |
| Autonomous in Lebanon | 3 | 2 |

The second table contains the characteristics that indirectly relates to the violence. "Fundamental/ extremist," "Autonomous in Lebanon," and "Supported by Iran and Syria," have the content of violence. Fundamental/extremist Muslim reminds the audiences of Al-Qaeda and being Autonomous in Lebanon means Hezbollah is an illegal party in its states. The character "supported by Iran and Syria" contains the name of two already introduced dangerous states as threats for the global security based on the US politicians and media[12]. At the same time, Israel supported by the US and other Western states have the right of occupying Lebanese territory and capturing many Muslims but Hezbollah doesn't have the right to defend itself and its country.

---

10. As mentioned above, 50 reports from the CNN have been read for this study
11. The number associated with each characteristic includes the number of times that characteristic was repeated within a single report as well as within all 50 reports.
12. For example see:
http://www.cnn.com/2006/WORLD/europe/12/08/newspapers/index.html?iref=newssearch.

ENGAGING TERROR

Table 3: The non-violence characteristics defined for Hezbollah[13]

| Character[14] | BBC | CNN |
|---|---|---|
| Social Welfare | 2 | 3 |
| Lebanese | 4 | 2 |
| Political Party | 12 | 10 |
| Organization/ Group (without specification) | 2 | 6 |

Let's compare this table with the previous ones. This table contains the non-violent characteristics. But as we can see the BBC and the CNN very rarely talked about the social missions of Hezbollah or even its nationality.

These tables show that the most important characteristic for Hezbollah that the BBC emphasizes is its relation with Iran and Syria, whereas for CNN, the militant aspect of Hezbollah is of most importance. The second feature that the BBC refers to is the militant base of Hezbollah whereas the CNN refers to the support that Hezbollah receives from Iran and Syria. Also, for the BBC being Muslim in general and Shiite in particular as well as being politically active are all equally important in identifying what Hezbollah is, while for the CNN being Muslim is more important than being Shiite, and Hezbollah's political activity is considered less important than its religious aspects. As we can see, there are not many differences between the BBC and CNN in their representation of Hezbollah's characteristics in this war. Although these two news agencies make the distinction between the religious features of a Muslim community and its political and military characteristics, by mentioning these features in conjunction audiences do not separate these features from each other, and Islam becomes equated with illegal military actions, which is defined as terrorism. Furthermore, by confounding these different characteristics, the BBC and CNN work to legitimize Israeli attacks on Lebanon; the reports not only focused on the negative and militant characteristics of Hezbollah, but also emphasized the illegality of these actions. Thus, when a militant group engages in illegal activity a powerful country can gain legitimacy to control the enemy, especially in this case where the news media have declared that Hezbollah is a terrorist group which threats global security.

---

13. As mentioned above, 50 reports from the CNN have been read for this study
14. The number associated with each characteristic includes the number of times that characteristic was repeated within a single report as well as within all 50 reports

These news media do not make a clear distinction between the religious, political, and military aspect of Hezbollah although they use different terms for introducing Hezbollah fighters such as terrorist, militant, Shiite Muslim, or Lebanese. As Said (1997) implied, this kind of coverage is misleadingly full. "It [western news coverage] has given consumers of news the sense that they have understood Islam without at the same time intimating to them that a great deal in this energetic coverage is based on far from objective material" (Said 1997, li). As a result, the news media spread hatred towards a group without mentioning that some information is missing from their report; most audiences absorb this information as is, without questioning its accuracy.

## Analyzing News Content
There are some methods in the media for covering and reporting news and events in their own preferred ways such as: simplification of the events, over lexicalization in defining the news, lack of history in the news, using double standard evaluation, and generalization.

### *Simplification*
The BBC and CNN usually draw a line between the bad and the good side of a critical situation. In these kinds of wars between Israel and Muslims (in this case, with Hezbollah) the CNN and BBC base their position on old stereotypes about Muslim communities. The following example is one of the CNN's reports after an attack on Qana during which many Lebanese civilians were killed by Israel's air-strike. What is remarkable here is that despite the fact that Israel killed many civilians, Lebanon is defined as the guilty party.

> We [Israel's nation and IDF] are dealing with a ruthless, cynical, cruel enemy [Hezbollah], one of the most monstrous terror organizations this world has known. They [Hezbollah] have no regard for Israeli life, and they have no regard for Lebanese life… Clearly, we did not know the civilians were in the way, said IDF spokesman Jacob Dalal, who added that Israel was exercising its right to defend itself with its campaign of airstrikes[15].

Representation of Israel as the good side of this war and Hezbollah as the bad side repeats the historical labels, as seen in Western movies and news, of Arabs as the bad guys (Shaheen 2001). Through these points one can claim that the CNN and BBC try to characterize Hezbollah in a specific way: as a threat and a source of fear, even in its own country. This emphasizes the historical stereotype of Arabs as a brutal nation. By claiming this, the bloody

---

15. http://www.cnn.com/2006/WORLD/meast/07/30/mideast.main/index.html?iref=newssearch

attacks of Israel on Lebanon, like what happened in Qana[16], can be made acceptable. Israel becomes an innocent who was only responding in kind to Hezbollah's attacks; in contrast, Hezbollah is the guilty perpetrator of chaos in the region. These kinds of statements play a main role in legitimizing the war and Israeli attacks.

The other related issue here is the concept of defense, which is identified as a positive aspect of Israel and a harsh aspect of Hezbollah. When the CNN and BBC refer to the war, it is suggested that Israel has the definite right to respond to Hezbollah with force, but unacceptable for Hezbollah to use force even if the Lebanese army is told not to take part in the war[17]. Who, then, should defend Lebanon? Do other Muslim nations have the equal right to defend themselves as Israel and Western nations do?

## *Over Lexicalization*

Referring to the text of the reports by the BBC and CNN, we can identify some of the most popular characteristics that they use to identify Hezbollah. For instance:

> Hezbollah, a fundamentalist Shiite Muslim militant group, emerges as a force in Beirut, the Bekaa Valley and southern Lebanon. Sponsored by Iran, modeled after Iran's Revolutionary Guards and supported by Syria, Hezbollah aims to establish a Shiite Islamic state in Lebanon and force Western interests like Israel and the United States out of the region[18].

The main characteristics mentioned in this paragraph are: "fundamental," "militant," "force," and "sponsored by Iran's Revolutionary Guard"; all of these include aspects of violence. Other characters are repeated several times in one sentence, such as "militia" and "force." These two are almost synonyms, and repeating them only serves to further emphasize the violent aspects of Hezbollah's nature. Linguists call this redundancy or over-lexicalization. What over-lexicalization does is reinforce the dominant meaning through repetition and reiteration. Also, this paragraph mention Hezbollah's demand to "force Western interests like Israel and the United States out of the region"[19] while defining the goals and demands of the weaker side of a conflict or of terrorist actions is found only on the odd occasion in the news reportages. Consequently, when audiences consider the previous information

---

16. http://www.cnn.com/2006/WORLD/meast/07/30/mideast.main/index.html
17. See, For example, "The Lebanese army has been ordered not to respond to the Israeli attacks" in http://news.bbc.co.uk/go/pr/fr/-/2/hi/middle_east/5192036.stm
18. http://www.cnn.com/2006/WORLD/meast/07/14/israel.lebanon.timeline/index.html?iref=newssearch
19. Ibid

given in the last paragraphs of the same report, Hezbollah and its aims comes to be seen as intrinsically violent. Meanwhile, when the CNN and BBC refer to the U.S. and Israel's aim to remove Hezbollah from the region, they do not mention it as a violence and illegal aim and action.

Another example of how the BBC represents Hezbollah is in an article entitled "Profile: Sheikh Hassan Nasrallah,"[20] which begins with the following statement:

> Hezbollah's military wing is believed to have been behind a large number of deadly attacks, hijackings, kidnappings of Westerners, including Terry Waite, and the bombing of the U.S. Marine barracks in Beirut which killed 241 people in 1983[21].

"Military wing," "deadly attack," "hijacking," "kidnapping," and "bombing" are the major words with which Hezbollah has been identified. Similarly to what we said about the last example, in this article the BBC repeatedly words that are synonyms to each other, such as "deadly attack and bombing," to emphasize this characterization of Hezbollah as perpetuating violence and threat. But what makes this phrase noteworthy is that although the BBC mentions the "military wing of Hezbollah," it doesn't provide any explanation as to what the other wings of Hezbollah might be. Also, Western media like the CNN and BBC rarely talk about Israel in this way. They never provide a report called "who is Israel" or "what is IDF" or "what are the U.N.'s resolutions regarding Israel regarding the matter of Palestine or Lebanon?" It is assumed that everyone already knows who Israel is; at least these questions remain unanswered through the reports about this war.

## *Double Standard Evaluation*

These news agencies, backed by Western politicians, use a double standard in portraying Hezbollah as opposed to Israel. Why is it so important for the West that Israel should be able to defend itself, but neither Lebanon with its Army, nor Hezbollah and its militia can defend Lebanon? Isn't it Western countries and other political pressure that forces Hezbollah to act as a violent group? This may guide us to seek out more important questions such as: what is the role of Western societies, and Israel, in identifying a group like Hezbollah as fundamental and terrorist?

Israel's ambassador to the United Nations, Dan Gillerman, called it a "horrible, tragic incident." But Gillerman said the dead were "victims of Hezbollah," which he said was using civilian buildings as cover to launch rockets into Israel. "We are dealing with a ruthless, cynical, cruel enemy, one of the most monstrous terror organizations this world has known" he said.

---

20. http://news.bbc.co.uk/2/hi/in_depth/5176612.stm
21. Ibid

"They [Hezbollah members] have no regard for Israeli life, and they have no regard for Lebanese life. Clearly, we did not know the civilians were in the way," said IDF spokesman Jacob Dalal, who added that Israel was exercising its right to defend itself with its campaign of airstrikes.

## *Lack of History*

In the BBC and CNN's eyes the reason for this war is really simple; Hezbollah captured two Israeli soldiers and Israel attacked Lebanon to force Hezbollah to free their soldiers. As Bush simply defined it:

> Hezbollah started the crisis on July 12 when the terrorist group Hezbollah launched its raid into Israel that led to the kidnapping of two soldiers. Israel than began its offensive and Hezbollah rocketed Israeli targets. 'I believe sovereign nations have the right to defend their people from terrorist attack, and to take the necessary action to prevent those attacks,' Bush said, also emphasizing that 'we have called on Israel to continue to exercise the greatest possible care to protect innocent lives'.[22]

The memory of these news media as well as Bush—as a political leader—only goes back four weeks to when the soldiers were arrested but no further. According to their logic, Hezbollah operated a terrorist action, so firstly, it is not strange that Israel should defend itself, and secondly, Hezbollah has become a global threat that should be removed as soon as possible. These kinds of reports want to provide an acceptable explanation for this war. Based on the explanation they have given, this is a global war intended to spread and defend global values, but whether these Western values are really global values is a debatable issue. More importantly, how can the U.S. and other Westerners bring peace by making war? Simplifying the situation is a technique that Western media like the CNN and the BBC always use for portraying one side as innocent and the other as fatal. For instance, in another report on the CNN, we read:

> Hezbollah militants cross into Israel, kill three Israeli soldiers and kidnap two others in a bid to negotiate a prisoner exchange, a demand rebuffed by Israel. Another five Israeli soldiers are killed after the ambush. Israel responds with a naval blockade and by bombing hundreds of targets in Lebanon, including Beirut's airport and Hezbollah's headquarters in southern Beirut[23].

---

22. http://www.cnn.com/2006/WORLD/europe/07/22/saturday/index.html?iref=newssearch
23. http://www.cnn.com/2006/WORLD/meast/07/14/israel.lebanon.timeline/index.html

In this phrase it is Hezbollah who captured two Israeli soldiers and killed three others, and Israel has the right to respond to these actions with lethal force.

But in this kind of report the CNN never mentions that the conflict between Israel and Muslims has a long history in the Middle East. Occupying southern Lebanon for many years and capturing many Lebanese and Palestinians by Israel are only a few examples of this historical conflict. This is mentioned very rarely in Western media as a potential reason for this war. The BBC and CNN suggest that the only reason for Hezbollah's action to capture Israeli soldiers was in order to exchange them for its prisoners being held in Israeli jails. But they ignore that the reason for capturing those Israeli soldiers could be the huge number of Lebanese and Palestinians seized by Israel and liberation of South Lebanon from Israeli occupation completely[24].

### *Generalization*
The other method that the news media used for providing excuse for Israel's attacks on Hezbollah is the suggestion that a relationship exists between Hezbollah and other fundamental/terrorist organizations, such as Al-Qaeda. So, for example, one CNN report claims:

> Hezbollah, a Shiite militia, and al-Qaeda, a Sunni group, share a common enemy, but they have long been wary of each another. Despite their differences, al-Zawahiri tells the Muslims in Lebanon and Palestinian territories, 'Stand with us and we will stand with you'... 'Nowhere is safe from al-Qaeda attacks', he warned, saying that 'the whole world is an open field for us.' ... 'As they attack us everywhere, we will attack them everywhere. They gang up to wage war on us; our (Islamic) nation will fight them and wage war on them,' al-Zawahiri said[25].

This process of generalizing and linking Hezbollah to al-Qaeda, which has become the most aggressive power after 9/11, specific attributes to all Muslims, especially to Shiite in this case, paints the entire Muslim community as one that poses a threat to the whole world. Although the CNN doesn't ignore the division between Sunni and Shiite in regards to their beliefs, it suggests to us how they are equal in sense of their actions and in their support of one another. The CNN quotes al-Zawaheri, who is a member of al-Qaeda and a strict Sunni, and mentioned that although Shiite and Sunni are different in some of their rituals, "they share a common enemy." By default, this enemy is the West and modernity, and so we can easily find the implication that

---

24. http://www.youtube.com/watch?v=249JaIaubVw
25. http://www.cnn.com/2006/WORLD/meast/07/27/zawahiri.tape/index.html?iref=newssearch

the Muslim community is a threat to Western society because all of them share this specific enemy. But CNN never talks about whether or not Hezbollah shares this belief and accepts being identified as al-Qaeda's ally. This is one of the important methods that the media apply for proving their information. Although al Zawaheri said that al-Qaeda will defend all Muslims against the West's attacks, one cannot find any report to confirm that Lebanese, Palestinian, and other Muslim countries support al-Qaeda in this case in CNN and BBC's reports.

## Conclusion

Globalization, as a process intended to create a more peaceful atmosphere for social affairs on both small and large scales, has various physical agencies and institutes furthering its goals. That making and keeping peace in global society is a desired goal of globalization is revealed though the international agreements on banning and limiting the usage of many kinds of weapons and through peace negotiations which are increasing in quantity, but not quality.

The information flow, which is one of the main flows in globalization process, has its physical agencies; one of the most important agencies is the media. The media play a significant role in educating people about other societies and belief systems, and they also have the important role of transferring the news to the whole globe. If we consider that the media are the most important tools in shrinking time and space, we can understand how it is vital for politicians to control this flow.

Because global society is stratified, powerful countries have greater access to information sources and technologies, while weaker states only consume this information. The point being that this unequal flow from the North to the South means that only the Northern states have the opportunity to propose their way of thinking to their own people and to people in other countries. In this sense, how Northern states, especially the U.S., define events in a critical situation like a war shapes most of the world's thinking and reacting about those events. Although the news media claim that they are free and independent in their news reportages, they are bonded to the political hegemonic system and their own historical biases. This is particularly true considering what has happened in the Middle East and how the mainstream news media have reported on it. In fact, the Western media have many kinds of biases against the Middle East/Muslim countries, and these are represented in their news reports; "the orient has uniformly been considered an inferior part of the world" (Said 1997, 4) in these news media. The media, if they are not directly playing the role of anti-peace maker in the globalization process, nevertheless do not help the making and keeping of peace because they portray only a single specific image of the group in question—Shiite Muslims in this case. Thus, the media just spreads feelings of hatred towards that group.

Analyzing the qualitative and quantitative data, we can now answer the main question that was raised at the beginning of our research. In the coverage of the war between the IDF and Hezbollah by the BBC and CNN, many historical stereotypes were repeated, and there is no doubt that these two news agencies published their news with little attempt to analyze the situation equitably. The war coverage emphasizes only the violent aspects of Hezbollah. In looking at the CNN reportage defining Hezbollah as a group of militants, guerrillas, and fighters, or that of the BBC defining Hezbollah through its allies, we can declare that these two news agencies, as the representatives of Western media, transfer specific concepts based on their ideology. Their ideology, as we see in their news reports, is that the West has secular values while Hezbollah has a religion devoid of values. Therefore, this war is portrayed as a confrontation between values and religion. More specifically, Shi'im is depicted as an important sect of Islam, and defined as an anomic community.

Besides the biased content of these reports, the BBC and CNN's websites also apply many techniques to emphasize their goal to prove that Hezbollah is the perpetrator of the war and to legitimize Israel's attacks. They use "simplification" to reduce the situation of war to one where there is a bad side who attacks, and a good side who just defends itself. The BBC and CNN try to show that in this war, Hezbollah is the attacker and Israel just defends itself. Meanwhile, because of the important situation of Israel in the Middle East, it shouldn't be characterized as a weak victim. Therefore, only Israeli and Lebanese civilians are the victims of this war and IDF is defender. The BBC and CNN never mention the historical and economic bases of this war. They never talk about why there are so many Lebanese in Israel prisons or why the U.S. and Israel were not in any rush to assert a cease-fire[26].

The other technique used in these kinds of reports is that they use big bold titles for reports which are meant to promote the ideological bases for the BBC and CNN. Titles like "formidable enemy,"[27] "ominous threat,"[28] and "violence mixed with social mission"[29] are only used for Hezbollah but not Israel. The BBC and CNN, as the most powerful and effective news agencies, shape the way of thinking for a large group of audiences who is not taking part in the war and who does not know anything of Hezbollah or Islam and Shiite Muslims beyond this news coverage.

---

26. See, for example, http://news.bbc.co.uk/go/pr/fr/-/2/hi/middle_east/5218210.stm and http://www.cnn.com/2006/WORLD/meast/07/19/mideast.diplomacy/index.html?iref=newssearch.

27. http://news.bbc.co.uk/2/hi/middle_east/5177346.stm

28. http://news.bbc.co.uk/go/pr/fr/-/2/hi/middle_east/5185586.stm

29. http://www.cnn.com/2006/WORLD/meast/07/13/hezbollah/index.html?iref=newssearch

In general, the discourse analysis for this research (qualitative method), based on content analysis data (quantitative method), reveals that not only is the news coverage regarding this war unfair, but it also emphasizes stereotypes like the violent character of Arabs and Muslims. Consequently, although the media, as a strong tool of information flow, could potentially play the role of peace-maker/keeper and further the free flow of information, they do not do so in practice.

# References

Adler, E. "Condition(s) of peace." *Cambridge University Press* 24 (1998): 165-192.
BBC News: http://news.bbc.co.uk/.
Castells, M. 2000. *The rise of the network society.* Cambridge: Blackwell Publishers.
CNN News: http://www.cnn.com/.
Darby, J. and R. MacGinty. 2003. *Contemporary peace making.* New York: Palgrave Macmillan.
Eagleton, T. 1991. *Ideology: An introduction.* London: Verso.
Fairclough, N. 2003. *Analysing discourse: Textual analysis for social research.* New York: Routledge.
Hall, S. et al. 1980. *Culture, media, language: Working papers in cultural studies. 1972-79*, Abingdon: Routledge.
Holsti, O. R. 1969. *Content analysis for the social sciences and humanities.* Don Mils, Ontario: Addison-Wesley Publishing Company.
Karim, H. K. 2003. *Islamic peril.* New York: Black Rose.
Macionis, J. J., & Gerber, L. M. 2005. *Sociology.* Toronto: Prentice Hall.
Marquardt, M. J. "Globalization: The pathway to prosperity, freedom and peace." *Human Resource Development International*, 8 (2005): 127-29.
McCombs, M. 2004. *Setting the agenda: The mass media and public opinion.* Cambridge: Polity Press.
Mekata, M. 2000. "Building partnership toward a common goal: Experiences of the international campaign to ban landmines." In *The third force: The rise of transnational civil society,* ed. A.M. Florini, 143-76. Tokyo/Washington, DC: Japan Center for International Exchange/Carnegie Endowment for International Peace.
Norton, A. R. 2000. "Hizballah and the Israeli withdrawal from Southern Lebanon." *Journal of Palestine Studies*, 30 (1): 22-35.
Nye, J. S. 2004. *Soft power: The means to success in world politics.* New York: Public Affairs.
Prince, R. 1998. "Reserving the gun sights: Transnational civil society targets land mines." *International Organization*, 52 (3): 613-44.
Riffe, D. et al. 1998. *Analyzing media messages: Using quantitative content analysis in research.* Mahwah, N.J.: Erlbaum.
Rydell, R. W., and R. Kroes. 2005. *Buffalo Bill in Bologna: The Americanization of the world, 1869-1922.* Chicago: Univ. of Chicago Press.
Said, E. W. 1997. *Covering Islam.* New York: Vintage Books.
——— 1979. *Orientalism.* New York: Vintage Books.
Schafnner, C., and A. L. Wenden. 1995. *Language and peace.* England: Dartmouth Publishing Company Limited.
Scholte, J.A. 2005. *Globalization: A critical introduction.* Basingstoke: Palgrave Macmillan.

Schudson, M. 2002. "The news media as political institutions." *Annual Review of Political Science*,(5): 249-69.

Thussu, D. K. (2000). *International communication: Continuing and change.* New York: Hodder Arnold.

Thussu, D. K. and D. Freedman. 2003. *War and the media: Reporting conflict 24/7.* London: Sage Publications Ltd.

Wolsfeld, G. 2002. *Political communication in a new era.* Abingdon: Taylor & Francis Ltd.

# THE MEDIA IN THE SERVICE OF TERRORISM

*Dario Kuntić*

The aim of this paper is to illustrate the way in which modern terrorists use the media to spread terror all around the globe.

First, it is necessary to briefly define the terms used in this work. The term *terrorism* denotes premeditated violence perpetrated against combatant and noncombatant targets by violent groups or individuals, usually intended to influence an audience, in order to achieve political or religious goals. Although there is no single definition of terrorism, this one should be appropriate for this paper. The term *media* encompasses newspapers, radio, television, and the Internet.

It is also necessary to mention that "the communication" between terrorists and public is not restricted only to the modern times. The Assassin Sect of Shia Islam, which attempted to sow terror in the Muslim world in the Middle Ages, relied upon word of mouth in the mosques and market places to relay news on their attacks; similar methods of transmitting fear were used by the Russian and Balkan terrorists of the nineteenth century.[1] And the Palestinian group Black September carried out spectacular terrorist action at the Munich Olympic in 1972, which attracted worldwide media attention of approximately 500 million people. Modern terrorist groups, such as al-Qaeda and its affiliated organizations, just improved this communication, in the most lethal and terrifying way. Although terrorism has changed and has become a global threat, the relationship between the media and terrorism has not changed. Moreover, it is stronger then ever.

Since the media presents the main public informative service, terrorists through newspapers, television, radio and the Internet strive to influence the public in order to accomplish their goals. Terrorists must have publicity in some form if they are to gain attention, inspire fear and respect, and secure favorable understanding of their cause, if not their act.[2] Paul Wilkinson indicates that in using TV, radio, and the print media, terrorists generally have four main objectives: 1) To convey the propaganda of the deed and to create extreme fear among their target group/s; 2) To mobilize wider support for their cause among the general population, and international opinion by em-

---

1. Terrorism: Q&A, Terrorism and the Media, Council on Foreign Relations, at http://cfrterrorism.org/terrorism/media.
2. Perl, Raphael F. "Terrorism, the media, and the government: Perspectives, trends, and options for policymakers," CRS Issue Breief, 1997, at http://fas.org/irp/crs/crs-terror.htm.

phasizing such themes as righteousness of their cause and the inevitability of their victory; 3) To frustrate and disrupt the response of the government and security forces, for example by suggesting that all their practical anti-terrorist measures are inherently tyrannical and counterproductive; and 4) To mobilize, incite and boost their constituency of actual and potential supporters and in doing so to increase recruitment, raise more funds, and inspire further attacks[3].

The scholar Brian Jenkins stated in 1974 that terrorism is a theatre. That can be confirmed by the statement of Timothy McVeigh, who was found guilty and convicted of the 1995 Oklahoma City bombing that killed 168 people. He said that he chose the Murrah Federal Building as a target because it had "plenty of open space around it, to allow for the best possible news photos and television footage." The Italian leftist Red Brigades liked to stage attacks on Saturdays to make it into the Sunday newspapers, which had a higher circulation. And the Palestinian group Black September took Israeli athletes hostage at the 1972 Munich Olympics because television sets worldwide were already tuned in to the games and the concentrated foreign press would amplify the story.[4]

Modern terrorist groups use media to accomplish their goals much more than their predecessors. There is no better proof than the attack on the United States in September 11, 2001, when approximately 3,000 people were killed. After these attacks, all the media attention had been focused on these terrifying events and the whole world stood in front of their TV sets. Dramatic footage of hijacked planes crashing into buildings of the World Trade Center, the collapsing "twins," and the Pentagon in flames spread to the world, and al-Qaeda got all the attention it wanted. Attacks on the U.S. emphasized the fact that terrorism has become a communicative violence, which uses media as a main means of communication with the public. Referring to these attacks, professor Barbie Zelizer said that terror depends on visibility and this attack got incredible visibility because it was staged in such a brilliant fashion. It just kept coming. The pacing of it was astounding. It started at the end of Good Morning America and then, when we all ran to the TV to see it, it all happened again.[5]

Besides mass casualties, huge media attention has also been supported by the fact that terrorists choose symbolic targets. Attacks on symbolic targets have been the subject of interest for many terrorist groups because these kinds of targets attract broad media and public attention. If these symbolic

---

3. Wikinson, Paul. "The media and terrorism: A reassessment, terrorism and political violence," Vol. 9, No. 2, (Summer 1997), 51-64, FRANK CASS, London.
4. Terrorism: Q&A, Terrorism and the media, Council on Foreign Relations, at http://cfrterrorism.org/terrorism/media.
5. Collier, Gene. "It's time to quit helping terrorists spread fear," *Pittsburgh Post-Gazette*, at http://www.post-gazette.com/columnists/20010919geneo919np1.asp.

targets are destroyed, then the insurgent has succeeded in isolating individuals from the society in which they formerly felt secure and protected.[6] After the September 11 attacks, no one could feel safe. Islamic terrorists carried out attacks on the World Trade Center because it represented the economic power of the U.S., their biggest enemy. The second attack on September 11 was aimed at the Pentagon, a symbol of U.S. military power, and third, which ended unsuccessfully, was directed probably towards the White House or State Department, symbols of the American political strength.

If the terrorist comprehends that he is seeking a demonstration effect, he will attack targets with a maximum symbolic value[7]. In the case of September 11, terrorists tried to demonstrate their strength and operational capability as well as American vulnerability. After the September 11 attacks and their big media coverage, America felt insecure. But the news spread fast, and the fear overtook the rest of the world. People thought if terrorists can attack America, an imaginary untouchable fortress, then they can attack any country they wish. The illusion of an untouchable America was bursted like a soap bubble.

Previous attacks on a U.S. Air Force housing complex in Saudi Arabia in 1996, bombings of the U.S. embassies in Kenya and Tanzania in 1998, and an assault on the USS Cole in Yemen in 2000 have also been monitored by the world media, but the public considered them as a part of regional conflicts. September 11 showed that Islamic terrorists think and operate on a global scale and that no one can be safe from their retaliation. Afterward, brutal terrorist attacks in Madrid in 2004 and London in 2005 just confirmed this claim. The western public for the first time asked themselves "who are these terrorists" and "why do they hate us so much?" For Islamic terrorists, that was the real victory, because eyes of the entire world, helped by the huge media coverage, have been focused on them since.

With their bloody attacks, modern terrorists also showed that terrorism has changed and has a new face. Expert Brian Jenkins in 1995 famously said that "terrorists want a lot of people watching, not a lot of people dead"[8]. After the attacks in New York, Madrid, and London this thesis is no more applicable, at least not towards modern terrorists. In this case, they have been led by retaliation and mass killings of the civilians.

Modern terrorists use the media not only as a means for sending their messages to the public, but also to show their brutality. Decapitations of

---

6. Thornton, Perry Thomas, "Terror as a weapon of political agitation in internal war: Problems and approaches, ed. Harry Eckstein, New York: Free Press of Glencoe, 1964, 73 in *Information age terrorism: Toward cyberterror* by Matthew J. Littleton, at http://www.fas.org/irp/threat/cyber/docs/npgs/terror.htm.
7. Littleton, Matthew J., Information Age Terrorism: Toward Cyberterror, at http://www.fas.org/irp/threat/cyber/docs/npgs/terror.htm.
8. Hoffman, B., "Re-thinking terrorism in light of a war on terrorism," before the Subcommittee on Terrorism and Homeland Security, September 26, 4.

prisoners and various massacres recorded on tapes and sent to the media networks show that terrorists have found a new tool for spreading terror and fear. And this is where they significantly rely on the Internet. Recent advances in communications and information technology had a big impact on terrorists' ability to spread terror, as well as to improve their communications. By its very nature, the Internet is in many ways an ideal arena for activity by terrorist organizations. Most notably, it offers easy access; little or no regulation, censorship, or other forms of government control; potentially huge audiences spread throughout the world; anonymity of communication; fast flow of information; inexpensive development and maintenance of a web presence; a multimedia environment (the ability to combine text, graphics, audio, and video, and to allow users to download films, songs, books, posters, and so forth); and the ability to shape coverage in the traditional mass media, which increasingly uses the Internet as a source for stories.[9]

As the Internet has become the fastest source of information and has become available to millions of people, modern terrorists widely use this latest source of communication to spread propaganda. Pictures and recordings of roadside bombings, decapitations, and other violent acts circulate on the Web and are accessible to almost everyone. Terrorists also abuse the Internet to share information, spread ideology, plan attacks, raise funds, and recruit. According to Haifa University's Gabriel Weimann, whose research on the subject is widely cited, over the last 10 years the number of terrorist sites has jumped from less than 100 to more than 4,800.[10]

But all of that would be pointless without freedom of the media. Terrorist groups are in favor of the media only in democratic countries. Democratic countries are big advocates of the freedom of speech and expression, and terrorists are widely using that fact. In antidemocratic countries, the media are under the state control and access to the information can be easily restricted to the public. In that case, authorities are able to influence the editing policy of particular media, and by that to marginalize, reshape, omit, and even deny particular news. However, in the modern world as global village it is difficult to stall information, particularly due to ever growing access to the Internet, even in the third world countries. But the control of media is not a characteristic of the antidemocratic countries alone. In the 1980s, for example, Britain banned the broadcasting of statements by members of terrorist organizations or their supporters, following then Prime Minister Margaret Thatcher's argument that the surest way to stop terrorism was to cut off "the oxygen of

---

9. Weimann, Gabriel, "How modern terrorism uses the Internet," United States Institute of Peace, at http://www.usip.org/pubs/specialreports/sr116.pdf

10. Kaplan, Eben, "Terrorists and the Internet," Council on Foreign Relations, 2006, http://www.cfr.org/publication/10005/#4

publicity."[11] Nevertheless, democratic countries usually avoid this kind of pressure and "sometimes ask media organizations to voluntary hold back-either for national security reasons or to deny terrorist an outlet for their political views." Following the September 11 attacks, for example, the Bush administration asked U.S. networks not to air videos of Osama bin Laden because the government said they might contain coded messages with instructions for further attacks.[12] States can also appeal to the media organizations not to report on possible homeland security vulnerabilities or not to indicate other possible targets, which could become objects of new attacks in the near future.

Still, the media have always been addicted to dramatic reports and possible government appeals can easily be neglected. For as long as terrorists commit violent acts, the media "will continue to scramble to cover them in order to satisfy the desire of their audiences for dramatic stories in which there is inevitably huge public curiosity about both the victimizers and their victims"[13]. The media in open societies advocates the freedom of speech and public right to be informed and by that media organizations can ignore some government appeals or limitations. But problem lies in the fact that the media sometimes can directly or indirectly jeopardize an action directed to prevent or repulse particular terrorist action. For example, during the Iranian Embassy siege at Princess Gate, London, in 1980, the Metropolitan Police were particularly concerned to ensure total secrecy and surprise for the hostage rescue by the SAS. However, one ITN film crew defied police instruction and succeeded in filming the rescuers as they were abseiling down the walls of the Embassy. If those pictures had been shown live on TV, they could have jeopardized the entire hostage crisis.[14]

But, the media seek shocking news to attract the public and maximize revenues, as terrorists seek the media attention to send their messages and to spread fear among the population. It can be said that the media and terrorists live in some kind of symbiosis. Terrorist organizations use the media "as a conduit for their political message to be heard by the target audience, whilst supplying 'exiting news' for the media"[15]. Without the media attention, terrorist actions would have more than a limited influence on the public. Without attention, a terrorist act is a tree falling in the forest with no one to hear and

---

11. Terrorism: Q&A, Terrorism and the Media, Council on Foreign Relations, at http://cfrterrorism.org/terrorism/media.
12. Ibid.
13. Wikinson, Paul. "The media and terrorism: A reassessment, terrorism and political violence, Vol. 9, No. 2, Summer 1997, 51-64, FRANK CASS, London.
14. Wikinson, Paul. "The media and terrorism: A reassessment, terrorism and political violence, Vol. 9, No. 2, Summer 1997, 51-64, FRANK CASS, London.
15. Lockyer, Adam. 2003. The relationship between the media and terrorism, The Australian National University.

it's pointless.[16] The press is very important to the terrorists in terms of getting their message out, generating sympathy and support for their cause, furthering their demands, and pressurizing governments and population to respond.[17] On the other hand, violent actions such as plane hijacks, mass killings, or property destruction provide an endless source of news to the media. Terrorism fits perfectly into the scheme of what is newsworthy and what sells newspapers, because it provides powerful pictures and dramatic stories about good and evil.[18] Bad news sells newspapers much more than good. In the world ruled by fierce competition, media companies are struggling for an audience because more sold press issues or higher TV ratings mean higher revenues.

At the end of this work it can be concluded that modern terrorist groups greatly benefit from the media. Although experts disagree about whether the media helps terrorists, recent events had shown that the huge media coverage of violent acts helped al-Qaeda and its affiliated groups to spread terror. Some experts claimed that "the media coverage is mostly unfavorable to the terrorists . . . and has a heavy influence on the policy against them"[19]. But this thesis is not applicable to modern terrorists who do not care for sympathies or bad publicity, but only strive to provoke mass casualties in order to achieve their goals.

With the September 11 attacks Islamic terrorists had attracted the huge public attention of the world population and had shown that America is not invulnerable. Although al-Qaeda provoked a drastic response by the U.S. and its allies, and lost its main stronghold in Afghanistan, its network spread throughout the world. Attacks on America had shown that "great Satan" can bleed, which means it can be defeated. And thanks to the publicity al-Qaeda's leader Osama bin Laden has received, "he has unfortunately become a cult figure across much of the Islamic world, perceived as a Muslim David defying the American Goliath."[20] A similar situation happened after the Madrid attack, when Islamic terrorists killed 191 people and wounded more than 1,800, as well as the London attack, in which more than 50 people were killed. After the attack, Spain withdrew its troops from Iraq, and the British public started to loudly protest against the Iraq war. In these attacks, terrorists did not want to avoid bad publicity. They wanted to be heard in the most horrible way.

---

16. White, Timothy. "The terrorist threat to the American presence abroad," University of Virginia, at http://www.healthsystem.virginia.edu/internet/ciag/reports/report_terr_media.cfm?printfriendly=1&.
17. Madhok, Rayat. 2004. "Are terrorists manipulating the world media?"
18. Fog, Agner. 2002. "Why terrorism doesn't work," Draft article, 4.
19. Altheide, D. L. 1991. The impact of television news formats on social policy, *Journal of Broadcasting and Electronic Media* 35 (1): 3-21.
20. Madhok, Rayat. 2004. "Are terrorists manipulating the world media?"

As long as modern terrorists enjoy wide media coverage their acts will be severe. And as long as the media will be dependent on their readers, it will publish shocking news. This is a circle without an end.

## References

Altheide, D. L., "The impact of television news formats on social policy." *Journal of Broadcasting and Electronic Media* 35 (1): 3-21.

Collier, Gene. "It's time to quit helping terrorists spread fear." *Pittsburg Post-Gazette*, at
http://www.post-gazette.com/columnists/20010919gene 0919np1.asp.

Hoffman, B., "Re-thinking terrorism in light of a war on terrorism." Before the Subcommittee on Terrorism and Homeland Security, September 26, 4.

Kaplan, Eben. 2006. "Terrorists and the Internet." Council on Foreign Relations, at http://www.cfr.org/publication/10005/#4.

Littleton, Matthew J. "Information age terrorism: Toward cyberterror," at http://www.fas.org/irp/threat/cyber/docs/npgs/terror.htm.

Lockyer, Adam. 2003. *The relationship between the media and terrorism.* The Australian National University.

Madhok, Rayat. 2004. "Are terrorists manipulating the world media?"

Perl, Raphael F. 1997. "Terrorism, the media, and the government: Perspectives, trends, and options for policymakers." CRS Issue Brief, 1997, at http://fas.org/irp/crs/crs-terror.htm.

Terrorism: Q&A, terrorism and the media, Council on Foreign Relations, at http://cfrterrorism.org/terrorism/media.

Thornton, Perry Thomas, "Terror as a weapon of political agitation in internal war: Problems and approaches." ed. Harry Eckstein, New York: Free Press of Glencoe, 1964, 73 in *Information Age Terrorism: Toward Cyberterror* by Matthew J. Littleton, at
http://www.fas.org/irp/threat/cyber/docs/npgs/terror.htm.

Weimann, Gabriel. "How modern terrorism uses the Internet." United States Institute of Peace, at
http://www.usip.org/pubs/specialreports/sr116.pdf

White, Timothy. "The terrorist threat to the American presence abroad." University of Virginia, at
http://www.healthsystem.virginia.edu/internet/ciag/reports/report_terr_media.cfm? printfriendly=1&.

Wikinson, Paul. "The media and terrorism: A reassessment, terrorism and political violence, Vol. 9, No. 2, Summer 1997, 51-64, FRANK CASS, London.

# LIBERALISM AND GOVERNMENTALITY IN THE WAR ON TERROR

*Matthew Morgan*

In the post-September 11th world, Western liberal democracies find themselves engaged in a global war on terror. In the supposed fight to eliminate terrorism and make the world "safe for democracy," liberal states have invaded and occupied two states, killing thousands, while subjecting their own populations to greater levels of surveillance and control. The space for political discourse within liberal democracies has progressively narrowed, as the population has become increasingly fearful by the depth of hostility that seems to confront the policies their governments pursue internationally in their name. Liberal governments have sought to manipulate this fear through the creation of what Didier Bigo terms a *governmentality of unease*. This new liberal form of governmentality has been created not only as a means for liberal states to gain consent for their international policies, but also to ensure that citizens are aware of their own actions and govern themselves in ways appropriate to the war on terror context. To further enforce the governmentality of unease, surveillance and social sorting is used to classify as dangerous those that resist the policies of their governments, or those that simply don't fit into the new framework of governance that the liberal state has sought to create post-September 11th.

The surveillance techniques that the liberal state has employed operate through the extraction of information from the body. "The body itself has emerged as a legitimate surveillance target because of the immense level of detail and truth about the person it is thought to provide."[1] Notions of biopolitics thus become extremely important in contemporary societies as the information acquired through surveillance is used to control the body in the pursuit of securitizing society. Through the application of these technologies, the body becomes a political object to be acted upon by the state. In the racially charged atmosphere of the war on terror, the appearance of a body determines whether one is ranked as a low risk or a high risk individual.

Although these actions may appear malicious, they pale in comparison to the policy of containment, depoliticization, and death inflicted upon those considered to be outside the confines of liberal society; the individuals which reside within these spaces are commonly referred to as either terrorists or

---

1. Kirstie Ball, "Organization, Surveillance and the Body: Towards a Politics of Resistance," in *Theorizing Surveillance: The Panopticon and Beyond*, ed. David Lyon (Portland: William Publishing, 2006), 299.

unlawful combatants. The sovereign power of the state has been utilized to construct territories outside of the legal realm of the state where the laws and norms of liberal society no longer apply. While this may appear to be a contradiction, the creation of such spaces is in fact inherent to liberal societies. Although Guantanamo Bay may the archetypal form of such a space, the extending assemblage of calculation and control employed by the liberal state in the war on terror means that the number of individuals as well as the number and extent of these spaces of exception will continue to expand.

The strategy pursued by liberal societies in the war on terror does not represent a break with liberalism, but is rather an intensification of particular elements inherent within the liberal mode of governance. To understand the operation of liberal governmentality in the age of the war on terror I will follow Dider's definition as the war on terror creating a governmentality of unease within liberal societies. Intimately connected to propagation of a governmentality of unease are the practices of exceptionalism, profiling, and containment, which have characterized the contemporary period. My concern is with how the majority of liberal society is regulated in the war on terror through the application of surveillance techniques, the process through which individuals are depoliticized and transformed into homo sacer placed within spaces of exception, and how spaces of exception gradually become regularized throughout society and within the legal framework. In my argument I will refer frequently to liberal societies. I define such societies to be those from which Enlightenment thought developed or where it quickly took root. Such societies are territorially based in the Western Europe and North America, and I believe that the governmentality of unease can be used, broadly, to characterize these societies in the present period.

As my discussion of the war on terror will be grounded in a Foucauldian analysis, I will begin my paper with a discussion of Foucault's concepts of governmentality, biopolitics, and technologies of government to prepare for their use analyzing liberal societies in the war on terror. Foucault's interest lay in determining how liberal principles were used to inform a method of governance adopted by the state. Foucault termed the strategies employed through which society was governed *governmentality*. Modern states differed sharply from previous political organizations because they were concerned primarily with the control of their own populations, as opposed to the defense of sovereign borders. "In contrast to sovereignty, government has as its purpose, not the act of government itself, but the welfare of the population…this is the new target and the fundamental instrument of the government of population: the birth of a new art, or at any rate of a range of absolutely new tactics and techniques."[2] Foucault developed the concept of go-

---

2. Michel Foucault, "Governmentality," in *The Foucault Effect: Studies in Governmentality*, ed. Graham Burchell, Colin Gordon, and Peter Miller (Chicago: University of Chicago Press, 1991), 100.

vernmentality to describe the art of government within Western societies. For Foucault, liberalism itself was not equated with governmentality; rather it represented the further rationalization and extension of the power of the sovereign over society. Governmentality has progressed through several phases, with modern societies now utilizing liberal technologies of control.[3]

The sovereign applies liberalism "not as a theory, an ideology, a juridical philosophy of individual freedom, or a particular set of policies adopted by a government...Liberalism is a particular way in which the activity of government has been made both thinkable and practicable as an art."[4] Under liberalism the constitution of and the perpetuation of government becomes an end in itself. The sovereign is no longer primarily concerned with maintaining control over the space that it has claimed as its territory, but rather with the control of the population, which exists within that territory. The sheer complexity of modern societies creates new problems as to how they can be governed and controlled. In modernity, "The governed substance is a materiality drenched with thought. It is hence not a question of either a pure materiality or a pure ideality; it is both and at once . . . We thus seek to act upon a materiality rendered governable through a grid of intelligibility and calculation."[5] As an art and a discipline, liberal governmentality seeks to develop solutions, strategies, and tactics for the control of individuals continually exposed to new thoughts, new relations, and new experiences. Liberal governmentality thus seeks to expand the framework of control exercised by the sovereign through the development of new technologies of the self.

What is unique about the liberal mode of governmentality, as opposed to other previous modes, is that rather than the sovereign directly acting upon and exercising its power over individuals to force them to conform to its framework of governance, the sovereign instead strives for the construction of a self-conforming liberal political subject. Thus power in liberal societies is typically not exercised in a direct fashion upon subjects, but is rather used to mold them to follow particular paths of action, although as well will see below, power is increasingly being employed directly, in highly repressive manners. Power in liberal societies is also not expressed in a singular format, but rather through multiple technologies of the self and multiple methods of containment and control. Foucault conceptualized power in modern societies as

---

3. Michel Foucault, "The Birth of Biopolitics," in *Ethics: Subjectivity and Truth*, ed. Paul Rabinow (New York: The New Press, 1994), 74.
4. Graham Burchell, "Liberal Government and Techniques of the Self," in *Foucault and Political Reason: Liberalism, neo-liberalism and Rationalities of Government*, ed. Andrew Barry, Thomas Osborne and Nikolas Rose (Chicago: The University of Chicago Press, 1996), 21.
5. Mitchell Dean, "Foucault, Government, and the Enfolding of Authority," in *Foucault and Political Reason: Liberalism, neo-liberalism and Rationalities of Government*, ed. Andrew Barry, Thomas Osborne and Nikolas Rose (Chicago: The University of Chicago Press, 1996), 222.

an encompassing mesh which was capable of assuming a number of forms and responding in a variety of ways to societal events. "A society is not a unitary body in which one power and only one power exercise itself, but in reality it is a juxtaposition, a liaising, a coordination, a hierarchy too, of different powers which nonetheless retain their specificity."[6] The sheer complexity of modern societies prohibits the sovereign from directly exercising repressive control upon a significant portion of its subjects. Within liberal societies a unique relationship between the sovereign and its subjects exists, as compared to earlier societies organized upon different bases of control. "Liberalism . . . constructs a relationship between government and the governed that increasingly depends upon ways in which individuals are required to assume the status of being the subjects of their lives…"[7] To assist in the creation of subjects which deem the governance (in particular ways) of their own lives as their primary responsibility, the sovereign seeks the development of technologies of the self, which allow individuals to act upon their bodies and hence their soul and mind, to transform themselves in order to attain a certain lifestyle.

To create these technologies of the self, the development of new technologies of governance, or new government apparatuses and techniques is required. "The coercion of bodies, their control, their subjugation, the way in which power is exerted on them directly or indirectly . . . requires an organ of generalized and constant oversight; everything must be observed, seen, transmitted"[8] Modern society seeks the level of control necessary to shape bodies into agreement with the social relations required for the reproduction of society. Modern governance thus seeks to inscribe its system of control upon the body of the modern subject. The production of these biopolitical subjects requires that government adopt a sense of calculability about the world and its inhabitants. This calculability is used to inform the political rationality of liberal governmentality to assist in the creation of a "schemata for representing reality, analyzing it and rectifying it, as a kind of intellectual machinery or apparatus for rendering reality thinkable in such a way that it is amenable to political programming."[9] Liberal societies thus place a vision of

---

6. Michel Foucault, "The Meshes of Power," in *Space, Knowledge and Power: Foucault and Geography*, ed. Jermeny Crampton and Stuart Elden (Aldershot: Ashgate, 2007), 156.
7. Graham Burchell, "Liberal Government and Techniques of the Self," in *Foucault and Political Reason: Liberalism, neo-liberalism and Rationalities of Government*, ed. Andrew Barry, Thomas Osborne and Nikolas Rose (Chicago: The University of Chicago Press, 1996), 29.
8. Michel Foucault, "The Punitive Society," in *Ethics: Subjectivity and Truth*, ed. Paul Rabinow (New York: The New Press, 1994), 35.
9. Nikolas Rose, "Governing Advanced Liberal Democracies," in *Foucault and Political Reason: Liberalism, neo-liberalism and Rationalities of Government,* ed. Andrew Barry, Thomas Osborne and Nikolas Rose (Chicago: The University of Chicago Press, 1996), 42.

reality upon the world to encourage their subjects through the application of various means to pursue this liberal vision in their own way. As long as subjects ascribe to the tenets of liberal societies[10] or are believed to ascribe to them by the sovereign, the subject may enjoy the measure of freedom extended to them to govern their own life.

However liberal societies have historically and as well as within in the current war on terror context, been highly intolerant of those who are deemed illiberal. "Liberal ideas of what constitutes a peaceful society, what forms of life are compatible with the existence of liberal peace, and are thus deemed worthy of the title of the human have developed through a state of continual antagonism . . . with rival life forms."[11] While liberal societies are supposedly organized on the basis of achieving peace, they have become a dominant form of governmentality through their efficient and ruthless prosecution of war to eliminate rivals as well as ensure conformity within society. *Human* is defined as that which subscribes the framework of thought common to liberal societies. Thus while expressing tolerance of difference, liberal societies are in fact unable to understand, let alone engage with, societies outside of their own. Liberal societies have however been highly adaptable and quick to eliminate those viewed as threats due to their failure to adopt liberal modes of thinking.

The paradox then at the heart of liberalism is a dynamic of inclusion and exclusion. While liberalism develops this dynamic in a particular way, it is by no means unique to liberal societies. Determining who is to be included within a society and those, who because of their characteristics, are deemed outsiders has existed ever since political organizations were established. In past centuries, as well as today, this logic is primarily informed by the creation of territory, which a specific people claim as their own. As opposed to space, which exists naturally and does not require the creation of social relations driven by dynamics of power to bring it into existence, the production of territory occurs through the operation of power and social claims over a particular space. Through this process territory becomes something more complex and differentiates itself from space. "Territoriality is always socially constructed. It takes an act of will and involves multiple levels of reasons and meanings. And territoriality can have normative implications as well. Setting places aside and enforcing degrees of access means that individuals and groups have removed some activities and people from places and included others."[12] The creation of territory thus requires the creation of an exclusio-

---

10. Broadly defined here as support for a free market economy, legal equality, and viewing the individual as the basis for society.
11. Julian Reid, *The Biopolitics of the War on Terror: Life Struggles, Liberal Modernity, and the Defence of Logistical Societies* (Manchester: Machechester University Press, 2006), 8.
12. Robert Sack, *Human Territoriality: Its Theory and History* (Cambridge: Cambridge University Press, 1996), 26.

nary dynamic. The formation of political organizations required that they be able to successfully make and defend a claim over a particular space, in the process transforming it into a territory. The construction of these defensible territories was informed and justified by the ideology of nationalism, which constructed the political unit of the state rooted in a specific territory. As Anderson demonstrates through his masterful analysis of the development of the ideology of nationalism the state has always been based upon an exclusionary and limited logic: "The nation is imagined as limited because even the largest of them, encompassing perhaps a billion living human beings, has infinite, if elastic boundaries beyond which lie other nations. No nation imagines itself coterminous with mankind."[13] The creation of territory resulted in the formation of the political organizations that came to comprise the modern state. These organizations were informed by an exclusionary logic that denied membership to large segments of the human population due to their failure to satisfy particular criteria. Politically then, modern society is defined by the fragmentation of global space into a number of different territories over which the political apparatus of the state exercises dominion.

Societies are of course more complex than simple claims over a territory. Those who live within a particular territory tend to have shared customs, beliefs, and a way of viewing the world. Therefore in claiming that you belong to a particular society, you place yourself within a specific territory and set of assumptions about the world. However within modernity, the situation is not so clear, as individuals may claim that they belong to multiple societies, by for example, tracing their heritage and following the traditions of one society while at the same time living within a different society and adopting some of its norms as well. A central part of what is portrayed in any definition of territory is the existence of rigid borders delineating the inside and outside. These borders are however frequently transgressed. "Any transcendence of territorial limits, whether this occurs through intervention and the imperial projection of power, through transnational institutional practices aimed at the government of populations, or through modes of transnational affiliation, is but a confirmation of the primacy of the spatial imaginary in modern life and its effects in institutional practices and lived experience."[14] In some sense then the traditional inclusion/exclusion dynamic is being overcome, as linkages grow and strengthen across different cultures, through the overcoming of territorial borders. Yet at the same time the threshold that must be passed to be deemed a member of a particular society continues to rise. "Modern civilizations given their technical complexities . . . become functionally intolerant of the lack of basic competencies that they at the same time, fail to generate

---

13. Benedict Anderson, *Imagined Communities: Reflections on the Origin and Spread of Nationalism* (Verso, London, 2006), 7.

14. Vivienne Jabri, "Michel Foucault's Analytics of War: The Social, the International, and the Racial," *International Political Sociology* 1(1) (2007): 70.

on a universal level. They establish conditions for normal participation that continue to be ever more demanding."[15] As modern societies become more complex not only through historical development, but also through interactions with other cultures, the formerly simple claim over a space and by extension a people, becomes more complicated and confused. How is one to know what a liberal subject is, when the conditions of our existence alter at a progressively rapid pace?

One solution, which has unfortunately become predominant in the war on terror period, is the attempt to reinvigorate the inclusion/exclusion dynamic through the creation of new claims as to what a liberal subject is. Ironically this process has occurred in a highly illiberal manner. "the liberal direction itself is not altogether liberal. It requires a commonwealth of believers whose dogmatism is as corrosive of its own account of freedom as its policing is corrosive of its free institutions . . . Instituting such a commonwealth creates a violently divided loyalty: that between local political communities and the global civil community."[16] Rather than adopting a broader view of what it means to live within a liberal society and be defined as liberal, the definition of liberal has become increasingly hardened and inflexible. Although this process had been going on well before September 11th, since that fateful day this process has only intensified.

In the context of the war on terror new technologies of the self and government have been developed to profile, contain, and eliminate threats to the liberal order. These new practices can be placed under the framework of a new governmentality of unease, which has characterized liberal societies in the present period. This development is justified because of the new spectrum of threat liberal societies face. The enemy is both within and without, and it is not clearly discernable who exactly the enemy is. "The terrorist is seen as all the more threatening because he (or she) cannot easily be identified, separated, and labeled. Very often, he is already amongst us . . . How tempting, then, to find a way of separating out the terrorist, identifying him on a map, and attacking him!"[17] Hence, the fear that a threat may exist within a society is used as justification for attacks outside the society upon states from which acts of terrorism are said to originate (Afghanistan), from states which supposedly sponsor terrorism and serve as nodes within the international terrorist network (Iraq), and finally against states which may in the future develop weapons that may be employed by terrorists or used by a state

---

15. Claus Offe, "Modern Barbarity: A Micro-State of Nature?," in *Biopolitics: The Politics of the Body, Race, and Nature*, ed. Agnes Heller and Sonja Riekmann (Aldershot: Avebury, 1996), 28.
16. Michael Dillon, "Governing Terror: The State of Emergency of Biopolitical Emergence," *International Political Sociology* 1(1) (2007): 23.
17. David Keen, *Endless War? Hidden Functions of the War on Terror*. (London: Pluto Press, 2006), 89.

that is defined as a terrorist state (Iran).[18] An outside is thus created that is excluded from liberal society and can be justifiably attacked.

Although the creation of this international situation is a byproduct of the governmentality of unease is itself concerned with the regulation and control of individuals within societies and can be characterized by three criteria: practices of exceptionalism, acts of profiling, and containing foreigners.[19] The governmentality of unease is rooted in the application of biopolitical techniques through which the state categorizes and controls its subjects.

> A skin color, an accent, an attitude and one is isolated, extracted from the unmarked masses, and evacuated if necessary. Policing is thus an affair of the margin, of cleanup, and needs concern itself only minimally with norms.... The advantage for the unmarked masses is that they have the impression of being free, to the benefit of the institution, and since control only bears on a few, it is more economical.[20]

The application of these techniques is informed by the belief that those who belong from a particular territory viewed as outside of liberal society are a threat because of their supposed illiberal convictions, which imperil liberal society. The difficulty is that these techniques are applied to those whose heritage may be traced back to societies outside of the liberal domain, but who have spent their entire existence within liberal society, or to those who are for all intents and purposes liberal, but are determined to be attempting to subvert the liberal project.

The necessity of creating a distinction between who is and is not a threat requires the creation of profiles to determine against whom the coercive mechanisms of the state shall be applied. These profiles are created through the application of surveillance technologies to the population. The information gathered within a profile is then used to classify an individual and determine if he or she poses a threat.

> Surveillance has to be understood today as social sorting, which has exclusionary consequences. Watching others has become systematic, embedded in a system that classifies according to certain pre-set criteria, and sorts into categories of risk and opportunity...Such classification is very important for people's life-chances and choices.

---

18. The media has of course played a pivotal role in fostering the conceptions and hysteria that exists surrounding the actions and policies of these states.
19. Didier Bigo, "Globalized Insecurity: The Field and the Ban-opticon," in *Translation, Biopolitics, Colonial Difference*, ed. Naoki Soloman and Jon Soloman (Hong Kong: Hong Kong University Press, 2006), 110.
20. Ibid., 140-141

> Surveillance is becoming a means of placing people in new, flexible, social classes.[21]

In the modern era the entirety of liberal society is observed and analyzed, surveillance is "now omnipresent, with people from all segments of the social hierarchy coming under scrutiny"[22] Although everyone within liberal society is exposed to some general level of surveillance, certain segments of society are surveilled more heavily, either due to previous information which has been collected within their profile which marks them as dangerous, or because their appearance does not coincide with how a liberal subject should present themselves.

Although it conflicts with liberal notions of equality, an analysis of the effects of the war on terror on liberal societies must include an analysis of its biopolitical elements because the process through which profiles are created and individuals are placed within social classes strongly depends upon the visible characteristics of that individual. More than any other site airports embody a constructed territory traversed by a border whose regulatory framework is informed by the profiles assigned to travelers.

> Airports are spaces of policing that also represent the constitutive gate of entry into the population. Airports are spaces that represent the policing power of the sovereign state, that contain the dangerous or risky elements of the unknown, and that render certain mobilities visible and others impossible or invisible. The trick of the modern airport is to present immobility as mobility, stagnancy as efficient, and incarceration as freedom.[23]

Regarding life-chances, one particular example of the manner in which the liberal subject is conceived concerns mobility rights and how freely one may travel.

> Constructions of high and low risk travelers are highly gendered, racialized and class-based. They enable populations to be subdivided into groups and managed according to differential mobility rights. Low-risk travelers, for example, are constructed around the identity

---

21. David Lyon, "Everyday Surveillance: Personal Data and Social Classifications," in *The Surveillance Studies Reader*, ed. Sean Hier and Joshua Greenberg (New York: Open University Press, 2007), 371.
22. Kevin Haggerty, "Tear Down the Walls: On Demolishing the Panopticon," in *Theorizing Surveillance: The Panopticon and Beyond*, ed. David Lyon (Portland: William Publishing, 2006), 29.
23. Mark Salter, "Governmentalities of an Airport: Heterotopia and Confession," *International Political Sociology* 1(1) (2007): 53.

of economically advantaged professional and business elites, often male and white[24]

Those whose bodies do not display the appropriate characteristics are singled out for further surveillance as potential threats. The body thus becomes a determining factor in one's social status. "The image of my body has now become the mirror image of my social rank in society . . . rather than what it should be ideally; the house of the spirit."[25] The creation of what is defined as a good liberal subject thus incorporates specific notions of gender, race, and class.

While one's appearance is an important factor in the level of surveillance and suspicion one is subject to, the nature of the threat challenging liberal societies is so amorphous and vague that progressively greater portions of society come to be viewed as threats. "The spectrum of threat expands beyond what are presented as the contemporary incarnation of totalitarianism (e.g., terrorists, the Axis of Evil) to subsume anything that at a particular moment in time is seized upon by paranoiac imagination as constituting a threat"[26] While only a minority of the population may be targeted and excluded from liberal society, the sphere of exclusion created by the governmentality of unease is continually expanding. This expansion should be thought of not only in terms of the exclusion of individuals and the narrowing of their life-chances through their placement within lower social classes due to their exhibiting of characteristics which result in the creation of an unfavorable profile, but also as the creation of states of exception; zones where the norms and laws that underpin liberal societies no longer apply.

The term *homo sacer*, or bare life, has been used to refer to those that dwell within these states of exception. These individuals are no longer human in the liberal sense, as they have been completely depoliticized and abandoned, existing as a pure object, exposed to the full capacity of organized violence contained within the state. The primary characteristic of homo sacer is that they may be killed without cause or consequence. Homo sacer exists within a dual state, still physically alive, but politically and legally dead. In a sense their life is a sacred life, as their death is neither a homicide, nor can it serve as a sacrifice to some political ideal.

---

24. Kim Rygiel, "Protecting and Proving Identity: The Biopolitics of Waging War Through Citizenship in the Post-9/11 Era," in *(En)Gendering the War on Terror: War Stories and Camouflaged Politics*, ed. Krista Hunt and Kim Rygiel (Aldershot:Ashgate, 2006), 155.
25. Peter Gyorgy, "The Order of Bodies," in *Biopolitics: The Politics of the Body, Race, and Nature*, ed. Agnes Heller and Sonja Riekmann (Aldershot: Avebury, 1996), 43.
26. Kyle Grayson, "Persistence of Memory? The (New) Surrealism of American Security Policy," in *The Logics of Biopower and the War on Terror: Living, Dying, Surviving*, ed. Elizabeth Dauphinee and Cristina Masters (New York: Palgrave Macmillian, 2007), 101.

> What defines the status of homo sacer is therefore not the originally ambivalence of the sacredness that is assumed to belong to him, but rather the particular character of the double exclusion into which he is taken and the violence to which he finds himself exposed. This violence, the unsanctionable killing that, in his case, anyone may commit, is classifiable neither as sacrifice nor as homicide.[27]

The creation of homo sacer is the direct result of a decision by the sovereign to cast him or her outside of society. Homo sacer is thus an exiled figure, excluded from society and abandoned.

Although in the war on terror this act of exclusion has been preformed by supposedly inclusive liberal societies, the decision to exclude, to ban an individual or a portion of the population from society is, in the final analysis what sovereignty and society is based upon. "the production of bare life is the original activity of sovereignty. The sacredness of life, which is invoked today as an absolutely fundamental right in opposition to sovereign power, in fact expresses precisely both life's subjection to a power over death and life's irreparable exposure in the relation of abandonment."[28] The core of sovereignty power is determining who is to be included within society. Those who are included within society are political subjects because they express the ability to express and develop themselves. In addition political subjects may influence the way society is constituted and the manner in which it projects itself in the world. Those who are excluded from society are not political, because they are not given the opportunity to express themselves; they are bare life, as they are prevented from portraying any of the characteristics that we would associate with life. Existing as only a simple biological entity those "at the level of bare living are stripped of any criteria that would make this life (this thinking, this dreaming, this world) familiar."[29] Bare life is humanity at its most basic form, forcibly removed from politics, the process through which humanity has separated itself from bare life through the creation of a society of rules, norms, and regulations. However the base instinct towards declaring some life as unworthy of the political and marking it as bare life still exists within modern societies as the process of excluding individuals from society naturally creates states of exception.

In the war on terror, states of exception are territories specifically created by an act of sovereign power where the normal rules of liberal society no longer apply. States of exception are a territory, rather than simply a space,

---

27. Giorgio Agamben, *Homo Sacer: Sovereign Power and Bare Life* (Standford: Stanford University Press, 1998), 82.
28. Ibid.,83.
29. Thomas Wall, "Au Hasard," in *Politics, Metaphysics and Death: Essays on Giorgio Agamben's Homo Sacer*, ed. Andrew Norris (Durham: Duke University Press, 2005), 32.

because their creation and continued existence results from the decision of the sovereign.

> The sovereign is revealed only in or after the decision on the exception, the decision whether or not a state of exception exists and, therefore, the decision whether the normal order exists. That decision will relate to an indeterminate area and cannot be figured in advance.[30]

In the creation of states of exception the sovereign places itself outside of the legal order that it has constructed. The territory in which the state of exception exists is created by the sovereign, but the creation of a state of exception cannot be construed as a normal legal action, because the state of exception serves as an area where the rules by which the sovereign normally bounds itself no longer apply.

> The violence exercised in the state of exception clearly neither preserves nor simply posits low, but rather conserves it in suspending it and posits it in excepting itself from it…Sovereign violence opens a zone of indistinction between law and nature, outside and inside, violence and law. And yet the sovereign is precisely the one who maintains the possibility of deciding on the two to the very degree that he renders them indistinguishable from each other.[31]

The state of exception can then be viewed simply as an area where the normal legal order is suspended. However the state of exception is more complex than this, because when the sovereign declares the existence of a state of exception, suspends the legal order, and depoliticizes those who exist within the state of exception, the sovereign issues a special legal order to do so.

The manner the law functions in practice clashes with the way liberalism envisions the operation of the law occurring. Similar to the application of surveillance within society, where different segments of the population are exposed to varying levels of surveillance; the law is not applied uniformly throughout society. Rather the law is full of divergences and contradictions, which are used to govern different aspects of society. "Embedded within the law are a rich and complex set of maps of social life. Legal categories are used to construct and differentiate material spaces which, in turn, acquire a legal potency that has a direct bearing on those using and traversing such spac-

---

30. Peter Fitzpatrick, "Bare Sovereignty, Homo Sacer and the Insistence of Law," in *Politics, Metaphysics and Death: Essays on Giorgio Agamben's Homo Sacer*, ed. Andrew Norris (Durham: Duke University Press, 2005), 58.
31. Giorgio Agamben, *Homo Sacer: Sovereign Power and Bare Life* (Standford: Stanford University Press, 1998), 64.

es."[32] Placement within a particular legal category is determined by the social class of an individual, which as discussed above is strongly influenced by the profile ascribed to an individual as a result of the application of surveillance methods.

In addition to legal categories of law, inherent within the law is the conditions for its own negation, in particular situations. As it is the sovereign who creates the law, the sovereign can decide when the law does and does not apply. "The paradox of sovereignty consists in the fact that the sovereign is, at the same time, outside and inside the juridical order...the sovereign, having the legal power to suspend the validity of the law, legally places himself outside the law."[33] The sovereign thus constitutes and is contained with the legal order, yet at the same time the sovereign possess an extra legal ability, which allows it to step outside of its own legality to make decisions unbound by previous legal precedent. It is these actions that create a state of exception.

Liberal societies deny both the possibility for a state of exception to occur and the multifaceted nature of the law. These denials arise from the failure of liberal forms of governmentality to truly encompass the contingent nature of modern society. This failure is rooted in the establishment of the liberal social order, which is presented as the natural progression of humanity. The foundation of liberalism is thus posited as based upon transhistorical norms, when in actuality these norms are historically constituted and are promoted by sovereign power. "The metaphysical image that a definite epoch forges of the world has the same structure as what the world immediately understands to be appropriate as a form of political organization. The determination of such an identity is the sociology of the concept of sovereignty."[34] In striving to encompass the contingent nature of modern society liberal governmentality attempts to obscure the foundations its continued stability rests upon, with only partial success. The denials are necessitated because "The stabilization of order depends on the operation of the conversion of the act of its contingent and undecidable foundation into the presence or positive foundations, i.e. the conversion of exteriority into interiority, of transcendence into immanence."[35] The basis of society must be viewed as stable and capable of projecting itself into the future in order to ensure in the minds of the populace both the continued existence of society and the mechanisms that govern it. In extreme circumstances the sovereign retains the ability to act outside of the structure that it has created, by declaring the existence of a

---

32. Nicholas Blomley, *Law, Space, and the Geographies of Power* (New York: The Guilford Press, 1994), 54.
33. Giorgio Agamben, *Homo Sacer: Sovereign Power and Bare Life* (Standford: Stanford University Press, 1998), 15.
34. Carl Schmitt, *Political Theology: Four Chapters on the Concept of Sovereignty* (Cambridge: MIT Press, 1985), 46.
35. Sergei Prozorov, *Foucault, Freedom and Sovereignty* (Burlington: Ashgate, 2007), 88.

state of exception, however in doing so the fictional narrative that serves as the basis for society is destroyed.

While the initial decision of the sovereign to move outside of the legal framework, creating a state of exception make be a unique action initially, over time the state of exception becomes normalized as it is brought into the legal framework. "The state of exception is not meant to produce or confirm the rule, it tends rather to coincide with it, that is to say, to blur with it."[36] As the state of exception becomes regularized the possibility that it may expand and encompass greater aspects of society increases.

The form that a state of exception assumes and the manner in which it is gradually permeated throughout the legal apparatus are unique to each society. Thus the governmentality of unease through which liberal societies presently organize and view themselves through has its own particular states of exception. Within the present war on terror context, the obvious example of a state of exception is Guantanamo Bay, where several hundred supposed terrorists are held outside of the legal realm, "stripped of every political status and wholly reduced to bare life . . . in which power confronts nothing but pure life, without any mediation."[37] However, as shocking as the existence of Guantanamo Bay may appear to a society with liberal sensitivities, it has gradually been transformed from a place in which the legal order was suspended, to a place for which new laws are created to regulate its operations and normalize its existence. A recent law passed by the American Congress symbolizes this transition, while at the same time, greatly expanding the state of exception to potentially include those who are commonly assumed to be an integral part of any society, citizens. The law that is referred to is the Military Commissions Act (MCA) of 2006.

The Military Commissions Act performs a number of functions; it "incorporates, for the first time, the notion of illegal enemy combatant into the law and extends the scope of the crime . . . the MCA authorizes naming any American or foreigner living in the United States as an illegal enemy combatant."[38] The concept of illegal enemy combatant was a term created to refer to the individuals defined by the military order of November 13, 2001 as those who have "caused, threaten to cause, or have as their aim to cause, injury to or adverse effects on the United States, its citizens, national security, foreign policy, or economy"[39] Being marked as an illegal enemy combatant within the

---

36. Giorgio Agamben, "The State of Exception," in *Politics, Metaphysics and Death: Essays on Giorgio Agamben's Homo Sacer*, ed. Andrew Norris (Durham: Duke University Press, 2005), 293.
37. Erik Vogt, "S/Citing the Camp," in *Politics, Metaphysics and Death: Essays on Giorgio Agamben's Homo Sacer*, ed. Andrew Norris (Durham: Duke University Press, 2005), 79.
38. Jean-Claude Paye, "Enemy Combatant or Enemy of the Government?," *Monthly Review* 59(4) (2007): 6.
39. George Bush, "Military Order of November 13, 2001: Detention, Treatment, and Trial of Certain Non-Citizens in the War against Terrorism," *Federal Register* 66(222) (2001): 57834.

discourse of the war on terror marked an individual as extremely dangerous and was used to justify their placement within an alternative legal framework designed specifically for them. These individuals were, at the time, explicitly defined as non-citizens. However as the war on terror has progressed, those who can be defined as illegal enemy combatants has expanded to include citizens as well. As discussed above, this is not usual, as states of exception tend to become normalized within the law.

The enforcement of a state of exception within the United States, as recent presidential memos reveal, specifically an October 23, 2001 memo authored by the Office of Legal Counsel and sent to both the Defense Department and the White House, would be done through the explicit disregarding of the Fourth Amendment of the American Constitution, therefore allowing for unlimited searches and seizures. The contemplation of such an action demonstrates the inherent instability that exists within not only liberal, but all societies, when the foundational document of a nation can be voided under the proper circumstances. Such an event would demonstrate, in crystal clear terms, the tedious foundations upon which modern society rests. The legal status of the memo itself reveals the malleability of the law, as it has not been formerly withdrawn and remains a secret, but *unclassified* document, according to a Justice Department spokesman.[40]

These measures are portrayed as acting in the defense of society, due to the unorthodox threat facing society. "In the discursive constitution of the war on terror, the state is clearly cast in terms of the defender of society, and so great is this particular threat that the instrumentality of the state must become extraordinarily extensive and intrusive."[41] The justification is in a war, a war against terror, where the normal rules no longer apply. The disregarding of current rules and the creation of new rules during a war to respond to the threat presented by the war is of course nothing new. However because of the diffuse nature of the present conflict, "it is not clear whether the U.S is at war in a literal sense. If this is merely war in metaphor, then war rhetoric turns largely flat, and a more precise term for the conflict against terrorists might more appropriately be police action."[42] However, if the struggle against terror is merely a police action, a common occurrence within society, then no justification is provided for the creation of new state powers, the formation of states of exception, and the prosecution of war internationally against terrorist regimes.

---

40. Dan Eggen and Josh White, "Administration Asserted a Terror Exception on Search and Seizure," *The Washington Post*, April 4, 2008, A04.
41. David Mutimer, "Sovereign Contradictions: Mahar Arar and the Indefinite Future," in *The Logics of Biopower and the War on Terror: Living, Dying, Surviving*, ed. Elizabeth Dauphinee and Cristina Masters (New York: Palgrave Macmillian, 2007), 171
42. Michael Brough, "Legitimate Combatancy, POW Status, and Terrorism," in *Philosophy 9/11: Thinking about the War on* Terror, ed. Timothy Shanaham (Chicago: Open Court, 2005), 206.

The solution to these problems is the governmentality of unease, which creates a rationalization for the expansion of the instrumentality of the state by provoking fear of the other, of dangerous social classes. Thus "exceptionalism is not only linked with the derogatory measures and special laws against presumed terrorists, but also with a specific form of governmentality. The governmentality of unease increases the exception and banalizes it."[43] Through the application of new surveillance techniques, the governmentality of unease classifies a threat by the creation of profiles. The individuals that fit into these profiles are then targeted and gradually excluded from society as their life chances are reduced. However, this applies only to individuals viewed as liberal subjects, those viewed as illiberal have the potential to have their political character stripped from then and interned for an indefinite period within a sovereign created state of exception. Changes in the law normalize these processes and extend their potential reach within society. Understanding the operation of these dynamics and how they make the metaphorical war on terror possible allow us to unravel the forces that create and sustain it and hopefully allow us to actualize some of the, as yet, unrealized promises of liberalism. All while retaining the knowledge that the constructed order of liberal societies remains unable to achieve this future and actively seeks to obscure and discourage its fulfillment.

---

43. Didier Bigo, "Security, Exception, Ban, and Surveillance," in *Theorizing Surveillance: The Panopticon and Beyond,* ed. David Lyon (Portland: William Publishing, 2006), 47.

**References**

Agamben, Giorgio. 1998. *Homo sacer: Sovereign power and bare life.* Stanford: Stanford University Press.

—— *State of exception.* 2005. Chicago: The Univ. of Chicago Press.

Anderson, Benedict. 2006. *Imagined communities: Reflections of the origin and spread of nationalism.* Revised Edition. London: Verso.

Balland, Kirstie and Frank Webster. 2003. *The intensification of surveillance: Crime, terrorism and warfare in the information age.* London: Pluto Press.

Barry, Andrew, Thomas Osborne, and Nikolas Rose. 1996. *Foucault and political reason: Liberalism, neo-liberalism and rationalities of government.* Chicago: The Univ. of Chicago Press.

Blomley, Nicholas. 1994. *Law, space, and the geographies of power.* New York: The Guilford Press.

Burchell, Graham, Colin Gordon, and Peter Miller. ed. 1991. *The Foucault Effect: Studies in Governmentality.* Chicago: Univ. of Chicago Press.

Bush, George. "Military Order of November 13, 2001: Detention, Treatment, and Trial of Certain Non-Citizen in the War against Terrorism." *Federal Register* 66(222) (2001): 57833-57836.

Crampton, Jeremy and Stuart Elden. ed. 2007. *Space, knowledge and power: Foucault and geography.* Aldershot: Ashgate.

Dauphinee, Elizabeth and Cristina Masters. 2007. *The logics of biopower and the war on terror: Living, dying, surviving.* New York: Palgrave Macmillan.

Dillon, Michael. "Governing terror: The state of emergency of biopolitical emergence." *International Political Sociology* 1 no.1 (2007): 7-28.

—— "Governing through contingency: The security of biopolitical governance." *Political Geography* 26 no. 1 (2007): 41-47.

Eggen, Dan and Josh White. "Administration asserted a terror exception on search and seizure." *The Washington Post* (April 4, 2008), A04.

Foucault, Michel. 1995. *Discipline & punish: The birth of the prison.* New York: Vintage.

—— 1994. *Ethics: Subjectivity and Truth.* New York: The New Press.

Heller, Agnes and Sonja Riekmann. ed. 1996. *Biopolitics: The politics of body, race and nature.* Aldershot: Avebury.

Hier, Sean and Joshua Greenberg. 2007. *The surveillance studies reader.* New York: Open Univ. Press.

Howell, Alison. "Victims or madmen? The diagnostic competition over terrorist detainees at Guantanamo Bay." *International Political Sociology* 1 no.1 (2007): 29-47.

Hunt, Krista and Kim Rygiel. ed. 2006. *(En)gendering the war on terror: War stories and camouflaged politics.* Aldershot: Ashgate.

Jabri, Vivienne. "Michel Foucault's analytics of war: The social, the international and the racial." *International Political Sociology* 1 no.1 (2007): 67-81.

Keen, David. 2006. *Endless war? Hidden functions of the war on terror.* London: Pluto Press.

Lyon, David. ed. 2006. *Theorizing surveillance: The panopticon and beyond.* Portland: William Publishing.

——— 2007. *Surveillance Studies: An Overview.* Cambridge: Polity Press.

McGrath, John. 2004. *Loving big brother: Performance, privacy, and surveillance space.* London: Routledge.

Norris, Andrew. ed. 2005. *Essays on Giorgio Agamben's homo sacer.* Durham: Duke Univ. Press.

Paye, J. C. "Enemy combatant or enemy of the government?" *Monthly Review* 59, no. 4 (2007): 1-11.

Pettman, Ralph. 1981. *Biopolitics and international values: Investigating liberal norms.* New York: Pergamon Press.

Prozorov, Sergei. 2007. *Foucault, freedom and sovereignty.* Burlington: Ashgate.

Reid, Julian. *The biopolitics of the war on terror: Life struggles, liberal modernity and the defense of logistical societies.* Manchester Univ. Press, Manchester.

Sack, Robert. 1986. *Human territoriality: Its theory and history.* Cambridge: Cambridge Univ. Press.

Salter, Mark. "Governmentalities of an airport: Heterotopia and confession." *International Political Sociology* 1, no.1 (2007): 49-66.

Schmitt, Carl. 1985. *Political theology: Four chapters on the concept of sovereignty.* Cambridge: MIT Press.

Shanaham, Timothy. ed. 2005. *Philosophy 9/11: Thinking about the war on terrorism.* Chicago: Open Court.

Soloman, Naoki and John Soloman, ed. 2006. *Translation, biopolitics, colonial difference.* Hong Kong: Hong Kong Univ. Press.

Wiegele, Thomas. 1979. *Biopolitics: Search for a more human political science.* Boulder: Westview Press.

# COMBATING TERROR OF LAW IN COLONIAL INDIA: THE LAW OF SEDITION AND THE NATIONALIST RESPONSE

*Aravind Ganachari*

> *"My experience of political cases in India leads me to the conclusion that in nine out of ten the condemned were totally innocent. Their crime consists in the love of their country . . . the administration of law is thus prostituted consciously for the benefit of the exploiter . . . Section 124-A under which I am happily charged is perhaps the prince among the political sections of the Indian Penal Code designed to suppress the liberty of the citizen . . . Holding such a belief I consider it to be a sin to have affection for the system . . . .I am endeavoring to show to my countrymen that violent non-cooperation only multiplies evil and that as evil can only be sustained by violence, withdrawal of support of evil requires complete abstention from violence . . . I submit to what in law is a deliberate crime and what appears to me to be the highest duty of a citizen."*
> 
> —Mahatma Mohandas K. Gandhi[1]

## I

Terror could broadly be defined as a method or the theory behind the method, which seeks to achieve its avowed aims chiefly through the systematic use of violence. Terrorism is an emotionally charged word that is frequently used to politically and socially denigrate one's opponents. When a repressive regime forces its citizens into total obedience, uses violence, or the credible threat of violence, it becomes intolerant of incongruent ideas and puts persons belonging to such groups on a state of chronic fear or terror. The chief aim is to produce disorientation and /or compliance, or to instill a wholesale fear in the hearts of the general populace by the gross display of repressive power of the State. A working definition of 'terror' ought to constitute three parts—method, target, and purpose or motivation behind the action.

It must be remembered that the formation of the Colonial state in India was the result of not just political as well as territorial conquest and consolidation, but it was an invasion of epistemological space as well. In this regard, it would be apt to discuss, rather reiterate in agreement, the arguments advanced by Bernard S. Cohn in his celebrated work—*Colonialism and Its Forms of Knowledge*.

---

1. M.K. Gandhi, *The Law and the Lawyer*, pp.113-122; Also, *Young India*, 27 March 1930.

At the outset, in his 'Foreword' Nicholas B. Dirks outlined Cohn's premises[2]:

> Colonial conquest was not just the result of the power of superior arms, military organization, political power, or economic wealth—as important as these things were. Colonialism was made possible, and then sustained and strengthened, as much by cultural technologies of rule as it was by the more obvious and brutal modes of conquest that first established power on foreign shores... colonialism was itself a cultural project of control. Colonial knowledge both enabled conquest and was produced by it; in certain important ways, knowledge was what colonialism was all about. Cultural forms in societies newly classified as "traditional" were reconstructed and transformed by and through this knowledge, which created new categories and oppositions between colonizers and colonized, European and Asian, modern and traditional, West and East. Ruling India through a delineation and reconstitution of systematic grammars for vernacular languages, representing India through the mastery and display of archaeological memories and religious texts, Britain set in motion transformations every bit as powerful as the better-known consequences of military and economic imperialism.

It was Michel Foucault who advanced a premise, in which knowledge and power were inextricably linked, a thought that was opened up for discussion by Edward Said. In this sense, Cohn argues that "The colonial state is seen as a theatre for the state experimentation, where historiography, documentation, certification and representation were all state modalities that transformed knowledge into power."[3] Therefore, he felt that the conquest of India was a conquest of knowledge that included gathering, its ordering and classifying, and then transforming it into usable forms. Implicit in this is not only acquiring and controlling the channels of information so much needed for governance of the colonized, but to show and assert the superiority of the Colonizer's institution, thereby legitimizing their right to govern.

One of the important sites of colonial power that give the impression of being both benevolent as well as most susceptible to indigenous influences but in fact became responsible for institutionalizing peculiar British notion about how to regulate a colonial society made up of "others," was 'law.'

---

2. Bernard S. Cohn, *Colonialism and Its Forms of Knowledge–The British in India*, Oxford University Press, Delhi, 1997, p. ix. Nicholas B. Dirks is the Franz Boas Professor of History and Anthropology at Colombia University and his other work is The Scandal of Empire: India and the Creation of Imperial Britain, Harvard University Press, 2006.

3. *Ibid.*, p.XI.

Unable to stem the surging tide of Indian nationalism at the turn of the nineteenth and the early decades of twentieth century, the British Indian Government sought to contain 'sedition,' on the one hand, by a wholesale prosecution of newspapers repressed any hostile criticism of its rule by ever widening the legal scope of the term 'sedition' and also by inventing legal traditions by amending the Indian Penal Code (IPC) and Criminal Procedure Code (Cr. PC); applying different existing laws and enacting new cognate laws such as the Sea Customs Act (1878), the Seditious Meeting Act (1908), and the Indian Press Act (1910), to name a few; to bring those newspapers' editors and printers under official net. In this scheme of things, the colonial administration grossly abused the judicial procedure and secured the convictions through officially tainted judicial officers.

In tracing the evolution of the Indo-British Law of Sedition, namely Section 124-A of the Indian Penal Code, which the colonial state so deftly used and Mahatma Gandhi so poignantly referred to as 'evil' only sustained by legal 'violence', this paper seeks to argue that the Colonial state thereby not only terrorized the masses by using 'law' as an effective instrument of coercion but also subverted the judicial procedure to achieve the desired aim, namely, to humble the colonized into total submission. The term 'sedition' which earlier equated with treason and felony, and which so far people abhorred to think, now became a handy weapon of the State to terrorize the people. The Anglo-Indian press generally acted as an agent of the state.

It also seeks to argue that the law of sedition and the Indian nationalists acted and reacted on each other. The nationalists, on the other hand, questioned the very basis of the 'terror of law'. With forces of repression let loose and no legitimate means of ventilating grievances, the nationalists found different ways of disseminating ideas of 'freedom' other than the press since the government came down heavily upon them, through the medium of *melā* songs, the theatre, *kirtans, pravachanas* and public lectures. The ideas of freedom were thus couched in indigenous tradition that soon became a part of their public memory.

The paper attempts to compare the approach of two the towering nationalists—Lokmanya Bal Gangadhar Tilak and Mahatma M.G. Gandhi— towards British Indian law and argues that Lokmānya B.G. Tilak, whom the colonial administration considered its irreconcilable foe, deftly used sedition cases against him to arouse political consciousness of the masses. The fundamental moral question he raised: Was it sedition of the people against the British Indian Government (*Rājdroha*) or of the Government against the Indian People (*Deshdroha*).[4]

---

4. *Rajdroha* means 'sedition' against a lawfully constituted government and Deshdroha means treason against people represented by the State. *Bombay Presidency Police Abstracts of Intelligence (hereafter BPPAI)*, 1907, Vol. XXI, No, June 20, 1907, Para 537 (c).

With the experience in South Africa as well as from the lessons drawn from the Tilak trials, Mahatma Gandhi adopted totally a different strategy. He questioned the very nature of the colonial law: *"Is moral law, the law of conscience, higher than the law of the State which is oppressive?"* He, unlike Tilak, did not work within the British framework of law; in fact, he set the agenda, which was designed to defy law and the legal system, and even to ridicule it. In this, the British authorities could not anticipate Gandhi. By inaugurating an 'era of Satyagraha' he sought to attack the very basis of British rule—the 'oppressive' law. His individual Satyagrahas, No-tax campaigns, Non-cooperation, Civil disobedience, culminating into Quit India Movement, were illustrative of the design. With the progressive mobilization of mass participation in the national movement the 'terror of law' so characteristic of the earlier phase was lost, and thereby knocked the most important pillar of British imperialism in India.

The paper is based on the sources located at the Maharashtra State Archives, the contemporary writings, and also the state intelligence reports.

## II

The law of 'Sedition' was an import during the colonial period from English law into the Indian Penal Code, which consisted of partly the Treason-Felony Act, the Common law with regard to seditious libels' and the law relating to the seditious words.[6] The clause on 'sedition' stood as Section 113 in Macaulay's draft Indian Penal Code (IPC) of 1837[7], and was shelved for 20 years

---

5. For an excellent analysis of how the Law of Seditious Libel was used in England during the period 1890-1832, see Philip Harling, "The Law of Libel and the Limits of Repression, 1790-1832", *The Historical Journal*, 44, I, 2001, pp.107-134.

6. The measures of 1835 drafted by Macaulay were explained by Charles Metcalfe as an "Act to establish perfect uniformity in the laws... Every person would be at liberty to set up a newspaper without applying for previous permission; but no person would be able to print or publish sedition or calumny without imminent risk of punishment". Quoted by Walter Russell Donogh, *The History and Law of Sedition and Cognate Offences in India*, Thacker Spink and Co., Calcutta, 1914, 2nd ed., p.180. This book is mainly based on official Law Reports and presents the British administrative viewpoint.

7. A very perceptible view regarding the making of Macaulay's draft Code is given by David Skuy. He argues that though Macaulay claimed to be very original and that his code was an attempt to modernize a primitive Indian indigenous law tradition, was in fact based on the effort concurrently carried out in England to reform primitive English law. However, he does not mention about the way the Law of Sedition was drafted in IPC –Section 113 by Macaulay. See David Skuy, "Macaulay and the Indian Penal Code of 1862 : The Myth of the Inherent Superiority and Modernity of the English Legal System Compared to India's Legal System in the Nineteenth Century", *Modern Asian Studies*, Vol. 32, No. 3, July 1998, pp. 513-557. In India, colonial law operated on the heavily guarded border between the hermetic categories of colonizer

until the enactment of IPC in 1860. But when enacted, the said clause was curiously omitted despite the tumultuous happenings of 1857-58, only to be inserted into the IPC by way of an amendment in 1870.[8]

Interestingly, while introducing the amendment Sir James Stephen, the Law Secretary to Government of India, justified on the pretext that it aimed to bring about uniformity and remove incongruities in the existing law. He pointed out that the new section (124-A) aimed to punish attempts to excite feelings of 'disaffection' against the Government and made a distinction between 'disaffection' and 'disapprobation'.[9] In reality, the insertion of a section on 'sedition' was prompted by the increasing Wahabi activities between 1863-1870.[10] To book these 'agents of sedition', E.C. Bayley, Secretary, Home Department, Government of India (GOI), suggested "the necessity of amending law with the object of enabling the government to deal more satisfactorily with seditious proceedings not amounting to waging, or attempting to or abetting to wage war against the Queen, that it cannot now do under the provisions of the Indian Penal Code."[11] The Bill containing the law of sedition, i.e. Section 124-A, was passed on November 25, 1870 as Act XXVII, an amendment to the IPC and continued to remain in force unmodified till 18 February, 1898. Thus, Section 124-A read as follows:

> Whosoever by words, either spoken or intended to be read or by signs or by visible representations or otherwise excite or attempts to excite feelings of disaffection to the Government established by law in British India, shall be punishable with transportation of life . . . to three years to which fine may be added.

In the initial years, while the administration was discreet in not using the law of sedition against criticism of official measures, though it dealt severely with any attempt of uprising, however negligible. Criticism in Indian press

---

and colonized. What was Law of Seditious Libel only in England became just the Law of Sedition in Indian Colonial context.

8. Some possible clues to the questions such as- Why was the said clause on sedition omitted in 1860 while enacting the IPC despite the Revolt of 1857? And, what prompted the Government to insert the clause by an amendment in 1870?, have been discussed in Aravind Ganachari, "Evolution of the Law of 'Sedition' in the Context of The Indian Freedom Struggle : 1837 – 1922" in *Nationalism and Social Reform in a Colonial Situation*, Kalpaz Publication, New Delhi, 2005, pp.54-55.

9. Disapprobation or disapproval of any official measures was allowed so long as it was compatible with a disposition to obedience to Government.

10. For more details see R.C. Majumdar (ed.) *British Paramountcy and Indian Renaissance*, Part I, Bharatiya Vidya Bhavan, Bombay, 1963, pp. 883-901; Also, Narahari Kaviraj, *Wahabi and Farazi Rebels of Bengal*, People's Publishing House, New Delhi, 1982.

11. *Maharashtra State Archives (MSA)/ Judicial Department (JD)*, Vol. 14/767; No. A-52, March 24, 1869.

largely reflected against some official measures and did not aim at the Government itself. After 1870, the administration did not amend the law of sedition until 1898 but sought to cover disapproving criticism by enacting two cognate laws, i.e. the Dramatic Performances Act XIX of 1876 (DPA) and the Vernacular Press Act (IX) of 1878. Hence, these Acts were termed 'preventive measures'. While the first of these laws was enacted due to two allegedly seditious plays[12], the Vernacular Press Act of 1876—was brought about by Lord Lytton to suppress sharp criticism of British policies as a result of the events of 1875-76, namely, the Deccan Agricultural riots of 1875-76 and the failure of relief measures. It aimed to control the publishers and printers of periodical magazines in native languages by means of a system of personal security.[13]

## III

How the law of 'sedition' gradually became an instrument of terrorizing the colonized can be illustrated by discussing a few landmark cases. The first trial on record for sedition under the section 124-A was Queen Empress v. Jogendra Chander Bose & Others, more commonly known as the *Bangobasi* case of 1891. This case brought up the question of limits of legitimate criticism in the press against the official measures. The *Bangobasi*, a newspaper edited by Jogendra Chandra, while reacting to the passage of the Age of Consent Bill (1891), raised the cry of 'religion in danger', and charged the Government for Europeanizing India by brute force, and held it responsible for the economic deprivation of Indians. However, it also stated that Hindus neither believed in rebellion nor were they capable of it.[14]

The question that was discussed in this case was: Did the *Bangobasi* exceed the bounds of legitimate criticism? The prosecution charged that the intention was to bring the people into a frame of mind, namely, 'we would rebel if we could', and that the religious feelings of the people were so excited that public peace was imperiled. The defense disapprovingly argued that there was no reference to 'rebellion', and that it only differentiated between "European and native method of thought." However, the judge 'thought that *Bangobasi* excited the feelings of ill-will against the Government and attempted to

---

12. The two plays were: *Cha-Ka Durpan* (The Mirror of Tea Planting) by Girish Chandra Ghosh in Bengali and *Malharraoche Natak* by Narayan Bapuji Kanitkar in Marathi. *MSA/JD/1876/Vol.24/398*.

13. The only prosecution in Maharashtra for seditious writing under this Act was of *Pune Vaibhav* in 1881, which had commented in the editorial note that, 'the failure of his (Irish leader Parnell's) efforts in Ireland only suggest the futility of such civilized methods'. The proceedings were turned down because the thinly veiled seditious allusions did not carry force.

14. Donogh, *op.cit.*, pp. 38-9.

hold it up to the hatred and contempt of the people."[15] In the meanwhile, the accused tendered an apology and the proceedings were dropped.

Two cases made innovative contribution to the evolution of the law of sedition in 1897—The Tilak Case and the *Pratod* Case. The agricultural distress and epidemic of bubonic plague of 1896-97, the hostile criticism of the vernacular press against the failure of government remedial measures and the growing popularity of Bal Gangadhar Tilak, alarmed the government. The officials decided him to fix him by any means but within the legal framework. On 12 June 1897, Tilak took the lead in celebrating the Shivaji Coronation ceremony with lectures and patriotic songs. Although the function went off peacefully, the report of this function which appeared in *Kesari* and was followed by the murder of Plague Commissioner W C Rand and Lt. Ayerst on June 22. Legal proceedings were then pressed against Tilak on the charge of sedition. This case is important on several counts: firstly, it was a classic example of how the imperialist Anglo-Indian press goaded government into arresting Tilak on charges of sedition and also prejudiced the judiciary; secondly, it illustrated how the law and legal system were distorted to suit the official design; and lastly, it precipitated the amendment to the existing law of Sedition [Section 124-A of IPC] to make it more comprehensive and draconian.

The legal proceedings against Tilak were precipitated by a venomous campaign launched by the Anglo-Indian newspapers—the *Times of India* and *Bombay Gazette*. Not only the editorials but also letters under the pseudonym of 'Shackles' and 'Justice' connected Tilak to Rand's murder and thereby suggested his complicity in the murder. The Anglo-Indian press advocated to the Government on July 6, to prosecute Tilak under Section 124-A. Tilak's retort to such mischievous writings appeared in the *Kesari* of June 30 but in vain.[16] As expected, he was arrested on charges of sedition on August 27th and the trial began on September 8th, 1897.

Since the government was hell-bent in bringing Tilak within the legal ambit, the administration transferred and promoted the obliging Justice James Strachey to High Court. Justice Strachey, who was the junior most on the bench and was known for his bias against the natives, was especially - asked to preside over the case. Significantly, while applying Section 124-A, Justice Strachey rejected the defense argument that the articles describing the sufferings of the people were quite consistent with loyalty, the object of the accused was to "create a national sentiment" and that "no suggestion to overthrowing the British Government" was made. Further, he transcended the argument of the prosecution and gave his own inventive interpretation by

---

15. *Ibid*, p.40.
16. S. S. Setlur and K. G. Deshpande (ed.), *A Full and Authentic Report of the Tilak Case (1897)...at the Criminal Sessions*. n.d., pp. 90-6. Also, Queen Empress vs. B.G. Tilak, *Indian Decisions*. New Series, Vol. XL, 1897-98, pp. 656-683.

widening the scope of the law regarding the 'feelings of disaffection': "it meant "hatred, enmity, dislike, hostility, contempt and every form of ill-will to the Government." He equated disaffection to disloyalty, comprehending every possible form of bad feeling and held that "the amount or the intensity of the disaffection is absolutely immaterial except perhaps in dealing with the question of punishment." On the 'disapprobation' allowed in the explanation to clause 124-A, he commented, "It does not apply to any writing which consists not merely of comments upon Government measures, but of attacks upon the Government itself, its existence, its essential characteristic, its motives, or its feelings towards the people."[17] In view of this judicial innovation, the obvious necessity of importing plainer language into the law of sedition was at once recognized and legislation speedily followed in 1898 to update the clause to his interpretation. Justice Strachey's remarks were very often cited in subsequent cases and confirmed.

Tilak was aware that the case for prosecution was weak but he feared the bias of a non-Marathi knowing and European dominated jury. He knew that the law was twisted to suit the administration.[18] A new legal tradition was invented by convicting Tilak under the widened scope provided by the new meaning of the law and then an amendment was suggested to bring the law to that effect. The native press throughout the country unanimously condemned it as "the Strachey Law."

The *Pratod* case concerned with a newspaper from Islampur in Satara district that published an article titled "Preparation for becoming independent" (27 May 1897). The article described Canadian nationalist resistance to colonial exploitation and the manner by which Canadians acquired political democratic rights, and urged the Indians to follow the suit. The Judge, H.F. Aston sentenced the first accused, R.N. Kashalkar, the publisher, to transportation for life and the other, K. D. Hamalkar, the printer, for seven years' rigorous imprisonment. Aston's remark explains generally held predisposition against Indians: "The sentence should be such as to bring home to the minds of all, the gravity of the offence committed by those who seek to undermine the foundation on which the greatest strength of the Government in India rests."[19]

When this case came up on appeal to the High Court before the full bench consisting of Chief Justice Farran, Justice Parson and Justice M. G. Ranade, a few months after the Tilak Case, it was unanimously held that the animus was to excite a feeling of aversion and hatred against the Government. They believed that the attack was not against any particular act or measure of Government or its officers, but was an outcome of a vague disaf-

---

17. Donogh, *op.cit.*, pp.47-50.
18. Setlur and Deshpande, *op.cit*, Appendix-D, pp.30-1; Tilak's apprehensions reflect in the letter quoted in The Indian Nation of Calcutta, Sept. 1897.
19. *MSA/JD/*1897/ Vol.233/2039.

fection against the existing political system. Significantly, the judges made a further inventive interpretation of the terms 'disaffection' and 'disapprobation' but within the framework provided by 'the Strachey Law'. Justice Farran felt that the word "disaffection" used in Section 124-A "cannot be construed as meaning an absence of or the contrary of affection of love, that is to say dislike or hatred." It is an attempt "to excite political discontent and alienation from their allegiance." He concluded the enigmatic exposition by saying that "the article as a whole has the object of making its readers impatient of their allegiance to a foreign sovereign and creating in them the desire of casting off their dependence upon England." The conviction of both the accused was confirmed, but the sentences were found to be disproportionate to the gravity of the offence; and were reduced to one year's and three months simple imprisonment respectively. These two cases give an idea of how in the altered political conditions law could be powerfully used for terrorizing the people.

Against this background, the *raison d'etre* of the amendment to the law of sedition—Section 124-A, was provided by Mr. Chalmers, the member in charge of the Bill. He said, "recent events in India have called prominent attention to the law relating to seditious utterances and writings. We have had anxiously to consider the state of law regarding these matters and to decide whether, and in what respects, it required an amendment . . . But we are also determined that the law shall not be a dead letter." He made references to the defense arguments in the Tilak Case that "resort to actual violence was not advocated," and therefore thought that the law be expressed in clearer and less equivocal terms."[20] In the amended Section 124-A, the words 'hatred and contempt' were inserted along with the term 'disaffection'. The expression 'disaffection' was made inclusive of 'disloyalty and all feelings of enmity'. Besides, new sections such as 153-A and 505 were inserted into IPC and Criminal Procedure Code.

Immediately after the enactment of the amendments, the Bombay Government charged a host of newspapers on grounds of sedition. Proceedings were instituted against the *Sudharak, Muslim Herald, Arunodaya, Kalidas, Indu Prakash* and *Gurakhi*, to name a few. In the case *Indu Prakash*, the Poona district officials started proceedings under Section 153-A; i.e. class-hatred, for describing Englishmen as "adept in the art of trickery."[21] The Solicitor General felt that such a comment, could incite a hot-headed Englishman to assault the editor of *Indu Prakash*.

In the midst of such repression was the case of Imperatix v. Henry Wilson, which evoked considerable criticism in the vernacular press. Henry, the accused, was a stud-keeper of the Governor of Bombay, who caused the death of one Bapu bin Raoji, a servant of the stud farm, by what was termed

---

20. Donogh *op.cit.*, pp.60-1.
21. *MSA/JD/*1899/ Vol. 147/619 (Confdl.) pp.889-90.

as a "rash and negligent act." Judge H.F. Aston, who had earlier awarded a harsh sentence in the *Pratod* Case, fined Rs.25/—for fatally attacking Raoji. This was glaring instance of judicial discrimination on the basis of race. Such bias against Indians was held by many European officials of the ilk of Aston.[22]

While in the Tilak Case (1898), the Anglo-Indian press pressurized the Bombay government into initiating proceedings, but in the *Kal* Case (1900-4) it acted as an agent of the Bombay government. Unable to acquire prior approval of the GOI to prosecute *Kal* newspaper since many cases did go up to conviction, the Bombay government leaked information to the *Times of India* to cry foul so that the hesitant GOI would give necessary prior sanction. But the government was put in a quandary when the vernacular Indian press made the exposé. The GOI termed the action of the Bombay Government as "a somewhat unfortunate error of judgment" and reasserted the need to take prior sanction. It was only in 1908, that Professor S.M. Paranjape, editor of the *Kal* could be convicted for seditious writings

Against the background of the Partition of Bengal (1905), the happenings in Barisal, the Swadeshi Movement with its programme of *Swadeshi*, boycott, national education, and temperance, any veiled criticism in the native press against the official repressive measures caused much consternation to the Government. The said Section 124-A was further reinterpreted in the case against the newspaper *Bhala* and its editor B.B. Bhopatkar, to suit official repression. Within the limits of disapprobation, the published article—"A Durbar in Hell" (Oct. 11, 1905)—was an allegory applying to no government but giving a description of Hell and its rulers. But in Justice Blatty's opinion Bhopatkar had made allusions to the forgery committed by Robert Clive and the treatment meted to the Begam of Awadh, thereby did attempt to create hatred and disaffection against the Government. He further clarified, "Disaffection is a feeling and not the want of feeling. It is not the absence of affection. It is not indifference but a positive emotion not necessarily prompting to action, but with a tendency to influence conduct just as all our feelings do . . ."[23] Bhopatkar was sentenced to six months imprisonment, and the scope of Section 124-A was further enlarged.

The tumultuous events of 1905-7 in Bengal and its ramifications all over the country, the arrest of Lala Lajpatrai and Ajit Singh in Panjab by Governor Denzil Ibbetson, and the triumph of Extremism at Surat Congress led to more severe official repressive measures. The native press became more vocal in its criticism and even tacitly admired revolutionaries. The administration came out with two repressive legislations in early 1908 against sedition related

---

22. *MSA/JD/*1899 /Vol.145-A/139-A (Confdl.)
23. Emperor Vs. S.S. Dev, *The Bombay Law Reporter*, Vol. XII. pp.675-88. Keshav N. Damle was the author of the Ekshlokigita and was father of the famed Marathi poet Keshavsut. S.S. Dev was the publisher.

offences—the Newspapers (Incitement to offences) Act VII and the Seditious Meeting Act. The first, empowered the District Magistrates to confiscate the printing press used or intended to be used for, publishing seditious matter.[24] The very title of the second was self-explanatory. The nationalists quickly understood the hidden intentions and organized protest meeting. Tilak felt no necessity for such an act when empowered with Section 124-A but aptly described nationalists' perception in the following words:

> Government of India is giving itself powers to stop meetings where more than twenty people assemble . . . It will create tyranny on people . . . Such things are done in Russia...*they have made up their mind to pass the Bill into law. We only meet and discuss for formality's sake . . . The police can enter the house where such a meeting is held, arrest its promoters without a warrant. If there are 18 persons, the police will supply remaining two to make up the complement. It is not that I am suggesting this idea to the police. It will suggest itself to them.*[25]

Tilak feared that such oppressive laws might compel the people to find out ways and means to evade them, and forewarned the administration that too much of repression breeds revolution. But the Government was relentless.

When the Muzzafarpur bomb incident took place, the *Kesari* wrote strong articles pointing out the evil effects of repression. It was aware that Krishnaji Prabhakar Khadilkar had written the articles but judging from Tilak's conduct in the past they knew that, if prosecuted, he would own responsibility as editor.[26] Proceedings were initiated against Tilak as editor for publishing two articles—"*Deshache Durdaiva*" ('The Country's Misfortune', May 12, 1908) and "*He Upaya Tikau Nahit*" ('These Remedies Are Not lasting', June 9, 1908). Two separate cases were filed for the two articles under Section 124-A and 153-A. The case was committed to the High Court by Judge Aston Jr. on both charges. It came up before Justice D.D. Davar, who was elevated to the bench just before this case, and who was assisted by a non-Marathi knowing European dominated jury. The government took adequate care to see that no European was involved in handing Tilak a harsh sentence, lest it may draw public flak. Tilak defended himself. Branson, who had defended him in the Barve Defamation Case in 1882, appeared for the State. In 1908, Tilak was the only leader of note among the Extremist leaders yet to be sent to jail. Ti-

---

24. A case was registered under this Act against D.K. Phadke. He printed the newspaper Hindu Punch, which had carried a seditious article. The press was confiscated. *The Bombay Law Reporter*, Vol. XII, pp.120-121.
25. BPPAI/ 1907/ xx/No.43 /12 Nov. /Para 1113.
26. BPPAI/1908/xxi/No.27/July 11/ Para 674.

lak's arrest on July 24 evoked nation-wide protests. In Bombay, it resulted in the mill-hands strike and disturbances.[27]

Justice Davar did not depart from the line suggested by Strachey. Tilak was sentenced to six years rigorous imprisonment with transportation, three years in each case, to be undergone simultaneously. Tilak's reply to the judge is too well known to be repeated. Justice Davar went over-board in accomplishing the official task and his harsh remarks exuded venom. He said:

> it must be a diseased mind, a most perverted mind, that can think that the articles you have written are legitimate articles in political agitation. They are seething with sedition: they preach violence, they speak of murders with approval. I say such journalism is a curse to the country . . . I have decided to pass a sentence which I consider will be stigmatized as an instance of what is called misplaced leniency[28]

On the heels of Tilak's conviction, came the conviction of S.M. Paranjape, the editor of *Kal*. The significant feature of this case was that "for the first time in the history of prosecution for sedition in India, *patriotism was recognized in the jury-box to be a ground for palliation of sedition.*"[29]

In 1916, Tilak was again prosecuted under the charges of sedition, for delivering objectionable speeches. Barrister Mohammed Ali Jinnah ably defended Tilak and secured his acquittal. He argued that criticism of English bureaucracy did not represent 'disaffection' against the Government.

## IV

The Indian intellectuals were equally sharp to understand sly ways of British invasion of India's culture, which was designed to undermine it; to dwarf it by making evaluation in cultural scale; making value judgments that showed inherent backwardness of Indian tradition. Naturally, while the Indians sought introspection in the light of cultural criticism, they also came forward to defend against the cultural denigration. Many Indian intellectuals began to see in it as a cultural conflict that involved both restructuring as well as defending their past. With press being gagged and prosecutions of editor galore,

---

27. *MSA/JD//*1910/Vol.99/1562.
28. Emperor v. B.G. Tilak, *The Bombay Law Reporter*, Vol. X, pp.848-903. The full case was immediately published in Marathi and it became a means of spreading Tilak's message. Sitaram K. Damle, *Tilak Yanchyavaril Rajdrohacha Khatala* (1908), National Publishing, Bombay, 1908. This book was later proscribed. Sitaram K. Damle was Keshavsut's younger brother.
29. *Source Material for a Freedom Movement in India*, M.R. Palande (ed.), Government of Bombay, Bombay, Vol. II, 1958, pp.647-55.

the nationalists devised novel and varied means of disseminating patriotic thought through the medium of indigenous traditions. One of the most innovative features of such means since 1895 was introduction of the *Mela* movement of singing- parties, which produced a salutary effect on large and eager audiences. The British government saw a sinister design in this development and started licensing *the mela* songs in 1896.[30]

How the Government used judiciary to scuttle the *mela* songs within the legal framework is illustrative from the case—Emperor v. Ganesh Damodar Savarkar in 1909. G.D. Savarkar had authored a book of Marathi poems called *Laghu Abhinav Bharat Mala* in 1908 of which four poems came under official scan. He was charged under Section 121 and 121-A, i.e. waging war against the State and abetting to wage war, and also 124-A of IPC.[31] The defense argued that the poems charged had no reference to the British Government or the present times, that they did not constitute abatement to waging war, and that the "poems are puerile and must not be taken very seriously . . . at the very worst the poet inculcates revolutionary ideas into minds of readers." Though Justice N.G. Chandavarkar of the High Court admitted that the poet "has in mind the *Ganapati Melas* of the present times," but charged that "the venom is too transparent to be mistaken for anything else than to call people to wage (and) . . . preach war against the present Government." He held the invocation to Lord Ganesh, Rama, Krishna and Shivaji to destroy the 'foreign demons' as 'unmistaken innuendoes against the Government.' Justice Heaton further interpreted that it was "an instigation of an unknown person," for the author had sold three thousand copies of the book. Both the judges held Savarkar and sentenced him to transportation and two years rigorous imprisonment. The judges not only invented interpretation to oblige the government but skillfully used law with a view to terrorize the nationalists. When Indian judges like Justice Chandavarkar[32] gave such an interpretation, they became the target of public ridicule for obsequiously obliging their white masters.

In the late 1890s, when government tried to scuttle the press and *Mela* movements, the Marathi theatre made an intelligent use of dramatic art through sarcasm and allegory, to create anti-colonial feelings and to promote nationalism. The Maratha and Rajput histories and the epics provided suitable themes. Not until 1897, did the Government find anything objectionable in such dramas. But in the altered situation, particularly due to Tilak's arrest,

---

30. Richard L. Cashman. *The Myth of Lokmanya*, University of California Press, 1975, pp.81-2.
31. *The Bombay Law Reporter*, Vol. XII, pp. 105-21. The sedition charges were with regard to poems Nos. - 5, 7, 9, 17.
32. Soon Justice Chandavarkar was rewarded with Vice Chancellorship of Bombay University.

they came to convey a different meaning to the government and more so to the public.[33]

During the heyday of militant nationalism (1897-1916) as many as 39 dramas were prosecuted for dissemination of sedition, 32 of which were eventually banned and 16 were proscribed. The Government banned these dramas under one or the other provision of law. Wherever the Dramatic Performances Act (DPA) (1876) could not be used since the enforcement required prior sanction from the GOI, it applied the District Police Act (1890), Bombay City Police Act (1902), the IPC, Cr. C P, and even used extra-constitutional methods. Dramatists such as G.D. Kane, K.H. Dixit, and K.P. Khadilkar were harassed and blacklisted. Actors were sent to jail under the IPC and a few of them Were bound Section 108 of Cr. CP. Descriptive rolls of the members of the theatrical troupes were maintained by the Intelligence Department, as they were suspected to be conduits between the nationalists and the revolutionaries.

Another indigenous method of spreading national sentiment that the nationalists followed and the government found difficult to curb, was through *Kirtans* and *puran* [religious/spiritual discourses] reading, The confidential *Bombay Presidency Police Abstracts of Intelligence* are replete with such information. Apart from the *Bhagwat Gita* and the *Purans,* the most common themes of the *kirtans* and *pravachanas* were the life and teachings of Shivaji and Ramdas. The Government, which had kept a close surveillance on the Arya Samajists, maintained descriptive rolls of even *Haridasas,* the *Ramdasi Sadhus,* the swamis of Ramkrishna Math and termed them as "political Sadhus." In 1910, it prosecuted Keshav N. Damle and Shankar S. Dev for authoring and printing respectively, the *Ekaslokigita*[34] under Section 124-A. Later many commentaries on *Bhagwatgita* were brought under official ban and proscribed.

However, frustrated by the meek attitude of Government of India, officials like J.B. Morrison, Under Secretary, JD, Bombay Government, disgustingly recorded,

> I do not agree that the line of action suggested here are suited to present condition in this Presidency. *We are past the stage where persuasion, private reproof or warnings can stem seditious movements; and the only safe policy at least for some time to come is stern repression of the very sign of sedition.*[35]

---

33. Aravind G. Ganachari, "The Contribution of Marathi Theatre to The Growth of Nationalism- 1897-1916", *Proceedings of the Indian History Congress,* 54th Session (1993), Delhi, 1994, pp.582-590.
34. Emperor v. S.S. Dev, *The Bombay Law Reporter,* Vol. XII. pp.675-88. Keshav N. Damle was the author of the *Ekshlokigita* and was father of the famed Marathi poet Keshavsut. S.S. Dev was the publisher.
35. *MSA/JD/*1910/ Vol.235/1553.

## V

Mahatma Gandhi adopted totally a different strategy. He, unlike Tilak, did not work within the British framework of law; in fact, he set the agenda, which was designed to defy law and the legal system, and even to ridicule it. In this, the British authorities could not anticipate Gandhi. By inaugurating an 'era of Satyagraha' he sought to attack the very basis of British rule—the 'oppressive' law.

The South African experience (1893-1914) of Mahatma Gandhi contributed in a number of ways to the foundation of his ideology and methods to fight every form of injustice and oppression.[36] In all the three trials he faced in South Africa, he used the weapon of *Satyagraha* to peacefully disobey the oppressive laws. He showed a definite pattern in approach and method by showing the hollowness of the law and of legal procedure. He wrote in 1908 that 'the laws of the land are not inviolable' and that "The selfsame law is now about to fall apart."[37] He later recalled,

> In opposing the atrocious laws of the Government of South Africa, it was this method that we adopted ... no State is possible without two entities, the ruler and the ruled. When we are not subjects, you are not the sovereign either ... If you make laws to keep us suppressed in a wrongful manner and without taking us into confidence; these laws will merely adorn the statute-books. We will never obey them. Send us to prison and we will live there ...[38]

This became the pattern even in India, but on a large scale. In Champaran (1917), he decided to disobey the externment order of the District Magistrate W.B. Heycock to quit Champaran as he was termed as 'danger to the public peace'. The bureaucratic correspondence unfolds official un-preparedness in dealing with Gandhi. In fact, the bureaucracy reprimanded Heycock for "unjust Magistracy."[39] The nationalist press condemned the order and hailed Gandhi as a hero, which endeared him to the title *Mahātmā*.

---

36. He faced three trials there in South Africa: in 1907 for violating Transvaal ordinance on compulsory registration and passes for Indians; in 1908 for disobeying the order of the Court to leave the Colony; and in 1913 over immigration restrictions, the de-recognition of non-Christian marriages and the 3 pound tax on ex-indentured labourers.
37. "Triumph of Truth," Indian Opinion, February 8, 1908. In *Moral and Political Writings of Mahatma Gandhi* (hereinafter MPWMG), Raghavan Iyer (ed.), Vol. III, Clarendon Press, Oxford, 1987, pp.28-30.
38. Ibid. July 27, 1916, Pp.40-43.
39. Judith M. Brown, *Gandhi's Rise to Power-Indian Politics*, 1915- 20, Cambridge University Press, 1972, p. 27, pp. 52-83. She takes the approach of Cambridge School. Her book is full of observations calculated to undermine the importance of Gandhi and over-emphasize the role of British administration.

While leading the distressed peasants of Kaira (1917), the Magistrate served him with an order to quit the district. He disobeyed and told the Court, "I have ventured to make this statement not in any way in extenuation of the penalty to be awarded against me, but to show that I have disregarded the order served upon me, not for want of respect for lawful authority, but in obedience of the higher law of our being—the voice of conscience."[40] In his statement, Gandhi raised the most fundamental issue: *Is moral law, the law of conscience, higher than the law of the State, which is oppressive?* The officials were confounded, one said, "Gandhi is, this time, on a thoroughly bad wicket." Lord Willingdon, the Governor of Bombay, called him "honest, but a Bolshevik & for that reason very dangerous."[41] However, Gandhi advised his volunteers, "We are opposing the intoxication of power, that is, the blind application of law, and not authority as such."

Gandhi was sincere in offering co-operation in war efforts. But he was soon disillusioned with the introduction of Rowlatt Bills. He quickly learnt the lesson and told the Secretary of State, "This retention of Rowlatt legislation in the teeth of universal opposition is an *affront* to the nation. Its repeal is necessary to appease national honor."[42] Quickly followed the *hartals*, mass courting of arrests and Satyagraha throughout the country. Chelmsford's reaction to Gandhi's call was one of a confused person. He told Montagu, "I think he is trying to frighten us and I propose to call it a 'bluff'. In any case no other course is open to us." He finally said, "I am quite happy in defending my present position."

The article that Gandhi wrote in Navjivan during Non-Cooperation movement is very illuminating as to why the lawyers in particular should boycott the courts. He wrote:

> It is my firm belief that every Government masks its brute force and maintains its control over the people through civil and criminal courts, for it is cheaper, simpler and more honorable for a ruler that, instead of his controlling the people through naked force, they themselves, lured into slavery through courts, etc., submit to him of their own accord ... every State tries to perpetuate its power through lawyers.[43]

Gandhi's belief in the absolutism of ethical values, that moral norms are absolute and are objective and eternal, and completely removed from the canons of expediency and opportunism, was unquestionable. If he found

---

40. 'Statement Before the Court', *The Leader*, April 22, 1917.
41. Brown, *op.cit.*, pp.110-11., 164 & 168.
42. *Ibid.* p. 164.
43. Cited in *MPWMG*, 'Non-Cooperation', Navjivan, July 4, 1920, pp. 127-8 & 140.

the Moderate's method unworkable, nevertheless condemned violence in no uncertain terms.

Gandhi was arrested in March 10, 1922, on charges of sedition, for publishing certain articles in *Young India*.[44] Unlike Tilak, Gandhi never disclaimed his disloyalty towards the Government and that there was no halfway between active loyalty and active disloyalty. In the editorial, "Duty of disloyalty" (27 March 1930), he wrote, "When you are disloyal you seek not to destroy persons but institutions. The present State is an institution that can never evoke loyalty. It is corrupt . . . They represent not the interest of the people but those of their foreign masters . . . Disobedience to the law of an evil State is therefore a duty."[45] Gandhi, thereby, called the British Indian State as an evil empire and questioned the very basis of its existence. In doing so, he removed the spell of fear of the "terror of law" from the hearts of the people, which became so characteristic of all of his movements, and thus knocked off an important pillar of imperialism. Countless people went fearlessly to prisons, which Gandhi called "His Majesty's Hotels." He struck at the very root of British imperialism in India.

He then addressed the Judge, "The only course open to you is either to resign your post and thus dissociate yourself from evil, if you feel that the law that you are called upon to administer is an evil . . . ; or to inflict the severest penalty (on me)." Finally, he thanked the Judge for associating his name with the Late Lokmanya Bal Gangadhar Tilak.[46]

During the Civil Disobedience movement, he urged the masses not only to non-cooperate, but to breach the evil, unjust, and oppressive law. In 1942, he was not just condemning the evil law or the system that perpetrated it, but felt that the evil British Government ought to go out of India.

Gandhi's method created a dilemma for the British. Throughout, he first condemned violence in any form and subtly pointed out the role of repression that produced it. Even a faint justification of it would have helped the authorities to deal with him in the same manner as Tilak. They found that neither indifference nor repression really worked against Gandhi. Furthermore, the bureaucracy at various levels was at pain to maintain legal fiction, while using every conceivable means to suppress nationalist agitation. Equally, he was as bewildering to the Indian political elite of the day as it was to the British authorities.

---

44. The articles were published in *Young India*, entitled – "Disaffection a Virtue" (15 June 1921), "Tampering with Loyalty" (29 September, "The Puzzle and Its Solution"(15 December) and "Shaking the Manes" (23 February 1922).
45. *MPWMG, Young India*, 27 March 1930.
46. M.K. Gandhi, *The Law and the Lawyer*, pp.113-122.*Young India*, 27 March 1930.

## Conclusion

The chain reaction between the repressive law of sedition and the cognate laws and the Indian nationalists continued until Mahatma Gandhi inaugurated an 'era of *Satyagraha,* when the 'terror of law' was lost. The bureaucracy at various levels was at pains to maintain a legal fiction while using every conceivable means to suppress nationalist agitation. The law of sedition as it came to be applied to the Indian situation reflected a tension between the British adherence to democratic ideas in theory and its actual recourse to repression as a means of political survival. Likewise, Anglo-Indian press generally acted as an agent and the judiciary as the coercive arm of the executive.

The difference between Lokmanya Tilak and Mahatma Gandhi was that while Tilak consistently contended in 1897, 1908 and 1916 against the charge of committing sedition and thereby being 'disloyal' to the State. Gandhiji pleaded guilty. He called the British Indian State evil and removed the spell of fear of the 'terror of law.' This was also the measure of distance that the nationalists had traveled in relation to the "law of sedition."

# Terror, Outlawry, and the Experience of the Impossible

*Mary Bunch*

St. Augustine asked "Remove justice and what are states but gangs of bandits on a large scale? And what are bandit gangs but kingdoms in miniature?" (*City of God*, 4.4). The question of what differentiates law from outlawry is still relevant in a world where it is sometimes difficult to distinguish justice from injustice, and acts of terrorism from the legitimate actions of sovereign nations. There exists an apparently permanent crisis on both national and international scales, as is evident in the "war on terror" with its murky extralegal territories and identities. This indefinite state of global crisis is characterized by a resort to political praxis in the space outside of the law. Building on Walter Benjamin's "Critique of Violence" and Derrida's concepts of the "mystical" in law and the *avenir* (to-come) of justice, this paper investigates the concept of outlawry and the experience of the impossible—a striving for justice in the context of terror.

There are numerous ways to conceptualize 'terror.' The term is derived from the Latin *terrorem*, meaning "great fear, dread." Its use in relation to political violence and "government intimidation" began in association with the French Revolution's 'Reign of Terror.' As Robespierre remarked in a speech to the French National Convention of 1794 justifying the use of terror, (just a few short months before losing his own head):

> If the spring of popular government in time of peace is virtue, the springs of popular government in revolution are at once *virtue and terror*: virtue, without which terror is fatal; terror, without which virtue is powerless. Terror is nothing other than justice, prompt, severe, inflexible; it is therefore an emanation of virtue.

While currently there is no precise consensus on terrorism in the international community, Robespierre's association of terror with justice is generally reversed. Terrorism is popularly conceived as violent actions that invoke a state of fear and dread in the population, that the perpetrators justify with a political or ideological rationale of justice. Terrorist acts are distinguished from legitimate actions by their status outside the law, where the law is associated with justice. However, the legitimacy of violent actions is a matter of perspective—what one group sees as terrorism is a fight for freedom and justice from another point of view.

That said, it is not my intention to reduce the concept of terrorism to pure relativism. Instead, what strikes me is that regardless of the relative position of the actors—whether they are a recognized state or a clandestine organization, for example—the activities of "terrorism" and the "war on terror" take place outside of the law. As it is commonly understood, outlawry indicates both the withdrawal of legal rights and protections, and a refusal to obey or recognize the law. Thus, in the context of the war on terror, outlawry encompasses, on the one hand, the indefinite detention, torture, and withdrawal of *habeas corpus* from detainees at Guantanamo Bay and other extralegal actions by states, and on the other, suicide bombings, the attacks of 911 and other such clandestine actions worldwide. Outlawry is enacted in the space outside the bounds of the law, yet it is distinct from criminality, which is internal to the economy of the law. Outlawry is not so much illegal as it is extralegal. It maintains a relation to the law, and has significance in terms of sovereignty and justice, and not merely transgression, guilt and punishment.

Walter Benjamin noted that the public regards outlaws with both fear and admiration because outlaws bear witness to the violence of the law, and they threaten a new law (284). In "Critique of Violence" Benjamin argued that the law derives its legitimacy in retrospect—in the moment of its action there is no distinction between an act of violence that breaks the law, and one that makes the law (280). Outlawry is thus simultaneous to the law as its possibility and impossibility—its potentiality to be law and to be not-law. As such, outlawry is part of what shapes our experience of the political and of our striving for justice, and it plays a role in the founding and eradicating of political power.

Derrida's reading of Benjamin's "Critique" helps clarify outlawry's simultaneous relationship to the law. He proposes that if legality is determined in retrospect, then the law's legitimacy must be artificial. Borrowing a term from de Montaigne, he dubs this artificiality the "mystical foundation of authority." People obey laws not because they are just, but because they have authority, and because they consent to that authority through *belief* in its legitimacy. Derrida writes: "[the mystical] is in law, what suspends law. It interrupts the established law to found another. This moment of suspense, this epokhe, this founding or revolutionary moment of law is, in law, an instance of non-law...But it is also the whole history of law" ("Force of Law" 269). The mystical signifies a fundamental undecidability and iterability in the concept of the law, and this is precisely why designations such as terrorist and freedom fighter are so ambiguously dependent on perspective. The law is not a concrete, fixed, and universal entity, but is variable, temporary, and particular. Moreover, the law has an illegitimate twin with whom it sporadically switches place. Thus, I argue, the mystical does more than merely suspend the law—it suspends the difference between the law and its other, outlawry.

The suspension that Derrida terms the mystical, and that signals the presence of outlawry in, over and against the law is more than a temporary exception to the law, as Giorgio Agamben argues in *State of Exception* and *Homo Sacer*. Theories of exceptionality specify a situation in which the law is still force, but its application is interrupted to allow the state extralegal powers to deal with a situation of war or civil unrest. Agamben discusses the exceptional as a "suspension of the juridical order" (*State of Exception* 4), with suspension meaning "no longer applying ... withdrawing" (*Homo Sacer* 17-18). Agamben's approach reflects a presumption that the law is always prior to the exception, and that this prior rule of law represents a normal situation: "The state of exception is ... not the chaos that precedes order, but rather the situation that results from its suspension" (17-18). In contrast, a Derridean approach would employ a multifaceted understanding of the term "suspended" that rejects the presumption that the law is always prior to the exception, and that this prior rule of law represents a normal situation. The mystical suspension is ongoing, occurring in a moment that is always in process where one law is destroyed and another founded. Suspending the difference between the law and outlawry, the mystical ceaselessly hangs the threat and promise of another law over whatever law is currently in force.

While situations of conflict in the war on terror may heighten this threat to the law and make us aware of it, it is nonetheless present even in "normal" circumstances. Where exceptionality allows the law to continue, even when suspended, the mystical demands attention to the impermanence and arbitrariness of law, and its relation to an outlaw sister who is always waiting in the wings to seize the throne. Thus pressed the law never rests complete; instead it continually founds itself. The mystical is consequently not reserved for emergencies (perpetual or not). It always includes, as a potentiality, nonlaw as a part of law, the result of which is as suspenseful as it is suspended. For this suspense imbues the concept of law with the uncertainty, doubt, anxiety and excitement of the promise and threat of a new law.

The ambiguity between law and outlawry is not merely a reflection of the crises of our times, but is a manifestation of the performative structure of a law that continually founds itself. Derrida referred to the law as a performative force in "Force of Law" arguing that: "The very emergence of justice and law, the instituting, founding, and justifying moment of law implies a performative force, that is to say always an interpretive force and a call to faith [*un appel à la croyance*]" 241-242. In this remark we find the two elements of the performative that constitute the hybrid construct of the law and outlawry. The first is force, the violence that destroys, institutes, and justifies; and the second is fiction, the interpretive aspect of this violence, its duplicity and its deceptions. Derrida addresses this double character of the law in his reworking of de Montagne's concept the 'Mystical Foundation of Authority'. He argues that people obey laws not because they are just, but on two other accounts: because they have authority, and because they consent to that authority through belief in its legitimacy—which is to say that the legitimacy on which the law's authority is based is fictional. Force and fiction thus comprise the law, superseding various elements attributed to law in western legal theory, for instance morality, normativity, or justice.

Performativity is distinguished from other speech acts by the elemental inclusion of force in its structural integrity as a speech act. Force involves transformative power, so that the performative utterance has the power to produce and transform reality. When Derrida conceptualizes the law as a performative force, he sees it as the "exercise of force in language itself" ("Force of Law" 237). Outlawry disrupts a pure conceptualization of the law from the outset, for as Derrida continues, the exercise of force in language occurs in "the most intimate of [the law's] essence, as in the movement by which it would absolutely disarm itself from itself" (237). This disarming intersection of force and fiction is an internal movement of the law, and it is also outlawry; the law constitutes and is constituted by what it would forbid, exclude and deny. As a performative force, the law is a structure that lives only insofar as it reasserts itself through its continual citation. Yet it is also a structure that continually undoes itself through a consequent iterability. This continual undoing may be either catastrophic, or mundane. For instance, even when it is not being overthrown in a revolution, the law always changes, for instance through jurisprudence.

Outlawry thus retains a persistent relation to the law, rather than being exceptional or illegal. It is a useful lens for understanding the war on terror precisely for this reason. Moreover the threshold between the law and outlawry has implications for political praxis and for justice. Derrida and Benjamin both sever the law from justice, which has led some critics to accuse them of glorifying violence, and refusing human responsibility for injustice (Cornell), as if, like Robespierre, they implicitly advocate the outlaw tactics of terror if performed for just ends. At first glance there are some similarities between Robespierre's equating of terror with a justice that is "prompt, severe [and] inflexible" and the Benjaminian association of justice with immediate and expiating violence. For Benjamin and Derrida alike the law is not only potentially unjust, it is always unjust because the law generalizes, whereas justice must be immediate and specific, since what is just in one situation may not be valid in another (Critique of Violence 294; "Force of Law" 244). Benjamin associates outlawry with justice through the immediate, boundless violence that destroys the law—violence that he nominates 'Divine.' In this gesture he transforms the divine character of justice from the law of the Father to a messianic mode, a justice of devastation and transformation. He attributes two opposing powers to outlawry, the imminent and destructive forces of justice and the teleological, mediating forces of power, writing: "Justice is the principle of all divine end-making, power the principle of all mythical law-making" (295).

Yet by no means do either Benjamin or Derrida align themselves with Robespierre and contend that insurrections or acts of terrorism are just by virtue of being outside of the law. Indeed, the law destroying powers of outlawry are followed by nothing less that its law-making powers and the inauguration of a new law in which the hope for justice is suspended, once again. The justice of the outlaw does not lie in his or her illegitimate violence, but rather in the great criminal's exposure of the law's violence and fraudulent tie to justice. Justice is no more graspable via outlawry than it is through the law, for, as Derrida elaborates, the essence of justice is elusive. It is a deferment to the future; the promise of a justice to come (*avenir*). The concept of justice to-come (*avenir*) oversees the suspension between outlawry and law not as a synthesizing agent but as a compelling force of action/disruption directed at the future. Outlawry is in this sense a paradoxical concept; it swallows itself, cancels itself out, without ever actually disappearing. This is the same cannibalistic gesture by which power (realized in the form of the law) exercises a constant erasure of justice, but never succeeds in expunging justice, for Divine justice remains always out of reach.

Justice is only possible when the generalities of law are suspended in favor of the "fresh judgment" of a decision that has passed the test of the undecidable. Derrida writes: "for a decision to be just and responsible, it must [*il faut*] ...be both regulated and without regulation, it must preserve the law [*loi*], and also destroy or suspend it enough to have [*pour devoir*] to reinvent it in each case" (251). The suspension of the law occurs at the threshold between the law and its bracketed other, outlawry. Thus it follows that justice is not opposed to outlawry. On the contrary, without possessing justice (for justice is impossible), outlawry somehow opens the aporia (non-path or non-experience) that divides the law and justice, summoning the possibility of the experience of the impossible. Outlawry heralds this (im)possibility, because justice depends on the undecidable, which characterizes the différance of outlawry, and the associated movement of reinvention that traverses the space between the suspension of law and its maintenance. Undecidability disallows the binarity between the law and outlawry (and any synthesis between them), even as it defines the limits of decidability within the order of the law as a calculable space. But more importantly, the undecidable "calls for a decision in the order of ethical-political responsibility" (116). Herein lies the affiliation between outlawry and justice. Outlawry is the shock, the ghost of illegitimacy and the promise of something other that wrenches our attention from the mythicism and mysticism of our narratives with the urgency of the immediate. Outlawry is what, in law and outside of law, demands an ethical-political decision.

The law and outlawry are thus both possibilities that stand in contrast to justice, yet potentially strive for justice. There is a suspended suspense that interrupts and disrupts the flow between them, something in the expiatory and generative powers that erupts in their interstices that activates the call for justice. As the possibility of otherness embedded in the performative utterance, the outside of the law is that structurally (non)present possibility that demands the law's responsibility to a justice that is strived for but never realized (248-249). This moment of suspense is what Derrida terms an epokhe. The Epokhe that hinges the law to outlawry in that elusive dance with justice is a complex moment. To paraphrase Derrida, it perpetuates a suspense that brims over itself in anguish, cracking open spaces of metamorphosis and revolution. The epokhe of (out)lawry is what motivates the impossibility we understand as justice—it is a shock, an impulse for transformation, a summoning of all the hidden possibilities of *différance*. Although it is structurally integral to the law, it is that other side that appears not as a lack but as the affective force that constitutes the law's possibility and impossibility alike. The *epokhe* is the liminal tension that activates the aporia of justice —as Derrida puts it, that "experience of the impossible: a will, a desire, a demand for justice...a *call* for justice" ("Force or Law" 244). Where the law strives for the predictability of the rule, outlawry, in both its dystopic and utopic forms (threat or promise) heralds the "to-come" (*avenir*) of justice, demanding a constant refounding of law and politics (256). Propelled by anticipation, surprise, shock and catastrophe, justice waits on the horizon and summons our responsibility to pierce the suspense and strive toward it.

# References

Agamben, Giorgio. 1995. *Homo sacer: Sovereign power and bare life.* Trans. Daniel Heller-Roazen. Stanford: Stanford Univ. Press.

——— *State of exception.* 2005. Trans. Kevin Attell. Chicago: Univ. of Chicago Press.

Augustine. 1972. *Concerning the city of God against the pagans.* Trans. Henry Bettenson. Harmondsworth:Penguin Books.

Benjamin, Walter. 1978. "Critique of Violence." *Reflections: Essays, aphorisms, autobiographical writings.* Trans. Edmund Jephcott. New York: Schocken Books.

Cornell, Drucilla. 1992. "The violence of the masquerade: Law dressed up as justice." in *Working through Derrida.* Ed. G.B. Madison. Evanston, IL: Northwestern Univ. Press.

Derrida, Jacques. 2002. "Force of law: The mystical foundation of authority." In Jacques Derrida's *Acts of Religion.* Ed Gil Anidjar. New York and London: Routledge.

——— "Signature, event, context." 1972. *Limited Inc.* Samuel Weber and Jefry Mehlman Trans. Evanston IL: Northwestern Univ. Press. 1-23

Robespierre, Maximilien. "Justification of the use of terror." In Paul Halsall, *Modern History SourceBook.* http://www.fordham.edu/halsall/mod/modsbook.html. last revised 9/22/2001.

# WHAT'S IN A NAME? INTERPRETING TERRORISM FROM THE PERSPECTIVE OF PERSONAL CONSTRUCT THEORY

*James Horley and Ian McPhail*

*"True or false, that which is said of men often occupies as important a place in their lives, and above all in their destinies, as that which they do."*

(Hugo 1887, 1)

## Introduction

Since its introduction in the late 18th century to describe the conductors of "The Terror," or the period of killings immediately following the French Revolution, the term "terrorist" has been applied to a variety of individuals engaged in a wide variety of violent activities. Many frequent users of the term, such as U. S. President George W. Bush (see Singer 2004), may believe firmly that they understand the "true" meaning of the term, and that they apply it appropriately and consistently, but the modern English meaning of the term is far from clear. According to Turk (2004), it appears clear that terrorism is constructed socially, yet few social scientists have attempted to examine the manners and mechanisms by which we have arrived at our current understandings of terrorism. Rather than engage in an etymological exercise to discover or to derive the best definition of the term, as some investigators (e. g., Jenkins 2003) have attempted, we intend to analyze terrorism in terms of some of its implicative meanings. Perhaps more importantly, we will consider probable common outcomes or actions based on the broad, contemporary meanings of terrorism. In order to accomplish our constructivistic project, we will employ a well-established if rather unconventional psychological theory, personal construct theory (PCT).

PCT was developed and presented by Kelly (1955, 1963, 1970) as a theory of personality with direct relevance to the fields of personality assessment and clinical psychology, as well as many other indirect connections within psychology and the social sciences (see Adams-Webber 1979; Walker and Winter 2007 for reviews of research). Unlike most personality theorists, Kelly (1955) explicitly formulated the epistemological assumptions underlying his approach. His principle of constructive alternativism asserts that reality does not reveal itself to us directly, but rather it is subject to as many alternative ways of interpreting it as we ourselves can invent. In this way, we can explain the rich diversity of human experience. According to Kelly (1955, 1970), all of our current representations of events are anticipatory in function.

In order to predict our future experience, each individual develops a unique personal construct system and attempts to accommodate it to the unknown structure of reality. This system, including complex subsystems, affords the underlying ground of coherence and unity in the ongoing experience of each person. It is comprised of a finite number of bipolar constructs (e.g., light versus dark, hard versus soft), some of which likely defy verbal labeling, and some of which are likely not polar opposites, however much opposition may help us to interpret experience.

Although any particular sequence of events lends itself to a variety of different interpretations, some ways of construing probably will prove more useful for anticipating similar events in the future. As events do not directly reveal their meanings to us, it must be the anticipatory constructions or hypotheses that we impose on them that endow them with whatever significance they may have in relation to our own behavior. Each individual is responsible for choosing what specific constructions of events will inform his or her actions. In developing this model, Kelly eschewed any distinction between 'scientists' and the 'subjects' of their inquiries. He claimed that all persons, as scientists, seek to understand their experience and anticipate future events. Kelly applied his constructivist model of scientific activity to the explanation of all human behavior. Each individual not only constructs his or her own hypotheses for anticipating events, but also evaluates and revises them in the light of the results of behavioral experiments based on these hypotheses.

PCT has been employed in a variety of different studies and analyses of violence (e.g., see Horley 2003, 2008; Winter 2003). Most of this work, however, with the possible exception of Kelly (1965), has involved individual construct analysis (i.e., examination of the meanings of individuals) as opposed to collective construct analysis (i.e., examination of the meanings of social groups). We intend, here, to present a very brief example of the latter by considering common, contemporary, Western understandings of the notion of terrorism.

## Various Meanings and Implications of Terrorism

The definition of any term occurs within socio-political and historical contexts. This is certainly the case for a term like terrorism (Jenkins 2003; Gergen 1998; Turk 2004). Terrorism, as a socio-political label, has become central in much contemporary Western discourse on international relations and especially the relationships between so-called developed and developing nations. The level of the discourse, however, appears to be slipping beyond mere labelling and moving into non-productive, indeed dangerous, territory involving name-calling and demonising.

The frequent use of terrorist-related terminology by world leaders and media has led to a rather fascinating and frightening alteration in the English-language use of terrorism in recent years. A variety of sources, very public and pervasive if not always extremely credible, have colored our understanding of terrorism by associating it with a number of extreme terms. A terrorist or terrorist-credited act is frequently described as "brutal," "cowardly," "crazed," "evil," "irrational," and "unjustified," among other ways. There are idiosyncratic and even bizarre interpretations that can become associated with the term. Bush's view of Islamic terrorists as "jealous" of United States' successes and values provides one example (Singer 2004). Whatever the source of the description, we have come to associate the person who resorts to violent opposition to predominantly Western governments and influences as an extremist who is driven by irrational beliefs and who is irredeemable, worthy only of torment and death.

It is not just world leaders or local politicians using the term frequently these days. Social scientists, too, especially over the past several years, have begun to use the term more often, and often very loosely and worryingly. Miller (2006), for example, has presented a psychological analysis of terrorists that, while attempting to avoid simplistic typologies of terrorists as either evil or crazy, views them as "wicked" (257) and "personality disordered" (261). Such twisting of terminology and jargon should make a thoughtful reader wonder if we have really come very far over the past 30 years from psychological perspectives that described terrorists as "crusaders, criminals, or crazies" (Hacker 1976). Fortunately, in the so-called field of "psychology of terrorism," there have been some analyses with more nuance. Victoroff (2005), for example, reminded us that there is much heterogeneity among those labeled terrorists and much of the research is merely anecdotal. Terrorists, too, have made their way into our very homes here in the West in the form of "intimate terrorists" (see Frye, Mangenello, Campbell, Walton-Moss, and Wilt 2006). Intimate terrorism—a term that seems to post-date September 11, 2001, although the term "patriarchal terrorism" (Johnson 1995) appears to predate 9-11 by a few years—has been used to refer to repeated, escalating domestic abuse between couples, contrasted with situational couple violence. This division of inter-spousal violence into two separate and distinct types may be far too simplistic, but it seems to have some resonance (and grant-generating ability?) in post-9/11 America.

From the perspective of personal construct theory, we can understand the construct "terrorist versus not-a-terrorist" as a superordinate construct pair. As mentioned, constructs are related in an ordinal, hierarchical manner. Constructs that are "higher" or subsume other constructs when employed are superordinate, while "lower" or subsumed constructs are described as subordinate (Kelly 1955). In a sense, superordinacy allows for conceptual conciseness or efficiency insofar as any element that can be construed using a superordinate construct can be 'set aside' (i.e., further consideration in terms of related subordinate constructs is unnecessary). Terrorism has come into a superordinate position following repeated use by Western leaders and the media, among others, until its use is now commonplace and commonly recognized. It is no longer necessary to refer to other associated terms, such as cowardly and irrational, because they are now subordinate, in general terms, to terrorism; by calling an act or actor "terrorist," all subordinate constructs are subsumed and applied. Conceptual efficiency is thereby gained, although at a cost.

An example of a subsumed or subordinate construct pair is "legitimate violence" versus "illegitimate violence" (Ahmed 2003). An act of violence by a "terrorist" organization is understood as illegitimate in the media because it is conducted by an irrational individual, whereas an act of military violence is portrayed as legitimate because it is conducted by an identifiably legitimate institution such as the United States government. This subordinate construction of illegitimate violence is assumed when the news media presents a story concerning an act involving anti-state violence due largely to frequent rejection of any forms of acceptable violence aside from state-sponsored violence.

Not only does terrorism appear to be a superordinate construct, it appears to be used in a very pre-emptive manner in most contemporary uses. In other words, all elements (i.e., people, acts, events) that are described as "terrorist" take on the aspect of "terrorist-and-nothing-but-terrorist." People viewed as terrorists cannot also be construed as fathers, concerned citizens, or liberators because they are restricted to a single role or aspect. Failure to construe terrorists in any other social role leads to the inability to engage in genuine social interaction that can serve as a productive encounter because there is no basic assumption of the totality of the other person. We also forfeit the ability to construe the terrorists' construct systems, which is a fundamental step in social interactions according to PCT (Kelly 1955). The capacity of the labelling actor to predict accurately the other's behavior is thus diminished or removed completely. Hence, when we narrowly define someone as a terrorist, we lose the ability to understand how he or she might act in everyday social interactions. Extreme constructions of terrorists as only evil and violent leave little room for debate of what sort of actions we can take to bring them in line with the desires of Western nations. If a terrorist is evil and unreasonable, they can only comply through fear or defy through violence. There is no room for a reasonable and rational dialogue between two opposing parties because of this construction (Lloyd and Potter 2007).

## Prescribed Responses to Terrorism

The superordinate and pre-emptive use of the construct "terrorist versus not-a-terrorist" has many implications for subsequent behavior, most of them seriously troubling. Narrow, pre-emptive construing undoubtedly produces a quick, automatic action or reaction. This is not necessarily maladaptive because, in certain contexts, equivocation can be deadly for the equivocator. As Horley (2008) noted, a maximum-security prison often produces pre-emptive thinking where, for example, a prison informer becomes "rat-and-nothing-but-rat." Appropriate behavior when confronting an informer must be decisive and violent unless an inmate is willing to be construed as "like a rat" or "weak," neither of which is likely to lead to longevity in the violent world of most maximum-security prisons. The battlefield, too, is a setting where equivocation can be fatal, and pre-emptive thought is no doubt adaptive. With respect to terrorism, it is not likely accidental that conflict with armed opposition is framed often as a "war" or a "battle" against the terrorist because such a construction promotes further pre-emption.

A major distinction should be drawn, however, between total institutional life of the prison or combat on the battlefield and the world of international relations. Use of the term terrorist at the bilateral or international negotiating table probably terminate discussion. Indeed, use of the terrorism label is likely to produce a violent response from any party involved in a conflict. George W. Bush is well known as a staunch supporter of military pre-emptive strikes when it comes to dealing with those he construes as terrorists (Singer 2004). Bush and former British Prime Minister Tony Blair appear to accept that, because terrorists cannot be reasoned with, and they are likely to strike Western targets at any time, it is better to attack terrorists first and talk, or not, later (Lloyd and Potter 2007). For them, and for us, the issue of importance becomes when to respond and not how, negating an important part of international relations.

Unfortunately, it is not just a single evangelical Christian leader of the United States, one who views the world simplistically as either good or evil (Singer 2004), or a small number of Western leaders who is likely to act violently and without consideration with respect to anyone considered a terrorist. Troops on the ground, too, will likely engage in ill-considered acts (e.g., torturing detainees, summary executions), and public responses will be swift and extreme (e.g., support for war, vigilante justice). Crelinsten (2003) has provided a good analysis of the construction and acceptance of physical torture use. The process does not start and end with identification and objectification of a particular enemy; it involves centrally a lengthy process of fomenting hatred and dehumanisation via careful choice of words used in propagandistic rhetoric. What follows the violent response, whether by national leaders ordering a military strike or an individual military interrogator employing physical torture, is the creation of more victims, possibly construed by some as martyrs. With more provocations come more martyrs—or more terrorists, depending on your perspective—and the cycle of violence will continue and expand. The cycle of violence, however, is neither acceptable nor inevitable.

The main difficulty with narrow, pre-emptive understandings of opponents is that they do not permit any significant understandings of others. Allowing that an opponent may also be a devoted father, a concerned citizen, and dedicated campaigner for social justice might negate swift and violent responses, but such a view may open the doors to more nuance and insight when construing the constructions of the other. One plausible outcome of expanding the number of perspectives involved in the discussion surrounding terrorism is a widening of the influences that act upon other social actors, to say nothing of more and less violent responses to opposition. We may begin to include the cultural and environmental influences that act upon individuals involved in politically motivated violence (Hewer and Taylor 2007). In the language of PCT, we must stop tight and pre-emptive construing of terrorists and expand what roles, behaviors, and characteristics we ascribe to these individuals. The use of just a few, or just one superordinate construct to characterise the mysterious strangers we are often at odds with cannot continue. We need to begin to take a holistic approach to how we construe and behave towards terrorists and predict the outcomes of our interactions with them. Coming to an understanding of this violence through an awareness of the cultural and historical context removes the self-imposed ignorance of narrow, pre-emptive constructs. This gives us a more complete construction of the causes of this type of violence, permitting more flexible and adaptive ways of predicting the others' behavior, as well as behaving in accordance with this new interpretation (Hudson 1999). We must note here that the endeavor to understand is not a way of justifying violent behavior, but rather an attempt to create a richer tapestry upon which to base our future behavior. A violent act may demand a violent response, but it must be a reasoned response selected, perhaps quickly and decisively, from an array of possible reactions.

## Conclusions and Recommendations

Although far from the only source of power (see Horley 2008), the ability to persuade others of the "right way" to think—really, defining social reality—is an important power base (Epting, Pritchard, Leitner, and Dunnett 1996). Propagandistic definitions of terrorism serve to structure and define social reality, and they are important means of presenting the "appropriate" perspective to any audience. Of course, the line between propaganda and information, if indeed a line exists, is a very fine one (Hewer and Taylor 2007; Turk 2004). We would argue that, at this point in time in the West, a term like "terrorist" must be considered a propagandist's tool. Political leaders and media in the West have used this term to construct a common understanding of a terrorist as an irrational, barbaric outlaw for politically-motivated reasons (Mohammad 1999). The use of terrorist appears to have gone well beyond a designation of disdain to describe armed and dangerous opponents but a statement of absolute moral condemnation, one that carries with it the requirement that those so labelled be contained and killed as quickly as possible. No dialogue, discussion, or negotiation is possible with individuals named as terrorists because these hard and fast characteristics spread by the media and political leaders work to demonise the terrorist or their host states (Hewer and Taylor 2007). Given the wide usage of terrorism, including black-market dealing described as "economic terrorism" and rape viewed as "sexual terrorism" (see Jenkins 2003), we seem to be painting ourselves into a small corner where we must respond violently to many others who surround us on a daily basis. Terrorism is not only a broad designation today, but it is a potentially deadly one as well.

Viewing definitions of terrorism from the perspective of PCT may allow the observer to understand the personal and cultural biases that the rhetoric is based upon. Illumination of the tight constructions that reveal themselves in the speech of world leaders, such as Bush and Blair, provides a basis to challenge the supposed characteristics of terrorists and the negative actions that these constructions urge an audience to undertake (Lloyd and Potter 2007). By adopting this critical approach, intended audiences or communities of action can negate the influence that ethnocentric, negative and narrow definitions of terrorism can have. This perhaps can have the effect of shrinking the influence that government and politicians have in defining other cultures and social actors, which is perhaps out of their realm of credible knowledge. As Gergen (1998) suggested, the challenge to the relational sphere of the social world is to come to be co-inhabited by a variety of disparate voices. Applied to the current discussion, a deconstruction of the understandings by the political elite of terrorism may lead to a multiplicity of voices being included and considered in the debate surrounding how we construe violent acts and, consequently, how we react to them as a culture and as individuals.

We would suggest that, rather than redefinition, terrorism and terrorist should be given a very long hiatus at the very least. Better yet would be assignment to the garbage bin, much in the way that some groups assign offensive words in any language to the trash (e.g., Lake Superior State University's annual list of "Words banished from the Queen's English"). This might permit renewed or even initial dialogue between many political and ideological rivals.

## References

Adams-Webber, J. R. 1979. *Personal construct theory: Concepts and applications.* New York: John Wiley and Sons.

Crelinsten, R. D. The world of torture: A constructed reality. *Theoretical Criminology,* 7 2003: 293-318.

Epting, F. R., S. Prichard, L. M. Leitner, and G. Dunnett, 1996. Personal constructions of the social. In *The construction of group realities: Culture, society, and personal construct theory.* ed. D. Kalekin-Fishman and B. Walker, (pp. 309-322). Malabar: Krieger.

Frye, V., J. Manganello, J. C. Campbell, B. Walton-Moss, and S. Wilt. 2006. The distribution of and factors associated with intimate terrorism and situational couple violence among a population-based sample of urban women in the United States. *Journal of Interpersonal Violence,* 21: 1286-1313.

Gergen, K. J. 1998. Constructionist dialogues and the vicissitudes of the political. In *The politics of construction.* ed. I.Velody and R. Williams (pp. 33-48). Sage: London.

Hacker, F. J. 1976. *Crusaders, criminals, and crazies: Terror and terrorism in our times.* New York: W. W. Norton.

Hewer, C., and Taylor, W. 2007. "Deconstructing terrorism: Politics, language, and social representation." In *Just war: Psychology and terrorism.* ed. R. Roberts. (pp. 199-212). Ross-on-Wye: BCCS Books.

Horley, J. 2003. "Forensic personal construct psychology: Assessing and treating offenders." In *International handbook of personal construct psychology.* ed F. Fransella. (pp. 163-170). Chichester: John Wiley and Sons.

———— 2008. *Sexual offenders: Personal construct theory and deviant sexual behavior.* Hove: Routledge.

Hudson, R. A. 1999. *The sociology and psychology of terrorism: Who becomes a terrorist and why.* Washington: Federal Research Division, Library of Congress.

Hugo, V. 1887. *Les Miserables.* New York: Thomas Y. Crowell and Company.

Jenkins, P. 2003. *Images of terror: What we can and can't know about terrorism.* New York: Aldine de Gruyter.

Johnson, M. P. 1995. Patriarchal terrorism and common couple violence: Two forms of vio-lence against women in U.S. families. *Journal of Marriage and the Family,* 57: 283-294.

Kelly, G. A. 1955. *The psychology of personal constructs* (2 volumes). New York: W. W. Norton.

———— 1963. *A theory of personality: The psychology of personal constructs.* New York: W. W. Norton.

———— 1965. "The threat of aggression." *Journal of Humanistic Psychology,* 5: 195-201.

———— 1970. "A brief introduction to personal construct theory." In *Perspectives in personal construct theory.* ed. D. Bannister. (pp. 1-29). London: Academic.

Lloyd, J., and S. Potter. 2007. "Relational psychology in the war speeches of Bush and Blair: Beyond 'Us' and 'Them.'" In *Just war: Psychology and terrorism.* ed. R. Roberts. (pp. 140-159). Ross-on-Wye: PCCS Books.

Miller, L. 2006. "The terrorist mind: Typologies, psychopathologies, and practical guidelines for investigation." *International Journal of Offender Therapy and Comparative Criminology,* 50, 255-268.

Shakespeare, T. 1998. "Social constructionism as a political strategy." In *The politics of construction.* ed. I. Velody and R. Williams, (pp. 168-181). Sage: London.

Singer, P. 2004. *The president of good and evil: The ethics of George W. Bush.* New York: Dutton.

Turk, A. T. 2004. "The sociology of terrorism." *Annual Review of Sociology,* 30, 271-286.

Victoroff, J. 2005. "The mind of the terrorist: A review and critique of psychological approaches." *Journal of Conflict Resolution,* 49, 2-42.

Walker, B. M., and D. A. Winter. 2007. "The elaboration of personal construct psychology." *Annual Review of Psychology,* 58, 453-477.

Winter, D. A. 2003. "A credulous approach to violence and homicide." In *Personal construct perspectives on forensic psychology.* ed. J. Horley, (pp. 15-53). Hove: Brunner-Routledge.

# ON TERROR CONSIDERED AS ONE OF THE FINE ARTS

*Milo Sweedler*

An analysis of the attack of September 11, 2001, in Manhattan from an aesthetic point of view risks shocking if not outright offending some people, while striking others as apolitical dilettantism. It is not in the aim of belittling the horror or the geopolitical impact of the event that I propose to undertake such a study. It is, on the contrary, in an effort to understand it. For the assault on New York was less a military maneuver per se than a media phenomenon of unrivalled success. And this "mediated" side of the event, which constitutes an integral component of contemporary terrorism, goes hand in hand—such, in any case, is my hypothesis—with the aesthetic quality of the event. Aesthetic and not symbolic. Jean Baudrillard is undoubtedly right to insist on the symbolic importance of the choice of targets of September 11, especially the World Trade Center, center of global capitalism. But the "success" of the terrorist attack on New York is irreducible to the destruction of the symbol of American economic power that the Twin Towers represent. It derives especially from the spectacular aspect of the event; for the more spectacular the destruction, the more effective—in other words, the more *terrifying*—the attack.

The montage we saw in September 2001 of planes crashing into twin skyscrapers, framed in low-angle shots of sky blue, bright orange, and clouds of black, intercut with shots of the city belching smoke, of desperate victims jumping to their death, and of the collapse of two the buildings which disappear virtually without trace into the ground—these images are horrible, but they are dazzling. Why, one might ask, did the attack on the Pentagon, center of the military power of the United States, fascinate no one? Why did television stations broadcast only short clips of that smoking building, interspersed here and there among the sequences repeated *ad nauseum* of the two towers burning, then collapsing? Is it not because the sight of a four-storey building of reinforced concrete spread out over 29 acres with an enormous hole in its side is nothing compared to the spectacular destruction of two identical skyscrapers of 110 storeys, glass and steel glistening in the sun, which was reduced before our eyes, by an almost perfect implosion, floor by floor, to nothing? Yet, it is not merely the images that are spectacular. The images are fascinating because the event is. The pages that follow situate the 9/11 attack of New York in relation to a wide array of aesthetic theories and artistic movements—from classical tragedy to the performing, environmental, and plastic arts of our day—in an effort to understand how and why the demolition of the Twin Towers constitutes the greatest terrorist act of our times.

When, at 9:30 in the morning of September 11, 2001, President Bush calls the attack on the World Trade Center "a national tragedy," he gives the event a lasting designation. Since Bush's speech, the media and politicians have repeated this word "tragedy" with such frequency that it has almost become the event's official appellation. The collapse of the Twin Towers, which instantaneously killed some three thousand innocent people, is undoubtedly a tragedy, but what does this word mean? The noun *tragedy* signifies first and foremost a genre of theatre, born in ancient Greece from the dithyramb; then, by metaphor, a lamentable event or catastrophe. Does Bush therefore have recourse to a figure of rhetoric when he calls the attacks of 9/11 a tragedy? One does not have the impression that Bush wants to insinuate that we are dealing here with a work of art. No more than Jacques Chirac, who, during his speech of September 11, has recourse to the same term that his American counterpart used several hours earlier to bring into relief the gravity of the events of the day: events that Chirac qualifies nonetheless as "dramatic"—another term borrowed from the theatre, skewed, once again, from its original meaning. Neither in Bush's speech nor in Chirac's does one have the sense that the heads of state wish to assimilate the destruction of the Twin Towers to a work of art. Yet in order to underline the magnitude of the event and communicate its gravity, the word that the two leaders choose designates, almost by antiphrasis, a genre in the arts. It is as if, even among those who had no interest in introducing the slightest equivocation between art and life when speaking of the destruction in Manhattan, one could only assimilate it to a sublime spectacle. A simple question of semantics, one might argue: one clearly sees that the two orators mean "catastrophe" when they evoke the "tragedy" of 9/11—an objection to which one might provisionally respond by noting that the word "catastrophe" also derives from the language of theatre.

Since it is a question here of tragedy, qualified or not as "dramatic," synonym or not of "catastrophe," it might behoove us to recall from the outset the famous definition that Aristotle proposes of this term in the *Poetics*.

> Tragedy . . . is an imitation of an action that is serious [*spoudaias*], complete, and of a certain magnitude; in language embellished with each kind of artistic ornament, the several kinds being found in separate parts of the play; in the form of action, not of narrative; through pity and fear effecting the proper purgation of these emotions. (61/1449b)

This definition of tragedy seems to fly in the face of the meaning of the word in Bush's and Chirac's speeches. Whereas Aristotle writes of the imitation of an action, the politicians evoke the action itself. In short, the philosopher speaks of fiction; Bush and Chirac, of a real event. Moreover, the action represented receives, in Aristotle's treatise, the qualification of *spoudaias*, which Butcher translates as "serious" and others have rendered as "good," "heroic," or "noble." This precision opposes tragedy to comedy, but would it not by the same token oppose it to the senseless crashing of planes into buildings? One is, of course, free to side with the terrorists. Just as one might identify, depending on one's inclinations and sympathies, with Creon or Antigone, Dionysus or Pentheus, one might just as easily take the side of either the Americans or the highjackers. But one would not use the word "tragedy" in the latter case. If one sided with the terrorists, if one saw in their destruction an act of heroism, one would not qualify the event as "tragic." Saying that 9/11 is a tragedy is tantamount to an identification with the victims, not the perpetrators. The only way to see in the events of September 11 both a tragedy and "an action that is *spoudaias*" would be, it strikes me, to see in American *hubris* a fatal flaw leading ineluctably to the fall of the country.

The catastrophe of such a drama—"catastrophe" understood here in the theatrical sense of the turning point of a tragedy—would be the collapse of the Twin Towers: a collapse which would provoke, according to Aristotle's theory, emotions of pity (*eleos*) and terror (*phobos*). Such is the interpretation that Fredric Jameson offers of the spectacle of the flaming towers: "fear comes from putting myself in a victim's place, imagining the horror of the fire and the unimaginable height outside the windows; pity then sets in when we remember we are safe ourselves, and think of others who were not" (298). It is precisely on such emotions that the delegates of the 9/11 Commission, who, following the lead of Bush and Chirac, qualify once again the events as "tragic," insist when they declare, in the opening sentences of their report on the terrorist attacks, that "September 11, 2001, was a day of unprecedented shock and suffering in the history of the United States" (xv). If Chirac, in his speech of September 11, qualifies the "tragedy" as "dramatic," as if to seal, undoubtedly despite his intentions, the aesthetic connotation, do the authors of the *9/11 Commission Report* not evoke here, barely modified, the key Aristotelian terms of *phobos* and *eleos*? Once again, the destruction of the two towers would not produce such emotions in the spectator unless he or she imaginarily put him- or herself in the place of the New Yorkers. The collapse of the buildings would provoke neither terror nor pity if one simply celebrated the highjackers' actions. In order to feel such emotions, one would have to have to identify with the victims. For, everything works here by identification: the shorter the distance between the subject-spectator and the contemplated object, the more effective the work. Whence the famous Aristotelian notion of *catharsis*, the purging of terror and pity. In order to purge oneself of these sentiments, one must first feel them; and in order to do so, one must have identified, while watching the piece, with the action presented before one's eyes.

However, as Roselyn Dupont-Roc and Jean Lallot point out, "for Aristotle, *eleos* and *phobos* are painful emotions. . . . But—and herein lies the paradox—instead of pain (*lupē*), it is pleasure (*hēdonē*) that the spectator must feel" (189 n.3; my translation). We have already called attention to the sort of *Schadenfreude* that the destruction of the Twin Towers could provoke in the spectator: a *Schadenfreude* to which Baudrillard unequivocally attests when he affirms that the terrorists "*did it*, but we *wished for* it" (5). But the pleasure evoked here by Baudrillard is foreign to the one that Aristotle discusses. What the philosopher brings into play is, rather, the pleasure of contemplating the mise en scène of one's one demise: ultimately, of seeing oneself die on the stage, and surviving. One needs, therefore, a certain distance from the spectacle. This critical distance of the audience from action represented differs radically from the Brechtian *Verfremdungseffekt*, that "distanciation effect" which prevents the viewer from identifying with the action portrayed. It is a question, rather, for Aristotle, of the pleasure that one feels in the reflection that accompanies the identification of the spectator with the spectacle.

In contrast to Brecht, who strives to remove the public from the action depicted on the stage by inhibiting the spectator from identifying with the drama and thereby compelling him or her to reflect on the dramatic action of the play, Antonin Artaud, the anti-Brechtian par excellence, pursues a form of theatre in which all distance, critical or other, is eliminated between the audience and the stage. This pursuit leads the theorist to dismiss virtually every mimetic aspect of theatre, beginning with the embellished language that Aristotle advocates. Whereas Aristotle specifies that tragedy represents an action "in language embellished with each kind of artistic ornament, the several kinds being found in separate parts of the play," Artaud, the innovator of "theatrality," invents a new language, specifically theatrical, in which the audio-visual elements of the performance (gesture, mise en scène, lighting, music, costume, masks, and the like) take precedence over the text. Instead of *representing* an action, Artaud strives to *present* it: to bring it to life directly on the stage—or, rather, *in the space*, for among the theatrical innovations envisioned by Artaud figures a reconfiguration of the physical disposition of the performance space: "We intend to do away with stage and auditorium, replacing them by a kind of single, undivided locale without any partitions of any kind and this will become the very scene of the action" (74). For what Artaud *dreams of* is a destruction of the distance separating the spectator from the spectacle. Hence the call, in his work, for terror and cruelty: Artaud seeks brutal jolts and violent shocks that would wake the public from its everyday slumber. If Artaud himself never realized his theories on the stage, Peter Brook, founder of the Theatre of Cruelty, a theatre troupe named in homage to Artaud, pursued diverse means to put the directives of his master into practice. Among the director's dramatic experiments: "I fire a pistol at a spectator—I did so once—and for a second I have a possibility to reach him in a different way" (54).

This attempt to "reach the spectator in a different way" animates innumerable avant-garde movements of the twentieth century. Almost the entirety of what has taken place over the past decades under the name of "performance art" is dedicated to such an endeavor, from Yves Klein's *Leap into the Void*, in which the artist threw himself from the second storey of a building, twisting his ankle in landing, to the performance pieces of Chris Burden, who, over a period of five years, "had himself shot, electrocuted, impaled, cut, drowned, incarcerated, and sequestered not to make a grand social, political, or religious statement or to reveal a deep psychological meaning, but just because he knew he could" (Schimmel 98). However, the moment in which performance art transgresses most clearly the limit separating life from art—and almost from death—may be Marina Abramović's *Rhythm O*, a performance piece of six hours in which the artist, having laid out instruments of torture on a table, invites the spectators to use the various instruments as they see fit, assuring them that she will remain motionless throughout the duration of the piece. After having removed the young artist's clothes with razors, members of the audience used the same instruments to cut into her skin, from which blood flowed. At hour four of the piece, when a visitor put a revolver in the artist's hand and placed her finger on the trigger, a group of protectors intervened in the young woman's defense, leading to a brawl in the museum between her torturers and her defenders, during the course of which Abramović, loyal to her art, remained completely passive (Schimmel 101). In contrast to Brook, who executes in his own way "the simplest surrealist act," Abramović and company turn the violence against themselves.[1] What these experiments have in common is the attempt to reach the spectator at any price, by any means.

Obvious differences separate this sort of spectacle from the massive destruction that took place in Manhattan in 2001. To start with, in one case, the participation of the public is voluntary; in the other, completely against its will. Even if the spectator-participants of *Rhythm O* did not know what to expect, even if the poor spectator on whom Brook conducted his dramatic experiment could not know that he made himself a human target in buying his admission ticket, they could have chosen not to attend the performance. Nothing of the sort on the floors of the World Trade Center. But on the one hand, the idea of the "happening" crosses, by the simple gesture of leaving the museum, the threshold separating private space from public space, making of the entire world a prospective stage. "A Happening can be anywhere, any time, of any duration: nothing is required, nothing is taboo" (Brook 55). On the other hand, does not earth art—dedicated in general either to raising consciousness about the fragility and beauty of the natural environment or simply, as Christo and Jeanne-Claude claim, to decorating the world—

---

1. The reference here is to André Breton's notorious sentence at the beginning of the *Second Manifesto of Surrealism*: "The simplest surrealist act consists of dashing down into the street, pistol in hand, and firing blindly, as fast as you can pull the trigger, into the crowd" (125).

transform the planet into a living museum? And if, according to Brook, "the theory of Happenings is that the spectator can be jolted eventually into new sight, so that he wakes to the life around him" (55), could one not say the same for works of earth art, especially those of Christo and Jeanne-Claude, who, in contrast to the vast majority of artists who work in the domain, do not limit themselves to interventions in the natural environment but also work urban space? They would undoubtedly deny it, but when Christo and Jeanne-Claude wrap the Pont-Neuf in Paris or the Reichstag in Berlin with cloth, when they erect 7,500 canvas gates along the 37 kilometers of paths that weave through Central Park, intervening therefore directly in public space, do they not jolt the spectator into new sight, waking him or her from his or her everyday slumber and changing thereby his or her relation to his or her milieu? Is it not, moreover, to such a reconfiguration of urban space that a news commentator makes reference late on the evening of September 11, 2001 when he proposes that on the next day New Yorkers will wake up to a new skyline? As Frank Lentricchia and Jody McAuliffe affirm, commenting on the altered horizon of Manhattan: "The famous anchor was in effect predicting that New Yorkers would have an experience of the sort prized by the most advanced imaginative writers and art theorists of the last two centuries": the terrorists had punched "a hole in the familiar" (350).

These diverse attempts that one finds in the work of Artaud and Brook, of Burden and Abramović, and, in a very different way, of Christo and Jeanne-Claude, to punch, each in his or her own way, "a hole in the familiar" find perhaps an analogous gesture, in the domain of the plastic arts, in Damien Hirst's "tank pieces," that series of dead animals cut into sections, preserved in formaldehyde, and exposed to the museum-going public. I remember the response of Marilyn Zeitlin to the sight of one such work: "It is only a matter of time before some one puts a human cadaver in one of those tanks" (personal communication). It may then come as no surprise that Hirst, the most famous British artist of his generation, reacted with an almost jubilatory enthusiasm to the attack on New York: "There's something surreal about the idea of taking a means of transport like an aeroplane and crashing it onto a building. . . . The thing about 9/11 is that it's kind of an artwork in its own right. . . . It's visually stunning." These comments by Hirst follow two interrelated paths. On the one hand, the conjunction of means of transportation and skyscraper constitutes a surrealist image, beautiful, if you will, "as the chance meeting on a dissecting-table of a sewing-machine and an umbrella." On the other hand, the moment that the plane strikes the building is "visually stunning": the image of the blow that the towers receive, strikes, so to speak, the eye of the spectator. In both cases, Hirst admires the encounter of planes and buildings, not the reduction of the towers into rubble, which perhaps softens to a certain extent his remarks. But would it not be above all the collapse of the two skyscrapers that merits the qualification of "surreal"? Who would have believed it? Who did not have the impression, upon hearing the news of the disappearance of the Twin Towers, that it was impossible, that there was surely some misunderstanding? It was unimaginable, and yet it was true. It is as though we arrived, on that morning of September 11, at "the future resolution of these two states, dream and reality" evoked by Breton in the first *Manifesto* (14).

If Hirst celebrates the "surreal" visual beauty of the planes crashing into the towers—and not the demolition of the buildings as such—for the German composer Karlheinz Stockhausen, on the contrary, who proclaims, in a press conference of September 16, 2001, that the event that had taken place five days before was *das größte Kunstwerk, das es je gegeben hat*, "the greatest work of art that has ever existed," it is the destruction of the towers, complete with the death of some three thousand people, that is ravishing.

> Minds achieving something in an act that we couldn't even dream of in music, people rehearsing like mad for 10 years, preparing fanatically for a concert, and then dying, just imagine what happened there. You have people who are that focused on a performance and then 5,000 people are dispatched to the afterlife, in a single moment. I couldn't do that. By comparison, we composers are nothing.

Whereas Hirst puts the accent on the visual side of the piece, Stockhausen goes into ecstatic raptures over the work in its entirety, from the conception to the performance, including the final catastrophe of the mass murder.

These remarks by Stockhausen call to mind Hans-Jürgen Syberberg's thesis that Hitler is "the greatest film-maker of all time": "the man whom they called 'Gröfaz,' *Größter Feldherr aller Zeiten*, the 'greatest general of all time,' [was] the greatest film-maker of all time" (109). According to Syberberg, Hitler's interest in cinema is irreducible to the ends of propaganda. Rather, one might wonder, he suggests, whether Hitler "did not merely organize Nuremberg for Leni Rieffenstahl . . . and, taking the argument a little further, whether the whole of the Second World War was not indeed conducted as a big budget war film" (cited in Lacoue-Labarthe 63). The entirely of the war—not only the Führer's speeches and the rallies of the troops but the battles as well—meticulously recorded on celluloid, would be led, according to this interpretation, in the aim of creating a spectacular film, with a cast of hundreds of thousands and extraordinary visual effects. From this perspective, it would not be the case that Hitler made films in order to incite the German people to go to war; on the contrary, he went to war in order to create a sublime film. As Philippe Lacoue-Labarthe remarks, "though [Syberberg] rejects the Hollywood stereotype of the catastrophe movie, he accepts the inverted form: 'catastrophe as film'" (65)—an affirmation echoed in the interpretation that Slavoj Žižek, commenting on Stockhausen's September 16 press conference, offers of 9/11: "the 'terrorists' themselves did not [attack the World Trade Center] to provoke real material damage, but *for the spectacular effect of it*"

(11). In these conditions, would not Bin Laden, the *Gröfuz*, the *Größter Feldherr unserer Zeiten*, the greatest general of *our* times, he who was able to realize, at the price of several thousand lives, the *größte Kunstwerk, das es je gegeben hat*, "the greatest work of art that has ever existed," be the greatest artist of all time?

Once again, it is not to diminish the horror of the attack in New York that I am comparing it to a work of art. It is, on the contrary, in the aim of understanding the specificity of that particular attack, the most successful of its type. Stockhausen's response to the massacre of September 11 may be repugnant, but the composer is not completely crazy. That his affirmation is in poor taste, that it is insensitive to the victims and their families, and that it disregards the geopolitical context of the event is irrefutable. But his remarks help us to perceive another, primordial element of the attack: the destruction of the Twin Towers came to us in the form of an immense spectacle. And without entering into the authorial intentions of Bin Laden, could one not imagine that this "spectacular" side of the event was precisely, as Žižek suggests, the aim of the destruction? In order to spread terror, one must create it. What better means than reducing gigantic twin skyscrapers to rubble?

One sees, then, the extent to which the destruction in Manhattan merits the name of "tragedy," in all senses of the word. But the event goes well beyond Aristotle's generic theory. When Baudrillard proposes in passing that September 11 "is *our* theatre of cruelty" (30), he puts into play a fundamental difference separating ancient Greek tragedy from the post-Aristotelian tradition inaugurated by Artaud. Whereas classical playwrights strove to represent an action through specific mimetic techniques, the performing arts of the twentieth century break all the rules in an effort to touch directly the spectator. When Artaud explains that "in order to affect every facet of the spectator's sensibility, we advocate a revolving show, which instead of making stage and auditorium into two closed worlds without any possible communication between them, will extend its visual and aural outbursts over the whole mass of spectators," he surely was not envisioning showering the audience with bursts of glass and steel (66). He takes, rather, as his paradigm "the marvelous explosion of the plague" that ravaged Europe in the eighteenth century. But whether it comes from a viral pandemic or by means of the spectacular destruction of two buildings, the result amounts to more or less the same thing: what Artaud envisions is a direct assault on the senses and sensibilities of the audience. Terror would be one of the theatre's doubles.

The attack on the World Trade Center seems to constitute, in sum, the culmination of a current that has nourished the cultural history of the West for decades: the one that Žižek calls, borrowing an expression from Alain Badiou, "the passion for the Real." But as both Baudrillard, who affirms that if the violence of the real seems to outstrip fiction, "this is because it has absorbed fiction's energy, and has itself become fiction" (28), and Žižek, who notes that "the problem with the twentieth-century 'passion for the Real' was not that it was a passion for the Real, but that it was a fake passion" (24), this attempt to go directly to the heart of experience and to break down the barriers separating human beings from the world around them, goes hand-in-hand with another cultural current—call it "postmodernism"—where the virtual seems to devour all "real" reality, which consequently appears to us as a weak simulacrum. It is, moreover, the same socio-historical device, motored by the same technical apparatus, which provides, on the one hand, the brutal reality of the demolition of the Twin Towers and, on the other, its spectral, "unreal" image: the cinema, or more precisely the television, which, especially in recent years, has integrated the aesthetic innovations that the cinema developed over the years, adding to them the global diffusion of images in real time. The cinema has the singular capacity to implicate the spectator, by way of a system of codes more or less invisible to the viewer, into the spectacle—to "suture" him or her into the dramatic action of the film to the point that he or she forgets for a couple of hours that he or she is experiencing a work of art. Hollywood is an unparalleled "identification machine," mobilizing an array of techniques dedicated to the elimination of the critical distance that classical playwrights strove to maintain between the spectator and the spectacle, by means, for example, of a "language embellished with each kind of artistic ornament, the several kinds being found in separate parts of the play." Yet a strange thing occurs under these conditions: the elimination of the distance between the viewer and the film world seems to entail, as if it were its inevitable corollary, a concomitant reduction of the discernable distance between the world outside of the cinema and the one on the screen. The shorter the distance between the world presented on the screen and the non-filmic world, the more the world outside of the cinema starts to resemble a film, to the point that even the brutally *real* destruction of the Twin Towers, that "absolute event," as Baudrillard calls it, "the 'mother' of events," takes on a resolutely unreal allure.

In a first moment, then, by combining, radicalizing, and pushing to the extreme tendencies implicit in the performing, plastic, and environmental arts, the attack on Manhattan in September, 2001 seems to attack directly the spectator's senses. But in a second moment and as though a counterpoint to the first, this immediate assault is perceived precisely *as a spectacle*. The destruction of the Twin Towers seems to belong to two heterogeneous, almost diametrically opposed traditions: on the one hand, it animates a specter that has haunted the most daring avant-garde movements for decades; on the other, it resembles the most banal Hollywood films. 9/11 is perhaps the *Gesamtkunstwerk* of the new century, the contemporary realization of the "total work of art" announced by Richard Wagner in the middle of the nineteenth century: the one that incorporates within it all the other arts. Wagner thought that the *Gesamtkunstwerk* was the opera. Numerous critics since his time have thought that the cinema—the "seventh art," in which the other arts are brought together in a single work—represents the culmination of Wagner's theory. Add to that the destruction of two twin skyscrapers of monumental proportions and the real death of several thousand people, and one has the recipe for an unrivaled spectacular event, producing emotions of terror and pity while leaving an emotional escape valve for the spectator, who assimilates the horror only too easily to a catastrophe film. Whether we like it or not, the attack on the World Trade Center comes to us as a work of art, perhaps the greatest that has ever existed.

# References

*The 9/11 Commission Report: Final Report of the National Commission on Terrorist Attacks upon the United States.* New York: Norton, 2004.

Aristotle, *Poetics.* 1961. Trans. H.S. Butcher. Intro. Francis Fergusson. New York: Hill and Wang.

Artaud, Antonin. 1970. *The theatre and its double.* Trans. Victor Corti. London: Calder and Boyars.

Badiou, Alain. 2007. *The century.* Trans. Alberto Toscano. Malden, MA: Polity.

Baudrillard, Jean. 2002. *The spirit of terrorism.* Trans. Chris Turner. London: Verso.

Brecht, Bertolt. 1964. *Brecht on theatre.* Trans. John Willett. New York: Hill and Wang.

Breton, André. 1972. *Manifestoes of surrealism.* Trans. Richard Seaver and Helen R. Lane. Ann Arbor: Univ. of Michigan Press.

Brook, Peter. 1968. *The empty space.* New York: Touchstone/Simon and Schuster.

Bush, George W. "Remarks by the President after two planes crash into World Trade Center." Sept. 11, 2001. March 26, 2008. <http://www.whitehouse.gov/news/releases/2001/09/20010911.html>

Chirac, Jacques. "Allocution du Président de la République." Sept. 11, 2001. March 26, 2008. <http://www.ambafrance-us.org/fr/actu/statmnts/2001/terroriste/terreur2.asp#1>.

"Documentation of Stockhausen's Comments re: 9/11." Sept. 22, 2001. March 26, 2008. <http://www.osborne-conant.org/documentation_stockhausen.htm>.

Dupont-Roc, Roselyne and Jean Lallot. 1980. *Notes to* La Poétique *by Aristotle.* Paris: Seuil, 1980.

Jameson, Fredric. "The dialectics of disaster." *South Atlantic Quarterly* 101 no. 2 (2002): 296-304.

Lacoue-Labarthe, Philippe. 1990. *Heidegger, art and politics.* Trans. Chris Turner. Oxford: Basel Blackwell.

Lentricchia, Frank, and Jody McAuliffe. "Groundzeroland." *South Atlantic Quarterly* 101 no. 2, (2002): 349-59.

Schimmel, Paul. 1988. *Out of actions: Between performance and the object.* London: Thames and Hudson.

Syberberg, Hans-Jürgen. 1982. *Hitler: A film from Germany.* Trans. Joachim Neugroschel. Preface Susan Sontag. New York: Farrar, Strauss and Giroux.

Žižek, Slavoj. 2002. *Welcome to the desert of the real.* London: Verso.

# Some Thoughts on Political Terrorism and Film Music

*Panayiotis Demopoulos*

The rituals of theatre and the representational arts are known to, or at least thought to, have preceded historiographies in all cultures; some theatre is also thought to have played an actual historiographical role in pre-scriptorial societies. Producing dramatic representations for audiences appears to have been a continuous practice through the ages; the origins of this activity are not to be defined with accuracy by the archaeologist, the anthropologist, or the historian: they are themselves a likely fiction which defines the drama of social development.

Nevertheless, there were those pivotal points in historical time that defined the relationship of human society with its rituals. Some have vague dates and temporal boundaries demanding a prehistory and a sense for prophecy, others are purely historical, i.e. moments that are described by their horizontal placement in a linear narrative of events. Take, for instance, the various stages of graphical invention. They outline the course of progress in information rituals; that is to say that technical invention transpires to be poetically potent because it assumes the role of pre-historic requirement. On the contrary, the unknown precise latitude of the origins of tuning theories makes their pre-history inaccessible and so tuning theory is a latitude itself, a *Deus ex machina* of compasses, which punctuates the succession of musical progressions.

With regards to drama and theatre, the development of dramatic thought was influenced equally by pure fiction, semi-mythological events, oral traditions, historical struggles, first performances of plays, the births and deaths of patrons and artists; so our Western historiographies have us believe, at any rate.

Still, the one absolute constant in the history of drama has been the communion between dramatist and audience. The stage appears as a fiction that happens in real life, in real time and in a visceral counter-reality in front of the audience. This constant is common in epic or oral traditions, in storytelling but also in the theatrical world: the ritual requires a living teller or signifier and a living listener or receiver.

Subsequently, one may consider what level of dynamic change the introduction of recorded performances brought about in theatrical ritual. Even if the first cinemas were called theatres, they were not theatres. Indeed, soon the word 'theatre' was dropped, because it became so obvious that something inherent in theatre, namely the perceptive sensibility of the spectacle's animate constituents, had now been annulled. Very much like recorded sound, recorded images were simply a series of photometric animations that meant nothing in the pure ritualistic sense of the theatrical tradition. Now, years later, the discourse has been further informed by the multifarious doctrines of technocracy and the—valid yet contrived—inauguration of film as a fine art. By deeming all rhetoric that was concerned with anthropocentric psychographies as archaic and obsolescent, a value judgement was made that the 'human soul' was only a convoluted notion, a basic Romantic delusion that demonstrated neither a hint of logic nor a capacity to escape the realms of naturalism and theocracy.

Needless to say, the economical possibilities that this removal of theatre offered to those engaged in the commerce of spectacle were too great to ignore. Within a few years, cinema departed from its socialist and urban, working-class roots to arrive at its 21$^{st}$ century corporate milieu.

Essentially, the cinema is a religion in its most pure, emblematic form, or more accurately, a faith that need not recognise itself as a religion. It promises ecstasy through extreme phantasmagoria, and it delivers immortality through the negation of temporal finitude; the dead do dance, whether they can or not is not one of film's concerns. If theatre had an Olympian quality to it, or a socially illusory purpose since it allowed the interaction of mortals and their fiction, it did so through the placement of heroes in adversity and through enabling direct empathy with its audience. But film speaks for newer, less conscious Gods. It delivers its spectacle and message but it will not listen to the sounds of agony or pleasure that the receivers may cry silently when blood is shed in horrid manners, or when colours and shapes work their sensual wonders on the screen. It need not do so, for its only contact with humanity is to display a heroic ideal, to exhibit a simple image, or to portray an epic dimension. Film is morphing to signify various things and is ever seeking to be appeased by a consuming crowd. We are dealing then with a truly post-Homeric God because film speaks a Law and will not consider the reasons why a Law may be broken. The system of values it contains is set in magnetic tape and light not in secret dialogue, prayer and subtle interaction.

The mimetic analogies between the representations of Adam and Oedipus for instance cannot be captured by film, for they not only require an understanding of the drama, but its fulfilment by a sense of shame, guilt, remorse, repentance, and all these primordial emotions that require a mirror not available to the cinema screen or the amoral conscience. Furthermore, they are most unwelcome by the conscience, which, guided by successive doctrines focused on social emancipation, negates any ethically derived authority.

Of course, such is the nature of machine, to be a medium; the media of image and sound have long supplanted the critical function of both user and end, obliging the user to an endless cycle of self-punishment. Could this be what an ever-fraudulent Andy Warhol meant when he said that he 'painted as he did because he wanted to be a machine'?

The unanswered, and all too frequently asked, question is if the self-induced mechanisation of mankind demands mankind's happiness or its bankruptcy. Terminologies are crucial in any ethical discourse: the corrupted of today are the visionaries of tomorrow and vice versa, however the rich of today are miraculously the rich of tomorrow; this poor, plain and perfectly pointless little comment on the economy of things should suffice for the discerning and patient reader as the core idea of this essay. Yet, the unanswered question is a question of values for the unmechanized conscience and an utterly indifferent one for the mind that scorns humanity. Moreover, it is a question a machine may not be able to ask, for the design of our machines seems to reflect, largely, on our obsession with fratricidal assertion.

We shan't be attempting to portray film as an art form that is inadequate or somehow unable to withstand a set of value judgements here. On the contrary, this writer views film as a relatively new beast, but one not so new as to be threatening one's bourgeois sensibilities. Film defies the hermeneutics of traditional drama and so it is an imperative to examine its functions and techniques fairly independently of traditional readings of the history of Art. It may serve the reader to remember that Da Vinci's machines were not utilities and so art and machine are by no means historical antagonists. After all, even if the cinema destroyed drama, there is no greater satisfaction for the usurper than to be compared with the usurped. Let us do the academic unthinkable and allow the possibility for a filmed fiction *in vacuo*, outside Teutonic mythologies, outwith Wagner's *Gesamtkunswerk* spell on the educated ranks. Before that, let us hear the music that translates such free, disassociated imagery and story-telling into something familiar. But let us first define what is familiar.

Redirecting our attentions to the more general and familiar picture for a moment, an axiom concerning subject and object is a necessary irritant: terror is a terrible thing, literally. Its political function is dependent on the antinomies inherent in the use of popular terminologies and identity theories as well as the existence of a consistently unjust system of values. Historically, political terror was once produced in palaces and towers, administered by a ruler or governor and absorbed physically in dungeons by the historically unfortunate or those who sought to challenge established rule. Nowadays it is produced in academic think-tanks, delivered by a so-called administration or other and absorbed everywhere (where think-tanks do not dwell) by a new generation of historically unfortunate peoples who seem unable to adopt the social *modus operandi* they are ordered to conform with. In short, political terror has only transformed in quantitative scope: where it was once brought about by a multitude of local terrorisms it is now a single oecumenical force disguised in a plural patchwork of banners.

The fears which political terror employs can be of a theological, social and historical origin or of a purely biological form in their final analysis. Even if it is assumed that film acts as curator of a thin, universally accepted moral surface, the terrorist mentality, so often cultivated during the screening of a film, is in itself a paradigm of moral discontinuity between the gehalt and inhalt of 21st century politics.

It can be deduced from plain and undirected social observation that the successful transformation of local folklores into peripheral tourism and the negative identification of morality with an inferior past has diminished the role of non-mercantile traditions to an extent already. Disengaging the two notions of fear and guilt from our social perspective or metaphysical traditions simplifies matters and objectifies chance as the sole arbiter of all psyche-related rhetoric; chance is a notion which always defuses rational conditions—it is thought of as incomparably less pertinent to man than say divinity or fate. Surprisingly it is also a crystalizing factor. Chance need only be described not explained. It stands uncontrollable and unthinkable, an untouchable, extraneous infinity of events which refuses communion with human thought: after all, any human thought is happening by chance; the totalitarian rage of this severe dispute of our ability to question and invent is truly extraordinary and truly present on much popular film.

Political terror is a naturalist trick based on violence and it speaks an incomplete *dictum*: 'we must violent,' omitting the words that might complete the sentence: 'perhaps we only truly desire to be peaceful.' In this respect the death penalty is the reference of the terrorist mindframe to a circle of punishment and its utter ignorance of the notion of reconciliation: judicial terror is a veil, a refined obfuscating apparatus that divides the constituents of causality and informs them with utilitarian purpose, so that the death of people, for example, can be a useful event, provided they are guilty of something. Of course, inventing or proving guilt has never been much trouble for us.

For the culture industries, all this immediacy between the theories of political terror and their results indicates progress in the communication and information technologies. In this light, the cinema, an industry itself, becomes a most prototypical tool of global political terrorism. Besides the obvious propaganda it may facilitate, there are those subtle semantics a film inundates our collective memory with, which merit some consideration. If French horns sound each and every time noble and generous behavior is displayed on the screen, does that mean that societies which make no use for French horns in their musical folklore are less than noble? Of logical course, the answer is no. The syllogism, however, is not what concerns a viewer. We have established before, if in a somehow scant manner, that syllogisms and logical discourse are not political *officium* for the screen. And yet, if at least one of the statements made above stands true, that cinema is a religion, then what of its psalms and chants?

Recent examples, that are the majority of films in the 21st century, indicate that heroic models call for a puppetization of representation, i.e. the sedation of representational agency or to use the flattering words of von Kleist 'the infinite knowledge, the being without conscience, the opposite of divinity'.[1]

The super-ego of a memory without a past, which is precisely what music portrays when reproduced during a film screening, can then be used to terrorise the audience by way of refusing it its innocence and grace as well as a right to the fear and guilt of knowledge. The terror we are all subjected to when Sylvester Stallone ran up those famous stairs of white hope in *Rocky*[2] is the landscape which is neither political in nature, nor does it function by way of its implied aesthetic absolutism. Terror ensues when a stereotype erases knowledge and innocence at once: the hero is typified, his struggle is only a matter of utility and, consequently, heroics lay on a shelf in a super-market. We can still assume that the 300 of Thermopylae were historical heroes, but after their stylised transformation into visual objects of voyeurism, their heroism is relegated to the realm of lethal athletics very effectively and very essentially.[3]

Terror is certainly not caused by fear or guilt, for these emotions are its symptoms; its true origins are the tremors brought about by pluralist eulogies. In short and in confident messianic dialect, the quest for a world without ethics is a terrorist state of being. Evidently, upon its arrival this quest is no longer concerned with its politically cynical mechanics: such concerns are purely ethical and dismissible as aphoristic or axiomatic. Traditionally, we name this progress irony.

To find illustrative content of film music practices one need not search for long. Take for example the *Lord of the Rings—The Return of the King*[4] soundtrack. As much as the content of the tale is a second-hand mythology, so is the music score generic pseudo-Wagnerian writing. Besides the technical quality of expression or lack thereof, however, it is the ideological impressions that the soundtrack makes on the viewer which are of the greater interest. It seems odd that in a fictional world the forces of Good look consistently pale and listen to Celtic music whilst the forces of evil mound elephants, look dark and listen to Oriental instruments. Perhaps only the suspicious, ruined and conspiratorial mind may see harm in such coincidence, but any enthusing viewer will identify Ork-like brutality as the enemy of Celtic music henceforth. There is no reason to suggest that these choices of Apollonian and Dionysian stereotyping occur on purpose, nor is that investigation of much interest.

Nevertheless, whatever the cause, the result induces a terrorist mentality in the viewer. It is clear that Celtic music was wisely used to suit the content of the film as we hear one of the heroes speak: "Something stirs in the East.

---

1. Heinrich von Kleist, *On the marionette theatre*, 1810
2. *Rocky*, dir. by John Avildsen, 1976
3. *300*, dir. by Zack Snyder, 2006
4. *Lord of the Rings – The Return of the King* dir. by Peter Jackson, 2003

A sleepless malice. The eye of the enemy is moving." And would it be possible for Chinese or African to be employed after these words are spoken? Clearly, the political agenda of such audio—visual lingo is to appeal to prejudices by the emphatic, if not central, projection of stereotypes—even if the film's ethical influence varies upon reception. We may all come to believe that Welsh, Scottish and Irish accents are reserved for caricatures of men, dwarves, hobbits and other underlings and that the wise only speak Oxbridge English. On the contrary, in North American films, villains speak with English accents and naïve or vulnerable people with non-native tongues. In *Munich*[5], a film about terrorism, the cast speak English with Middle-Eastern accents—in fact when two groups of militant terrorists from Israel and Palestine find themselves in the same room, it is only Al Green, the American singer who intervenes by way of a radio broadcast to defuse the situation. In *Gandhi*[6] the portrayal of men's intentions and characters through their relation with the racial and colonial norm is further magnified, if more soberly treated. When Gandhi dresses up as an Indian again, the soundtrack moves from the symphonic element to the tablas, so that no man in a tie can be said to listen to such music regularly, and no Indian peasant can be said to understand Mozart as well as an Austrian would without committing treason. Swiftly, music has been put back in its boxes and our ears in theirs.

This linguistic and para-musical counterpoint is a political issue—certain sounds mean certain things in strict *Affektenlehre* fashion; without exaggeration, without doubt either, the basis for political terrorism is born right there, in the manufactured identification of evil and the classification of people, of certain sounds and manners, of a certain music, or character of speech. Not surprisingly, the legitimacy of war is a very passionately defended ideal in many North American films, ranging from the endless series of Vietnam-related pieces to the *Rambo*[7] saga and the stylised sophistication and realism of *Saving Private Ryan*[8]. In many of these films one witnesses a great deal of military fetishism in the musical devices that project the ideology of *Pax Americana*. A will for noble sacrifice, a capacity to reserve poignancy and to share confession, all these respectable and understandably admirable emotions and qualities of the many soldiers who possessed them no doubt, are fetishized in the name of coercing the audience to believe in causes which override a human code of honour. The flag of the United States of America waves in the background, a snare drum and a brass quartet play military music when, gradually, a cemetery and a tearful face of an old man appear on the screen. Legitimising military invasion and distant death is not just a means to political terrorism but a terrorist bluff in itself: it coerces the animated and vulnerable

---

5. *Munich*, dir. by Steven Spielberg, 2005
6. *Gandhi*, dir. by Richard Attenborough, 1982
7. *Rambo I-IV*, dir. by various, 1982-2008
8. *Saving Private Ryan*, dir. by Steven Spielberg, 1998

viewer to suspend history to a moment of human purity, justifying the antithetical barbarism it serves.

Occidental culture abandoned the ideals of natural order as soon as it adopted a legalist attitude towards rationality. It had previously abandoned rationality, in the Middle Ages, on account of a legalist attitude towards metaphysics. The bipolar energies of Western philosophies contrast since the beginnings of Western culture, and it is there, *in utero* where we may trace both the creative dynamism which has driven so much of our artistic production, including cinematography, but also the shortcomings of an inherent perjury. In the words of Adorno 'Art's double character, its autonomy and *fait social* is expressed ever and again in the palpable dependencies and conflicts between the two spheres.'[9]

Above all, art needs to discern the causes of political terror if it is to perform any political role. Music is a technique for the cinema. A device, not an art—perhaps a craft at best. As such it is terrorized itself by the pragmatic burden it is forced to carry. There can be little doubt that militant terror is constantly generated by the more abstract political terrorism; the negation of autonomy in the arts for instance, or an exclusively mercantile relationship with sound can be very elementary factors in promoting ecliptic artistic practice. It would be an error to expect much from words in explaining this process; the prohibitions of the culture industry, ever enforced in the name of pluralism, accentuate the impotence of criticism and philological resistance. There are no enigmas concerning the terrorism inflicted upon music by its commodification, however many times this commodification may be declared the emancipation of music. All that may be argued here is the rigorism of 'old' art:

> *A poem should be palpable and mute*
> *As a globed fruit,*
> *Dumb*
> *As old medallions to the thumb*'[10]

Representational art expresses a sensual primacy and its themes and intentions are composed of an immanent meaninglessness and a very determined aesthetic relevance at the same time. It seems that this dualism permeates the symmetries of film from its early days to today. Take the work of three film-makers from three different eras, say Hans Richter, Alfred Hitchcock and Béla Tarr for example: they all adhere to a principle of relating the intention's obscurity and the truth of the sensual result, simply because they do not divorce their intention from the process and the structure of the result. It may be a little formalist and Germanic to show such irrevocable faith

---

9. *Aesthetic theory*, by Th. Adorno, 1970
10. from *Ars poetica* by Archibald McLeish, 1925

in cohesion and the logical array of heteronomous elements. Nevertheless, the absence of this cohesion has a demagogical effect: in the place of structure, style is offered as an alibi, but style is a surface and accidental decoration of an artwork. It offers a semblance of distinction in the form of immediately recognisable attributes, which are empty of any content and which are themselves devices or symptoms.

Stylistic art is an advertisement of itself: the severe terror advertising achieves is its exclusively kinetic condition. It is ironic that stasis and kinesis should be the subject of the concluding paragraph, but for the cinema and its ever moving images, the teleological hypothesis is a fundamental truth. The progress of artistic suicide, the principle of *Durch leiden freude* describes a progressive taboo: becoming is not just different but more important to being. Affirming that the exorcism of static art, of iconography, photography, or long concert hall music is sedimented in the philosophical doctrines of common sense, is a point of first recognition of political terrorism as an ethical problem.

Before a true correspondence with the dialectic terrorism of film music ensues, one must experience or at least imagine a non-functional music and a socially powerless contemplation of art in general. In the consumerist domain such atonement with art is not accessible, nor is a departure from the utilitarian pre-conceptions of atomism. Therefore, an ahistorical, non-schematic and anonymous response seems the sole claim to recapturing the substratum and content of our affinity with sound. Ultimately, it is possible to think of music—and much of it—which has been written for the cinema and which is neither a produce of political terror, nor a cause of it; but it is still impossible to accept, without protest, that any music should ever have to be either of those things.

# RE(CON)fiGURING THE SPECTACLE: STATE FLEXIBILITY IN RESPONSE TO IMAGED TERROR

*Rebecca A. Adelman*

The spectacle, as a visual phenomenon, is the contradictory sum of two assertions: it is the bald lie of the police state that coerces us to concede that 'there is nothing to see here' (Rancière 2001) added to the propaganda that promises revelation of the full truth. To this strange arithmetic, September 11th is no exception: citizen-spectators were required both to look away out of respect and to stare transfixed in performance of an affective patriotic duty. Governmentally, this spectacle was similarly paradoxical: it was both the ultimatum for all political choices and the empty signifier that took the place of real deliberation. In order to understand the dynamics of the spectacular instantiation of American terror, it might seem that we have to pick a side and claim either that September 11th incapacitated the American state, or that September 11th galvanized it. Rather than accept the apparent incommensurability of these conceits, however, in what follows, I explore the extent to which they are co-constitutive and compatible, by charting a broader array of state[1] responses to the spectacle of imaged terror, rejoinders that counter the spectacular affront, but do not replicate its form.

Among the most eloquent diagnoses of the state's inability to cope with the spectacle is that put forth by the Retort collective in their 2005 volume, *Afflicted Powers: Capital and Spectacle in a New Age of War*. As an unavoidable result of its collaborative authorship, the text contains and acknowledges some internal disagreements, but one point about which the authors, Iain Boal, T.J. Clark, Joseph Matthews, and Michael Watts, are unequivocal is that September 11th was a spectacular 'image-defeat' for the U.S. "Spectacularly," they write,

> the American state suffered a defeat on September 11. And spectacularly, for this state, does not mean superficially or epiphenomenally. The state was wounded in September in its heart of hearts, and we see it still ... flailing blindly in the face of an image it cannot exorcize

---

[1]. The 'state,' as I conceptualize it, is a governmental authority. It is distinct from a nation, which is defined in large part by cultural commonalities, even though these entities might overlap. For the purposes of this analysis, the state is both banal (collecting taxes, supervising education, providing infrastructure) and insidious (producing and policing subjects with whom it interacts in intimate and instrumental ways).

and trying desperately to convert the defeat back into terms it can respond to (2005, 25).

According to Retort's calculations, the hijackers are insuperable in this regard, because "there is no answer to [their] image-victory" (2005, 27). For this reason, the authors continue, the state campaigned to censor the images of 9/11, but this repression only made the images more potent. Thus, in their assessment, the United States faces a crucial, existential dilemma. As a "spectacular state," it "is obliged ... to devise an answer to the defeat of September 11th. And it seems it cannot" (2005, 34). So, the state labors fruitlessly in the long "shadow of defeat" (2005, 37) cast by the hijacked planes, the collapsed Towers, and the wrecked Pentagon. Insofar as it achieved an eclipse of unprecedented darkness and duration, the authors contend, September 11th is absolutely unique.

There is ample evidence to support their widely persuasive interpretation, which illuminates the importance of appearance in the Global War on Terror (GWOT). In such a model, the U.S. is in dogged pursuit of an image coup. "Shock and awe"; the dethroning of Saddam Hussein's statue in Firdos Square; the orchestrated rescue of Pfc. Jessica Lynch; President Bush's declaration of victory aboard the *U.S.S. Lincoln* in May 2003: all of these aggressively stage-managed events early in the war clearly signal that the administration realized the importance of spectacular sights and stories. Indeed, at times the state explicitly invokes the language of the spectacle in its discourses on terrorism. In *The 9/11 Report*, for example, the Commission describes Khalid Sheik Mohammed's original plans as "theater. A spectacle of destruction with KSM as the self-cast star—the superterrorist" (2004, 222), while last summer, government agencies warned American citizens to brace for a 'terror spectacular.' Although the arrest of KSM was high-value and high-profile, the capture of this bedraggled and pajamaed superterrorist was not especially photogenic, and concrete proof of plans for the foretold extravaganza never materialized.

Spectacular victories like dramatic arrests and heroic, highly visible efforts to thwart imminent attacks have been in short supply, and yet the War on Terror persists, and the state makes do. Even if it limps from time to time, the very perseverance of the U.S. in its anti-terror campaign despite the absence of spectacular success suggests the need to recalculate the importance of the spectacle in state responses to terror. In so doing, it will be necessary to divest ourselves of two assumptions: first, the notion that the state wishes only or even primarily for a spectacular victory, and second, the idea that it would be sated if one were achieved. As an alternative to these rather superficial claims, I suggest that the state can derive as much pleasure and power from *suppressing* the spectacle as it can from creating it.

Indeed, the fact that the U.S. has engaged so willingly with the language of the spectacular suggests that it is undaunted by it. Crucial to Retort's argument about the spectacle is that it is difficult to handle, that blowback, as it were, is a very real risk in spectacular politics. Certainly, the U.S. has struggled in its GWOT, even as it has secured some substantial victories. Overall, however, the U.S. has been surprisingly candid in its confrontation with the images of 9/11, which Mitchell describes as the "image cloned repeatedly in the collective global nervous system" (2007, 284). This very frankness about the images, I argue, is indicative of the state's ability to manage, to govern their spectacular consequences. Certainly, states must promise and boast of grand victories; this is, as Retort reminds us, a consequence of their obligation to manage spectacular and military objectives simultaneously. Still, it is plausible, and even likely, that such rhetoric, while politically convenient, may not be a transparent window on the state's desires. There is no reason to assume that the state would take the occasion of its defeat to begin telling the truth.

Although acts of terror are, by their nature, sudden and unexpected, their instant impact may not necessarily correspond to an equally immediate loss of government control. It is possible that just as states can appear to be in control when they really are not, that the reverse could be true. This means that the illusion of stunned inefficacy (e.g., the oft-circulated video footage of President Bush proceeding with his elementary-school visit after receiving news of the attacks) might obscure a state mechanism that, while it may not be functioning smoothly, is functioning nonetheless.[2]

Consequently, I would argue that the state is capable of rehabilitating the spectacle and the spectacular defeat into a variety of counter- or even antispectacular measures that facilitate its war project more ably than even a spectacular victory could. Oppressive regimes, as Elaine Scarry observes, alternately employ under- and over-exposure of particular images and events (1999, 288) to cultivate conditioned, predictable affective and ethical responses in the populace. If the state can manage the visible and the invisible (and after all, the ministries of information for even the most ineffective states can usually handle this), hypervisible spectacular victories are not always necessary or even particularly useful.

Spectacular victories are, by their nature, costly and ephemeral. State success, then, might come from the employment of the anti-spectacle for similar ends, both strategic and ideological, in ways that are more durable and, ultimately, more gratifying. Although terror, as most of us[3] experience it, is large-

---

2. Thanks to my colleague Michael J. McVicar, who provocatively observed that states do not ever function smoothly. This observation coheres with Retort's description of the state as a "clumsy, lurching apparatus" (2005, 81) that often operates precariously and invigoratingly close to the "edge of failure" (2005, 89), and also with that of Deleuze and Guattari in *Anti-Oedipus*, that "it is *in order to function* that a social machine must *not function well*" (1983, 151).

3. Certainly, the un*mediat*ed experience of terror torments the subject through all sorts of corporeal affronts. But most people in the U.S. will never encounter terror

ly a visual phenomenon, insofar as every invocation of 'terror' necessarily and vividly "evokes images" (Routt 2003 93), the state's visual response to it may not be similarly automatic. The U.S., in its current anti-terror campaign, has charted a divergent relation to the visual, a tactically flexible subversion of the spectacle comprised of strategies that have in common their transformation of spectacular 'defeat' into unprecedented administrative control.

First among these is the proliferation of surveillance, a perverse and generative love affair with visuality. State surveillance has long attended terrorism[4] in a relationship that is anticipatory and prophylactic. Anti-terror surveillance is underwritten by faith that sufficient panopticism will prevent terrorism in both imagination and deed. In the U.S., this new infatuation with the visual has taken a range of forms, as in the elaborated inspection procedures at the airport checkpoint, a threshold where visual screening[5] is the primary rubric of threat. The anti-spectacular logic of surveillance has also functioned figuratively in the use of wiretaps and other monitoring mechanisms. Concern over phone calls, as in the recent wrangling over the Foreign Intelligence Surveillance Act (FISA), does not pertain explicitly to the visual, but is built nonetheless upon a lopsided form of visuality, in which the state, by concealing itself, gains access to the way that people act when they believe no one is watching. Rather than manipulating images with the goal of spectacular success, this is a subtle and insidious form of visuality. Yet even as the state might love the visual when surveillance is expedient, this is not the same as courting the spectacle. Moreover, that practice is in many ways unique among the other courses it might pursue, where the suppression of the visual is the source of the state's pleasure.[6]

Chief among these vexed technologies of visuality is secrecy. Like surveillance, secrecy balances sight and the unseen in a calculation aimed at preventing future spectacular defeats. By now, the penchant of the present administration for secrecy in its anti-terror campaign is well-documented. From the outset, it operated under the logic that "the public had no right to know anything, no matter how innocuous" because any bit of information could ultimately become a security risk (Savage 2007 94). Stealth and invisibility have become the preferred ways to fight a war in a moment where nearly every-

---

so directly, and in common parlance, 'terror' is what we see on television, or the abstract entity upon which we declare a Global War.
4. For a compelling account of this phenomenon, see Allen Feldman's work on the visual in Northern Ireland (2006).
5. Of course, if the visual inspection turns up something suspect, secondary measures that then ensue rapidly become far more tactile and incorporate a radically expanded realm of sensory interrogation and experience.
6. The claim that the state feels (and seeks) pleasure might not be an intuitively graspable one. But in this formulation, I am relying upon the extensive body of scholarship that charts out the importance of pleasure for the visual, and the visual in pleasure.

thing else is imaged. This orientation away from political stagecraft has evolved gradually, provoked in large part by changing tactical exigencies of the GWOT. Spectacular sights were easier to orchestrate at the beginning, but eventually became inadequate to the task of bolstering public opinion, and superfluous to the real work of prosecuting the war. Many of what Judith Butler (2004) describes as the legal 'innovations' of the GWOT, like the creation of the category 'enemy combatants' and the use of indefinite detention, emerged long after the American flag had been removed from Saddam Hussein's face and Pfc. Lynch was returned safely home to West Virginia. These measures are not glamorous, but they are crucial. They are effective because they "reanimat[e] a spectral sovereignty within the field of governmentality" (Butler 2004, 61); in this context, the spectral is atavistic and haunting, but also wraithlike, and barely visible, a series of shadowy machinations.

Attending processes like indefinite detention is the use of disappearance. Disappearance, whether in the form of extraordinary rendition or the network of top-secret prisons (perhaps now defunct) for holding high-value detainees like KSM, combines surveillance and secrecy. The sum, however, is zero visibility. Certainly, the U.S. did not invent political disappearance, but has nonetheless employed it liberally as a rejoinder to the spectacle, taking terrorists like KSM and punishing their very capacities for image-creation and spectacle-making by keeping them from appearing at all. Practically, of course, disappearance is useful: such ultimate invisibility, according to Ariel Dorfman (2007), is a thoroughgoing form of social death, absolute removal from the protection and accountability of social or legal oversight. It is especially convenient when these disappearances take place nowhere. As Charlie Savage (2007) observes, Guantánamo Bay (one of the sites where is the most nothing to see), is unique because it is American land on foreign soil, borrowed indefinitely from a government with which the U.S. has no diplomatic ties: in such a no-place, no domestic or international laws can apply. There is nothing there, simply the dark matter left behind after the spectacular explosion.

Despite all of this, certain images do seem to exceed the state's control: in the American context, the apparent limit-case came in the form of Abu Ghraib. The photographic evidence of American soldiers torturing Iraqi detainees that surfaced in the spring of 2004 looked at first like a course of shock therapy for the state that, according to Retort, "was entrapped in its own apparatus of clichés" (2005, 23). They argued that the circulation of these images compounded the spectacular defeat of 9/11. "The Towers," they wrote, "keep falling; and now they are joined by the imagery of Abu Ghraib" (2005, 35). As an ostensible antipode to 9/11, the release of these images (even more than the images themselves) *seemed* to indicate that the state was flailing, helpless again before a torrent of sights. Such a contention found purchase in a variety of anti-war quarters, and there are good reasons for taking it seriously. However, I would like to explore some alternate consequences of the Abu Ghraib photographs, in light of Agamben's contention that the post-9/11 "politics of security secretly works toward the production of emergencies" (2002), which ultimately amount to little more than costs of doing business.

Undeniably, the photos were a liability: ideologically, politically, diplomatically. But in reality, they also provided a mechanism by which to gauge public tolerance for this kind of behavior and, more precisely, its display. Even if it was the latter that provoked more outrage than the former, as Haim Bresheeth (2006) and others have noted, that outrage was, ultimately of little consequence. Disgust, at least before it eroded into desensitization and then gave way to acquiescence, became a kind of ethical barometer, proof of one's anti-war credentials, but ultimately a useless one, and perhaps even, as Susan Sontag would have it, an "insult" to the gravity of the situation (2004). Sontag described this phenomenon as an "orgy of self-condemnation" (2004). This characterization is particularly apt in light of Elizabeth Cowie's assertion that "squeamishness ... is not at all an ethical response, but on the contrary [is] a symptom of an anxious enjoyment in unpleasure" (2003, 36). Indulgence in discomfort is the very thing that allows us to keep looking.

Looking, in the end, became a kind of rite of passage, a way of establishing one's stoicism in the face of the spectacular hellishness of warfare.[7] This defiant staring seemed to be a resistant gesture against a state that *seemed* determined to prohibit it. However, insofar as the photos depict a carefully orchestrated 'institutional' practice, as Julie Gerk Hernandez contends (2007), then the looking that they provoked, must also have been, engineered or at least anticipated by the state that feigned terror at that very thing. Given this, Sontag and others may have overestimated the power of these images to arrest the state in its capacity for war-making or image-management.

The state has another option for combating the spectacle, for it can (and will) mirror its spectacular brightness into a blinding reflection. In the face of this awful luminosity, there is nothing for a citizen to do but squint, or avert her gaze. "Terror of the eyes," as Routt describes it, can take the form of "static blindness, nothing to look at, vision unmade" (2003, 93). When vision itself becomes agonizing and indeed impossible because of the surfeit of things to see, what is there to do but close our eyes? The state that can police the field of perception can, in Rancière's terms, construct a 'partition of the sensible' (2001). So, as easily as it can erect a barricade or a checkpoint, the state can "install" what Feldman describes as "public zones of perceptual amnesia" (1994, 103), places where seeing or feeling anything is simply and sometimes mercifully impossible.

---

7. Parenthetically, we might also question the ethics of the satisfaction that so many opponents of the war seemed to take in finally having evidence of the rightness of their cause.

And so it is that, as Butler points out, the Department of Defense willingly published certain interrogation photos from Guantánamo, in order to "make known that a certain vanquishing had taken place" (2004, 77). If those photos were hard to look at, that was the point—all the state needed to show was that it had achieved something and recorded it. Even when the state seems to lose control over the image, as when the first Abu Ghraib photos were 'leaked,' the very excess that provided evidence of the state's grotesquerie and so threatens to make them unmanageable is precisely what makes them bizarrely palatable. Hernandez (2007) argues that it was the sheer obscenity of the Abu Ghraib images that enabled the administration to disavow them; it could camouflage itself behind the ruse that a state so spectacularly ruined could not accomplish such a spectacular show of domination.

Thus the Abu Ghraib example demonstrates the resilience of the state in the face of spectacular defeat. It also suggests that the state is never fully thwarted by the spectacle, even if the spectacle constrained the options available to the state in response. Once the photos appeared, the only logical course available to the state was denial. And so the state set to work doing the only thing that it could, distinguishing itself rhetorically and disengaging itself institutionally from the people depicted in the images. But in the very process of calling them "rogue," as Wendy Kozol and Rebecca DeCola point out, they justified the need for more state intervention (2006, 185), which appeared to be the only adequate protection against future atrocities. The spectacle thus became an accomplice at the very moment when it would seem to be an adversary. In this case, where the state and the spectacle seem to be at their most antagonistic, the state can simply reach out and engage its enemy in a tenuous alliance, just as, perhaps, the U.S. has made its most substantive security gains in Iraq by cooperating with the very same militia fighters that were previously the 'insurgency.'

The willingness of the state to compromise strategically, then, leads to two conclusions about its relation to the spectacle of imaged terror, one methodological and the other rather more theoretical. In the first instance, it suggests the need to *refigure* the role of the spectacle in our theorizations of state responses to imaged terror. Particularly in a war where so little has been proportional, there is no reason to expect that the spectacular affront and the counter-spectacular response will exhibit either congruity or symmetry. Powerful states are flexible, and even if they might wish for a counterstrike that looks as decisive and astonishing as the terror itself, I think it important to remain open to the possibility that they can redirect their need for vengeance by utilizing the visual in lethally unspectacular ways.

This is not to suggest that the spectacle goes to waste; it is, instead, *reconfigured.* Paradoxically, even at its most incriminating, the spectacle might still provide an alibi. In the glare of 9/11 and Abu Ghraib, the state's vulnerability was illuminated, but it was also shrouded. For the conning hypervisibility of the spectacular affront serves also as a screen, behind which the consolidation of executive power (manifested in anti-spectacular and extra-legal initiatives) continues apace, out of sight and shielded from scrutiny, so that the grim business of retaliation might there continue unimpeded.[8]

---

8. In addition to the thoughtful commentary provided by the audience members in the conference session where I presented this paper, I have been fortunate to receive the insights of a variety of generous interlocutors. In particular, Dr. Philip Armstrong in the Department of Comparative Studies and various readers in the Comparative Studies Dissertation Writing Group have provided crucial, incisive feedback on drafts of this document.

## References

Agamben, Giorgio. 2002. "Security and terror." Translated by Carolin Emcke. *Theory and Event* 5 (4).

"Anaesthesia." In *The senses still: Perception and memory as material culture in modernity.* ed. C. Nadia Seremetakis, (87-107). Boulder: Westview Press.

Bresheeth, Haim. 2006. Projecting trauma: War photography and the public sphere. *Third Text* 20 no.1: 57-71.

Butler, Judith. 2004. *Precarious life: The powers of mourning and violence.* New York: Verso.

Cowie, Elizabeth. 2003. "The lived nightmare: Trauma, anxiety, and the ethical aesthetics of horror. In *Dark thoughts: Philosophical reflections on cinematic horror*, eds. Steven Jay Schnider and Daniel Shaw, (25-46). Lanham, MD: The Scarecrow Press.

Debord, Guy. 1995. *The society of the spectacle.* Trans. Donald Nicholson-Smith. New York: Zone Books.

Deleuze, Gilles and Félix Guattari. 1983. *Anti-Oedipus: Capitalism and schizophrenia.* Trans. Robert Hurley, Mark Seem, and Helen R. Lane. Minneapolis: University of Minnesota Press.

Dorfman, Ariel. 2007. Globalizing compassion, photography, and the challenge of terror. *CLCWeb: Comparative Literature and Culture* 9, no. 1, http://docs.lib.purdue.edu/cgi/viewcontent.cgiarticle=1014andcontext=clcweb (accessed May 28, 2008).

Feldman, Allen. 1994. From desert storm to Rodney King via Ex-Yugoslavia: On Cultural.

——— 2006. "Violence and vision: The prosthetics and aesthetics of terror." In *States of Violence*, eds. Fernando Coronil and Julie Skurski, 425-468. Ann Arbor: Univ. of Michigan Press.

Hernandez, Julie Gerk. 2007. The tortured body, the photograph, and the U.S. war on terror. *CLCWeb:Comparative Literature and Culture* 9, no. 1, http://docs.lib.purdue.edu/cgi/viewcontent.cgi?article=1019andcontext=clcweb (accessed May 27, 2008).

Kean, Thomas H. and Lee H. Hamilton. 2004. *The 9/11 Report.* New York: St. Martin's Press.

Kozol, Wendy and Rebecca DeCola. 2006. "Remapping the war on terrorism: 'U.S. internationalism' and transnational citizenship." In *Rethinking global security: Media, popular culture, and the "war on terror."* eds. Andrew Martin and Patrice Petro, 179-205. New Brunswick, NJ: Rutgers University Press.

Mitchell, W. J. T. 2007. "Picturing terror: Derrida's autoimmunity. *Critical Inquiry* 33 no. 2: 277-290.

Rancière, Jacques. 2001. Ten theses on politics. *Theory and Event* 5 no. 3.

"Retort" (Iain Boal, T.J. Clark, Joseph Matthews, and Michael Watts). 2005. *Afflicted powers: Capital and spectacle in a new age of war.* 2nd ed. London: Verso.

Routt, William D. 2003. Who dances when terror strikes? *Postcolonial Studies*, 6, no.1: 91-105.

Savage, Charlie. 2007. *Takeover: The return of the imperial presidency and the subversion of American democracy.* New York: Little, Brown, and Company.

Scarry, Elaine. 1999. The difficulty of imagining other persons. In *Human rights in political transitions: Gettysburg to Bosnia.* eds. Carla Hesse and Robert Post, 277-309. New York: Zone Books.

Sontag, Susan. 2004. Regarding the torture of others. *The New York Times Magazine.* http://www.nytimes.com/2004/05/23/magazine/23PRISONS.html (accessed February 19, 2008).

# "DON'T SAY THE ZED WORD!" TOWARD A LINGUISTIC CONSTRUCTION OF SOCIAL CLASS IN THE CONTEMPORARY *LIVING DEAD* FILM

*Leslie Russell Ashby*

In defining his first of seven theses of monster culture, that "the monster's body is a cultural body"—Jeffrey Jerome Cohen suggests:

> The monstrous body is pure culture. A construct and a projection, the monster exists only to be read: the *monstrum* is etymologically 'that which reveals,' 'that which warns,' a glyph that seeks an hierophant. Like a letter on the page, the monster signifies something other than itself: it is always a displacement, always inhabits the gap between the time of upheaval that created it and the moment into which it is received, to be born again. (4)

When George A. Romero's *Night of the Living Dead* first appeared in theatres in 1968, it heralded the beginning of a provocative strain of horror films that have been incorporated as much with sociopolitical commentary as they have with gore and terror. The films of Romero's *Living Dead* series, and the films that have followed in its footsteps, suggest a climate of apocalyptic destruction, infused with a metaphor for revolution. Essentially, the pre-existing social structure is thrown into chaos as a direct result of the literal and figurative uprising of a new social group, the Dead. The films of the *Dead*, as Romero and those that follow his model have conceived them, represent a common universe—an apocalyptic or post-apocalyptic world in which, as the character Peter in Romero's 1978 film *Dawn of the Dead* states, "when there's no more room in hell, the dead will walk the earth."

What follows is the establishment of a new social order, not only among the survivors, the Living, but also with respect to the Dead, who must be consolidated as a troublesome, and often unstable, new facet of the social structure. As Romero himself has frequently suggested, "I wanted to create a vision where a new world order literally rises up and devours the old. My films are about revolution." It is arguable that the Dead are a near-perfect example of the signification that Cohen describes, as he states:

> By revealing that difference is arbitrary and potentially free-floating, mutable rather than essential, the monster threatens to destroy not just individual members of society, but the very cultural apparatus through

> which individuality is constituted and allowed. Because it is a body across which difference has been repeatedly written, the monster seeks out its author to demand its raison d'être—and to bear witness to the fact that it could have been constructed Otherwise. (12)

While the Living are left to negotiate and define an entirely new social system, the tools they possess for defining this new system are grounded entirely within the parameters of the old system. Given that they must formulate an entirely new ideology, and given the basis of ideology in language, linguistic strategies play a key role in this reconstruction. The Living must use language to define their Living status and construct a boundary between themselves and the Dead. Language proves to be an effective tool for making such a distinction as the Dead, while communicative, are nearly always non-verbal. The non-verbal nature of the Dead is a fact upon which the Living can rely, and in a state of complete cultural distress, the Living will cling with both hands to anything that they can count as fact. However, Cohen also asserts that "the monster's destructiveness is really a deconstructiveness: it threatens to reveal that difference originates in process, rather than in fact (and that 'fact' is subject to constant reconstruction and change)" (7).

The Living, then, are faced with a linguistic problem. As George Lakoff and Mark Johnson suggest in their critical text, *Metaphors We Live By*:

> Each culture must provide a more or less successful way of dealing with its environment, both adapting to it and changing it. Moreover, each culture must define a social reality within which people have roles that make sense to them and in terms of which they can function socially...What is real for an individual as a member of a culture is a product both of his social reality and the way in which that shapes his experience of the physical world. (146)

The Living must, therefore, search for ways to define this new social class—the Dead—an entirely new phenomenon. They must attempt to define and acculturate that which is abject. As Julia Kristeva suggests in *Language: the Unknown*:

> While language is a practice realized in social communication and by means of it, it constitutes a material reality that, while participating in the material world itself, nonetheless posits the problem of its relation with what is not language, that is, with the *outside*—nature, society, etc.—that exists without language even if it cannot be named without it. (8)

The Dead do not make the Living's task a simple one. In fact, by virtue of the fact that the Dead are representative of a monstrous body, they are quite deft at defying categorization. As Cohen states:

> The monster always escapes because it refuses easy categorization...This refusal to participate in the classificatory 'order of things' is true of monsters generally: they are disturbing hybrids whose externally incoherent bodies resist attempts to include them in any systematic structuration. (6)

Given the Dead's status as literal walking corpses, Kristeva's words also bear significant weight as she writes in *The Powers of Horror: An Essay on Abjection*—"The corpse (or cadaver: *cadere*, to fall), that which has irremediably become a cropper, is cesspool, and death; it upsets even more violently the one who confronts it as fragile and fallacious chance" (3). Kim Paffenroth suggests, in *Gospel of the Dead: George Romero's Vision of Hell on Earth* that:

> Zombies bring the complete breakdown of the natural world of food chains, social order, respect for life, and respect for death, because all those categories are meaningless and impossible to maintain in a world where the most fundamental limen, the threshold between alive and dead, has become a threshold that no one really crosses all the way over, but on which everyone lives suspended all the time. (14)

There is a blurring of the boundaries between Life, Death, and Living Death that assist in the Dead's defiance of categorization. Their existence simply does not make logical sense, and thus, defies classification. As the villainous character, Kaufman laments in *Land of the Dead*, "in a world where the dead are returning to life, the word 'trouble' loses all meaning."

Under dire circumstances, the Living attempt to enact some level of power over the abject Dead through the process of naming. They attempt to construct metaphors that allow them some level of control, linguistically, at least. In choosing a lexical identifier for the Dead, the Living make use of lexical items ranging from the euphemistic to the pejorative. Notably, lexical identifiers for the Dead are only prominently featured in Romero's 2005 film *Land of the Dead*. This is likely attributable to the fact that the film is set in a post-apocalyptic environment, "some time" after the initial rising of the Dead and the characters have had significantly longer to accommodate the Dead linguistically. As April McMahon explains in *Understanding Language Change*, "psychological factors figure largely in taboo and euphemism. Often, religious concepts, dangerous animals, and acts or objects which are though of as unpleasant or distasteful become taboo; their names cannot then be used, and euphemisms are substituted, causing a semantic change in euphemistic expression" (181).

*Land of the Dead*'s protagonist, Riley, who is established throughout the film as the Living survivor most sympathetic to the plight of the Dead, always makes a point of referring to the Dead by the euphemism "walkers," therefore associating them with the most benign activity that they perform. The majority of other Living characters in the film refer to the Dead by the more pejorative term, "stenches." While pejorative, the term "stenches" still suggests that the Dead are fairly harmless, if a bit smelly. The term "zombie" is notably avoided. If it *is* used, then the speaker is typically an unsympathetic character. In thinking of the Dead as a distinct social, or even racial, group, the term "zombie," then becomes a type of racial slur. For example, the only character in *Land of the Dead* to use the term "zombie" is Kaufman, the clear villain of the film. Kaufman makes use of other racial slurs as well, as when he refers to a Latino character as a "spic bastard."

In exception to the conspicuous absence of the term "zombie" are the final scenes of Edgar Wright's 2004 film *Shaun of the Dead* that take place after the Dead have been effectively subdued by the Living. Earlier in the film, protagonist Shaun's best friend Ed uses the term "zombie" and is instantly rebuked by Shaun, who snaps "Don't say that! The zed-word!" When Ed asks why not, Shaun answers, "Because it's ridiculous." Given the satirical nature of the film, this sequence seems to cleverly reference the conspicuous absence of the term "zombie" from other films of the genre. In the aftermath of the Dead's uprising, however, the word "zombie" is used ubiquitously and has become the "official" term. As one character sits before the television, rapidly and aimlessly switching channels, the term is heard several times. The date of the rising has been termed "Z-Day" and a charity designed to provide disaster relief for the victims has been named "Zomb-aid." The use of the term in this context is meant ironically.

The majority of the characters in all films of the Dead make use of ambiguous lexical items to refer to the Dead. Many of the Living refer to the Dead simply as "those things." There is a good deal of variation in the usage of pronouns, as well, in which the neuter pronoun "it" is used in place of a gendered pronoun to identify one of the Dead. This strategy seems to reinforce the need of the Living to distance themselves as much as possible from the Dead by utilizing a pronoun that suggests asexuality, and thus, inhumanity. Given the complex cultural and linguistic environment within the films, and the fact that in none of the films is it possible for the Living to completely eradicate the Dead, how then, are the Dead acculturated as a new, viable social class? This problem is approached in different ways within the genre. For the purposes this discussion, I will describe the circumstances of three recent Dead films. First, though, it seems pertinent to acknowledge Kim Paffenroth's contention that, "zombies are the lowest, most 'peasant' type of monsters…but zombies enjoy greater success at annihilating humanity than any previous monster ever did" (16). Thus, the Dead, though higher in population, seem to begin their social existence at the lowest point of the social strata. While their initial coup is often devastating, the Dead often seem to land at the level of the lowest class.

Zack Snyder's 2004 remake, *Dawn of the Dead* is ambiguous in this respect. The downbeat, nihilistic ending of the film seems to suggest that the

Dead may actually be the only social group that remains—that their devastation is so great that the Living have been effectively extinguished. The four remaining survivors, having escaped a shopping center in which they were barricaded, board a boat in an effort to find an unpopulated island, yet another bounded place in which to segregate themselves. Shot on a handheld camera and meant to be a home video document of what took place on the boat, the final scenes show the survivors experiencing all manner of technical difficulties and biological hardships before finally landing on what appears to be a deserted island. As soon as the boat is docked, however, the survivors quickly discover that the island is already densely populated by the Dead and it is suggested that none of the survivors, for all of their struggles, is able to escape, or at least to remain a member of the Living.

In *Shaun of the Dead*, Edgar Wright chooses an alternative approach to acculturation. The majority of the film takes place in the space of about 24 hours, at the end of which the threat that the Dead represent has been effectively neutralized. The final sequence of the film takes place six months after "Z-Day," and the remaining Dead have been effectively incorporated into the cultural fabric. They appear on games shows, talk shows ("My Husband is a Zombie!"), and are staples of tabloid television. It is clear as the character watches television and flips rapidly through the channels, that the Dead are now regarded with little more than a passing ennui. Troublingly, though, the Dead have not staked out a true claim for themselves as a viable social class. Instead, they have become a spectacle—an inhuman source of entertainment, as well as a population of what are essentially slaves. They have been bound by chains and put to work, doing menial labor tasks. Reinforcing this subjugation of the Dead is the final treatment of the Dead Ed, Shaun's best friend, who is confined to the garden shed, "like an animal." While it is presumable that he is treated well by Shaun, the fact still remains that Ed has become little more than a pet.

*Land of the Dead* provides the most hopeful representation of the Dead as part of the social strata. This comes as little surprise, however, given the fact that the Dead as Romero has conceived them to possess the more humanity and characterization of any of the Dead featured in the other films. Romero's Dead seem to have more cognitive skills available to them, and thus, they are both more capable of fighting for their right to exists and easier for the Living to accept as functional members of the social order. During an exchange with another character, Mike, early in the film, Riley points out the primary similarity between the Living and the Dead, as they observe the Dead performing tasks and communicating non-verbally:

MIKE. They're trying to be us.

RILEY. No, they *used* to be us. [They're] learning how to be us again.

> MIKE. No way. Some germ or some devil got those things up and walking, but there is a big difference between us and them. They're dead. It's like they're pretending to be alive.
>
> RILEY. Isn't that what we're doing? Pretending to be alive?

As the Dead carry out their vendetta toward the Living, ultimately crossing the threshold into the city, enacting their justice, and learning to control their impulse to cannibalize, they are finally acknowledged, at least by the remaining members of the Living, as a functional social group. As the film winds to a close, Riley and his group are confronted with the problem of what to do about the remaining Dead. One of Riley's companions prepares to fire a weapon at the group of the Dead, but Riley stops her, as he insists that the Dead are "just looking for a place to go, just like us."

In the description of his seventh and final thesis of monster culture—"the monster stands at the threshold…of becoming"—Cohen concludes:

> Monsters are our children. They can be pushed to the farthest margins of geography and discourse, hidden away at the edges of the world and in the forbidden recesses of our mind, but they always return…These monsters ask us how we perceive the world, and how we have misrepresented what we have attempted to place. They ask us to reevaluate our cultural assumptions about race, gender, sexuality, our perception of difference, our tolerance toward its expression. They ask us why we have created them. (20)

The Dead created in Romero's image represent this reflexive construct. They not only symbolize and enact the deepest anxieties of our culture—they are, as Romero has repeatedly insisted, essentially "us." Though a fictional construct, the Dead play a vital role in the understanding of culture, just as monsters have done throughout the history of narrative. They are abject, amplifying some of culture's deepest fears and most inherent incongruities.

## References

Cohen, Jeffrey Jerome. 1996. "Monster culture (seven theses)." *Monster Theory: Reading Culture.* ed. Jeffrey Jerome Cohen. Minneapolis: Univ. of Minnesota Press, 3-25.

D'Agnolo-Vallan, Giulia. "Let them eat flesh." *Film Comment* 41(2005): 23-4.

*Dawn of the Dead.* Dir. George A. Romero. Perf. Gaylen Ross, David Emge, and Ken Foree. UFDC, 1978.

*Dawn of the Dead.* Dir. Zack Snyder. Perf. Sarah Polley, Ving Rhames, Mekhi Phifer, and Jake Weber. Universal, 2004.

*Day of the Dead.* Dir. George A. Romero. Perf. Lori Cardille, Terry Alexander, and Joe Pilato. UFDC, 1985.

Kristeva, Julia. 1989. *Language: The unknown.* Trans. Anne M. Menke. New York: Columbia Univ. Press.

—— *Powers of Horror: An essay on abjection.* Trans. Leon S. Roudiez. New York: Columbia Univ. Press, 1982.

Lakoff, George, and Mark Johnson. 1980. *Metaphors we live by.* Chicago: Univ. of Chicago Press.

*Land of the Dead.* Dir. George A. Romero. Perf. Simon Baker, Dennis Hopper, John Leguizamo, and Asia Argento. Universal, 2005.

McMahon, April M.S. 1994. *Understanding language change.* Cambridge: Cambridge Univ. Press.

*Night of the Living Dead.* Dir. George A. Romero. Perf. Duane Jones, Judith O'Dea, and Marilyn Eastman. New Line, 1968.

Paffenroth, Kim. 2006. *Gospel of the living dead: George Romero's vision of hell on Earth.* Waco, TX: Baylor Univ. Press.

*Shaun of the Dead.* Dir. Edgar Wright. Perf. Simon Pegg, Nick Frost, Kate Ashfield, and Lucy Davis. Rogue Pictures, 2004.

# FATE AND TERROR IN DON DELILLO'S *FALLING MAN*

*Christine Muller*

Two thin parallel lines bifurcate the title words "Falling Man" on the hardcover front of Don DeLillo's 2007 novel. On the back, an aerial perspective shows the top halves of the World Trade Center twin towers emerging in lonely solitude above a thick carpeting of cloud cover, vulnerably exposed to the vast expanse of a grainy blue sky. Below the clouds, unseen but of course implied, the towers' lower floors extend in structural continuity to underground foundations. The double lines and paired buildings that pierce and separate words and space evince the fluid but manifest distinctions between one thing and another, here and there, before and after. The prospect of crossing into troubled territory from which there is no return pervades *Falling Man*, and these pictorial components of the book's production evoke the formidable boundaries that come to demarcate person, place and time throughout the novel. Moreover, circumstances infuse these demarcations with a sense of forced and inevitable conclusion. As Lianne confronts her father's past and her possible future with Alzheimer's disease, Hammad succumbs to his role in predestined jihad, and Keith loses himself in endless, timeless, anonymous rounds of poker, daily life for these characters seems bounded by structured but uncontrollable peril, where the end is fated because root causes subtly and intricately conspire long before their effects are realized. Before these individuals might seize any opportunity for intervention or recognize whether any such opportunity even exists, and before the final instant actually arrives, the door has closed behind them.

Whether in the form of terminal disease, martyrdom, or surviving September 11, the specific end concerning each of these characters is the ultimate end: death. Psychiatrist Judith Herman has noted that experiences of powerlessness in the face of terror undermine survivors' and witnesses' ordinary notions of control, connection, and meaning (Herman 1992, 1997, 33). Essentially, psychologist Ronnie Janoff-Bulman has argued that traumatic encounters foreground human mortality, exposing what we ordinarily strive to ignore in the pursuit of lives not paralyzed by fear: our inescapable vulnerability and our potentially imminent destruction (Janoff-Bulman 1992, 59-61). When individuals are unable to avoid the circumstances or antagonism that result in their personal harm, they begin to question their ability to act in and make sense of a world now comprehended as intimately perilous. After trauma's foreshadowing of death, survivors and witnesses must reconstruct meaning about life that responds to both the reality that existence is subject to circumstantial whim and antagonistic will, and the need to continue living productively within that reality (Janoff-Bulman 1992, 115-141). In his formulations of logotherapy, Holocaust survivor and psychiatrist Viktor Frankl termed the "will to meaning" the paramount human motivation, a drive that becomes particularly acute and urgent when circumstances such as suffering set conditions beyond a person's control with which s/he nevertheless must contend (Frankl 1959, 1962, 1984, 119-157). In this context, meaningful action forms under the circumscribed conditions of mortality acknowledged as one's doom (Liechty 2002, 86-87).

*Falling Man* begins on September 11, 2001, with lawyer Keith Neudecker in shock navigating his escape from Ground Zero just after the towers in which he worked have collapsed. The novel follows him and his estranged wife Lianne in later days and years, attending early and often to Lianne's weekly meetings with early-stage Alzheimer patients at an East Harlem community center. She guides this group as they write about their lives and share those writings with each other, an exercise in their self-preservation as they gradually yield to an illness that specifically compromises the memory and thoughtful reflection that typically constitute conscious personhood. However, when she asks the supervising therapist if she could increase the number of sessions, he advises against it, cautioning her, "From this point on, you understand, it's all about loss. We're dealing inevitably here with diminishing returns" (DeLillo 2007, 60). His warning forecasts the course of the disease as an irreversible decline; once set in motion, progress moves in only one debilitating direction. From the therapist's point of view, Lianne's attempts to forestall the inevitable, to collect the matter of these patients' lives before illness' dissipation, arrive already too late. Every moment forward in time cements a further remove from the selves she wants to preserve; no present effort she makes can recover what has been lost or alter the path of decay. In this way, an Alzheimer's prognosis serves as a pronouncement of fate, of the insurmountable, accumulating separations between past, present, and future selves that culminate in a single predictable and unavoidable conclusion.

When Lianne was younger, her father was diagnosed with Alzheimer's. He decided he "did not want to submit to the long course of senile dementia" and instead, shot himself with a rifle (DeLillo 2007, 40). Although "she tried to tell herself he'd done a brave thing [, it] was way too soon. There was time before the disease took solid hold but Jack was always respectful of nature's little fuckups and figured the deal was sealed" (DeLillo 2007, 41). In effect, the diagnosis forced him to confront the interconnections between contingency and destiny; although the nuances of the disease's trajectory might be open to chance and change, he knew the final result was certain and closed. Given this choice that was no choice, since he could not choose whether to die but only how, he opted for a swift and comparatively painless finish rather than the slow and dire struggle determined by illness. "Died by his own hand" are the words Lianne uses to think about this decision (DeLillo 2007, 218), words that come to her mind the second time she sees a performance artist re-enacting a businessman's jump from the World Trade Center towers (DeLillo 2007, 169). She has observed in her father and in the personated businessman a parallel dilemma: the choice that was no choice, a shared reaction to the sound of a door shutting behind them. Later in the novel, a few years after September 11, Lianne finds herself compulsively counting backward from one hundred in increments of seven, so even if her medical tests fail to indicate the onset of Alzheimer's, she can detect early symptoms of mental falter (DeLillo 2007, 187-188). She is living "in the spirit of what is ever impending" (DeLillo 2007, 212), looking for the signs that will reveal her fate. As an affliction with inherited risk factors, the seeds of Alzheimer's lurk in a past beyond her will and contour a future she cannot fully control. For Lianne, for her father, and for the falling man, terror looms not in the crevices of what could happen, carved as discernible turning points with apprehended implications, but behind the solid door of what will be, the consummation of turning points that have passed unrecognized and unavailable to cognizant contestation.

DeLillo presents a different relationship between contingency and destiny through the character Hammad's preparations to hijack an airplane on September 11. In the forensic scrutiny of that day's events, investigators had found last instructions for the hijackers in the luggage of Mohamed Atta, which included exhortations to prayer and assurances that God's will would determine the outcome of their actions (Lincoln 2003, 93-98). Apparently, predestination provided a rationale that the hijackers could internalize over time to cohere as a group against dehumanized enemies whose own fate was also divinely preordained (Stern 2003, 261). This rationale could also have mitigated and contained any fear the hijackers themselves might feel during a murderous and suicidal undertaking; there might be comfort, after all, in feeling aligned with what God has prescribed. In *Falling Man*, DeLillo draws on excerpts of these instructions to suggest what might be going through the mind of a hijacker meeting his last moments (DeLillo 2007, 238-239). However, the principle of predestination also underlies the years of psychological training Hammad undergoes in anticipation of his mission.

Hammad first appears in *Falling Man* in Hamburg, Germany prior to September 11 as someone who listens attentively to other young men from his mosque as they gather together to discuss religion and politics. Although he harbors some initial uncertainty about their views (DeLillo 2007, 79), he listens particularly to Amir—the vocal leader in Hamburg, later identified as Mohamed Atta—who preaches, "The time is coming, our truth, our shame, and each man becomes the other, and the other still another, and then there is no separation" (DeLillo 2007, 80). This desired dissolution of any separation between them poses an alternative solidarity to the separation they feel from the rest of the world, "the all-enfolding will of capital markets and foreign policies" (DeLillo 2007, 80). However, contrary to this group's professed values, Hammad at this time continues a sexual relationship with a woman, prompting Amir to ask, "What is the difference between you and all the others, outside our space?" (DeLillo 2007, 83). Hammad accepts the criticism, and commits more fully to a patent distinction, through values and through actions, between himself and his Hamburg confederates and everyone else: "there were rules now and he was determined to follow them. His life had structure. Things were clearly defined. He was becoming one of them now, learning to look like them and think like them. This was inseparable from jihad" (DeLillo 2007, 80). In effect, he has encountered a more conscious turning point than Alzheimer's has made available to Lianne, but the path of this jihad features its own specific design. Once committing to this path, Hammad's opportunities for free choice fade in favor of a conformity in purpose and practice that accomplishes this group's singularity, signals their faithfulness to God's plan, and readies them for their final destination.

By the time Hammad and his co-conspirators begin living in the United States, he has embraced finitude, his own and that of the world receding from him, which he feels in his body with the weight and certainty of a bomb vest (DeLillo 2007, 172). At times Hammad senses that this outcome actually could be averted. One day he observes a car of laughing young people and imagines leaving his life and entering theirs, a volitional act that could have re-routed the progress of events in a different direction (DeLillo 2007, 172). Yet Amir manages to draw Hammad back to the furrows of a divine plan that renders human mortality a welcome duty rather than a dreaded horror. Amir insists, "The end of our life is predetermined. We are carried toward that day from the minute we are born….This is not suicide in any meaning or interpretation of the word. It is only something long written. We are finding the way already chosen for us" (DeLillo 2007, 175). Once he falls completely into the slotted folds of fate, Hammad ceases questioning the reasons for and the limits of his mission. His remaining days become not about thinking but only about doing, only about fulfilling the preordained plot. Action accepted as destiny becomes its own justification; as DeLillo writes, "All he saw was shock and death. There is no purpose, this is the purpose" (DeLillo 2007, 177). Even if alternative choices in fact remain, they go unrecognized because they have become irrelevant. As impact between his plane and the building approaches, Hammad recalls piecemeal directives from the hijackers' last instructions that focus his attention on the performance of martyrdom in a vacuum of completion apart from the immediate horror of its intended effects.

While death haunts Lianne's future with the specter of prolonged suffering and anoints Hammad's everyday routines with divine purpose, for Keith, it is a near-fact of his past that invades his present. When Hammad had asked Amir about the people they would kill, Amir had responded, "The others exist only to the degree that they fill the role we have designed for them. This is their function as others" (DeLillo 2007, 176). Keith and his co-workers, his friends, are those "others," the human beings on the receiving end of the hijacked planes' impact who share with the hijackers the time, place, and consequences of their fate, but not their foresight. In a modern era idealizing personal autonomy, sociologist Anthony Giddens characterizes fateful moments as "times when events come together in such a way that an individual stands, as it were, at a crossroads in his existence" (Giddens 1991, 113). However, Keith lacks the prescience of the hijackers and therefore any opportunity for conscious self-determination. Nevertheless, as Giddens argues, "They are moments when...a decision made, or a specific course of action followed, has an irreversible quality" (Giddens 1991, 114). With or without awareness of implications, Keith's presence at work on September 11 placed him on an irreversible track, a struggle with the aftermath of his friends' gruesome deaths and his own chance survival.

Giddens also attributes to the conditions of modernity a preoccupation with circumstance. He asserts, "For where contingency is discovered, or manufactured, situations which seem closed and pre-defined can again look open...The capability to disturb the fixity of things, open up new pathways, and thereby colonise [sic] a segment of a novel future, is integral to modernity's unsettling character" (Giddens 1991, 133). A few years after September 11, Keith is spending days and weeks at a time in casinos playing poker. An extended quote from *Falling Man* illustrates how the game enables Keith to compulsively re-enact his accidental survival of September 11, each hand reckoning anew Keith's ability to influence the circumstances that affect him:

> The cards fell randomly, no assignable cause, but he remained the agent of free choice. Luck, chance, no one knew what these things were. These things were only assumed to affect events. He had a measure of calm, of calculated isolation, and there was a certain logic he might draw on...But the game had structure, guiding principles, sweet and easy interludes of dream logic when the player knows that the card he needs is the card that's sure to fall. Then, always, in the crucial instant ever repeated hand after hand, the choice of yes or no. Call or raise, call or fold, the little binary pulse located behind the eyes, the choice that reminds you who you are. It belonged to him, this yes or no. (DeLillo 2007, 211-212)

At the poker table, Keith could tempt fate and assert choice over and over again, an intentional engagement with the incidental alignments that fell to him without warning at the World Trade Center.

About mid-way through the novel, Lianne discusses with her dying mother a painting that reminds Lianne of the twin towers and her mother of something "coming out of another time entirely, another century." Despite the apparent disagreement, her mother asks, "It's all about mortality, isn't it?"

to which Lianne responds, "Being human." Her mother echoes immediately, "Being human, being mortal" (DeLillo 2007, 111). The hijackers distinguish themselves from their victims by claiming, "We are willing to die; they are not. This is our strength, to love death" (DeLillo 2007, 178). Such a claim nuances the choices each character makes when confronting mortality; such a claim conjures questions of what it means as a human being to recognize death, in others but also in one's self. In *Falling Man*, the plight of the trapped victim in freefall looms as the neverending human condition of terror and doom that mortality poses, and which forms the premise of meaningful human life.

## References

DeLillo, Don. 2007. *Falling Man*. New York: Scribner.

Frankl, Viktor E. 1959, 1962, 1984. *Man's search for meaning*. New York: Pocket Books.

Giddens, Anthony. 1991. *Modernity and self-identity: Self and society in the late modern age*. Stanford: Stanford Univ. Press.

Herman, Judith. 1992, 1997. *Trauma and recovery: The aftermath of violence—from domestic abuse to political terror*. New York: Basic Books.

Janoff-Bulman, Ronnie. 1992. *Shattered assumptions: Towards a new psychology of trauma*. New York: The Free Press.

Liechty, Daniel. 2002. "The assumptive world in the context of transference relationships: A Contribution to grief theory." In *Loss of the assumptive world: A theory of traumatic loss*. ed. Jeffrey Kauffman, 83-93. New York: Brunner-Routledge.

Lincoln, Bruce. 2003. *Holy terrors: Thinking about religion after September 11*. Chicago: Univ. of Chicago Press.

Stern, Jessica. 2003. *Terror in the name of God: Why religious militants kill*. New York: Harper Collins Publishers.

# TERROR AS TEXT: DELILLO'S *FALLING MAN* AND THE REPRESENTATION OF POKER AS TERROR

*Charly Norton*

This is an extract from a larger study that analyzes the representation of terror and crisis in Don DeLillo's novel *Falling Man*.[1] For this paper, the focus will be upon the representation of poker as terror. Firstly, the term *terror* will be defined. There will then be a brief exposition of the novel. The paper will go on to examine the role of sex in controlling terror and how that fails for the protagonist, Keith Neudecker. This will be followed by an analysis of the place and tasks of poker in relation to terror and through that, the life of Neudecker. The paper will conclude with Hannah Arendt's theories on terror and terrorism applied to the textual analysis, thus proving that in *Falling Man*, poker is terror and why this subjugation is necessary.

Before an analysis of terror can begin, it is necessary to examine the terminology and define what exactly terror is, or perhaps, has become. It is my argument that terror was once a subjective emotion, one that could be applied to any aspect of the mundane; for example, I am in terror when I visit the dentist. However, after 9/11, terror became an almost unspeakable term, something that is objective, a part of the global narrative and an ideology that subverts mundane by its connection to terrorism. It is now second nature, a mimetic discourse that evokes connotations of 9/11, the July 7th bombings in the UK, the Madrid bombings and the War on Terror. It is almost as though Terror and Terrorism have become synonyms for Islamic fundamentalism in recent years, and the long history of worldwide terrorism has been set aside, forgotten. For example, the recent terrorist attacks in Spain by the Basque separatist group ETA do not seem to have received the media coverage that they once would have earned, something to think about for another paper on another day perhaps.

The protagonist of the novel, Keith Neudecker, has his story told through his relationships with his wife, Lianne, and his lover, Florence Givens, and through his relationship with poker. It is a story of Neudecker's escape from the Twin Towers and of how one man deals with the terror developed from what Baudrillard called, "the mother of all events."[2] Although this paper focuses upon Neudecker and poker, there are many intertwining

---

1. Don DeLillo, *Falling Man* (London: Picador, 2007)
2. Jean Baudrillard, *The Spirit of Terrorism* (London: Verso, 2002), 1

narratives within the novel revolving around him, Lianne, their son, Justin, a terrorist named Hammad, Lianne's mother and her long term partner and a fictional performance artist known as the Falling Man, but actually named David Janiak. It would not be possible here to examine all of these stories, but there are occasions in analyzing Neudecker's relationship with poker that they cross paths.

Before I talk of poker, I will need to talk about sex. In his pre-9/11 life, Neudecker lived through the subjective terrors of being a father, being a husband, of providing for his family. He dealt with this terror by turning to sex which ultimately, through him having many lovers, led to the demise of his marriage. He had so many affairs that he loses track of names. At one point, he mentions a fling as "Nancy, what's-her-name."[3] After 9/11, he attempts to return to that escape, that context for beating his terror. He returns to his estranged wife and at first, he cannot see her as anything other than sex.

> It wasn't just those days and nights in bed. Sex was everywhere at first, in words, phrases, half gestures, the simplest intimation of altered space. She'd put down a book or magazine and a small pause settled around them. This was sex.[4]

This fails to undermine his terror; however, he tries again when he meets Florence Givens, another Twin Towers escapee, by returning her briefcase which he had collected inadvertently as he made his way out of the towers. They soon become lovers and it is through sex that Neudecker saves Florence's life.

> Then she said, "You saved my life. Don't you know that?"
> He sat back, looking at her.
> "I saved your briefcase." And waited for her to laugh.
> "I can't explain it but no, you saved my life. After what happened, so many gone, friends gone, people I worked with, I was nearly gone, nearly dead in another way. I couldn't see people, talk to people, go from here to there without forcing myself up off the chair. Then you walked in the door."[5]

Eventually, Neudecker realizes that he cannot save himself through the same means. He can no longer use sex to escape terror as he once did because this terror is too specific and objective, overpowering all other terror. He played that card when terror was a lesser concept, and now that terror is much more, sex, no matter whom it is with, cannot control

---

3. Don DeLillo, *Falling Man* (London: Picador, 2007), 19
4. Ibid. 7
5. Ibid. 108

it. Neudecker leaves Florence, and in doing so, he regains his own memory of the event.

There is more to why sex can no longer succeed as the solution to terror; Neudecker needs something that replicates terror, something that articulates it. There is an inability to deal with terror through an emotional relationship, so the individuals involved rationalize events to their best ability, resulting in language that is stunted and nonsensical.

After 9/11, Neudecker isolates himself from all the relationships he developed during the period in between his separation from his wife to when the second tower fell. Admittedly, many of these people, such as his friend Rumsey, die in the event, but he also cuts himself off from those that live. He rejoins his estranged family; creates a connection of sorts with Florence and begins working for a new, and yet replica company to that of his company in the World Trade Center. It is once these things are in place that terror begins to take over and he extricates himself from 'normal' society.

Prior to 9/11, he played poker once a week with his friends. There were six players including Neudecker.

> Three of the card players were called by last name only, Dockery, Rumsey, Hovanis, and two by first name, Demetrius and Keith. Terry Cheng was Terry Cheng.[6]

They played every Wednesday night and the games were held at Neudecker's home. They started with every variant of poker going, and through the development of "a joke in the name of tradition and self-discipline [that] became effective over time," they limit it to only five card stud.[7] They also outlawed food and only allowed dark liquor or Beck's Dark beer to be drunk at the table. Of these six, only Neudecker and Terry Cheng survived 9/11 intact.

After 9/11, Terry Cheng and Neudecker find they have no way of communication without poker.

> Keith talked to [Terry Cheng] on the telephone, twice, briefly after the planes. Then they stopped calling each other. There was nothing left, it seemed, to say about the others in the game, lost and injured, there was no comfortable subject they might comfortably summon. Poker was the one code they shared and that was over now.[8]

Their initial telephone calls and attempts at continuing their relationship cease because they have no language with which to communicate. Poker was

---

6. Ibid. 149
7. Ibid. 96
8. Ibid. 129

the language that these six spoke. It was their language, and without all six participants in the discourse, the language as it was could not survive. It had to evolve to become a different language, one that epitomized and frame worked terror.

Neudecker cannot forget his experience of 9/11, however he can control the terror that the event instigated. The terror that Neudecker experienced before 9/11 is nothing; it is incomparable to the terror that results from the event. It is now inextricably linked to 9/11, to terrorism as an ideology. He cannot experience it in the same way. DeLillo cannot write of it in the same way also. DeLillo cannot talk of terror as something communicable after 9/11 because it is so divergent from the terror that came before. Therefore, what occurs is a displacement of terror, a subjugation of this ideology into this game, this job, this everything. Every day life and experience can no longer accommodate the terror that Neudecker experiences, so he turns to what once gave him happiness and inclusiveness, boundaries and structure.

Neudecker begins a new relationship with poker; it becomes a professional career, a new life of terror and control. He has a want to watch poker games and as this starts, Lianne states that, "It wasn't poker, it was television."[9] She can see the beginning of his self-inflicted alienation, his descent into isolation. This is the first hint that poker is not just poker, it is also something Other. This poker is more than a Wednesday night social and is alien to Lianne and something that she cannot be a part of; it is specific to Neudecker as is Neudecker's relationship to 9/11 and his terror derived from his experience of the event.

He then plays in a tournament at his local casino where he makes the discovery that underpins the argument of this paper that in this text, poker is terror: "This was never over. That was the point. There was nothing outside the game but faded space."[10] Poker is the all-encompassing totality of Neudecker's terror. There is nothing outside of terror, nothing outside of poker. It is this feeling, the isolating and consuming nature of the game that attracts Neudecker to it. It is terror in that it is isolation, it is fear; it is everything. This first tournament introduces him to the potential of poker, to what his life could be; something other than an existence, in which terror is a distant yet constantly present threat.

It could be said that poker is in fact a system for controlling terror by replicating a set of rule-driven emotions through the playing of the game; however, if this were so, then Neudecker would have played a simulacrum game, a friendlier version with similar colleagues to replace those missing. This new poker is something different, this is not something about rules, not a simulation of the past; it is about a simulation of the present, a replica of terror. If it were the former, then the new career games would not involve

---

9. Ibid. 117
10. Ibid. 189

the isolation that they do. Poker is a sociable game by its very structure. Neudecker needs other players for him to be able to play; however, there is a paradox whereby Neudecker can be isolated within the game's necessary sociability. He does not need to communicate or engage with the other players, he can remain isolated and alienated by his, as well as their professional involvement in the game, a concept I will discuss in more detail shortly.

Neudecker ups his interest in poker; he travels to Las Vegas to play in the desert. After months of "mastering the game," he is "finally making money, quiet amounts that began to show consistency."[11] His life is poker, and he only returns to his previous existence as father and husband sporadically, distancing himself from that reality. He meets Terry Cheng at one such tournament. By this time, he has a sort of permanency at the poker table. They discuss poker, poker games, and those that they knew before 9/11. However, this conversation is fictional in more ways than the obvious. Neither party is fully involved in the discourse, there are two conversations coinciding as if by chance. It is made up, necessary for both men to share that they exist and are a part of the same moment in time and space, but all the same, not real in any true sense. The closest we come to true meaning in this discourse can be found in this extract about the hotel waterfall.

> "There's a game getting started in Los Angeles. Same thing, stud and draw. Younger crowd. Like early Christians in hiding. Think about it."
>
> "I don't know. I'm not sure I could survive a couple of nights in that kind of social arrangement."
>
> "I think it was Rumsey. The one man," Terry said, "who smoked the cigarettes."
>
> Keith stared into the waterfall, forty yards away. He realized he didn't know whether it was real or simulated. The flow was unruffled and the sound of the falling water might easily be a digital effect like the water fall itself. . . .
>
> "Did you ever look at that waterfall? Are you able to convince yourself you're looking at water, real water, and not some special effect?"
>
> "I don't think about it. It's not something we're supposed to think about," Terry said.[12]

They are discussing reality and their self-imposed separation from that term and all it stands for. What is not evident here is *why*. It could be said that Neudecker does not want the pseudo-relationship with Terry Cheng that is shown here, as he states, he likes the casino tournaments due to the "cru-

---

11. Ibid. 197
12. Ibid. 203-204

cial anonymity of these days and weeks, the mingling of countless lives that had no stories attached."[13] This is also evidence of his isolation within the constructed society of the tournament. He chooses to separate himself from the other players within the world of poker tournaments. For him, they are peripheral to his life of poker, to his want of what poker *is* to him; they are necessarily present, but at the same time, non-existent in his world.

The further Neudecker becomes lost in the terror that is poker, the more he loses his grip on what is real and what is not. He realizes that there are times when he's not sure if he's watching live action or slow-motion replays on the television screens in the sports book, but he is not bothered by this, as shown here.

> There were times, in the sports book, when he glanced at one of the screens and wasn't sure whether he was seeing a fragment of live action or of slow-motion replay. It was a lapse that should have unsettled him, an issue of basic brain function, one reality versus another, but it all seemed a matter of false distinctions, fast, slow, now, then, and he drank his beer and listened to the mingled sounds.[14] (2007: 211)

His only understanding of reality is seen through a haze of poker, a shield of terror.

Lianne states that, "There was one final thing, too self evident to need saying. She wanted to be safe in the world and he did not."[15] He wants a simulation of *un*safe rather than the reality that he faces after 9/11. There is something paradoxical in this relationship with the game. It is reminiscent of the photographs of smiling inmates at Auschwitz, or perhaps the image of the iconographic cross formed by the debris of the World Trade Center. It is in this conflict of good accommodating bad that we find Neudecker's relationship with poker. In the terror of poker, there is a safety, like on a rollercoaster, and this is a part of the terror of terror. There is a memory of happiness and structure in poker that stems from Neudecker's previous relationship with the game. These pseudo-ideals no longer exist, but are the foundation for this changed experience of poker and allow Neudecker to have a sense of control, a sense that he is in charge of the game and as such, the terror.

Lianne refers to the game as "Like a séance in hell," understanding that there is nothing outside of this game for Neudecker, but nor is there anything within it either; to her, it is almost like the dead not knowing that they are dead, and being lost within empty space.[16] Perhaps, unbeknownst to him, Neudecker is dead on the inside, as he cannot live this life without this isola-

---

13. Ibid. 204
14. Ibid. 211
15. Ibid. 216
16. Ibid. 216

tion and terror. His experience has left him in another, alternate world to that of his wife and child, to that of his friends. Even Terry Cheng, who is a part of the same poker society, is constricted by the rules and etiquette of that society. He too is alienated much like Neudecker, but separately. They are dead to one another as well as society in general and they are not truly aware that this is the situation.

Hannah Arendt was writing in the fifties, a time when Nazism and the Second World War were a very recent memory (arguably, much more catastrophic than 9/11) and during the Cold War when Russia versus the West could at any point have escalated into nuclear war. Terror and fear were a big deal; fifty years on, and her work is again relevant, particularly now as the War on Terror is an everyday narrative of society and terrorism is our constant. Her concepts and ideas can now be used as a theoretical construct to analyze Neudecker and his obsession with poker post-9/11, in this new era of terror.

Arendt states that:

> Terror becomes total when it becomes independent of all opposition: it rules supreme when nobody any longer stands in its way.[17]

Neudecker does not stand in the way of poker; he allows it to consume him and his life. He alienates himself from all that came before, the reality of 9/11, the fiction of his reinstated marriage, the terror of everyday things. He chooses to encompass poker and what it means to him. Terror becomes something so real that it cannot be mediated by language. It thus becomes something Other; it becomes poker, a representation of the emotion of terror, a replication of the intense feelings derived from terror. As Neudecker becomes inseparable from the game, he states that "He was fitting into something that was made to his shape. He was never more himself than in these rooms, with a dealer crying out a vacancy at table seventeen."[18] He is acknowledging the fact that he cannot live without poker, he cannot survive without the terror that poker invokes and articulates. He needs it as nourishment, to underpin his existence. He is nothing without terror, and that is what developed from his escape from the Twin Towers. He had to find something else to mediate this terror, to vocalise it as he could not, and poker, with its high stakes, isolation and adrenalin, fills that hole.

Towards the end of the novel, poker, and therefore terror, supersedes all else.

> There were no days or times except for the tournament schedule. He wasn't making enough money to justify this life on a practical basis.

---

17. Hannah Arendt 'Ideology and Terror: A Novel Form of Government' *The Review of Politics*, Vol. 15, No. 3 (Jul., 1953) 310
18. Don DeLillo, *Falling Man* (London: Picador, 2007), 225

> But there was no such need. There should have been, but wasn't and that was the point. The point was one of invalidation. Nothing else pertained. Only this had binding force.[19]

As Arendt states:

> It has been frequently observed that terror can rule absolutely only over men who are isolated against each other.[20]

There is nothing for Neudecker but isolation, but poker. He isolates himself from everything, he stops looking out for Terry Cheng at tournaments, determined that he does not even want this connection with his time before terror. His terror rules him, he can no longer see any thing else, any outside to poker, to terror and this is what holds him together, what binds him as it were. He cannot exist in what is subjectively deemed as normality. His relationship survives with his wife, but only as something Other itself, another life in another fictionality, something that he partakes in as duty, and little more. He is isolated from this relationship by terror, therefore, poker.

Arendt continues:

> Isolation may be the beginning of terror; it certainly is its most fertile ground; it always is its result.[21]

In conclusion, it is the poker, and thus, the terror that not only creates, but also *is* the isolation of Neudecker. He, and therefore DeLillo, cannot articulate terror, it is unspeakable as it is no longer something that is subjective, that is relational to his personal experience. Terror has become a loaded term, complicated and a signifier of something Other, it is no longer a word for a simple, base emotion. It is possible to write of 9/11, to try and fictionalize it, however, the language required to articulate terror post 9/11 just does not exist, and so, terror has to become something Other for it to be included subjectively.

Isolation may be the beginning of poker; it certainly is its most fertile ground; it always is its result.

Terror is found in, and actually becomes poker, so that it can be a part of the narrative, a part of the personal discourse present in the novel. Now that terror is a part of our own global narrative, inextricably linked with the ideology and events of terrorism, for it to be subjective, it has to be represented as something else. Terror has to embody another entity, and for Neudecker, poker is this entity.

---

19. Ibid. 230
20. Hannah Arendt 'Ideology and Terror: A Novel Form of Government' *The Review of Politics*, Vol. 15, No. 3 (Jul., 1953) 321.
21. Ibid. 322

**References**
Arendt, H 'Ideology and Terror: A Novel Form of Government' *The Review of Politics*, Vol. 15, No. 3. Jul., 1953.
Baudrillard, J *The Spirit of Terrorism*. London: Verso, 2002
DeLillo, D *Falling Man*. London: Picador, 2007.

# CREATIVE ACTION:
# LANGUAGE AND GENDER BEYOND TERROR

*Stephanie Barann*

**Introduction**

We cannot express ourselves in inequality. Terror is maintained by the consistent reinforcement of patterns of inequality. When our ability to create new forms is blocked, we are forced into narrower paths of expression resulting in alienation and despair. When we no longer feel a part of that which we are invariably a part of, we become stuck and our ability to generate different processes of growth is lost. This results in limited functioning and the fragmentation of our communities. Instead of adding to our significance, we substitute things such as power for real action.

A popular feminist text, *Les Guérillères* by Monique Wittig urges the reader to think about the consequences of creating narratives that place the subject exclusively within the masculine. *Les Guérillères* also shows us what it means to be sustainable artists: we can harvest the meaninglessness of gendered practices as raw material, as compost, to help sow seeds that are free to grow past hierarchy. What is available to us is never limited to what is prescribed for us through current institutions.

Gendering is unfit and outworn for the patterns our bodies are now urging us to experiment with especially now in the 21$^{st}$ century as we see new forms of family, work, and sexualities emerging to name just a few. Feminism and pragmatism provide us with the opportunity to create new forms while dismantling both conceptual obstacles and oppressive circumstances that are holding us back. Our language, identities, habits, feelings, and bodies have all been shaped by gender—and gender is a forced form. We know it is a forced form because the feeling is there in the situation that these categories, oppositions and dichotomies are wrong. The body responds to patterns that do not fit or represent its situation appropriately.

It is possible to use processes of creation to negotiate our freedom and to resist oppressive circumstances. I understand gender, as gender diversity, or "attention to the ways in which women and men, boys and girls are not homogenous groups but intersected by cultures, religions, ethnicities, social class, sexualities, bodies and so on" (Lorber 2005a, 360).

Pragmatism and feminist thought share a vast ground. Multiplicity, experimentalism and fallibility shape the mutable configuration of insights and approaches necessary to improve our conditions. Building communities that are constituted by expansive and self-correcting processes of growth and learning requires energy and responsibility. It is true that understanding and becoming familiar with the fundamental aspects of our bodies highlights and renews a sense of feeling alive that carries with it the opportunity to expand into healthier identities, but we still have to slough off and turn over outworn symbols and meanings.

## The Conventional Novel

There are interesting parallels between a conventional novel and the idea that identities are fixed and innate. A conventional novel, according to writer Shelley Jackson is "a safe ride": "It is designed to catch you up, propel you down its track, and pop you out at the other end with possibly a few new catchphrases in your pocket and a pleasant though vague sense of the scenery rushing by."[1] Chapters divide time. Transitional phrases, like habits, guide the reader through a fixed plot and the characters and protagonists follow a linear pattern. The idea that one's gender is pre-determined, fixed or even natural is analogous to the development of characters and events in such novels. The characters of traditional novels fall into categories and sequences nicely, producing meaning within a linear existence.

Monique Wittig's *Les Guérillères* is an example of a literary text that successfully works outside prescribed gender norms as well as conventional forms of the novel. It pushes the reader to think at the edge. The relationship the author creates with its reader is unconventional and restless. Therefore, Wittig helps free us from the ways in which linear thought patterns often censor our emotions and reinforce gender oppression. By breaking free from the limits of the traditional novel, Wittig is also breaking free from the limits of a language encoded within gender, thus actively creating room for degendered languages that does not censor or limit our emotional response. To take responsibility for the meanings we as individuals create through language is one way to meet with the meaninglessness of social order based on division and make it meaningful—an idea inspired by Linda Zerilli: "Wittig insists that individuals take responsibility for the meanings they produce, specifically for the oppressive meanings they ascribe to those persons denied their subjectivity by being defined as a woman" (1990, 156).

It is useless to open up *Les Guérillères* and look at the first page to search for sequence.[2] Chapters do not divide time; there are no plots, protagonists or characters. Aphoristic paragraphs leave spaces and random pages are dedicated to scattered lists of capitalized names with no surname. There are also

---

1. Fragment from a speech by Shelley Jackson at an MIT forum. For the full lecture entitled "Stitch Bitch" see http://web.mit.edu/comm-forum/papers/jackson.html.
2. A direction found "hidden" in the book. Close paraphrasing: "Even then it is useless to open it at the first page and search for any sequence" (Wittig 1969, 53).

pages dedicated to the symbol and visual of a large **O** said to represent the vulva ring, "the zero."[3]

Monique Wittig's *Les Guérillères* is not a safe ride designed or equipped with transitional phrases or fixed plots. Rather, *Les Guérillères* consists of descriptive fragments about Amazonian women engaged in struggles and rituals for dismantling all meaning that is oppressive or universalized as masculine. Wittig levels the playing field by using the neutral French pronoun "on," instead of the gendered identified masculine "ils" or feminine "elles" to describe the English "they." Similarly, Ursula LeGuin a feminist author, responds to her analysis of her science fiction novel *The Left Hand of Darkness* in "Is Gender Necessary Redux" by saying: "If I had realized how the pronouns I used shaped, directed, controlled my own thinking, I might have been 'cleverer' (1989, 306). LeGuin goes on in a footnote to say she do not want to "mangle" the English language by inventing a pronoun and used the generic form "He" to denote the characters of her novel. She says that at the time she did not feel it was important, but now considers it very important. Monique Wittig does realize the importance of how language and parts of language shape our thinking. It is interesting to note that both writers were writing in the same year. Wittig's work was published in 1969 and LeGuin talks about her "utter refusal" to use "invented pronouns" in 1968.

The idea that we cannot play with forms and change them because it would insult tradition is a stigma employed to discourage rebellion. Experimenting, inventing and mangling allow us to actively challenge traditional notions and what these notions reflect. Marthe Rosenfeld's, "Language and the Vision of Lesbian-Feminist Utopia in Wittig's Les Guérillères" discusses the traditional novel as: "…The sequential development of fictional characters and events towards a specific ending [that] reflects the culture's inherent determinism." (1981, 6-9). Discussing novels in this way is in no way meant to dismiss the traditional novel as an art form.

**The Life Expectancy of Symbolism and the Paradox of Degendering**

Symbols, relationships and poetic imagery take precedence over unified structures or underlying unities in *Les Guérillères*. Instead of main characters, overarching plots or dialogue there are songs, lists of rhythmic words and textured imagery of things such as herbs, plants, tears, the body and the sun. The importance of unity is not found in the text but in the movement of the text, in the progression or carrying forward of meaning.

---

3. See also: Jardine, Alice A. *Gynesis: Configurations of Women and Modernity*. Ithaca: Cornell University Press, 1986. Similar to Wittig, Jardine, through an exploration of French feminisms and psychoanalysis, illustrates women's move from subordination in phallocentric constructions to subjectivity in feminist and postmodern social constructions.

The zero or **O** or vulva ring represents a starting place for the women; "they" are engaged in war against all oppressive meanings: "They say that all these forms denote an outworn language. They say everything must begin over again. They say that a great wind is sweeping the earth. They say the sun is about to rise" (Wittig 1969, 66). One result of the text's unconventional style is that the reader must constantly be alert and attentive. To be attentive and alert to the meaning the author is creating, to the women's symbols and rituals being created by the text, is, in essence, to train oneself to be attentive to relationships of meaning encountered as individuals and as communities on a daily, interactional basis—not just in reading or being attentive to a text, but in things like how and when we do gender. It is clear that the women are engaged in a powerful battle against oppressive meanings, and as long as they are and they do not rest, neither does the reader or individual.

If we are engaged in a battle against oppressive meanings because categories such as woman, man, masculine and feminine do not represent the living body or the experienced body, it will be to our advantage to create meanings that are living or active. What sounds like a vague or utopian ideal is a very reasonable approach to creating meaning that is not oppressive. The point is we will be better equipped to represent our experiences if we do not become attached to old symbols—to outworn and dead symbols. The symbols that help us grow cannot nourish us continually; we must nourish them or weed them out—whatever the situation calls for—to make room for growth and generation (especially within feminist movements). Such approaches could and would only work in areas of the world or communities or cultures in which people do experience a satisfactory degree of equality or opportunity, as elaborated by Judith Lorber: "A movement to eradicate gender divisions would not be a universally useful form of feminist politics. It would be most effective where women have achieved a high measure of equality" (2001, 131).

For many feminists, reading a novel that universalizes a woman's experience in any way is a drawback: "Glorifying womanliness consolidates female unity and power, but when pushed to extremes, it comes dangerously close to reviving the cult of true womanhood and the ideology of separate spheres" (Lorber 1994, 355). *Les Guérillères* works notoriously close to the edge. For example, "they" take enormous pride in the fruitfulness of their genitalia (Wittig 1969, 31): "The women say that they expose their genitals so that the sun may be reflected therein as in a mirror. They say that they retain its brilliance. They say that the pubic hair is like a spider's web that captures the rays" (Wittig 1969, 19).

In battle many of the women don their breasts as if armor: "Some laugh out loud and manifest their aggressiveness by thrusting their bare breasts forward brutally" (Wittig 1969,100). There is also an essentialism spoken of in regard to men if one interprets the tail in the following passage as being a penis: "The women say that men put all their pride in their tail. They mock them, they say that the men would like a long tail but they would run away whining as soon as they stepped on it" (Wittig 1969,106).

Despite such readings, Wittig suggests that the point of the book was not to "feminize the world, but to make the categories of sex obsolete in language" (Zerilli 1990, 167). The symbols and the praise of genitalia and specifically the vulva are denounced once "they" have outgrown the principles that have guided them thus far: "They say it is not for them to exhaust their strength in symbols." Symbols lose their strength; symbols have a life expectancy, especially when they are a part of a movement requiring restlessness at the front lines and patience in the meantime. While most feminist movements will be guided by principles and symbols that may universalize or generalize women's experiences in some manner, it will be necessary to discard them along the way:

"They say they must now stop exalting the vulva. They say they must break the last bond that binds them to a dead culture" (Wittig 1969, 72). What is necessary at an earlier stage will not be necessary at a later stage. The symbols and signs we use and are not fixed or rigid, but are alive and changing.

### Creating Fuel for the Fire: Rituals of Meaning

Snakes, as symbols, are prominent throughout the book. The snakes can be understood as representing the necessary shedding of old skin and consequently as the shedding of universalized or binary languages in the current context. The Amazonian women overthrow categories and conceptions that do not represent the body as honorable or as living.

Snakes can also be understood to have negative religious undertones especially as interpreted by the Judeo-Christian traditions alluded to in the following passage:

> The women say with an oath, it was by a trick that he expelled you from the earthy paradise, cringing he insinuated himself next to you, he robbed you of that passion for knowledge of which it is written that it has the wings of the eagle, the eyes of the owl, the feet of the dragon. He has enslaved you by trickery, you who were great strong valiant…He has invented your history. But the time approaches when you shall crush the serpent under your heel, the time approaches when you can cry, erect, filled with ardour and courage, Paradise exists in the shadow of the sword. (Wittig 1969, 110-111)

Eventually the women are able to use the snake as a shield, crushing the serpent's old, deceitful meaning. The role of rituals, chanting, screaming, crying and stomping the earth—throwing oneself onto the ground and rolling around are means by which the women cleanse and purge their energies along the way. Rituals allow for controlled conflict. This purging allows the energy to flow as opposed to becoming stuck.

The women are marching together into another world, "blowing up everything that will not burn":

> Distaffs looms rollers shuttles combs point-paper presses cams cloth toiles
>
> cashmere twill calico crepe chintz satin spools of thread sewing machines
>
> typewriters reams of paper stenographers' pads ink-bottles knitting-needles ironing boards machine tools spinners bobbin-winders staplers assembly lines tweezers blow-lamps soldering-irons bonders yarn for braiding for twisting knitting machines cauldrons great wooden tubs stew-pans sauce pans plates stoves brooms of every bristle vacuum-cleaners washing machines brushes et cetera. (Wittig 1969, 73)

These items are burned by the women and as a result no longer resemble women or women's work but a ritual in which all these "things" become meaningless—they become raw materials for creating meaning. They become fuel for the fire.

If we think about Wittig as a crafter, artist and a writer, then we can say that the meaninglessness of gendered languages provides raw materials for seeking a new language and for making a break from the conventional novel.[4] This is exactly what the women of *Les Guérillères* are doing. By overthrowing outworn symbols or meanings, "they" are able to take responsibility for the changes they want to make and the forms they want to participate and create with.

There is no mistaking that *Les Guérillères* embodies violent tones. The women spit blood and carry off war casualties from the fields. The saliva on their tongues is "covered with the dust of long travels" (Wittig 1969, 77). There is immense anger: "They say that they sing with such utter fury that the movement that carries them forward is irresistible. They say that oppression engenders hate. They are heard on all sides crying hate hate" (Wittig 1969, 116). To say that the women are in a war against all meaning is never to be taken lightly:

> The women say, the language you speak poisons the glottis tongue palate lips. They say, the language you speak is made up of words

---

4. I do not wish to allude to the manner in which many have come to see the Earth as nothing but "raw material" to be turned into commodities and profit. This is a much richer notion I am evoking here and hope that is clear in the context of the argument.

> that are killing you. They say, the language you speak is made up of signs that rightly speaking designate what men have appropriated. Whatever they have not laid hands on, whatever they have not pounced on like many-eyed birds of prey, does not appear in the language you speak. (Wittig 1969, 114)

But, there are also tones of forgiveness and immense sorrow for what has or had to be done: "The women address the young men in these terms, now you understand that we have been fighting as much for you as for ourselves" (Wittig 1969, 127).

War is among the many symbols or meanings or representations that will be discarded. What is necessary at one time will not be necessary at another. War is used to overthrow dominant positions. This is significant because just as we must take responsibility for the meanings we create, we must take responsibility for the destruction we create as well. The women are not engaged in non-violent protests. The message becomes hard to tackle: "They say, War rally! They say, War, forward! They say that once they have arms in their hands they will not yield them. They say that they will shake the world like thunder and lightening" (Ibid., 120).

However, there is a sense that wars are evoked not as a means to establish dominance but as a means to establish integration and balance. The violent undertones of Wittig's work are among the many things that make this a radical piece. Wittig's text successfully challenges conventional forms of language, writing and the body to generate rich and imaginative opportunities for change. The text also speaks of something not easily digested or perhaps too grave to consider:

> They say that they are more barbarous than the most barbarous. Their armies grow hourly. Delegations go before them when they approach the towns. Together they sow disorder in the great cities, taking prisoners, putting to the sword all those who do not acknowledge their might. (Wittig 1969, 130)

To start from zero, to sweep over the earth, to start over again involves a great deal of destruction.

**Anarchy as Possibility**
Wittig's *Les Guérillères* is not a practical outline of lived situations where we can find opportunities to dismantle traditional gender roles or a vision of what society would look like without gender. Wittig's work is radical but no less effective than more practical approaches. The main argument that without creating new meanings and killing off old ones we will easily fall back into them is important to remember when going through the daily motions of

societal interactions. Legality in *Les Guérillères* is not left up to court systems or the recognition of politics, but to the oppressed.

Lorber writes that "degendering means freedom from gender restrictions, but it does not mean anarchy" (2005b, 176). It is true that anarchy is often thought of as a demeaning connotation of chaos but the women of *Les Guérillères* are radical, feminist anarchists who:

> foster disorder in all its forms. Confusion troubles violent debates disarray upsets disturbances incoherences irregularities divergences complications disagreements discords clashes polemics discussions contentions brawls disputes conflicts routs debacles cataclysms disturbances quarrels agitation turbulence conflagrations chaos anarchy. (Wittig 1969, 93)

I think Ursula LeGuin would take a position in favor of feminist anarchy: "To me the 'female principle' is, or at least historically has been, basically anarchic. It values order without constraint, rule by custom not force" (LeGuin 1989, 302).[5] Anarchy and revolution are two themes woven into feminist art and theory. Historically we find writers like Emma Goldman who in 1910 wrote a series of essays on anarchism. According to Goldman: "No real social change has ever come about without a revolution. People are either not familiar with their history, or they have not yet learned that revolution is but thought carried into action" (2002, 411). If we are talking about changing the very structures on which our societies are built, we are talking about revolutionary possibilities.

Similar to Wittig's work, Goldman's essay "Anarchism: What it Really Stands For," embodies this notion of weeding away, of actively finding what prevents harmonious blending of individual and society and doing away with it. Goldman sees anarchy as rooted in nature's forces to destroy "not healthful tissue but parasitic growths that feed on the life's essence of society. It is merely clearing the soil from weeds and sagebrush, that it may eventually bear healthy fruit" (Goldman 2002, 406). Goldman describes government and the state as something to be done away with altogether because at best it has imposed "one single mode of life upon all, without regard to individual and social variations and needs" (Goldman 2002, 410).

## Conclusion

Feminism, pragmatism, semiotics and anarchy provide us with the opportunity to create new forms while dismantling both conceptual obstacles and oppressive circumstances that are holding us back. They also provide support and stability, necessary ingredients for individuals to be able to guide

---

5. For more on the current feminist anarchist movement: http://www.anarcha.org/sallydarity/LynneFarrow.htm

their possibilities without a sense of fear and/or intimidation or force. We are not powerless or tragic in the face of enormous power structures; we just need a sense of community to support our notions.

Just as we must recognize gender as something necessary only to justify treating members of a community differently and never as the way things naturally are, it is also important to recognize the fear and shame created to dissuade people from change. This fear and shame is only necessary to justify keeping things the way some invested in the current institutions want them; not as they are.

If culture is, as Judith Lorber notes, "one of the main supports of the dominant gender ideology," then feminists, pragmatists, activists will have to challenge languages of cultures that produce and reinforce gender (2005b, 174). Conceptions of ourselves that either create distance or isolation from each other or our bodily knowledge create intense oppositions to our regenerative growth. Treating each other as if we are merely places in society or as if we are static and unchanging has terrible consequences.

Although I have focused primarily on gender inequalities, all this also applies to other societal inequalities such as race, ethnicity, age, religion and sexuality. It is possible to create genderless communities, indeed communities of full equality and equity. In fact, anarchist collectives like In Our Hearts located in Brooklyn, New York exemplify what this might look like. However, this is a project without closure because the building of community is an on-going process.

## References

Gendlin, Eugene T. 1981. *Focusing.* New York: Bantam Books.

LeGuin, Ursula. 1989. "Is gender necessary redux?" In: *Dancing at the edge of the World: Thoughts on words, women, places.* New York: Grove Press Inc.

Lindsay, Cecile. "Body/language: French feminist utopia." *The French Review*, Vol.60, No.1. (October, 1986): 46-55.

Lorber, Judith. 2005a. *Gender inequality: Feminist theories and politics.* 3rd ed. Los Angeles, Roxbury Publishing Company, 2005a.

——— 2005. *Breaking the bowls: Degendering and feminist change.* ed. Jeffrey C. Alexander. New York: W.W. Norton and Company, Inc.

Lorber, Judith, and Lisa Jean Moore. 2007. *Gendered bodies: Feminist perspectives.* Los Angeles: Roxbury Publishing Company.

——— "It's the 21st century—Do you know what gender you are?" In *An international feminist challenge to theory*, ed. Marcia Texler Segal and Vasilikie Demos, *Advances in Gender Research*, Vol. 5, Greenwich, CT: JAI Press, 2001: 119-137.

——— "Dismantling Noah's ark." In: *Paradoxes of gender.* New Haven, CT: Yale Univ. Press, 1994: 355-369.

Rosenfeld, Marthe. "Language and the Vision of a Lesbian-Feminist Utopia in Wittig's, 'Les Guérillères'." *Frontiers. A Journal of Women Studies*, 6, no.1/2 (1981), National Women's Studies Association: Selected Conference Proceedings, 1980. (Spring-Summer, 1981): 6-9.

Wittig, Monique. 1969. *Les Guérillères.* David Le Vay, trans. New York: Avon Books.

Zerilli, Linda. "The Trojan horse of universalism: Language as a war machine in the writings of Monique Wittig (in the Phantom Public Sphere)." *Social Text*: no. 25 (1990): 146-170.

# COSMOPOLITAN HOSPITALITY IN POST-9/11 POPULAR FICTION: ASAD'S *THE RELUCTANT FUNDAMENTALIST*

*Amy Hildreth*

Cosmopolitan hospitality is a specific theoretical offshoot of Jacques Derrida's philosophy. As a macro-level version of the hospitality described by both Derrida and Emmanuel Levinas, cosmopolitan hospitality is the understanding that the state usurps the position of "home" and citizens are enabled as "hosts." The control that characterizes any interaction of hospitality is now repurposed into a framework that alienates the Others—who may include minorities as well as immigrants or other "guests" of the state.[1] This delineation between host and guest is newly charged in a cosmopolitan framework, as actions play out in an international scene—with amplified repercussions.[2] Even if no violence occurs, the inhospitality of the guest as a "limit figure" in the state violates any attempt to reach absolute hospitality—a perfectly opening, benevolent state.[3]

I discuss this theory briefly because it allows me to construct a method in which to analyze the various ways absolute hospitality fails in a political framework. Literature provides a focus for my thoughts—I see Asad's work as an investigation into the fragile world of international relations, with all the complexities, mistaken assumptions, and problems of real dynamics transposed. Changez, the protagonist of *The Reluctant Fundamentalist*, exhibits a series of maneuvers in his attempt to diagnose his guest's proclivity to violence and to appear sufficiently threatening himself. This demonstrates Derrida's statement that hostility and hospitality are codependent ends of the same axis.[4]

Frame narratives are what they appear to be—they are stories that surround and contextualize the main material of a novel, play, or other literary work. In *The Reluctant Fundamentalist*, the frame narrative is a dinner where the unnamed American and Changez, the protagonist, share a meal. From the reader's perspective, the American appears to be coerced by Changez, but

---

1. Meyda Yegenoglu, "Liberal Multiculturalism and the Ethics of Hospitality in the Age of Globalization" (*Postmodern Culture* 13.2, 2003), 9.
2. Beat Jahn, ed. *Classical Theory in International Relations* (Cambridge: Cambridge University Press, 2006), 89.
3. Nick Mansfield, "War and Its Other: Between Bataille and Derrida" (*Theory and Event* 9.4, 2006), 3.
4. Jacques Derrida, "Hostipitality." Trans. Barry Stocker and Forbes Morlock (*Anglaki: Journal of Theoretical Humanities* 5.3, 2000), 13.

one cannot be sure. The American may be a secret agent attempting to kill our "reluctant fundamentalist" as he occasionally hints at a predilection for violence. However, Changez deftly controls the dynamics of the dinner, insisting with barely concealed hostility that the American stay for several courses so that he may hear of his experiences in the United States. Analysis of the frame narrative is in two parts: first, the content of some of the remarks directed to the American during the dinner and second, awareness of the dinner as a scene of hospitality.

The novel begins with the question, "excuse me, sir, may I be of assistance?" which demonstrates Changez's hospitality to an Other.[5] Changez places himself in the role of the host, by introducing himself and offering knowledge of Pakistan in peaceful openness. Or wait—is his hospitality truly peaceful? The man is identified as an American only due to Changez's sense of his "bearing," and his idea that this man must be "on a mission."[6] Furthermore, when the American moves his head in a "steady tick-tick-tick" motion, Changez informs his readers it was like "the behavior of an animal that has ventured too far from its lair and is now, in unfamiliar surroundings, uncertain whether it is predator or prey."[7] This description tells us far more about Changez's evaluation of the situation than who the American is. Later on, this becomes even more apparent. He explodes into the statement that: "four thousand years ago, we, the people of the Indus River basin had cities ... while the ancestors of those who would colonize America were illiterate barbarians."[8] By his use of the term "barbarian," Changez chooses alienating terminology to show his anger at the lost prestige of Pakistan within the contemporary cosmopolitan politics. As "barbarian" is rooted in the cosmopolitan condition of the Roman Empire, etymologically it establishes a historical context of otherness.

As colonization is the foundational history to international politics today, cosmopolitan hospitality cannot ignore its ethical repercussions. In Mansfield's analysis Derrida claims that if sovereignty is the "master narrative" of Western culture, which people are able to claim it and why are central concerns. Derrida remarks that "a nation state is never properly itself, its territory is never its own." In other words, any claim after colonization is not fully legitimate, as historically all territory changes hands either peacefully or through war. Therefore, "all culture" becomes colonial when national boundaries are recognized as historical constructions created through force rather than natural designations.[9] The home of cosmopolitan hospitality was always originally the territory of another. A previous violence has always occurred, which in turn reiterates Derrida's claim that peace is an exception.

---

5. Mohsin Hamid. *The Reluctant Fundamentalist*. (Orlando: Harcourt, 2007), 1.
6. Ibid., 2.
7. Ibid., 31.
8. Ibid., 34.
9. Mansfield, "War and Its Other," 3.

This theme is picked up again much later as Changez's exposure to American hegemony grows through his international work experience. He says:

> I reflected that I had always resented the manner in which America conducted itself in the world; your country's constant interference in the affairs of others was insufferable. Vietnam, Korea, the straits of Taiwan, the Middle East, and now Afghanistan: in each of the major conflicts and standoffs that ringed my mother continent of Asia, America played a central role. Moreover I knew ... that finance was a primary means by which the American empire exercised its power.[10]

As Changez progresses through his narrative, he is able to correctly diagnose the functional basis of American hegemony as based in financial power even more than military intervention. As Changez combines information with ideology, he becomes more of a threat within the text. One must only look to the historical circumstances of September 11 to see the correlation the author draws.

This change also signals a switch to a cosmopolitan viewpoint. Instead of constructing an argument based on generalities, he becomes specifically historical. He also moves from implicitly aligning himself with Pakistan to explicitly considering himself part of a national Other by removing his elite status and constructing his achievements as another example of colonialism. This is the difference between what David Bennet describes as the "additive model" of nationalism, where "non normative citizens" are added to the state and a traditional interpretation of cosmopolitan hospitality where a foreign ally, new citizen, or resident alien are still separated as Others due to their difference.[11]

In addition, Changez sees his home, the "mother continent" of Asia, as scarred by colonial violence and the twentieth century.[12] In cosmopolitan hospitality, peace is dependent on the guest's recognition of the host's primacy. This violation through military and/or economic intervention disrupts the fragile relationships and roles. Although humans have "communal possession of the earth's surface," this statement does not imply communal ownership. As Derrida argues in "Hostipitality," the conduct of seeing land either "ownerless territories" or belonging to those who are worthy of dispossession, entails a normative violation that effects all and "is felt everywhere."[13] In full circle, twentieth-century warfare and economic oppression reinvigorates wounds created by colonialism.

---

10. Hamid, *The Reluctant Fundamentalist*, 156.
11. Yegenoglu, "Liberal Multiculturalism," 10, 2.
12. Hamid, *The Reluctant Fundamentalist*, 156.
13. Derrida, "Hostipitality," 5.

As this original violence was taken primarily out of consideration for expanding and enhancing American economic might, Kant would agree with Changez's diagnosis of these actions. Kant explains, "out of all the factors that are responsible for war . . . the greed for money and wealth are the most important factor[s]."[14] In other words, greed is both the original cause of violence and its primary motivation.

Each country listed by Changez represents a specific example of hospitality. Each context had the possibility of two results: either success, which is defined by hospitality and peace or failure, hostility or war. In all occasions, Changez points out, the latter occurred. Each Asian country offered hospitality to the United States and, in every example, the United States responded with violence rather than respect. The scale of this pattern is the primary charge of Changez's accusation.

Changez, however, realizes that the United States is not always the only guilty party. At the end of the novel, he reveals that his own nation has violated the norms of cosmopolitan hospitality:

> I learned recently that one of them had been arrested for planning to assassinate a coordinator of your country's effort to deliver developmental assistance to our rural poor. I had no inside knowledge—which was all the more perverse for its alleged targeting of an agent of compassion—but I was certain that the boy in question had been implicated by mistake . . . . I must say, sir, you have adopted a decidedly unfriendly and accusatory tone. What precisely is it that you are trying to imply?[15]

In this excerpt, Changez attempts to distance himself from possible culpability by expressing his distaste. His acknowledgement, however, is brief. The act is described as "perverse" for "targeting an agent of compassion," but Changez quickly begins a defense of both himself and the boy accused of the act.[16] The citation of American intervention on the behalf of the need of Pakistani citizens, while not at first glance a criticism, contains another problematic assumption. David Chandler states that the foreign Other is victimized when unmet needs are used as justification for usurping another nation's jurisdiction. Fulfilling the moral need to give to the Other is an effective mask for states that as international actors have a many motivations for their actions. In addition, Candler makes the additional point that this offer of help is framed "in the context of unmet needs" and "the weaknesses and incapacity

---

14. Ashok Vohra, "Perpetual Peace and Just War" (Puri, Bentu and Heiko Sievers, eds. *Terror, Peace, and Universalism: Essays on the Philosophy of Immanuel Kant*. New Delhi: Oxford University Press, 2007), 32.
15. Hamid, *The Reluctant Fundamentalist*, 181.
16. Ibid, 181.

of the Other.""[17] In other words, philanthropy often masks a belief in the Other's irrationality and inability.[18] As *The Reluctant Fundamentalist* does not give this interpretation further material, the reader has no choice but to believe the perspective presented by Changez that the Americans' offer of "provisional assistance" may not be entirely ethical.

When the citizens of another state are seen as irrational and unable to decide what is best for them, violence has occurred. It does not matter whether physical aggression has taken place. Citizens under the control of an alternative government are, by implication, characterized as irrational because the legitimacy of their rule—the representation of their ability to form a functional government based on politics, which is defined as decision-making—is neither respected nor recognized. This may in extreme examples result in the dehumanization as Others are seen as "less than" the citizens. Historically, nationalist constructions of identity often use this as a rhetorical ploy.

Within Kant's philosophical framework, the terrorist is a rational actor who uses his or her personal comprehension of society to inform the decision to react in a violent manner. While Kant does not approve of either suicide or violence, as demonstrated from his investment in the ideology of perpetual peace, his original understanding of rationality necessitates justifying all individual action as inherently rational.[19] The decision to break laws or normative practices is a result of the same decision-making process that created these constructions originally.[20] Although no laws have been broken and, presumably, no act of terrorism has occurred, it is important to recognize that both the American and Changez act intentionally. Their actions at dinner are calculated, however subtle they may appear. In this vein, I will discuss the second aspect of the frame narrative: the dynamics of the dinner itself.

Considering the American makes no overt action aside from showing up in "the district of Old Anarkali" making repeated nervous gestures and wearing a firearm which, in a complete suspension of judgment, could be the action of any nervous Westerner in a hostile foreign country, it is important not to take Changez's account on full faith.[21] The American is confronted and then forced to remain at the dinner table, not exactly a representation of ideal hospitality.

At first, Changez notes that his guest prefers the seat against the wall and declines to remove his jacket.[22] Then he reassures his guest to not look "so

---

17. David Chandler, "The Other – Regarding Ethics of the 'Empire in Denial'" (Chandler, David and Volker Heins, eds. *Rethinking Ethical Foreign Policy: Pitfalls, Possibilities, and Paradoxes*. London: Routledge, 2007), 163.
18. Rick Parrish, *Violence Inevitable: The Play of Force and Respect in Derrida, Nietzche, Hobbes, and Berlin*. (Lanham: Lexington Books, 2006), 17.
19. Puri, *Terror, Peace, and Universalism*, 14, 24.
20. John Brenkman, "The Cultural Contradictions of Democracy," (*Ibid.*), 86 and Sujata Miri, "The Kantian Terrorist," (*Ibid.*), 24.
21. Hamid, *The Reluctant Fundamentalist*, 2.
22. Ibid., 2-3.

suspicious" as "nothing untoward will happen to you, not even a runny stomach" when the tea arrives. However, Changez does not refrain from specifying what his guest's fears must be for he says later, "after all, it is not as if it has been *poisoned*."[23] By alternatively reassuring his guest and naming the source of his fears, Changez foregrounds the possibility of covert violence in the guise of his friendship. When he explains later in the novel that the source of his scar is a wax burn, he cannot fail to thoughtfully consider "what sort of training camp could have given a fellow" such as himself such a mark.[24] By casting the mundane as possibly menacing, Changez subtly reminds the American that he may be lying.

The American's frustration is largely ignored, but occasionally readers are given a glimpse of his reaction to the dinner. For example, Changez notes that his "fingers are tearing the flesh of that kebab with considerable determination."[25] The American, however, is not always a complacent, fearful guest. By the end of the novel, his gestures suggest hostile intent even though Changez chooses to read his actions as peaceable. The concluding lines of the book are:

> I know you have found some of my views offensive; I hope you will not resist my attempt to shake you by the hand. But why are you reaching into your jacket, sir? I detect a glint of metal. Given that you and I are now bound by a certain intimacy, I trust it is from the holder of your business cards.[26]

The roles have reversed. The American is now insinuating violence even though his actions can be considered benign. Frighteningly, there is a small likelihood that his actions are peaceable. After all, the American has been held hostage at the table of hospitality. Over the course of his evening with Changez, he has been subjected to a story that accuses his native country of ethical violations, violence, and greed. In addition, he has been given subtle reminders that he is an easy target for retaliation.

The end of Changez's tale parallels the fears of Schederazade, the mythic narrator of *One Thousand and One Arabian Nights*. Schederazade, who must speak in order to entertain the sultan and forestall execution, is like Changez for both employ storytelling out of desperation. Although readers are not left with a definitive knowledge of either Changez's fate, the American's true identity or motivations, or even Changez's real involvement with Pakistani fundamentalists, the overarching narrative structure reminds the reader of uncertainty at every level.

---

23. Ibid., 11.
24. Ibid., 46.
25. Ibid., 123.
26. Ibid., 184.

*The Reluctant Fundamentalist* performs itself. The reader picks up the novel, consumes a tale of cosmopolitan hospitality fraught by double motives and the narrator's rapidly changing sense of self, and then reaches a conclusion that opens the possibility of either peace or violence. While peace could occur on an individual basis if the American accepts Changez's hand, the tone is that the American would need at least to understand how his country has violated international ethical norms and feel empathy for Changez in order for the confrontation to be diffused non-violently. This does not seem to be likely. The end of *The Reluctant Fundamentalist* radically re-opens possibility by offering hospitality with an uncertain knowledge of which outcome will emerge. The reader, unsettled by this openness, is taught the insecurity which characterizes both roles. Does the host truly offer what he appears to give? Is the Other willing to accept the host's jurisdiction peacefully? In this manner, Hamid's text performs the very concerns that shape decision-making in international politics.

## References

Chandler, David and Volker Heins, eds. *Rethinking Ethical Foreign Policy: Pitfalls, Possibilities, and Paradoxes*. London: Routledge, 2007.

Derrida, Jacques. "A Discussion with Jacques Derrida." *Theory & Event* 5.1: 2001.

Derrida, Jacques. "Hostipitality." Trans. Barry Stocker and Forbes Morlock. *Anglaki: Journal of Theoretical Humanities* 5.3 (Dec. 2000): 3-17.

Jahn, Beat, ed. *Classical Theory in International Relations*. Cambridge: Cambridge University Press, 2006.

Kant, Immanuel. Toward Perpetual Peace and Other Writings on Politics, Peace, and History. Ed. Pauline Kleingeld. Trans. David L. Colclasure. New Haven: Yale University Press, 2006.

Hamid, Mohsin. *The Reluctant Fundamentalist*. Orlando: Harcourt Inc., 2007.

Mansfield, Nick. "War and Its Other: Between Bataille and Derrida." *Theory & Event*. 9.4 (2006).

Parrish, Rick. *Violence Inevitable: The Play of Force and Respect in Derrida, Nietzsche, Hobbes and Berlin*. Lanham: Lexington Books, 2006.

Puri, Bentu and Heiko Sievers, eds. *Terror, Peace, and Universalism: Essays on the Philosophy of Immanuel Kant*. New Delhi: Oxford University Press, 2007.

Rothfield, Philip ed. *Kant After Derrida*. Manchester: Clinamen Press, 2003.

Yegenoglu, Meyda. "Liberal Multiculturalism and the Ethics of Hospitality in the Age of Globalization" *Postmodern Culture* 13.2 (2003): 5-28.

# STEREOTYPING ISLAM: A CRITICAL STUDY OF TERROR IN JOHN UPDIKE'S *TERRORIST*

*Amal Al-Leithy*

From among the debris and ashes of the ruined Twin Towers of the World Trade Center in 2001 rose a menacing ghost of terror, heralding starkly the start of a new era for Islam and Muslims. In that post 9/11 epoch, Muslims in general, and those living in North America in particular, suddenly found themselves in a thankless situation. Caught in the quandaries of xenophobia, waves of ethnic discrimination, and hysterical ethnocentric conditioning, they were surprisingly considered as the national enemy and regarded as the evil 'Other.'

Reports of Islamic suicide attacks against Western targets in different parts of the world unpredictably flooded the media: aggressive acts carried out, terrorists thwarted before they could attack; assaults gone amiss; Muslims charged and convicted here and there. Even those living in the West were caught thrashing out against the civilized world they had often been part of. Suddenly, Islam was considered the instigator of terror and regarded as a religion that is at war with life and civilization itself.

On the Christian Broadcasting Network's *The 700 Club*, for instance, host Pat Robertson expressed a great concern that Americans need to "wake up" to the "danger" that Islam presents and wondered: "Whoever heard of such a bloody, bloody, brutal type of religion? But that's what it is. It is not a religion of peace."

Though some critics believe that up till now no writer could handle the post 9/11 trauma in the proper sense, certain works that address this tragedy drew considerable attention to themselves. In a series of subterranean episodes, John Updike delves into the inner workings of the mind of a young would-be terrorist in his novel *Terrorist*, focusing all the while on the condemned concepts of Jihad and martyrdom in Islam that lead to self-sacrifice. The novel tries to advance the thesis that the post-Soviet foreign devil is Islam, a religion whose physical immediacy and challenge to the West seems as diabolical and brutal now as it has never been before.

This paper aims to give a new insight into the process of terror-generation and shed light on the ways a work of literature can propagate a stereotyped image of a religion or a people. This analysis will hopefully lead to a better understanding of the 'Other' and a healthier appreciation of heterogeneity which characterizes most contemporary societies. It also seeks to encourage contemporary men of letters to assume their ethical and historical responsibility of enlightenment and education and objectively base their judgments on Islam on authentic sources and deep-rooted beliefs cherished by the majority of Muslims.

In *Terrorist*, Updike explores the theme of religious hysteria and disillusionment by linking Islamic fervor to an alleged heritage of violence through the story of a Muslim teenage student living in a run-down town in New Jersey. With Updike's considerable élan, overpowering style and yet sad finale, he depicts a moving picture of a quiet, polite and sensitive boy who finds his identity in a strong belief in Allah and an uncompromising faith. But, this protagonist, Ahmad Ashmawy, the son of a morally lax Irish-American mother and an Egyptian father, who left him when he was still three, does not venture into the world or plan for his education, or get into a serious relationship. He spends most of his time with a dubious imam at a small mosque whom he has many suspicions about and who exercises a huge effect on his decisions and life choices. From the very first line of the novel, Updike makes this paradox between Ahmad's faith and the godless life around him crystal clear: "Devils, Ahmad thinks. These devils seek to take away my God. All day long at Central High School, girls sway and sneer and expose their soft bodies and alluring hair" (Updike 3).

At school Ahmad's guidance counselor, Jack, is a depressed 63-year-old Jew who has a gruesomely obese wife and who only thinks about his approaching death. "The struggle then, the real agon [sic.], will be between Ahmad, with his merciless but glorious God, and Jack with his secular humanism and burned-out hopes" (Caldwell). Following the advice of his imam, Ahmad applies for a vocational truck driving license despite his high grades at school which would otherwise allow him to join college. Dissatisfied with the mediocrity of life around him, he is totally cut off from other people, even Muslim students, and has almost no one to know except for his sensuous classmate Joryleen Grant who sings in the choir of the church and is later revealed as whoring around for her boyfriend. Among this tumult of life and the merciless materialism of society, Ahmad's "chief solace," says Gail Caldwell, "is the Koran, however mangled by his teachers [sic.] into a text of cruelty and religious vengeance. So, Ahmad is a disaster waiting to happen."

He soon gets a job as a truck driver at a Lebanese furniture store and starts his real venture into the world. But, his unsavory Yemeni teacher, Sheikh Rashid, harangues him about the depravity of the west and the emptiness of the American culture: "Did you not discover that the world, in its American portion, emits a stench of waste and greed, of sensuality and futility?" (Updike 109). He is quickly thrust into the real test of his belief when his imam offers him the chance of executing a suicide bombing and becoming a martyr, which he surprisingly quickly accepts.

However, Updike intended to portray Ahmad with empathy as he says: "I think there are enough people complaining about the Arab menace that I can be allowed to try to show this young man as sympathetically as I can. He's my hero. I tried to understand him and to dramatize his world. Besides, it's not just young Muslims who are killing themselves. We have all these American high school students, steeped in Protestantism and Judaism, who bring guns to school and shoot up the cafeteria knowing they are going to die at the end of this rush." (Interview with Mudge). But Ahmad comes out as a completely vapid creation, lacking plausibility, humor and credibility and even understanding of what he wants and why he wants it. His faith in Islam is condemned as the source of terror and the number-one motivation for killing thousands. The readers are left without a clue as to why Ahmad offers his life so easily 'in the path of Allah,' and accepts to bomb himself in a tunnel, except for the conclusion that it is that faith that renders its followers so.

Unconsciously, Updike falls into the trap of stereotype. Stereotypes in general involve generalizations about the 'typical' characteristics of members of the same group. In *The Open Encyclopedia*, Zeeshan Muhammad defines stereotype in modern usage as "an oversimplified mental picture of some group of people who are sharing a certain characteristic (or *stereotypical*) qualities. The term is thus often used in a negative sense, with stereotypes being seen by many as illogical yet deeply held-beliefs that can only be changed through education."

While Updike is said by some critics and reviewers of the novel to have done his homework by studying the Islamic culture and the Qur'an thoroughly, it is obvious that he didn't give himself the necessary time to do so. "The novel features many quotations from the Koran in Arabic, with all the scholarly paraphernalia of diacritical marks, etc. But the end result is that Updike is unable to cut his brown characters loose from texts, scriptures and ideologies" (Ghosh). The text buzzes with many verses from the Qur'an, which are quoted to emphasize a point or convince the protagonist, but all of them reveal a desperate need to get more knowledge of this book and study it in more detail. Only the verses that tackle the issues of Jihad and martyrdom are quoted in the text. Moreover, most of these verses are de-contextualized to the effect that they all lead to one notion: Islam is a religion that preaches violence and turns the gentle soul of the hero who changes his route so as not to squash a bug, into a blood-sucking monster. It also shows how stereotyping is an ongoing process that secures that once the stereotype is activated, the traits equated with it easily come to mind. Although the same book, the Qur'an, says: "If one slew a person, it would be as if he slew the whole people, and if one saves the life of a person, it would be as if he saved the whole people" (Qur'an, 5:32) and says: "And God calls to the home of peace" (Qur'an 10:25). So, the author needs clearly to go back to the interpretations of these verses and study the comprehensive philosophy of Islam about war.

In his famous study *Orientalism*, Edward Said explains the process of stereotyping Islam and Muslim culture by depicting them in contemporary literature as "irrational, menacing, untrustworthy, anti-Western, dishonest, and—perhaps most importantly, prototypical" (207). The Muslim is seen as separate, abnormal, backward and lustful. The faith itself became accused of having a propensity towards tyranny and violence, and a tendency toward backlash against feminism in the male-dominated patriarchy it dictates. Its values are de-contextualized and judged in terms of western assumptions, which are—by nature—different. But it is worthy to note that the prophet of Islam, whom Ahmad is supposed to be following, never waged a war during the first phase of Islam's life in the city of Mecca, and was ordered to defend himself only in the second phase in the city of Medina. Even the early Muslims who stayed behind in Mecca never received an order from him to wreak havoc or carry out any act of violence against those who launched wars against him. The total picture in Islam dictates that war is only allowed for fighting oppression or for self-defense. Whether this religion was hijacked by people like Sheikh Rashid and Ahmad Ashmawy or not, the ethical responsibility of literature is to enlighten and enrich human experience by exposing the readers to the reality of the faith instead of helping produce terror by creating such stereotypes.

It follows that stereotypes of an object or a group often come from either cognitive sources or social categorization or the presupposed discrepancy between ingroup and outgroup characteristics, or 'us' versus 'them.' These factors do not give a chance to society members to learn about individual idiosyncrasies of outgroup members. So, a novel like *Terrorist* could rely in parts on cognitive sources, or immerse in social categorization that led to the fact that it supported in a way or another the sense of ominous fear in the reader's mind whenever the word 'Islam' is mentioned.

The depiction of the last moments of Ahmad's life before he carries on the terrorist attack came out lifeless and dull and added almost nothing to the reader's experience of terrorists. "Unfortunately," holds Michiko Kakutani, "the would-be terrorist in this novel turns out to be a completely unbelievable individual: more robot than human being and such a cliché that the reader cannot help suspecting that Mr. Updike found the idea of such a person so incomprehensible that he at some point abandoned any earnest attempt to depict his inner life and settled instead for giving us a static, one-dimensional stereotype."

Such kinds of depiction results in fostering a sense of prejudice against the stereotyped object, in this case Muslims. Thus, readers develop a tendency to organize the information they receive about the stereotype. The information that is "consistent with [their] prejudices (rather than inconsistent)," states Swim, "tends to receive more attention, is rehearsed more frequently, is more likely to be remembered . . . Prejudice often involves stereotypes, suggesting that all members of the group behave in certain ways and have certain characteristics" (Swim et al. 199).

A major factor, which contributes to Islamic stereotyping in the West, is due to the media's selection of some words that are used to characterize this faith such as: Islamic terrorist, Islamic fundamentalism, Islamic extremism, radical Islam, Islamic Jihadists, etc. It might sound odd to note that these words are misleading and mainly anti-Islamic. A real Muslim who is committed to the book of the Qur'an is not accepted as a Muslim unless he is at peace with everyone and everything around him, even with lesser creations like animals and insects (just as Ahmad is shown in the first chapter of the novel). If a Muslim exercises his power over others, he is condemned by the Qur'an and by the prophet of Islam who said: "The powerful person is not the one who bullies others, but rather the one who can control his anger," and also said: "The dearest of you to me and the closest of you to me on the Day of Judgment will be those who have the best morals" (Khan, 759).

Although Ahmad does not succeed in carrying out his mission, his mere acceptance of it leaves unanswerable questions in the readers' minds. Why he readily accepted to be a suicide bomber and why he unbelievably quickly rebelled against the very society in which he was born and raised and against his delicate nature that Updike now and then stresses is not clear in the novel.

*Jihad*, this fearful word that was manipulated by media reporters and writers to indicate 'holy war' means to struggle, and not necessarily military-wise. Jihad is so often apparent in the news and post-9/11 literature because the media thinks it is Islam's justification for war and violence. The word is stereotyped though it has many meanings. To give charity in Islam is a kind of Jihad as one struggles with his love to his fortune, and to fast is Jihad as one struggles with his natural desire to eat and to seek education is Jihad as one struggles with his laziness, etc. Since stereotypes are selective filters, supporting data is hoarded and any information to the contrary is ignored. So, Updike's real homework, like all other men of letters, is to shed light on the variations that could be found under the stereotype to achieve the goal of edifying readers and supporting efforts exerted to face terror. Because of the ongoing process of stereotyping in this novel and other works of literature produced in the aftermath of the 9/11 tragic events, readers are expected to attend more to stereotype-consistent information which activates attempts to confirm it. Vankin confirms that this process of stereotyping "affects social judgments about others, particularly minorities, and changes expectations regarding the probability of certain behaviors in the stereotyped group or target." So, one way to shape stereotypes into effective coping strategies is to bombard their devotees with 'exceptions,' contexts, and alternative reasoning and to educate readers and viewers about the 'other' without suspicion or anticipation.

## References

Caldwell, Gail. "Gods and monsters: *Terrorist*," *The Boston Globe*. June 4, 2006. From http://www.boston.com/ae/books/articles/2006/06/04/gods_and_monsters/

Ferguson, Tamara J. "Perceiving groups: Prejudice, stereotyping and discrimination." http://www.usu.edu/psy3510/prejudice.html

Findley, Paul. 2001. *Silent no more: Confronting America's false images of Islam.* Maryland: International Graphics.

Ghosh, Amitav. "John Updike's *Terrorist*." *The Washington Post*. 2006. http://www.amazon.com/Terrorist-John-Updike/dp/0307264653

Kakutani, Michiko. "A weak plot and cardboard cutouts make *Terrorist* implode," *New York Times* News Service. June 11, 2006. 19. http://www.taipeitimes.com/News/feat/archives/2006/06/11/2003313015/print

Muhammad, Zeeshan. 2003-2004. *The Open Encyclopedia*. http://open-encyclopedia.com/Stereotype

Muhammad, the Prophet. (His Traditions Translated) Sahih Bukhari. *Trans. M. Muhsin Khan* University of Southern California *Vo. 4, Book 56, Number 759*.

Said, Edward. 1978. *Orientalism*. New York: Random House.

―――. 1997. *Covering Islam: How the media and the experts determine how we see the rest of the world.* New York: Random House Inc.

Shiffrin, R. M. and Dumais, S. T. 1981. "The development of automatism." In *Cognitive skills and their acquisition*. ed. J. R.. Hiusdale, N J: Erlbaum, 111-140.

Swim, J. K. 1995. "Sexism and racism: Old-fashioned and modern prejudices." *Journal of Personality and Social Psychology*, 68: 199-214.

Robertson, Pat. 2008. "Media matters for America." Apr. 9, 2008. http://mediamatters.org/items/200804090011

Updike, John. 2006. *Terrorist*. New York: Alfred A. Knopf.

―――. "Holy terror: Updike goes inside the mind of a Muslim teen," (Interview) Alden Mudge. Book Page. ProMotion, Inc. <http://bookpage.com/0606bp/john_updike.html>

Vankin, Sam. *The merits of stereotype*. http://samvak.tripod.com/ stereotype .html

# THE TYRANNIZING ORDER OF MENTAL HEALTH PROMOTION

*Cindy Vander Meulen*

As a mental health counsellor in secondary schools I increasingly have become concerned with the current approach taken to mental health promotion in secondary schools and in particular by the theoretical framing of promotion strategies. As I start to think about better practices for health promotion I begin by raising questions about the effects of existing practices, how these practices direct the location of mental health problems thereby influencing their solutions, their moral implications and ultimately what is required to shift the theoretical framework such that I am less concerned about participating within the practices that it shapes.[1]

Mental health promotion strategies in secondary schools across Ontario, following "best practice" guidelines set out by the Centre for Addiction and Mental Health (2003)[2], presuppose the mental health profession's concepts and practices that are anchored in epistemological standards and research. This research transforms mental health into a medical problem; one that is treatable according to a disease model of human development, behaviour and functioning. Made apprehensive by now well-established suspicions and critiques of empiricism, three issues are most disquieting for me as a mental health professional when I notice wherein the technologies of mental health promotion are entrenched: 1.) Epistemological research glosses over the complexities of socio-historical, political and cultural contexts favouring in-

---

[1]. I wish to acknowledge the helpful comments of Anita Davies, Majid Malekan, Skip Hills, and especially Magda Lewis on earlier drafts of this paper.

[2]. According to the Centre for Addiction and Mental Health (2003), mental health promotion programs in schools ought to follow best practice guidelines that address and modify risk and protective factors that indicate possible mental health concerns; intervene in multiple settings; focus on skill building, empowerment, self-efficacy, individual resilience, and respect; train non-professional to establish caring and trusting relationships; involve multiple stakeholders; provide comprehensive support systems that focus on peer and parent-child relations; adopt multiple interventions; address opportunities for organizational change, policy development and advocacy; demonstrate a long-term commitment to program planning, development and evaluation; and finally, ensure that information and services provided are culturally appropriate, equitable, and holistic (Retrieved April 29, 2008, from http://www.camh.net/About_CAMH_Health_Promotion).

stead universal claims about individual ills. 2.) Individualizing mental health problems disguises socio-political problems that contribute to ill health. 3.) Medicalizing individual suffering subsequently prevents a.) noticing how our socio-political contexts cause problems and b.) conceptualizing about how to improve this problematic context for youth. I am left wondering about the oppressive consequences in mental health of overlooking the context of individual suffering, not addressing social arrangements and practices that cause suffering and, perhaps most important, what moral questions this leaves for a profession in the practice of assisting youth in their moral development and mental health.

Ultimately I am left calling for a conceivable alternative to conventional mental health promotion projects. This alternative should bring to light the relationships between social arrangements, structures, practices and individuals, the impact of these structures that cause suffering to youth, and the implication for mobilizing change that considers the interactions of people as having inextricable symbiotic connections to their social environments.

**Talking about Mental Illness within the Discourse of Epistemology**
When I first thought about actively promoting mental health in secondary schools I had been a counsellor for about five years and specifically a mental health counsellor in high schools for an additional one year. Also I was undertaking doctoral studies on the subject and had some theoretical considerations for what I wanted to do and how I thought it would be best to do it.[3] I had in mind workshops that would proceed to determine the "mental health"

---

3. Foucault (1972) appeals to alternative "knowledges" and prefers situated and local narratives which do not depend on "established regimes of thought" or a hierarchy of knowledge types. His 'insurrection of subjugated knowledges" rehabilitates local discourses, the first-hand participant in local struggles. Voice and speech, in feminist practice allow for one's self definition or construction of self; or, as Butler (1997) informs us it connotes an organic form of communication which signals the existence of the body in time and space, that is, in a socio-historical context. Foucault's and Butler's theories would turn to the everyday practices and lives of youth in creating and disseminating knowledge. Feminist standpoint theory generally, and Kathi Weeks' (2004) project of totality specifically, locates connections between people's everyday lives and a larger framework of social structures that involves a "methodological mandate" of relating and connecting, situating and contextualizing (p. 184). An amalgamation of these theorists informed my idea of how to promote mental health for youth: turn to them to express their experiences and allow their expression to provide the groundwork for future practices and focused promotion strategies. I had suspected, based on my experiences in counselling sessions with youth by that time, that they collectively would introduce varied manifestations of their subordination experiences, experiences differentiated by social class, sexual preferences, gender, race, or other like difference (which also comments on who is being "identified" and referred for "mental health counselling").

issues faced by youth at school, as defined by them through their stated local and contextual experiences. I would want to know how they perceive these experiences to affect their "mental health" (language that would no doubt direct their thinking but that was something that I was prepared to acknowledge and address, along with my status as a "mental health professional") and we would determine courses of action and perhaps even policy formation, as defined by youth, that would promote their well-being. I was pleased with myself. This inquiry would recognize the interplay between stage, gender and socio-cultural contexts for youth, their identity formation and general sense of well-being.

When I first inquired about promoting mental health in secondary schools I was directed by mental health professionals, school administrators, school counsellors, teachers, and even a few concerned parents to the Centre for Addiction and Mental Health's "all ready"[4] School Mental Health Program (2003), in particular to their promotion program known as Talking About Mental Illness (TAMI). This program focuses on defining, recognizing, and screening for risk factors and symptoms of serious mental illnesses, reducing the stigma attached to mental illness, disseminating information and resources on mental health and guides on how to make referrals and seek intervention and treatment for those individuals suffering from mental illnesses. I noticed that this approach to mental health promotion in schools has several taken for granted assumptions and underlying presuppositions: mental health sits within a disease model of interpretation and understanding; it is categorized into clusters of symptoms and syndromes that are readily identifiable; it is an individual problem; mental health promotion strategies endeavour to identify individuals with mental illnesses and direct those unwell individuals to mental health professionals; it is the responsibility of the professionals to treat mental health; treatment is understood as re-enfolding individuals into a social norm through psychological evaluation and management.

It is clear that biomedical explanations and understandings of mental illness dominate in scholarly, scientific, and psychotherapeutic worldviews and practices and these practices are well-established in our mental health profession; they also form the starting point for mental health promotion. The National Alliance for the Mentally Ill (NAMI) asserts, in pamphlets widely disseminated in secondary schools, that mental illnesses are disorders of the brain that disrupt a person's thinking, feeling, moods, and ability to

---

4. The phrase "always already" is common in philosophical discourse, and most notably popularized by Heidegger (1962). I use the term "already" to show that mental health promotion is conceived as being a certain way and as having been that way when I arrived at it or was directed to it; further, there is a sense that it perhaps should not be or cannot be otherwise (as implied by my having been directed there when offering to undertake mental health promotion).

relate to others. I could not but surmise, by virtue of the pervasive thinking about mental illnesses, that perhaps the only way that these problems can be recognized as "real", and perhaps be worthy of research, funding, and OHIP coverage, is if they are secured in the language of bio-physiology within an epistemological frame.[5] What I find disconcerting about this grounding of major psychiatric syndromes within medical confines is that it specifies mental illnesses as finite, predictable and consistent across contexts and time. Individuals, by extension, are conceived as being self-motivated, healthy or pathological, self-fulfilled or alienated and can be isolated, observed, diagnosed, and "improved" or "treated".

I wanted instead to engage the contextual complexity of youth suffering that is typically individualized and pathologized within an epistemic discourse. To begin I would need to acknowledge the contingency of scientific knowledge and its political, cultural and technological expressions. Thus, I sought to contest the discourse of expertise that informs current mental health theory and practice. To this end I needed to examine critically the beliefs that mental health research produces objective scientific "findings" and maintains that what is available to perception and study is an orderly system that is potentially the same for everyone. Further, I needed to challenge the view that scientific investigation will ultimately secure universal agreement about a thing's nature, predictability and control by objectively observing and measuring it using reliable and standardized techniques. Of course, my methodological leanings found good company in a wealth of scholarship pointing out how expert narratives surrounding psychiatric illness are reproduced through isolating ostensibly 'natural' elements from 'social' ones;. ... [and how] we have inherited the legacy of the eighteenth century when madness became an 'object', a thing-in-itself discoverable by dispassionate positivist inquiry" (Fee, 2000, p. 2).

It became clear to me that mental illness being an object for "positivist inquiry" has been passed on through dominant discourses and remains today as a methodology driven understanding of mental health, why ill health occurs and the reasons behind the way people act, that primarily focuses on biology for its etiology. This focus is arguably a direct result of the assumption that biomedical factors can be observed and measured in the most objective manner. Mental health is thus conceptualized in terms of physical processes (hor-

---

5. In a critical analysis of the epistemological assumptions of science and social science, Sandra Harding (1987) has defined epistemology as a theory of knowledge which sets out who may legitimately be deemed 'knower', what requirements information or beliefs must meet in order to be legitimated as 'knowledge', and what kinds of 'facts may be known' as 'real facts'. Epistemology therefore determines both methodology - the 'theory and analysis of how research does or should proceed' (Harding, 1987, p. 3) - and research methods - the techniques deemed legitimate or appropriate for gathering evidence or information.

mones, neurotransmitters, synaptic events, ovarian function, etc.) observable within the individual, wherein the problem may be located, following a model of cause and effect. While this frame of research reifies notions of mental health problems as discrete, consistent and homogeneous clinical units with identifiable symptoms; it ultimately facilitates specific arrangements of mental health disorders as "known" in the *Diagnostic and Statistical Manual (DSM)*.

When we talk about mental health promotion we invoke the tradition and interpretive frame of the mental health profession to define what we are talking about. This definition directs our inquiry into how to promote mental health in schools by outlining the strictures within which our inquiry may advance. It affects what we recognize as a mental health problem, how we articulate that problem and the question of what to do about it. We invite the profession's gatekeepers, the American Psychiatric Association, the publishing organization for the *DSM*, to bestow upon us consensus definitions of mental health problems, categorizations of deviance, and treatments according to an a-socio-historical medical model.[6] Yet the definitions, categories and cures, and the models of health and deviance that have been institutionalized in conventional mental health research and practice have not gone unquestioned. A range of critics such as anti-psychiatrists, poststructuralists, feminists and critical theorists from various ideological camps have subjected the profession to critique such that much of what has been taken for granted in mental health has been problematized.[7]

The limitations of epistemological methodology have been well documented (Gadamer, 1989; Harding, 1987; Harre and Secord, 1972; Henriques et

---

6. Philosopher Hans-Georg Gadamer warns that it is "the tyranny of hidden prejudices that make us deaf to what speaks to us in tradition" (1989, p. 270). The conceptions of tradition, interpretive frame, talking, and inquiry with which I am working are found in Gadamer's discussion of language and interpretation. He points out how we often fail to notice our stake in description and interpretation yet descriptions adopt and appropriate a way of viewing social phenomena; language or naming things brings them under scrutiny with the light of prejudices and tacit evaluations. Language equips interpretation with categories or names things as certain kinds of things and inevitably directs the course of our reflection about them in particular ways, informing what we are likely to perceive as the salient features of experiences and our questions in response to them. See *Truth and Method*. By invoking the mental health profession's interpretative frame of understanding mental illness, we set the parameters of our ideas for mental health promotion. We simultaneously limit our range of understanding of mental health while depending on the agreed upon methods and conclusions of the discipline of psychology.

7. The list of works criticizing psychiatric assumptions, ideology, biases, and methods is too long to enumerate. See Banton (1985); Broverman et al. (1970), Brown (1984, 1986), Chesler (1972), Conrad (1980), Costrich et al. (1975), Foucault (1965), Ingleby (1982), Laing (1985), Roesenhan (1973), Scheff (1984), Sedgwick (1987), Showalter (1985), and Szasz (1972, 1987).

al, 1984; Hollway, 1989; Ingleby, 1982; Shotter, 1975) and many critical theorists have argued that mental health can be conceptualized as socially constructed, based on value-laden definitions of normality, and created by a process of expert definition (Ingleby, 1982; Littlewood and Lipsedge, 1982; Szasz, 1961; Ussher, 1991). Parallel arguments have been made questioning the existence of many physical and psychological "disorders" or "syndromes" (Foucault, 1965; Sedgwick, 1987). As well, we know that what is understood as a sign or symptom of "illness" varies across cultures and time (Kleinman, 1980; Littlewood and Lipsedge, 1982; Payer, 1988; Sedgwick, 1987). In fact, there have been many critiques of the notion of the body, or biology, as objective realities which can not be understood as separate from socio-historical knowledge, experience or subjectivity (Foucault, 1979; Henriques et al., 1984; Stainton-Rogers, 1991). Individuals do not experience symptoms in a socio-cultural historical vacuum and the recognition or interpretation of these symptoms cannot be understood outside of their social and historical context (Martin, 1987; Ussher, 1991).[8]

It is not difficult to imagine why mental health problems remain contained within scientific methodologies despite numerous critiques. Embedding mental health in specific socio-historical contexts would challenge the privilege scientific positions secure. That is, if we "begin down the slippery slope" of contextualizing problems and locating mental health etiology outside of individuals we would "lose our grip on the powerful social status that is granted to scientific practices and theories" and "reverse the discipline's hard-fought gains to be seen as a medical science" (Cushman, 1995, p. 249). Shifting from a methodology of counting, measuring, "clinically proving", predicting, controlling, etc., to one of dialogue, leaves mental health professionals sounding less like medical scientists and more like philosophers. Mental health practitioners would be reduced to "soft" humanists, or philosophers discoursing about morality or the good life or underlying social conditions, a tenuous fate that threatens their place in the academy (not to mention the market place) in a world that values "hard" science.

If practitioners begin to question the exalted status of scientific inquiry they would have to volte-face their practices. It would mean admitting that perhaps universal agreement about self contained illnesses is not possible, that conceivably mental disorders do not exist entirely as objectively knowable biological things and that they are contextually more complex. This questioning would lead to a change of tack not only for the profession's healing

---

8. Social constructionists challenge the realist assumptions of traditional biomedical and psychological research, arguing that subjectivity, behavior, and the very meanings of 'health' and 'illness' are constructed within practice, language, relationships, and roles. Science is part of this constructive process, and, as a consequence, research or clinical intervention can never be seen as objective or neutral. This does not mean that scientific research is pointless, but merely that reflexivity in theory and practice is an essential part of the scientific enterprise (Usher, 2000, p. 216).

techniques, i.e. pharmaceuticals, self-help technologies, comodified training, registration, and supervision of the professional body, etc., but for their promotion templates and guidelines as well. Further, practitioners would recognize that world-shattering re-thinking would have to come about for the requisite shift out of the current epistemic frame of reference within which the psychotherapeutic tradition rests. Psychotherapists would need to rework their way of thinking and speaking and risk announcing themselves theorists not scientists.

**The Problem with Conventional Mental Health Discourse**
Arguably, it is because historical, political, wider societal factors or even the role of unconscious factors are not easily assessed and typically are addressed within social constructionist, hermeneutic or feminist critiques that are theoretically driven, they are not operationalized or "known" as causes of ill health and subsequently treated (Ussher, 2000).[9] What results is that individuals who present with mental health problems are positioned within the discourse or frame of positivism that denies the social and discursive context of their lives and they are left to make sense of their experiences by seeking help for their personal depression, anxiety, or other like disorder. Understanding symptoms or problems as related to current life events, lifestyle, the broader socio-historical, cultural, medical or psychological ideas about mental health, falls outside the epistemological standards of objectivity and replicability.[10]

Thus, when we raise the question of how to promote "mental health" in secondary schools we, in consequence, conceal the unexpressed or hidden

---

9. Feminist Standpoint theory critiques the notion that "speaking" from particular, historically specific and social locations can only obstruct and damage the production of legitimate scientific knowledge. The adequacy of scientific knowledge in the modern West depends on supposedly transcending the particular historical projects that produce it. As Sandra Harding aptly points out: standpoint theorists who avoid taking their research problems, concepts, hypotheses, and background assumptions from the conceptual frameworks of the disciplines or the social institutions that they serve are "outside the realm of the true" from the perspective of those disciplines and institutions (2004, p. 6). For a full discussion of this nature see *The Feminist Standpoint Theory Reader*.
10. Ussher (2000) makes this point: "The fact that women's accounts of mental health problems is considered to be biased or 'subjective' -yet researcher's are not - illustrates the absence of reflexivity in positivist/realist research. Yet, ... the ideological stance of researchers affects the research questions they ask, the epistemological stance and methodologies they adopt, and the interpretations of the data collected" (p. 215). See also Billig (1991) *Ideologies and Beliefs* and Hollway (1989) *Subjectivity and Method in Psychology*. Feminist research that challenges the dominance of biomedical models by directing attention to the social-political context of illness diagnoses (e.g. Chesler (1995)) is often dismissed by positivist/realist researchers as not meeting the criteria for "good science".

assumptions about what is mental health according to its gatekeepers. It has become impossible to discuss mental health as anything but a matter of psychological or mental disorders, such as personal difficulty coping with depression, anxiety, psychosis, that afflict individuals and have specific and most predominantly biological causes. The discourse on mental health has been medicalized, psychologized, and engulfed by epistemological practices within the social sciences. This realization allowed me to understand why I had been directed to an already packaged program for promoting mental health in schools. When I was talking about mental health promotion, based on my experiences as a counsellor who noticed that a lot of students were suffering often because of their social contexts not outside of them, I was in effect talking about school health promotion.

Improving the health of school environments would effectually promote mental health in schools. I arrived at this belief after discerning that several students who were "identified" and referred for mental health counselling were not suffering from a mental health disorder per se, but were describing social or political injustices and were living out the consequences of these injustices. Some who were referred for anger management were angry about those injustices; some were confused by them and "took them on" as their own private problem to be resolved; some had flouted the authorities who had perpetuated those injustices; some harmed themselves as a result of them. Fundamental components of our socio-political space in secondary schools includes injustices due to race, gender, class, size, ability and sexual orientation. If our promotion strategies preclude illuminating such social realities that cause harm to certain youth, then they misguide or even obstruct our advancement, worse, they perpetuate further harm. Social problems that are recast as individual ones, with no direct connection to the social realm, redefine public issues as the private problems of individuals (Furedi, 2004, p. 24-25). The inner world of the individual becomes the site where the problems of society are manifest but where it is perceived as the individual's own crisis to be worked out. Of course, this recasting or evaluation of the problem conceals oppression, power relations, tyranny, and sectarian interests that are unarticulated in a conventional approach to mental health, an approach that falls back into an unreflective endorsement of medicalized suffering.

An unhelpful narrowing of focus is predictable when the bias of the medical model prevails in mental health promotion. Promoting mental health requires more than a uni-focused reductionist myopia of symptom definition and recognition of ill health. While it includes biological factors associated with psychological symptomatology, it also embraces factors—sexism, racism, homophobia, classism, lookism—impacting at the corporeal level of gender, ethnicity, sexuality, class, and physical appearance. Expanding the form and content of psychological phenomena to larger socio-cultural factors opens up the need for social reform in order to improve psychological functioning or mental health in schools. Harmful grounds that foster injustice:

prejudice, egocentrism, violence, hypocrisy, repression, ethnocentrism, arrogance, disrespect, authoritarianism, need to be transformed. Beneficial grounds that promote safety in all forms need to be developed.

## The Implications of Individualizing Mental Health Promotion

I could not pretend that mental health transcends politics and culture. I realized that without a critical analysis of the interpretive frame of those who undertake mental health promotion in schools, primarily mental health professionals and, secondarily, school administrators, following guidelines or concepts of the mental health profession would commit that pretence. Even "best practices" that recognize that people's mental health is inextricably linked to their relationship with others, environment and lifestyle factors, and the degree of power that they have over their lives (Canadian mental Health Association, 1999, p. 7), remain focused on improving the psychological or emotional capability of individuals. For example, programs are designed to: enhance youth's social, emotional and ethical behaviour with interactive skills training; create opportunities for effective use of newly learned skills; help young people learn to recognize and manage their emotions; appreciate the perspectives of others; establish positive goals; make good decisions; handle interpersonal situations and conflicts; and develop responsible and respectful attitudes and values about self, others, work, health and their community (Weissberg, Kumpfer, & Seligman, 2003). A focus on the individual dominates healthy solutions for the individual. Even reviews of policies, institutional practices, and environmental supports relate to nurturing healthy individual behaviour through positive personal relationships with "pro-social" peers or adults who provide clear standards, high expectations, guidance and encouragement.

I had been trained in conventional counselling techniques that employ psychological principles to effect psychological changes in individuals. For example, challenging or changing cognitive processes to "reframe situations" so that one can change the way they feel; teaching negotiating and communication techniques to increase understanding and resolve conflicts; using displacement techniques to defuse negative emotions and aggression; taking up meditation to alleviate stress; learning self-control and personal responsibility to avoid addictions; employing behaviour modification to improve school performance and social behaviour; and applying principles of cognitive dissonance to alter attitudes or stereotypes. Yet I remained unsettled by the underlying belief in mental health promotion that efforts at changing individual psychology and behaviour would ultimately promote mental health in schools. The assumption I found bothersome is that if enough individuals are helped to improve their psychological competencies and cease their debilitating, antisocial behaviour, society as a whole will improve (Ratner, 2006, p. 33). The problematic effect is that mental health promoters cannot free themselves to improve directly the structural causes of local emotional ills or grasp their unintended involvement in perpetuating those ills.

## Reframing our Framework for Mental Health Promotion, Gazing at the Social

If, as mental health promoters, we want to get hold of a fresh approach to mental health promotion in schools, perhaps we may start by defining our task as promoting a principled framework of appraisal for school environments.[11] We situate ourselves as critics first and promote critical-mindedness. The practice of social criticism involves more than deriving premises based on knowledge within a given discipline. It involves reflecting on and illuminating assumptions that are taken for granted in social practices and our social positions. It notices how what is taken for granted makes domination possible and allows inequality, injustice, and persecution to pervade (Foucault, 1972). That is, social criticism examines how power relations operate, how power "is employed and exercised through a net-like organization" and is "deployed" through our practices impacting us and orienting our conduct, choices and beliefs (Foucault, 1972, p. 98). Through critical reflection one may comprehend human subjects as agents and effects of power relations where subjectivity is formed by a network of subjugations, imposed behaviours and manipulated desires.

We could introduce for examination human subjectivity as an effect of power that is disciplined by all social relations. Human behaviour may be understood as directed by the non-coercive power of cultural arrangements, dominant identities of self, moral commitments, and normative definitions that prevail over schools. We could then illuminate evaluations underlying social conventions or customs and assumptions that are presupposed therein; factors that have a deleterious impact on some students. We place our "gaze" on the social as well as on the individual.[12] We render our school environments as subjects for scrutiny, what their administrators, teachers, and inhabitants are doing thinking and saying and notice how this impacts on individuals, who in particular is impacted, and why.[13]

---

11. Paul Ricoeur allows us to modify perceptions through what he calls "impertinent predication", producing a kind of "semantic shock", by conjoining terms or ideas that otherwise do not come together. It in effect misuses language or description such that conventional meanings are challenged and thereby subsequent interpretations based on language may be problematized. For Ricoeur the process allows the interpreter to "get hold of something fresh" and lets new meaning or understanding to emerge (1977, p. 4). "Semantic innovation" disrupts, redscribes and reclassifies thereby revealing what hitherto was unexpressed or hidden. Redescribing and retelling allow us to imagine how current perceptions of social phenomena could be other than received. Refocusing an approach to mental health promotion to examine and improve the school environment disallows mainstream descriptions and categories of what is mental health that are located at the individual level.
12. See Parker et al., 1995, p.14.
13. French philosopher Michel Foucault proposes to reveal unperceived expressions of power from the standpoint of the situated critic or genealogist. Critical reflection

By framing mental health in the above terms, as embedded in prevailing conventions, we may better promote it, more globally. For instance, promoting health and safety for gay, lesbian, bisexual, transgendered/transidentified (glbtt) youth would involve scrutinizing the ways messages about gender roles are disseminated and how discrimination and persecution against these groups is encouraged in everyday social communications such as jokes and stories, television sitcoms and commercials, magazines, comic strips, movies and social conventions. It would include noticing that there are constructs of difference through social regularities that have implications for glbtt youth in school environments. It would thus come as little surprise that homophobia prevails considering the ways that heteronormativity is entrenched in gendered constructions of boys and girls. Repeatedly reinforced and regulated, the dominant discourse on gender and sexuality and processes of heteronormalization constitute gays, lesbians, transgendered, and transidentified youth as "other". Typically there are no resources for glbtt youth in school libraries and classroom curriculum. Same sex safe sex is not taught in physical education classes, library books contain descriptions only of heterosexual relationships, queer centred supports are left to "outside agencies" and are not the proper (read: conventional) domain of secondary schools. Gender is constructed in a "heterosexual matrix" (Butler, 1990). Noticing this, and then referring suicidal individuals who identify as queer, and *coincidentally* hate themselves, for mental health counselling to be treated with a self-esteem raising technology clearly is not enough.

Similarly, within a heterosexual matrix, the traditional script of femininity tells us that women live their lives through a man. For adolescent females following traditional scripts of femininity, to have a boyfriend, keep him happy, keep him to gain her own happiness (read: lose him and it is her fault) helps to understand her "depression" (read: self blame) when that relationship breaks up (because most adolescent relationships do end). Or, it may be put forth as one explanation for why she stays in a neglectful or violent relationship: women are taught to gain happiness through relationships, invariably with men, and they are taught that it is their fault if these fail (Ussher, 2000). We may frame a young woman's experience of reproducing a subordinate role with her boyfriend in terms of choice. Of course her choice is

---

for Foucault is "historical investigation into the events that have led us to constitute ourselves and recognize ourselves as subjects of what we are doing, thinking, saying' (1984, p. 46). To this end, his genealogical writings research the history and development of concepts, practices, and institutions prevailing over modern social interaction thereby illuminating assumptions and evaluations underlying social phenomena. In essence, he reminds us of the forgotten in our subjectivity and practices. Thus, genealogical inquiry disturbs, reveals, and dissolves social construction by reminding us of how constructions came to be formed. The effect is a denaturalization of our taken for granted or apparent perceptions and intuitions. See *The Foucault Reader*.

constrained by her complicity with particular social practices in her world attributed to the dominance of patriarchy and heteronormativity. We would encourage alternative practices in her resistance against conventional arrangements by scrutinizing those arrangements that direct her choice or provide a context not of her choosing. Referring her for cognitive therapy to treat her depression or narrative counselling for trauma is insufficient.

Likewise, identifying and referring stressed youth for treatment using individualistic psychological principles of relaxation, meditation, and stress-management would overlook socio-cultural origins of stressors. Education that aims to prepare youth for a competitive job market in a capitalist economy where they need to sell themselves and develop individual responsibility, requires a set of psychological competencies that is specifically tailored for them to participate in that system; it is not natural. It is stressful. They need to think abstractly; verbalize abstract concepts; control their attention in sterile classroom settings for an hour at a time; suppress emotions and bodily movement; respect a perhaps impersonal relationship with their teacher, memorize de-contextualized information; fulfill schooling requirements punctually; work quickly and independently; and recall information quickly (Ratner, 2006). Further, increased homework loads, pressures for good grades, competition to enter post-secondary institutions, mandatory volunteer hours, etc. increase stress levels among youth; but that "stress" reflects a difficulty in performing according to a consumerist, capitalist, production motif, not an inherent inability to cope that requires a generic treatment.

**Critically Appraising the Social**
I think it is important that my clients specifically and students generally reflect on the conventions, habits, or rituals and beliefs that speak to them, direct them, shape their identity and inform their responses to their world. Perhaps that is a good place to start in re-locating problems with social origins to their social domains. I believe it is imperative to deflect the psychological practice of placing social problems onto the shoulders of individuals. To this end I often engage students in larger questions that consider the social and moral or political framework of their world or terrain. I invite them to reflect on how their socialization is a process of learning the rules or norms of a particular terrain and how theses norms determine parameters for what is possible within their worlds.[14] Conceiving of mental health as taking

---

14. See Martin Heidegger (1962), *Being and Time*; Hans-Georg Gadamer (1985), *Truth and Method*. For a discussion of the concept of cultural terrain see Hubert L. Dreyfus (1991), *Being in the World: A Commentary on Heidegger's "Being and Time"*, and Georgia Warnke (1987), *Gadamer: Hermeneutics, Tradition and Reason*. I refer specifically to the horizonal nature of understanding. That is, our horizon of understanding is constituted by our everyday social positions and how these positions depend on the fact that others know them and also take them for granted. Looking over the "clearing"

place within a larger socio-political terrain allows us as mental health professionals to consider, along *with* students, how a proper way of being is taught through family, school, and media. Language, symbols, images and the power inherent in definitions and descriptions of the "other", advertising and fashion trends, newscasts, and celebrity personalities are processes that generate a psychological vulnerability to expectations of "normal".

Given how "proper" ways of being are configured and create certain expectations of youth, I ask youth what is possible and what is prohibited in their world; what locations are possible for them to occupy and how do they situate themselves? What does it mean to be a young woman and what does it mean to be a young man; what constitutes being a "girlfriend", a "boyfriend" and what is possible for boys or girls in their context. What does it mean to flirt with the opposite sex? Is it related to the marriage system? Would flirting happen in a context of arranged marriages? Can same sex couples openly flirt? What is the cultural function of my being jealous when my girlfriend cheats on me? Would I have this emotion in a different setting? What does it mean to compete with my classmates for grades? What does a white, middle class, North American female anorexic body say (that her words cannot) about cultural ideals of body shape, identity and control as they are exaggerated by her? With questions like "what is the socio-cultural function of a particular psychological competency or failing?" and "would I be engaging in these psychological competencies (or failing at achieving them) if I were in a different setting?" introduces "points for contestation" and can become important sources of critical insight (Ratner, 2006).[15]

Such questions, as instruments of critique, serve to de-naturalize what we take for granted. They reveal that representations of the proper self are adopted by individuals, performed, or acquired and how cultural approval, in accordance with dominant ideologies, imposes behaviours, dictates what psy-

---

before us, it is through our cultural beliefs and personal opinions that we unknowingly make it possible for certain things to be brought into view and for other things to be excluded. We place our "horizon" or situate ourselves in such a way as to make room in the terrain for some things to show up or we act as if some things do not exist if they are on the other side of the horizon. Having been "thrown" into the constructs of a particular world, we consider the world and experience it as reality, immutable and unchallengeable, and then we continually reconstruct it.

15. Feminist standpoint projects designed to see beneath or behind dominant ideologies and conceptual practices of powerful social institutions , especially research disciplines, reveal "moments of critical insight" into dominant or mainstream practices that are made to appear normal or even natural. Kathi Weeks explains: "the point is to create sites of contestation over the social construction of specific constitutive practices where we can raise questions about what we can do and who we can become" (2004, p. 186). The theoretical approach aspires to help us think about and cultivate the possible consequences of specific practices in particular places and times. See: "Labor, Standpoints, and Feminist Subjects".

chological competencies are required in order to adjust to society, and influences desires.[16] Conversely, critical reflection notices how difference is constructed by dominant discourses and what happens when individuals act in accordance with certain disavowed traits of the "other".[17] It notices how current arrangements of power and privilege create many victims in the course of everyday life and how structures cause many to be hated, attacked, ridiculed, or abused.[18] If as mental health practitioners we place the subsequent suffering that results for some in an epistemological discourse, then we disguise the socio-political source of this suffering. Psychologizing the effect of suffering caused by political realities, imagining the social terrain as being inhabited by isolated, internally driven individuals, and then maintaining an objective, privileged scientific method for producing truth about how to promote health for those individuals, overlooks the discipline's own domination or participation in reproducing the oppressions of the status quo (Cushman, 1995). What results is our promotion strategies pronounce a-contextualized truths about mental health and the visible symptoms of suffering while rendering invisible the causes thereof, simultaneously obscuring domination or oppression.

Veiled ideology is problematic since those who bring to bear its influence conceal its power. Therefore, by not critically analyzing the socio-political context of mental health, mental health promotion practices do more than just perpetuate the status quo. By wielding power while masking it, mental health practitioners become inadvertent participants in the socio-historical processes that replicate current problematic political arrangements in which

---

16. Notions of 'performativity' and 'performance' come out of work in queer studies, feminist theory, ethnography and post-structuralist thought, including Butler (1990) and Case (1990); see Haraway (1991) for a discussion of 'material-semiotic actors'. The insistence on 'the performative' resonates with the language of functionalism and symbolic interactionism in which concepts of 'social actor', 'social role', 'self-presentation', and 'role performance' were elaborated.

17. Gilman's (1985) analysis of how ethnic, racial, and sexual stereotypes have intertwined with the meanings of mental disorder in a range of historical contexts is important here. See *Difference and Pathology: Stereotypes of Sexuality, Race, and Madness*. Cushman (1995) also discusses how the dominant white Anglo-Saxon Protestant culture defines what is the improper way of being and locates it on the "other". Psychological processes of projection and displacement work in combination with the political needs of the dominant population to configure the self, Cushman argues; a combination of political strategies and psychological processes keep various discriminated-against populations in "unending political impotence" (p. 347).

18. As Hubert Dreyfus and Paul Rabinow (1984) write in *Michel Foucault: Beyond Stucturalism and Hermeneutics*: "Subjection, domination, and combat are found everywhere he looks. Whenever he hears talk of meaning and value, of virtue and goodness, he looks for strategies of domination. ... Instead of origins, hidden meanings, or explicit intentionality, Foucault the genealogist finds force relations working themselves out in particular events, historical movements, and history" (p. 109).

students are embedded. If as health promoters we conclude that our promotion strategies unknowingly have been colluding with political conventions that we contest, then we must alter our practices so that our work does not support that with which we disagree. We must instead conceive of social relations or political arrangements of which we approve. If we develop a better understanding of how socio-political environments are constructed and reconstructed, then we are better able to see unintentional contributions to that construction through our promotional practices (Cushman, 1995). We will be less naïve about claims of scientific authority and more able to mobilize effective efforts at getting beneath or behind the ideologies and practices that shape students lives. It enables us to enlarge the horizons of our explanations and understandings of our institutions and in this case, of how to promote health within it.

## Conclusion

Epistemological inquiry removes situations from the milieu; it applies rules in a deductive manner with a rigidity of procedures and scientific rigor effecting an alienated and disjoined framework through which mental health is viewed. An enhanced understanding would elucidate the messiness of social situations, their contexts, and specific standpoints from within that context that do not readily render themselves visible under the limited field of epistemological viewing. Confronting our understanding of mental illness, as fathomed and remedied by the scientific expert and disconnected from the cultural and social realms, as "a monologue of reason about" mental health allows us to address what is a "broken dialogue" (Foucault, 1965, pp. x-xi).

There is no dialogue between mental illness and human experience when an objective orientation to mental health surmounts a theoretical connection to underlying social conditions of ill health. If we imagine our methodology as standing to the culture on the model of a socially critical conversation, one-sidedness may be overcome through the practice of dialogue and questioning. It is through discourse that we communicate our perception of the cultural terrain and through practices that we re-create that terrain. What we permit into view, what we take for granted and believe are conclusions based on our location. Reflecting on our location through conversation and critique may not generate consensus but would assure fairness through an exchange of views that challenge rigid or dogmatic positioning. It gives all possible voices equal access to understanding such that no voice can retain a monopoly and try to limit in advance what we could know and learn; it thus acts against a reduction of diversity.

It is the nature of non-coercive power to restrict options or the perception of options. Promotion strategies that secure an optimal configuration for the self and of social life that is possible for youth is essential. Power advances on many fronts, assumes multiple forms and erodes autonomy in multiple increments. Conceiving of a social order that limits power and expands alternatives removes obstacles to individual choice on a system-wide basis and creates options in areas where persons—many of whose perceptions and preferences, owing to the workings of power, have been unduly circumscribed. Without pretending to aim naively for non-hegemonic environments, our promotion strategies need to aim to create a protected domain of opportunities for being, for all persons, while alleviating situations that find individuals immured in conditions of hegemonic authority and practices. Because we live in the shadow of racism, sexism, economic injustice, and the influence of consumerism, mental health promotion, without a situated critical reflection and moral framework, is complicit in the arrangements of our society. The status quo that is reproduced is insidious, complex, many sided and hard to locate. It is the product of many traditions and fundamental to society while not being immediately or easily visible. Mental health promoters are limited when not understanding that there are multiple perspectives of the causes of mental illness and comprehension is not awakened until prejudices to traditions are opened and horizons are expanded.

# References

American Psychiatric Association (1994). *Diagnostic and statistical manual of mental disorders* (4th ed.). Washington, DC: American Psychiatric Association.

Banton, R. (1985). *The politics of mental health*. Oxford: Macmillan.

Billig, M. (1991). *Ideologies and beliefs*. London: Sage Publications.

Broverman, I.K., Broverman, D., Clarkson, F., Rosenkraitz, P., & Vogel, S. (1970). Sex role stereotypes and clinical judgments of mental health. *Journal of Consulting and Clinical Psychology, 34*, 1-7.

Brown, P. (1984). Marxism, social psychology, and the sociology of mental health. *International Journal of Health Services, 14*, 237-64.

Brown, P. (1986). Diagnostic conflict and contradiction in psychiatry. *Journal of Health and Social Behavior, 28*, 37-51.

Butler, J. (1990). *Gender trouble*. New York: Routledge.

Butler, J. (1997). *Excitable speech. A politics of the performative*. New York: Routledge.

Canadian Mental Health Association. (1999). Retrieved March 14, 2008 from http://www.cmha.ca/mh_toolkit/intro/pdfintro.pdf.

Case, S.E. (1990). *Performing feminisms: Feminist critical theory and theatre*. Baltimore: Johns Hopkins University Press.

Centre for Addiction and Mental Health (2003). Retrieved April 29, 2008 from http://www.camh.net/About_CAMH _Health_Promotion.

Chesler, P. (1995). *Women and madness*. New York: Doubleday.

Conrad, P. (1980). On the medicalization of deviance and social control. In D. Ingleby (Ed.), *Critical psychiatry*. New York: Pantheon.

Costrich, N., Feinstein, J., Kidder, L., Mareced, J., & Pascale, L. (1975). When stereotypes hurt: Three studies of penalties for sex-role reversals. *Journal of Experimental and Social Psychology 11*, 520-30.

Cushman, P. (1995). *Constructing the self. Constructing America*. New York: Addison-Wesley Publishing Company.

Dreyfus, H., & Rabinow, P. (1982). *Michel Foucault: Beyond structuralism and hermeneutics* (2nd ed.). Chicago: University of Chicago Press.

Dreyfus, H. (1991). *Being-in-the-world: A commentary on Heidegger's Being and Time*. Cambridge: MIT Press.

Fee, D. (2000). *Pathology and the postmodern*. London: Sage Publications.

Foucault, M. (1965). *Madness and civilization: A history of insanity in the age of reason*. London: Tavistock.

Foucault, M. (1972). *Power/knowledge: Selected interviews and other writings 1972-1977* (C. Gordon, L. Marshall, J. Mepham, & K. Soper, Trans.). New York: Pantheon Books.

Foucault, M. (1984). What is enlightenment? In P. Rabinow (Ed.), *The Foucault Reader*. New York: Pantheon Books.

Furedi, F. (2004). *Therapy culture: Cultivating vulnerability in an uncertain age*. New York: Routledge.

Gadamer, Hans-Georg. (1989). *Truth and method.* (2nd revised ed) (J. Weingsheimer, & D. Marshall, Trans.). New York: Crossroad.

Gilman, S.L. (1985). *Difference and pathology: Stereotypes of sexuality, race, and madness.* New York: Cornell University Press.

Haraway, D. (1991). Biopolitics of postmodern bodies. In *Simions, Cyborgs and Women. The reinvention of nature.* New York: Routledge.

Harding, S. (Ed.). (1987). *Feminism and methodology.* Indianapolis: Indiana University Press.

Harding, S. (1991). *Whose science? Whose knowledge?* Milton Keynes: Open University Press.

Harding, S. (Ed.). (2004). *The feminist standpoint theory reader.* New York: Routledge.

Harre, R., & Secord, P.F. (1972). *The explanation of social behavior.* Oxford: Basil Blackwell.

Heidegger, M. (1962). *Being and time* (J. Macquarrie, & E. Robinson, Trans.). New York: Harper and Row.

Henriques, J., Hollway, W., Urwin, C., Venn, C., & Walkerdine, V. (1984). *Changing the subject: Psychology, social regulation and subjectivity.* London: Methuen.

Hollway, W. (1989). *Subjectivity and method in psychology: Gender, meaning and science.* London: Sage Publications.

Ingleby, D. (Ed.). (1982). *Critical psychiatry: The politics of mental health.* London: Penguin.

Keller, E.F. (1985). *Reflections on gender and science.* New Haven: Yale University Press.

Kleinman, A. (1980). *Patients and healers in the context of culture.* Berkeley: University of California Press.

Laing, R.D. (1985). *Wisdom, madness and folly: The making of a psychiatrist.* New York: McGraw-Hill.

Littlewood, R., & Lipsedge, M. (1982). *Aliens and alienists: Ethnic minorities and psychiatry.* Harmondsworth: Penguin.

Martin, E. (1987). *The woman in the body: A cultural analysis of reproduction.* Milton Keynes: Open University Press.

Parker, I., Georgaca, E., Harper, D., McLaughlin, T., & Stowell-Smith, M. (1995). *Deconstructing psychopathology.* London: Sage Publications.

Payer, L. (1988). *Medicine and culture.* New York: Henry Holt & Company.

Ratner, C. (2006). *Cultural psychology.* Mahwah: Lawrence Erlbaum Associates, Inc., Publishers.

Ricoeur, Paul. (1977). *The rule of metaphor: Multidisciplinary studies of the creation of meaning in language* (R. Czerny, Trans.). Toronto: University of Toronto Press.

Rosenham, D.L. (1973). On being sane in insane places. *Science* 179-258.

Scheff, T.J. (1984). *Being mentally ill: A sociological theory.* New York: Aldine.

Sedgwick, P. (1987). *Psycho politics.* London: Pluto Press.

Shotter, J. (1975). *Images of man in psychological research.* London: Methuen.
Showalter, E. (1985). *The female malady.* New York: Pantheon.
Stainton-Rogers, W. (1991). *Explaining health and illness.* Hemel Hempstead: Harvester Wheatsheaf.
Szasz, T. (1972). *The myth of mental illness.* London: Secker.
Szasz, T. (1987). *Insanity.* New York: Wiley.
Ussher, J. (1991). *Women's madness: misogyny or mental illness?* Hemel Hempstead: Harvester Wheatsheaf.
Ussher, J. (2000). Women's madness: A material-discursive-intrapsychic approach. In D. Fee (Ed.), *Pathology and the Postmodern.* London: Sage Publications Ltd.
Warnke, G. (1987). *Hermeneutics, tradition and reason.* Stanford: Stanford University Press.
Weeks, K. (2004). Labor, standpoints, and feminist subjects. In S. Harding (Ed.), *The Feminist Standpoint Theory Reader.* New York: Routledge.
Weissberg, R., Kumpfer, K., & Seligman, M. (2003). Prevention that works for children and youth: An introduction. *American Psychologist, 58,* 425-432.

# TERROR OF AIDS: RISKY SEXUAL BEHAVIOR OF MIGRANTS IN TWO CITIES OF INDIA

*Parveen Nangia*

Acquired Immune Deficiency Syndrome (AIDS) is a deadly pandemic which has terrorized humanity since the early 1980s. In 1981, several cases of some rare diseases like Kaposi's Sarcoma (a form of cancer), pneumocystis carinii pneumonia (a form of lung infection) and other life threatening infections were detected in the United States, initially in the gay community and later on in injecting drug users. Doctors were baffled at the sudden increase in such infections and causes of their transmission, but they had learned that infection was acquired due to certain behavioral practices. By the time a common name Acquired Immune Deficiency Syndrome (AIDS) was used in 1982 for these opportunistic infections and cancers, 452 such cases had already been reported (Kanabus and Fredriksson 2008). AIDS was dreaded because the medical fraternity did not understand its cause and increasingly large numbers of cases were being reported from other countries as well. By the end of 1983, the number of reported AIDS cases had increased to 3,064 in the USA out of which 1,292 had already died (Centres for Disease Control 1983, cited in Kanabus and Fredriksson 2008). Since then AIDS has assumed epidemic proportions and the number of persons detected with AIDS has grown rapidly. In 2007, all over the world, 2.1 million people, including 330,000 children, had died of AIDS. It is estimated that currently more than 33 million people in the world are living with Human Immunodeficiency Virus (HIV), the virus that causes AIDS. Everyday, more than 6,800 persons are infected with HIV and over 5,700 die from AIDS (UNAIDS 2007).

Earlier, when the causes of transmission of HIV were not fully known, the terror of AIDS was so strong that people would stay away from patients who had AIDS. Police officers wore special masks and gloves to deal with suspected cases of AIDS (*New York Times* 1983, cited in Kanabus and Fredriksson 2008), landlords evicted persons suffering from AIDS and the Social Security Officers interviewed patients by phone rather than face-to-face (David Spencer, Commissioner of Health, cited in Kanabus and Fredriksson 2008). Children with AIDS were banned from attending school (*Times Magazine* 1990, cited in Kanabus and Fredriksson 2008). Though the situation has improved now, the stigma attached to AIDS continues and many people still have misconceptions about the modes of transmission. In a study conducted in Nigeria in 2002, a large majority of the respondents knew that HIV could be transmitted through sexual intercourse with infected persons, blood transfusion, and by sharing contaminated skin-piercing instruments with infected persons; but a substantial proportion also had misconceptions that it could be transmitted by sharing personal items, such as clothes. More than half of the respondents believed that a cure was available for AIDS (Nwokoji and Ajuwon 2004). Gender gaps persist in many countries regarding awareness of AIDS. For example, in 1997, about 90% of the married men in Niger said that they had heard of AIDS compared to only 51% of married women. But in most Latin American countries, awareness of AIDS is almost universal and there is no gender difference in its awareness (*Population Reports* 1999).

In India, a recent national level survey conducted in the general population in 2005-06 shows that only 61% of the women (age 15-49) had heard of AIDS compared to 84% of the men. Thirty-one percent women and 44% men rejected the misconceptions that HIV can be transmitted by mosquito bites, hugging, or sharing food with infected persons (IIPS and Macro International 2007).

It is estimated that in 2006 the total number of persons living with HIV/AIDS in India was 2.5 million, with an adult HIV prevalence rate of 0.36 percent (0.43% for males and 0.30% for females). The HIV prevalence rate among high risk groups was much higher: for example intravenous drug users (IDUs) 8.7%, homosexual males 5.7%, and female sex workers 5.4% (NACO and National Institute of Medical Statistics n.d).

Many studies have shown that migrant men are more likely to engage in risky sex behavior and hence intensify the hazard of spreading HIV (Coffee et al. 2007; Gelmon et al. 2006; Hu et al. 2006; ICDDR, 2005). Migration in India has increased rapidly during the nineties, which is associated with fast economic growth after the liberalization of the economy in the early 1990s. New development projects are coming up in several cities, which are attracting migrants from less developed areas, particularly rural areas, to work in construction, manufacturing and other occupations. Economic migration in the country is mainly confined to males. From poor households one or two members move out to create an outside support system for survival of the family, whereas in better off groups, migration often means shifting of the entire family (Kundu 2007).

## Data and methods

The present paper is based on a survey that we conducted (Singh, Gupta, Lahiri and Nangia) in 2001 in two rapidly growing metropolitan cities of India, namely Greater Mumbai and Surat, which attract a large number of male migrants from various parts of the country. Mixed method approach was used in data collection. Qualitative approach was used to collect comprehensive information on sexual opportunities and drugs/alcohol availability in the study area, indulgence in risk behavior, and treatment seeking behavior. In-depth interviews were conducted with key informants and some of the migrants during the qualitative data collection phase. Quantitative approach was used to canvass a semi-structured questionnaire to collect information on causes of migration, extent of substance abuse, sexual behavior, knowledge of STDs and HIV/AIDS, their modes of transmission and methods of prevention. Interviews with men working in the organized economic sector were conducted in both cities. In Surat, stratification of industries was done on the basis of size (small, medium and large) and randomly 10, 7 and 5 industries were selected from the three groups. Selection of workers from the selected industries was done through probability proportionate to size (PPS) sampling design. In all 1,010 workers were interviewed of which 918 were migrants. In Greater Mumbai, three clusters were selected, namely Bhivandi, Tarapur and Navi Mumbai. In each cluster a list of workers in the organized sector was prepared and sample was selected through systematic sampling technique. In all 1,040 workers were interviewed of which 1,014 were migrants (Singh et al. 2002).

For the present paper, quantitative data from this study are used for preparing cross tables and further analysis. Two research questions are examined: 1. Are migrant men more likely to get engaged in paid/unpaid sex than non-migrant men? 2. Does perception about curability of HIV affect high risk sexual behavior of men? For this purpose chi-square tests are used to compare characteristics of migrant and non-migrant groups and logistic regression analysis is conducted to examine the effect of socio-economic and demographic characteristics on sexual behavior.

## Results

Out of 2,050 men interviewed in this survey 1,932 were migrants, 1,155 were currently married, 427 lived with their wives, 120 reported that they had sex at brothels, 59 said they had sex with street sex workers, 248 had sexual contact with other women (unpaid sex), 78 men used condoms with commercial sex workers, 66 used condoms with other women, and 205 ever used condoms with their wives. Information was not collected in this survey on use of condoms with every sexual act with commercial sex workers or other casual acquaintances.

## Background characteristics of sample population

Most of the workers (94%) in the selected sample were migrants.

Table 1 shows the background characteristics of migrant and non-migrant men. In terms of age distribution and marital status, migrants and non-migrants were quite similar. The educational level of non-migrants was significantly higher than migrants. It is easier for migrants with a lower level of education to get work in construction and manufacturing sector, the industries that got selected in the sample. A larger proportion of non-migrants were employed in professional and technical jobs compared to

**Table 1:** Percent distribution of migrants and non-migrants by background characteristics, Mumbai and Surat, 2001

| Characteristic | | Migrant | Non-migrant | Total |
|---|---|---|---|---|
| Age | Less or 24 | 44.0 | 40.7 | 43.8 |
| | 25—34 | 40.1 | 40.7 | 40.1 |
| | 35 or more | 15.9 | 18.6 | 16.0 |
| Marital status | Never married | 43.3 | 40.7 | 43.1 |
| | Married | 56.2 | 58.5 | 56.3 |
| | Divorced/separated/widowed | 0.5 | 0.8 | 0.5 |
| Education | Illiterate | 22.4 | 9.3 | 21.6 |
| | Middle (Elementary) | 43.2 | 33.1 | 42.6 |
| | Secondary complete | 29.0 | 36.4 | 29.5 |
| | Post secondary | 5.4 | 21.2 | 6.3 |
| Nature of work | Business | 1.1 | 2.5 | 1.2 |
| | Professional | 1.2 | 6.8 | 1.5 |
| | Technical worker | 28.4 | 44.1 | 29.3 |
| | Service worker | 17.9 | 16.9 | 17.8 |
| | Laborer | 50.2 | 23.7 | 48.6 |
| | Other | 1.3 | 5.9 | 1.6 |
| Monthly income (Rs.) | Low or 2000 | 21.8 | 22.9 | 21.9 |
| | 2001—3000 | 44.4 | 37.3 | 44.0 |
| | 3001—5000 | 28.5 | 28.0 | 28.4 |
| | Above 5000 | 5.3 | 11.9 | 5.7 |
| Savings (Rs.) | No saving | 7.3 | 31.4 | 8.7 |
| | Less or 1000 | 44.8 | 46.6 | 45.0 |
| | 1001—2000 | 38.1 | 12.7 | 36.7 |
| | 2001 and above | 9.7 | 9.3 | 9.7 |
| n | | 1932 | 118 | 2050 |

migrants and hence enjoyed higher levels of income. Even though migrants had lower earnings they were able to save some money to remit to their families left behind at the place of origin.

Nearly four-fifths of the non-migrants lived in their own houses, whereas more than two-fifths of the migrants lived in houses provided by their employers, another one-fifth lived independently in rented places and more than a quarter shared accommodations with friends or relatives. A substantially large proportion of migrants lived in crowded conditions. About one-fifth of the migrants shared accommodation with eight or more persons compared to less than one-tenth of the non-migrants (Table 2).

**Table 2:** Percent distribution of migrants and non-migrants by living arrangements, Mumbai and Surat, 2001

| Living arrangements | | Migrant | Non-migrant | Total |
|---|---|---|---|---|
| Place of living | Rental house | 19.0 | 11.0 | 18.5 |
| | Own house | 8.3 | 78.8 | 12.4 |
| | Sharing with relatives | 9.0 | 5.1 | 8.8 |
| | Sharing with friends | 18.0 | 1.7 | 17.0 |
| | Company house | 43.5 | 3.4 | 41.2 |
| | Other | 2.2 | 0 | 2.1 |
| Living with (number of persons) | Living alone | 8.4 | 0 | 7.9 |
| | Two to four | 42.9 | 43.2 | 42.9 |
| | Five to eight | 28.8 | 48.3 | 30.0 |
| | Above eight | 19.9 | 8.5 | 19.3 |
| n | | 1932 | 118 | 2050 |

## Social Relations

A small proportion of rural migrant men are able to bring their families to the cities due to lack of affordable housing and costlier life. Table 3 reveals that only one-third of the currently married migrant men live with their wives, whereas all of the married non-migrants live with their wives. Many people feel lonely when they stay away from their families. Proportion of migrants who generally or occasionally feel lonely is significantly higher compared to non-migrants. Their relations with neighbours are not that strong and they have fewer close friends.

Social relations can affect behavior of migrants in different ways. Having more close friends and good relations with neighbours may mean spending spare time with them, sharing feelings and concerns and overcoming loneliness and boredom. Some people also try to overcome their loneliness by taking refuge in alcohol, drugs, movies, and sex. Participation in such activities can trigger peer pressure.

## Lifestyle activities

Entertainment is another way of overcoming loneliness/boredom. Watching television is less common among migrants as many of them are unable to afford or unwilling to keep a television. A larger proportion of migrants compared to non-migrants visit video parlors[1], which are cheaper means

---

1. Small entertainment places in the poor neighborhoods where popular and/or pornographic movies are shown on video.

**Table 3:** Distribution of migrant and non-migrant men by social relations, Mumbai and Surat, 2001

| Social relations and feelings | | Migrant | Non-migrant | Total |
|---|---|---|---|---|
| Percent of currently married men living with wife | | 33.0 | 100.0 | 37.0 |
| n | | 1086 | 69 | 1155 |
| Have friends and relatives to visit | | 64.8 | 92.4 | 66.3 |
| Number of close friends | None | 5.1 | 1.7 | 4.9 |
| | 1—2 | 53.7 | 39.9 | 52.9 |
| | 3—5 | 27.8 | 39.0 | 28.5 |
| | > 5 | 13.4 | 19.5 | 13.7 |
| Relationship with neighbors | Good | 41.8 | 64.4 | 43.1 |
| | Neutral | 45.1 | 33.9 | 44.4 |
| | Bad or no relations | 13.1 | 1.7 | 12.5 |
| Feel lonely/bored | Generally | 17.7 | 7.6 | 17.1 |
| | Occasionally | 55.5 | 38.1 | 54.5 |
| | Never | 26.9 | 54.2 | 28.4 |
| n | | 1932 | 118 | 2050 |

of entertainment compared to cinema. In these video parlors an informal relationship develops between operators and clients who can request to rewind movie and watch interesting scenes again and again.

Use of tobacco and gutka[2] is very common among migrants and significantly higher than non-migrants. About one-fourth of the migrants and an equal proportion of non-migrants consume liquor. A negligible proportion of respondents reported use of intoxicating drugs (Table 4).

## Knowledge of HIV/AIDS

Most of the men in this study had heard of AIDS (88% migrants and 92% non-migrants), which is higher than what recent National Family Health Survey (NFHS-3) found (84% of men). This could be because the national survey covered both rural and urban areas, whereas our sample was from two large metropolitan cities. However, NFHS-3 showed that 95% of the urban men had heard of AIDS (IIPS and Macro International 2007), which is compatible with our findings. In urban areas, level of knowledge is much higher because media is used extensively by government and non-government

---

2. It is an intoxicant that is prepared from betel nuts, tobacco and other flavors. It is chewed like tobacco and considered to have carcinogenic and other negative health effects.

**Table 4:** Percent of migrant and non-migrant men by life style activities, Mumbai and Surat, 2001

| Life style | | Migrant | Non-migrant | Total |
|---|---|---|---|---|
| Entertainment | Usually watch TV | 42.7 | 83.9 | 45.0 |
| | Go to cinema | 59.7 | 59.3 | 59.7 |
| | Go to video parlors | 26.8 | 13.6 | 26.0 |
| Use of intoxicants | Chew tobacco/gutka | 62.3 | 42.4 | 61.1 |
| | Consume liquor | 25.3 | 25.4 | 25.3 |
| | Use drugs | 0.6 | 0 | 0.5 |
| n | | 1932 | 118 | 2050 |

agencies to disseminate messages about AIDS. Even though most of the men have heard of AIDS and a large majority of them know it is a serious health hazard, more than half of the migrants and less than a third of the non-migrants do not know that HIV causes AIDS. This could be related to educational differences between the two groups. Nearly one-fifth of all men think that HIV is completely curable (Fig. 1).

### Knowledge of HIV/AIDS

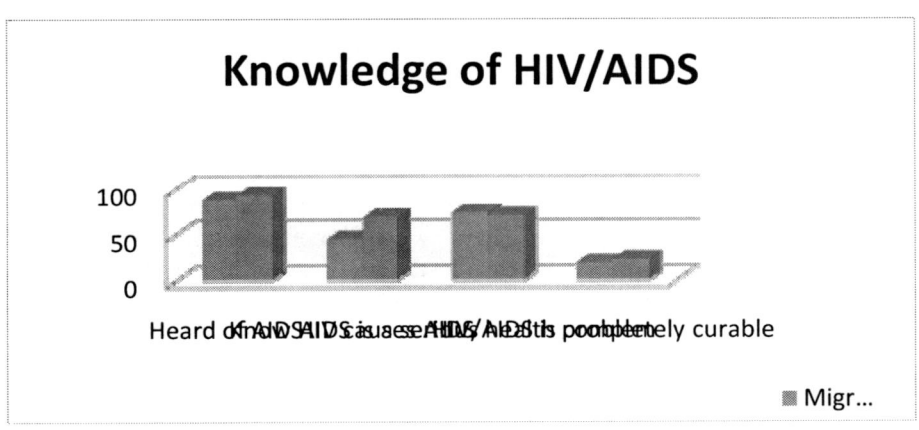

**Figure 1**

The major sources of information about HIV/AIDS are media (television, radio, newspapers, magazines, flyers, and wall hoardings), friends, relatives, community meetings and doctors. More than one in ten men in the study area was not aware of any mode of transmission. A considerable proportion also reported myths and misconceptions about transmission of HIV (Singh et al. 2002).

**Sexual Behavior**
In terms of sexual behavior, Indians are considered very conservative. Recent National Family Health Survey (IIPS and Macro International, 2007) reveals that among those aged 15-49 who had sex during 12 months period prior to the survey 2% of the men and 0.1% of the women reported to have had two or more sexual partners. Nevertheless, a higher proportion of men (5%) and women (0.2%) were involved in high-risk sex (sexual intercourse with someone other than a spouse or cohabiting partner). Among those who had sex during the past 12 months, the reported prevalence of multiple sexual partners was comparatively higher among never married men (18%), never married women (4%), and widowed/divorced/ separated/deserted persons (7% for men and 1% for women). Higher risk sex is also more prevalent in these marital status groups (IIPS and Macro International, 2007).

Studies on sexual behavior have become more important now in the context of HIV/AIDS, but data might be biased (underreported) due to sensitive nature of the issue. High risk population can spread infection to unsuspecting spouse and others sexual partners. For single male migrants ample opportunities are available in the big metropolitan cities for paid/unpaid sex. Peer pressure, exposure to pornographic material, use of intoxicants, lack of knowledge about STDs and HIV/AIDS may lead to sexual contact with commercial sex workers (paid sex) or other women who are casual contacts and not cohabiting partners (unpaid sex). In our sample we did not find any significant difference in the sexual behavior of migrant and non-migrant men. Only 7% of the migrant and 5% non-migrant men reported that they had sex with commercial sex workers, and 12% migrants and 9 percent non-migrants reported that they had sex with other women. Living with wife did not make any difference in the sexual behavior of married men (Table 5), however, never married men were more likely to have unpaid sex and widowed/divorced/separated were more likely to visit brothels and street sex workers compared to married men (Table 6).

**Table 5:** Percent of married men living with or without wife by sexual behavior

| Sexual behaviour | Living with wife | Not living with wife |
|---|---|---|
| Sex at brothels | 6.6 | 6.8 |
| With street sex workers | 2.6 | 3.1 |
| With other women (unpaid) | 8.2 | 8.6 |
| n | 427 | 740 |

**Table 6:** Sexual behavior of men by marital status

| Sexual behavior | Never married | Married | Widowed/divorced/separated |
|---|---|---|---|
| Sex at brothels | 4.8 | 6.6 | 18.2 |
| Sex with street sex workers | 2.8 | 2.9 | 9.1 |
| Sex with other women (unpaid) | 16.9 | 8.5 | 9.1 |
| n | 884 | 1155 | 11 |

When condoms are used during sexual intercourse, the risk of acquiring HIV can decline substantially. The majority of men, especially those who never married, usually do not use condoms when they have sex with commercial sex workers or other women. More than two out of five married men who had sex with commercial sex workers did not use condoms. Similarly, more than two-thirds of the married men who had sex with other women did not use condoms (Fig.2). These are the people who put their wives at a greater risk of acquiring sexually transmitted diseases, including HIV. A study conducted in 2004 estimated that 52% of female commercial sex workers in Mumbai were infected with HIV (UNDP, 2007).

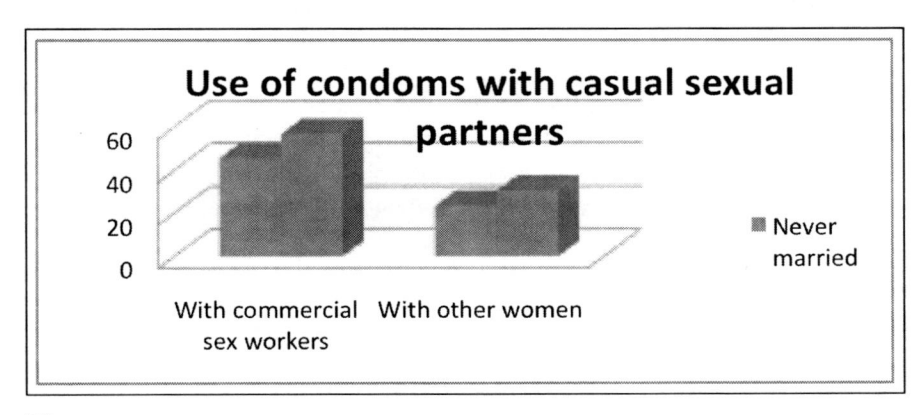

**Figure 2**

### Influence on sexual behavior

To understand the influence of characteristics of men on their sexual behavior, logistic regression analysis is used. Two models are tested for association between characteristics of men and their sexual behavior. In the first model, involvement in paid/unpaid sex and in the second model protected sex is taken as dependent variable. Independent variables considered in the two models are: age groups, migration status, income, perception about curability of HIV/AIDS, feeling of loneliness, and number of persons sharing accommodation with respondent. Some categorical variables are converted into binary variables because of the small sample in some of the categories. Results of logistic regression are presented in Table 7.

*Paid/unpaid sex*
Paid sex is sex with commercial sex workers (brothel based or street based) and unpaid sex is sex with other women, with whom one has casual or long term contact (certainly not wife or fiancée).

Younger men (age 25-34) are more likely to have paid/unpaid sex compared to older men (age 35+) (odds ratio 1.69). Young men seem to be looking for sexual adventures and pleasure, particularly when they have less restriction from their families and society. This is corroborated with the finding that migrant men are more likely to have paid/unpaid sex compared to non-migrant men (odds ratio 1.88). When they migrate their behavior is less likely to be noticed by those who are closely related to them and staying away. On the other hand, non-migrant men might be afraid of being found if they have socially unacceptable sexual behavior. Non-migrant married men also have the opportunity to be with their wives and therefore less likely to get indulged in paid/unpaid sex. Results of the analysis also show that married men are less likely to have paid/unpaid sex compared to non-married men (never married, widowed, divorced, or separated) (odds ratio 0.62). Those with higher incomes are more likely to engage in paid/unpaid sex (odds ratio 1.95). People with higher incomes have more disposable money and are in a better position to fulfill their desires.

Men who think that HIV/AIDS is curable are more likely to have paid/unpaid sex compared to those who think there is no remedy to this infection (odds ratio 1.47). Those who lack proper knowledge might think that even if they catch sexually transmitted infections they could get appropriate treatment.

Sexual behavior is also associated with feelings of loneliness or boredom. Those who occasionally feel lonely are less likely to have paid/unpaid sex compared to those who never feel lonely (odds ratio 0.74). In other words, some people overcome the feeling of loneliness and boredom by having paid/unpaid sex. When many people share accommodation loneliness is reduced, but it may increase peer pressure to have paid/unpaid sex. The findings of this study show that with increasing number of people sharing accommodation the likelihood of having paid/unpaid sex increases (odds ratio 1.04).

*High-risk sex*
High-risk sexual behavior entails sex with non-regular partners without using condom. This is a weak measure due to lack of knowledge about sexual behavior of regular partner (her other sexual contacts) and lack of information

**Table 7:** Odds ratio from logistic regression analysis showing the effect of selected characteristics on sexual behavior of men

| Characteristic | Paid/unpaid sex N = 1463 | High risk sex N= 236 |
|---|---|---|
| Age | | |
| Up to 24 | 1.49 | 0.82 |
| 25—34 | 1.69* | 0.99 |
| 35 and above | Ref. | |
| Migration | | |
| Non-migrant | Ref. | |
| Migrant | 1.88* | 0.29 |
| Marital status | | |
| Not married | Ref. | |
| Married | 0.62** | 1.50 |
| Income | | |
| Up to 3000 | Ref. | |
| More than 3000 | 1.95*** | 0.96 |
| Perceive HIV/AIDS as curable | | |
| Not curable | Ref. | |
| Curable | 1.47* | 0.38* |
| Feeling of loneliness | | |
| Generally | 1.09 | 0.86 |
| Occasionally | 0.74* | 0.72 |
| Never | Ref. | |
| Number of persons sharing accommodation with respondent | 1.04** | 1.11** |
| Constant | 0.02 | 4.37 |

*$p < .05$, **$p < .01$, ***$p < .001$. Ref.—reference category.

on use of condoms with each sexual act. It is very unlikely that people would use condoms with every sexual act. Even if they do it with strangers, they may not do so with their regular partners and they may still catch infection if their regular partners are not loyal to them.

High-risk sex does not show a significant relationship with most of the variables considered in this analysis. Men who think HIV/AIDS is curable are less likely to have high-risk sex compared to those who think it is not curable (odds ratio 0.38). Sometimes people take risk thinking that nothing will happen to them. With increasing number of persons staying together the likelihood of high-risk sex increases (odds ratio 1.11). It could be possible that these men are involved in sex with other persons staying in the same place. When people get an opportunity to have sex, condoms may not be available or there may be other reasons for not using condoms, such as affordability or disliking for condoms.

## Discussion and Conclusion

Even though most of the men have heard of AIDS, their knowledge about modes of HIV transmission is very limited. A substantial proportion of men in the sample were engaged in risky sexual behavior. One in seven married men claimed to have had extramarital sex. Over half of those who had paid/unpaid sex did not use condoms with their casual partners. More than two-thirds of those who had extramarital sex never used condoms with their wives. This indicates that a substantial proportion of women remain at risk of contracting HIV because of high-risk sex behavior of their husbands.

Sexual behavior of men is influenced by their socio-economic characteristics. Involvement of men in paid/unpaid sex is influenced by their income, migration status, age, marital status, belief about curability of HIV/AIDS, feeling of loneliness, and number of persons sharing accommodation. Migrants are significantly more likely to get engaged in paid/unpaid sex. These results support the findings of other studies, e.g. in a study in Bangladesh it was found that married men living away from their wives were 5-6 times more likely to get engaged in extramarital sex (ICDDR, 2005). Coffee et al. (2007) observed that migration increases high risk sexual behavior and influences spread of HIV. On the other hand, Gelmon and colleagues (2006) argue that migration does not change sexual behavior of people, but intensifies risk of contracting HIV because migrants move to cities where HIV prevalence rate is comparatively higher.

High-risk sex is influenced by belief about curability of HIV/AIDS and number of persons sharing accommodation. Despite so much publicity about causes of AIDS many people do not use condoms with their casual sex partners. Low condom use among men with multiple sex partners is also reported in other countries (Hu, et al., 2006; Zellner, 2003). From her study in Cote d'Ivoire, Zellner concluded that accuracy of knowledge about AIDS did not predict the likelihood of condom use. There are several reasons for not using condoms. Maes and Louis (2003) emphasize that even though many people recognize the seriousness of AIDS, they generally think that they will not get it even if they have sexual activity outside of a long-term relationship.

## Policy on AIDS

The government of India started its AIDS control program in the early 1990s and established National AIDS Control Organization (NACO). In the first phase of this program (until 1999) several STD clinics and blood testing centres were established. Emphasis was placed on creating awareness. Second phase (2000-06) focused on providing care and support to people living with HIV/AIDS. During this phase, this approach changed from creating awareness to changing behavior. Annual sentential surveillance and mapping of high-risk groups started in this phase. In the third phase (since 2007) emphasis is placed on preventing new infections and providing more care and support to people living with HIV/AIDS. Care, treatment and prevention infrastructure are being strengthened, particularly in the areas where incidence rate is high. Since 2004, government hospitals provide free anti-retroviral treatment (UNDP, 2007).

## Limitations

A large number of migrants are engaged in informal sector. Due to difficulties involved in the selecting sample from that group, it was decided to take samples from organized industries. In that sense sample is neither representative of population nor migrants.

Sexual behavior is a very sensitive issue and data are subject to underreporting. Qualitative interviews indicated that visits to commercial sex workers were more common.

It is difficult to estimate levels of high-risk sex in the absence of complete data on number of sexual partners, particularly commercial sex workers, and condom use with each sexual act.

## References

Coffee, M., M. N. Lurie, and G. P. Garnett, 2007. "Modelling the impact of migration on the HIV epidemic in South Africa." *AIDS*. 21, no.3: 343-350. Retrieved April 15, 2008 from
http://www.aidsonline.com/pt/re/aids/pdfhandler.00002030-200701300-00008.pdf;jsessionid=L8LGy1nJXTbJTzhngbthnLGSFTxJlnCLfnPq8xVC9Wby2LKszw91!195308708!181195628!8091!-1

Gelmon, L., K. Singh, P. Singh, P. Bhattacharjee, S. Moses, A. Costigan, J. and Blanchard. 2006. "Sexual networking and HIV risk in migrant workers in India." Paper presented at *16th International AIDS Conference*, Toronto, Canada. August 13-18, 2006. Retrieved April 15, 2008 from http://www.aegis.com/conferences/iac/2006/MoAco304.html

Hu, Z., H. Liu, X. Li, B. Stanton, and X. Chen. 2006. "HIV-related sexual behavior among migrants and non-migrants in a rural area of China: Role of rural-to-urban migration." *Public Health*, 120, no. 4: 339-345. Retrieved April 15, 2008 from http:// www.sciencedirect.com/science?_ ob=ArticleURLand_udi=B73H64J84 SW5-1and_user=1067249and_rdoc=1and_fmt=and_orig=searchand_sort=dandview=cand_acct=C000051240and_version=1and_urlVersion=0and_userid=1067249andmd5=83decb1feda77f49127f8788dabe1523

ICDDR. 2005. "Sexual risk behavior of married men and women who have lived apart due to the husbands' work migration." *Health and Science Bulletin*, 3, no. 4: 10-15. (December). Retrieved April 15, 2008 from http://www.icddrb.org/pub/publication.jsp?classificationID=56andpubID=6592

International Institute for Population Sciences (IIPS) and Macro International. 2007. *National FamilyHealth Survey (NFHS-3), 2005–06: India: Volume I.* Mumbai: IIPS.

Kanabus, A., and J. Fredriksson, 2008. "History of AIDS up to 1986." *Avert*. Retrieved May 14, 2008 from http://www.avert.org/his81_86.htm

Kundu, A. 2007. "Migration and exclusionary urban growth in India." *IIPS Newsletter*, 48, Nos. 3 and 4 (July): 5-23. (Prof. C. Chandrasekharan memorial lecture delivered in Mumbai on 2nd January).

Maes, C. A., and M. Louis, 2003. "Knowledge of AIDS, perceived risk of AIDS, and at-risk sexual behavior among older adults." *Journal of American Academy of Nurse Practitioners*, 15, no.11: 501-516. http://www.blackwell-synergy.com/doi/abs/10.1111/j.1745-7599.2003.tb00340.x

National AIDS Control Organization (NACO) and National Institute of Medical Statistics (Indian Council of Medical Research). (n.d.) *India—HIV estimates 2006: Technical report.* New Delhi: National AIDS Control Organization. Retrieved May 10, 2008 from http://www.nacoonline.org/upload/NACO%20PDF/Technical%20Report%20on%20HIV%20Estimation%202006.pdf

Nwokoji, U. A., and A. J. Ajuwon. 2004. "Knowledge of AIDS and HIV risk-related sexual behavior among Nigerian naval personnel." *BMC Public Health*, 4:24. Retrieved May 10, 2008 from http://www.biomedcentral.com/1471-2458/4/24

Population Reports 1999. *Closing the condom gap*. Vol. XXVII. No. 1 (April). Retrieved April 15, 2008 from http://www.infoforhealth.org/pr/h9edsum.shtml

Singh, S.K., K. Gupta, S. Lahiri, and P. Nangia. 2002. *Knowledge about HIV/AIDS and risk behavior of migrants in some selected development projects in Mumbai and Surat*. Mumbai: International Institute for Population Sciences.

UNAIDS and WHO. 2007. *2007 AIDS epidemic update*. Retrieved May 14, 2008 from http://data.unaids.org/pub/EPISlides/2007/2007_epiupdate_en.pdf

UNDP. 2007. "India at a glance." *Youandaids: The HIV/AIDS portal for Asia Pacific*. Retrieved May 10 from http://www.youandaids.org/asia%20pacific%20at%20a%20Glance/india/index.asp

Zellner, S. L. 2003. Condom use and the accuracy of AIDS knowledge in Cote d'Ivoire. *International Family Planning Perspectives*, 29 (1): 41-47.

# Addressing Terror Through Group Psyche

*Sophia C. Hughes*

I am offering a way that we can jointly and gradually work towards reducing the need for terror as a symptom of distress in our human society: a multi-sensory, multicentric, dialogic approach to terrorism and other frightening dynamics in the human community. Sand tray is a visual means of communication. It is a profound developmental process, and is a three dimensional, metaphoric means of expressing feelings, ideas and perceptions. It has demonstrated itself, when used as a psychotherapeutic tool, to be a positive process that gets us unstuck. In a sand tray session the psyche is naturally projected through the placement of miniatures by the participant(s) on a tray of sand. When a group participates in a sand tray session the group and wider cultural psyche is projected onto the tray, providing timely and pertinent material for group understanding and discussion. A well-facilitated group sand tray event, during which there is both verbal and non-verbal exchange of perspectives and information, results in greater understanding that will gradually pervade the system.

My computer's dictionary on terror: "1. Intense or overwhelming fear. 2. Violence or the threat of violence carried out for political purposes. 3. Some thing, event or situation that causes intense fear."

These definitions include action, emotion and an arrangement or entity that elicits strong emotion. Terror is induced, produced, felt and responded to. I have worked for years with domestic violence offenders and I know that explosions in anger often occur because of errors in thinking and failure to communicate effectively. Thoughts based on limited information are an important component of terror on both sides of the dynamic. Our fear, or the fear we produce, is based on surprise and expectation. Terror is an extreme at one end of a spectrum of feelings. Recently a psychologist who works with children in foster care pointed out that there is really nothing going on with any of us other than the wish for love and the fear that prevents it and causes our counterproductive actions[12]. A word that comes to mind in association with love is "inclusion." If we consider humanity as a whole, a terrorist act taking place in that whole is a form of self-injury. It has an emotional cause grounded in thinking, an emotional effect, and many after effects.

---

1. Heather T. Forbes and B. Bryan Post, *Beyond Consequences, Logic and Control* Orlando: Beyond Consequences Institute LLC, 2006.

# Engaging Terror

*Human community*

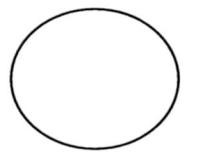

*Human community in conflict injures itself*

There are several reasons for a sand tray approach to the underlying sources of terror.

Collective psyche: We are trained to look at ourselves and each other as individuals, and as self and other.

We                They

In the wise words of the I Ching we see in hexagram thirty-eight:

K'uei / Opposition

Nine at the top means: Isolated through opposition,
> One sees one's companion as a pig covered with dirt,
> As a wagon full of devils.
> First one draws a bow against him,
> Then one lays the bow aside.

He is not a robber; he will woo at the right time.

As one goes, rain falls; then good fortune comes[3].

This hexagram points out the transformation of a negative projection to inclusion and the discovery the positive in someone or something we had previously seen as negative within our realm of experience. The Dalai Lama, new science and conscious studies point out that we must recognize self and other(s) as simultaneously central aspects of the whole of our experience.

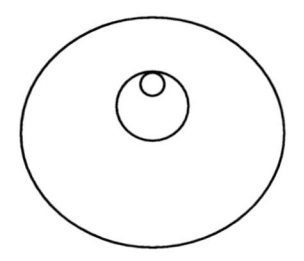

Self, community, world community in one

This new understanding empowers us as individuals, while giving us the challenge of respecting others and the consequences of our relationships to them since we are interdependent. We embody a group psyche, or unconscious interconnected causal relationships in a whole. Practitioners of family therapy understand this at one level of magnitude, at least. In a family or group each member has a broad spectrum of potentials, but expresses only those that fit the dynamic state of the group in order to compensate for each other. A group psyche, or collective, cultural, psyche is at the very least implied by Carl Jung's[4] collective unconscious, Kurt Lewin's group dynamics, Rupert Sheldrake's[5] morphogenetic fields, and James Lovelock's Gaia hypothesis, in which the whole planet is seen as an organism with interdependent parts including the species within it, such as our own.

---

3. Jung, Carl Gustav (Foreword), Hellmut Wilhelm (Preface), Richard Wilhelm (Translator), Cary F. Baynes (Translator), C.F. Baynes (Author), R. Wilhelm (Author) *The I Ching or Book of Changes*. http://www.onlineclarity.co.uk/html/wiltrans/wilhelm_translation.html

4. Jung, Carl Gustav (Foreword), Hellmut Wilhelm (Preface), Richard Wilhelm (Translator), Cary F. Baynes (Translator), C.F. Baynes (Author), R. Wilhelm (Author) *The I Ching or Book of Changes* http://www.onlineclarity.co.uk/html/wiltrans/wilhelm_translation.html

5. {Sheldrake, 1981, 1995 #4} Rochester, Vermont: Park Street Press.

When we see cars moving together in complex traffic patterns from a great height, or if we see starlings moving in swarms, we are convinced of a synchrony of movement that encompasses the individuals while expressing a larger, collective interplay. Terror is a component of the current interplay. We can consciously and unconsciously broadly address it through the group psyche. I want to emphasize that although each of us is an individual, as Jung pointed out we are all, deep down, capable of any human act, or at least we have some access to the feelings and thoughts that might produce it. Therefore we are all qualified to dialogue with or about it, no matter how slightly we believe it manifests itself in our own life. Since we are part of a connected whole, each and all of our human expressions have some impact on the whole. The word *holon* describes how our immediacy is to some as yet unknown degree pivotal in the larger world. Fractals and chaos theory illustrate this. What an individual brings to the group sand tray is unique, representative and highly pertinent. The same dynamics are occurring in their own particularity to some extent everywhere in the human community and we are all, in a sense, thinking together, too. Two scientists in different countries come up with almost the same insights within days of each other, suggesting that both are unique representatives, though in a specific sense outliers, of a collective mind. We are trying together to solve or dissolve the obstructions to health of all kinds, and improve the dynamics of our relationships to each other and the planet. Terror is an example of thinking at cross-purposes with the other due to limited information, a lag in information or misinformation. We are living in a time of swift globalization, with cultures that were once more separate are clashing due lack of familiarity and understanding. Certain topics have been taboo and we are often as groups in denial. There is a moral component to successful functioning of the Whole that can be seen most recently in the after effects of the sub-prime mortgages. Hidden dynamics can be discovered through sand tray.

## Information and perspectives

Generally each of us and each field of study has as its underlying ultimate mission the solution to human problems, but we each operate with limited information, a lag in information, or misinformation about each other's field of study or each other as individuals. Physicist David Bohm[6] has a concept of "active information" waiting to be assimilated through dialogue. In academia there is a growing awareness that interdisciplinary scholarship could help us better understand and solve our human problems. At the individual level we all benefit when we are heard by others. There is a strong attachment component to shared viewing[7] and being heard; the process increases empathy.

---

6. David Bohm. 1988. *On creativity*. New York: Routledge.

7. Alan Schore. 2003. *Effect of a secure attachment relationship on right brain development, affect regulation and infant mental health*. From http:www.healthychildrennetwork.lu/pdf/themes/schore_imhj_attachment

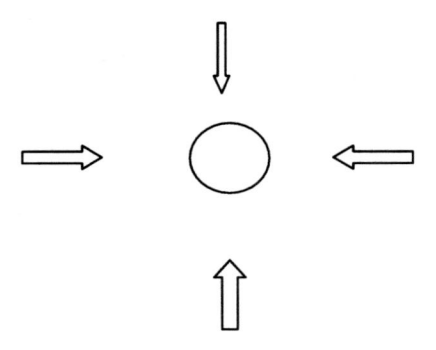

## Cumulative understanding

In a research project connected to my dissertation I noticed that information collected separately from members of a group is cumulative as if from an inverse prism, that is, each person, separately questioned, tended to have a new perspective to add about a topic, and together they led to a more comprehensive meaning picture. In other words, there is uniqueness and the potential to contribute in each of us as we meet and share information from our own experience and perspective.

"Blockages" is a term used by Margaret Lowenfeld[8], who, as far as we know, initiated the practice of sand tray or sandplay therapy. She used it to describe the impasses that confront the urge for well being in a child. A child, or an adult, has limited information or access to that which would benefit it due to misunderstanding, misinformation, or limited information. This skewed grasp of the world directs his or her behavior. Blockages to flow can be related to the term "dysfunction" in individuals, families and groups. Terror in its various forms is an especially intense and health destructive dynamic that maintains human misery either by maintaining the status quo or sending terrible new reverberations through the system. It is an ill-advised form of behavioral communication that would be better replaced by dialogue and play. The natural learning process through imaginative play is an effort to attain wellbeing or wholeness and is a healthy method of working through dysfunction. A child will play out a tea party or a war with miniatures as a way of propioceptively understanding and merging with the culture. In sandplay, a child, grownup or group can work through an impasse. Mihály Csíkszentmihályi's[9] concept of "flow" applies when we are functioning most freely, crea-

---

8. Lowenfeld, Margaret, "The non-verbal thinking of children." (Lowenfeld) and Non-verbal 'thinking' in child psychotherapy. (Trail and Rowles). London: Institute of Child Psychology, Ltd. 1964.
9. Mihaly Csikzentmihalyi,. *Creativity, flow and the psychology of discovery and invention.* (New York: HarperCollins, 1996).

ENGAGING TERROR

tively and productively. It is a feeling that often accompanies play because imaginative play is creative, healing and transformative.

At a remove: We often hear the phrase, "from outside the box." Einstein[10] pointed out that we can only understand where we are if we can see ourselves or our situation at a remove. This is difficult to accomplish in day-to-day life when our experience is more like that of a fish in water who doesn't know anything else. A sand tray and the miniature figures and objects that function in it as representatives of aspects of our world make it possible to profoundly share perspectives.

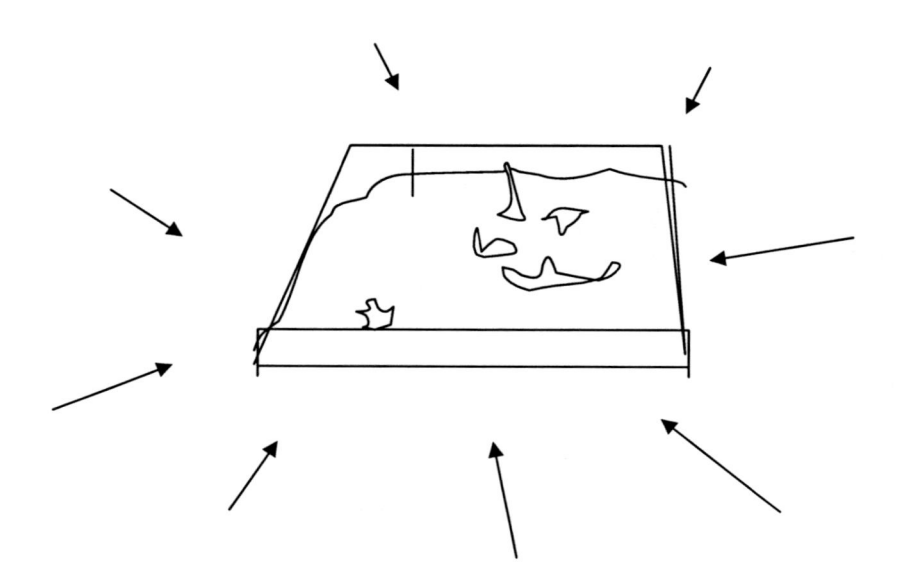

**Sharing perspectives from outside the box**
*Visual/multisensory:* Traditionally we have consciously focused on words and linear thought when solving problems. The sentences we read and speak are linear, but the right brain allows a more instantaneous understanding of or communication about a situation. Most adults can drive a car or do a complex physical task while thinking of any number of other things, which tells me that we can count on practiced visual assessment of situations to inform our next moves. Therefore a kind of visual discussion, using our right brain capacity, would be helpful when applied to the human condition (See J J Gibson[11], Enactivism and situated cognition).

---

10. Bernstein, James. *Einstein.* (New York: Penguin Books, 1973).
11. James J. Gibson, *An ecological approach to human perception.* (Hillsdale: NJ: Lawrence Erlbaum Associates 1986).

*Metaphor* is a longstanding aspect of communication, visually seen as early as cave paintings, that provides easy access often by tying a concept to an image. When expressed visually, metaphor has even more impact due to the relative comprehensiveness of our visual understanding. A conversation, verbal and spatial, about a three dimensional expression that includes visual metaphor is a highly communicative exchange, especially when its content is fully pertinent. This pertinence occurs through projection.

*Projection.* Freud called projection a defense mechanism whereby we see in another person or people the unrecognized aspects or dynamics of the self. This concept can be expanded, though, in a more positive framework as the appearance, in what we encounter, of what we are ready to learn and recognize, positive or negative, about our simultaneously central and interdependent existence. I think that negative projection or negative judgment can be viewed as a signal that there is something at hand that we had best learn from through some sort of dialogue. Through the lens of consciousness, projection is the next learning experience that arises for us. We can rely on this dynamic to produce exactly the right constellation in the sand tray for discussion about our shared strengths and current predicament.

*Catharsis.* As individual sandplay therapy shows, catharsis in sandplay allows a release of strong emotions or propensities for action that might otherwise have damaging effects though our behavior. In individual sand tray therapy a small boy who has a new little brother might play out, for example, a dragon devouring a smaller figure as a way of releasing his anger at his younger brother for taking his place as the baby in the family. This release will reduce or eliminate his urge to pinch his baby brother in secret in the future. His anger towards his brother was based on his own limited perspective that the baby brother is at fault for his arrival on this earth and perhaps came with the intention to make the older brother personally suffer. The group psyche, too, embodies a dynamic of emotions, thoughts and behaviors resulting in the current state of things that is based in both strengths and blockages. The miniature nature of the sand tray and its contents can allow for catharsis there if called for, a release of powerful emotions held by collections of individuals. I have noticed that the content of the projection, though it includes individual content rising from the experiences of the participants, actually draws from the collective with the participants becoming instruments of the group or cultural psyche, ready to productively process the material. The flow of exchange is positive and encourages more flow.

To review, we use both action and dialogue to communicate with each other in real life. In order to ease strong emotions in our global community that might lead to terrorist acts and the use of fear in order to control others, we can gather around the tray finding ourselves, in our holon, to be representatives of the wider culture. Through action and dialogue there, we can observe previously unrecognized dynamics, discover new information, and dissipate the misinformation that causes collective negative emotions. In the process we can assimilate that changed, more informed gestalt both consciously and unconsciously and adjust our behavior accordingly. With that more comprehensive world view our resultant behavior's reverberations will be more likely, as we return to our lives, to produce acceptance and wellbeing. Through repetitions of the activity the pressures in our increasingly global human community that lead to terrorist acts will be mitigated.

# References

Bernstein, James. 1973. *Einstein*. New York: Penguin Books.

Bohm, David. 1998. *On creativity*. New York: Routledge.

Csikzentmihalyi, Mihaly. 1996. *Creativity, flow and the psychology of discovery and invention*. New York: HarperCollins.

Forbes, Heather T. and B. Bryan Post. 1986. *Beyond consequences, logic and control*. Orlando: Beyond Consequences Institute LLC.

Gibson, James, J. 1986. *An ecological approach to human perception*. Hillsdale: NJ: Lawrence Erlbaum Associates.

Lowenfeld, Margaret, *The non-verbal thinking of children. (Lowenfeld) and Non-verbal 'thinking' in child psychotherapy. (Trail and Rowles)*. London: Institute of Child Psychology, Ltd.1964.

Jung, Carl Gustav (Foreword), Hellmut Wilhelm (Preface), Richard Wilhelm(Translator), Cary F. Baynes (Translator), C.F. Baynes (Author), R. Wilhelm (Author) *The I Ching or Book of Changes*. http://www.on lineclarity.co.uk/html/wiltrans/wilhelm_translation.html.

Sheldrake, Rupert. 1981, 1995. *The hypothesis of a new science of life: Morphic resonance*, Rochester, Vermont: Park Street Press.

Schore, Alan. 2003. *Effect of a secure attachment relationship on right brain development, affect regulation and infant mental health*. From http://www.healthychildrennetwork.lu/pdf/themes/schore_imhj_attachment

# CURING AND EDUCATING THROUGH TERROR (A COMPARATIVE CASE STUDY)

*Razvan Amironesei*

## Introduction

In the *Origins of Totalitarianism* (1951), H. Arendt shows that terror is the essence of totalitarian regimes that has its own rationality and the purpose to manufacture humankind. "Terror as the execution of a law of movement whose ultimate goal is not the welfare of men or the interest of one man but the fabrication of mankind, eliminates individuals for the sake of the species, sacrifices the 'parts' for the sake of the 'whole'". The suprahuman force of Nature or History has its own beginning and its own end, so that it can be hindered only by the new beginning and the individual end, which the life of each man actually is." (Arendt 1973, 465). In Arendt, terror has a double function. First, it is the essence of the totalitarian regime, and second it is law of movement which invalidates the action of citizens. Despite their differences, Arendt like Hegel argues that terror suppresses what is determined or singular. Whereas in Arendt terror is the law of movement that suppresses the singularity and accelerates the course of History and that of Nature, in Hegel terror emerges as the correlate of absolute freedom[1]. For both of them terror is not an individual or a group attribute, but rather is informed by a suprahuman necessity. According to Arendt, terror has an alienating function. It paralyzes, it divides and breaks any relation between humans. "The aim of totalitarian education has never been to instil convictions but to destroy the capacity to form any" (468). Totalitarian education does not seek consensus but instead pursues the atomization of individuals. Total terror deploys in the absence of any form of resistance[2].

---

1. See 'Absolute Freedom and Terror' in Hegel, 1977: 355-364. For a discussion of absolute freedom see Ch. 1 in Westphal :1992. For a discussion of terror in relation to the French Revolution, see : Schmidt, 1998: 4-32. and Wokler, 1998: 33-55.

2. According to Arendt, the totalitarian regimes use terror as a substitute for consent and forms of legitimacy. This position is indeed debatable. As Adamson shows, during the Communist era "the link between coercion and ideology was in fact rooted in discourses of violence." (Adamson, 2007: 569). In the respect he focuses on "strategies for building 'consent.' One of the findings of the present research suggests that the PCR [Romanian Communist Party] was engaged in an effort to achieve consent for its rule by means of a specific hegemonic strategy involving a discourse that was modified as it went along." (568). For a broad discussion on the formation of terror from a historical perspective see, (Deletant: 1999), and (Tismaneanu: 2003).

In this work, I will not discuss terror as a natural or a historical force, but rather I will see it as a historical practice inscribed in the study the modes of formation of violence. My aim is to show that violence is an effective political tool which should be analyzed in a positive manner. Violence is a political operator which transforms the individuals and which it has its own rationality. This paper contributes to what one would call 'the domain of historical perspectives of the rationalities of violence'. More precisely, I will show that fear and terror as practices of violence are at the same time effective political affects invested within a form of government of individuals. Using a genealogical interpretation, my aim is to see how a political technology using terror techniques operates and displaces in modern and contemporary Europe. In this respect, I will choose two seminal moments that occurred in different historical periods, but which are both similar in their articulation and mode of functioning. The first one deals with Leuret and Pinel asylum in France of the nineteenth century where the use of "moral treatment" included verbal menaces, interrogatory practices, cold showers etc. with the precise purpose to normalise the patients' relation to reality. In the second moment, I will show the investment of violence in an experimental prison from Romania in the middle of the twentieth century. The "Pitesti experiment" is known for breaking the prisoners' resistance through terror methods and for reinvesting the force of the "converted" individual in order to reproduce the terror effect on others.

Obviously, in these two political experiments terror plays a central role. As I will show in what follows, terror, deployed as an intense corporeal and psychic violence over resistant individuals, has a therapeutic and a pedagogical function. Following a juridical interpretation of violence one might argue that political violence is an unforeseen accident, a political residue sanctioned by our legal codes. My thesis is that on the contrary violence and specifically terror techniques should be inscribed in an economy of excess. Moreover, terror should be analyzed as a useful political tool in order to manufacture human minds and to elaborate docile political behaviors. In other words, terror techniques circulate and invest the social space with the objective to capitalize fear and reactivates forms of resistance, articulating this way the elements of a governementality of violence.

## Fear and Terror in Leuret and Pinel

As I already noted, in the first part of this paper I will provide two examples for the cure of the insane in Leuret and Pinel asylum between 1810 and 1840, in France. More specifically, I will focus on the formation of fear tactics in Leuret and the articulation of terror techniques in Pinel which function as therapeutic tools and regulated practices of violence. Michel Foucault notes in his *Histoire de la folie* (1961) that

> fear, in the eighteenth century, was regarded as one of the passions most advisable to arouse in madmen. It was considered the natural

> complement of the constraints imposed upon maniacs and lunatics; . . . But fear is efficacious not only at the level of the effects of the disease; it is the disease itself that fear attacks and suppresses. It has, in fact, the property of petrifying the operations of the nervous system, somehow congealing its too mobile fibers, controlling all their disordered movements; "fear being a passion that diminishes the excitation of the brain, it can consequently calm its excesses, and especially the irascible excitation of maniacs. (Foucault, 1988: 180).

However, during the nineteenth century he sees a displacement taking place in the investment of fear:

> fear is no longer used as a method for arresting movement, but as a punishment; when joy does not signify organic expansion, but reward; when anger is nothing more than a response to concerted humiliation; in short, when the nineteenth century, by inventing its famous "moral methods," has brought madness and its cure into the domain of guilt. (Foucault, 1988: 181-182).

From this moment, fear plays within a cure by passions and it is an important piece of now famous moral treatment which emerges at the end of eighteenth century in York Retreat asylum[3] under the recommendations of William Tuke (1732-1822).

François Leuret is one of the most known French physicians who made an efficient use of passion in therapeutics and of violent means within moral treatment. According to him, moral treatment of madness is grounded on "reason" and "experience" and it is "the reasonable use of all means which influence directly the mind and the passions of the insane" (Leuret 1840, 156), the only true remedy which has a "direct influence on the symptoms of the madness" (462). In order to prove the efficiency of this method of cure,

---

3. "Fear appears as an essential presence in the asylum. Already an ancient figure, no doubt, if we think of the terrors of confinement. But these terrors surrounded madness from the outside, marking the boundary of reason and unreason, and enjoying a double power: over the violence of fury in order to contain it, and over reason itself to hold it at a distance; such fear was entirely on the surface. The fear instituted at the Retreat is of great depth; it passes between reason and madness like a mediation, like an evocation of a common nature they still share, and by which it could link them together. The terror that once reigned was the most visible sign of the alienation of madness in the classical period; fear was now endowed with a power of disalienation, which permitted it to restore a primitive complicity between the madman and the man of reason. It re-established a solidarity between them. Now madness would never—could never—cause fear again; it would be afraid, without recourse or return, thus entirely in the hands of the pedagogy of good sense, of truth, and of morality." (Foucault, 1988: 245).

Leuret discusses in his book *Du traitement moral de la folie* (1840) the case and the treatment he offered to one of his patients, a treatment that invalidates the use of the physical treatment which supposes the existence of the organic lesions.

Mr. Dupré, a former officer in the French Army, is hospitalized in Charenton in 1824 "due to mental derangement"[4]. He becomes Leuret's patient in 1838 and is cured in February 1839. He relapses in May 1840. When he goes in therapy with Leuret, Dupré is indifferent to the external stimuli (he refuses people's company, he refuses to read, and the use of money). He identifies himself with Napoleon, and at the same time he believes is the exponent of a superior race and the victim of a vast conspiracy. Dupré also believes that he has an exceptional virility. Following his excesses, he was forced to retire to his 'châteaux' of Charenton, Saint-Yon and in Bicêtre. He thinks that he is the only man in the asylum while others are women in disguise. As Leuret sees it, his indifference is due to a disturbance of his intelligence and passions. The indifference of which Dupré suffers makes him opaque to the world and locks him up in his delirium. The question that Leuret asks is how to cure a madman who is "indifferent" (for he lacks passions like anger, joy etc.) and who is autonomous (he "does not ask for favours," 425). "How can we manage to pull him out of his torpor—to provide him with the right feelings; to make him to pay us attention?" (429). Thus, Leuret develops different strategies with the purpose to affect Dupré's behavior. The cure of Dupré involves several aspects. However, I will limit my analysis to the investment of violence through a therapy of corporeal pain and fear and the expected effect of obedience derived from the cure.

In the book that I just mentioned, Leuret defends himself against his critics and outlines that he does not aim to produce an unrestrained pain over the body, but he rather interprets pain as a useful tool which must affect the patient[5]. The pain produced through corporeal violence, repeated threats and fear seeks to unlock the internal resistances of the patient in order to cure him[6]. Precisely, this type of therapy involves a modulation of the capacity of

---

4. According to a medical bulletin of October 24, 1824 by Mr. Royer-Collard, the patient is able to think properly, to carry out a conversation, but it is consumed by sadness. In his occasional deliriums his father appears taking the face of other individuals. Progressively, he becomes apathetic and delirious. In 1836, Mr. Ferrus states that Mr. Dupré "suffers of chronic mania" and is declared incurable. (Cf. Leuret, 1840: 421).
5. In Leuret, pain involves a therapy of the body and a reformation of the soul. "Pain is useful to the lunatics, as it is useful in the ordinary course of life, as it is useful in education: it is one of the mobiles which eradicate the evil and pursues the good." (Leuret, 1840: 157).
6. "Do not employ consolations, they are useless; have no recourse to reasoning, it does not persuade; do not be sad with melancholics, your sadness sustains theirs; do not assume an air of gaiety with them, they are only hurt by it. What is required is

the body to endure pain[7]. Leuret submits Dupré to cold showers and effusions which act directly on his body and which regulate his unchained passions.

> It is true to say, however, that my fellow colleagues and myself, do not employ the showers and the effusions in the same circumstances nor completely with a same aim. With them, an inoffensive patient, a melancholic person, a monomaniac will never receive cold showers, unless he did commit some serious offence to the rule of the establishment or refused to be nourished. As far as I am concerned, I will not wait until the disease comes to this point to stop it. I will not give the patient the opportunity to fail, but instead I give him the shower and teach him what it must do to avoid it. And when I obtained a concession I am not satisfied. Each day I ask for more. If he concedes, I require more from him. And, if I foresee the cure, I stop only when it is obtained. (162)

Using cold showers, Leuret measures the body pain in order to quantify the patient degree of resistance and continuously tests his will to obey to his commands. When he approaches Dupré, he starts by blaming him for his numerous offences and his idleness, shakes him violently and asks him whether a woman could assault him the way he did[8]. This way, Leuret questions Dupré's hyper-masculinity.

In addition, within the process of the treatment, Leuret gives Dupré precise orders and threatens him of sever punishments[9]. Dupré must know that

---

great *sang-froid,* and when necessary, severity. Let your reason be their rule of conduct. A single string still vibrates in them, that of pain; have courage enough to pluck it." Leuret, François, *Fragments psychologiques sur la folie* (Paris, 1834), pp.308-21, cited in Foucault, 1988 : 182.
7. Leuret acknowledges that he exposed himself and his assistants to cold showers and effusions in order to quantify the degree of pain, which he allots to his patients. (Leuret, 1840: 160-161).
8. After this lively exchange of words, Leuret asks one of his assistants to slip purgative drugs in Dupré's food without informing him. By way of consequence, during night Dupré has abundant feces. The following day Leuret proves him that his actual weakness is a sign of fear. When Dupré denies his fear, Leuret's assistants pour water on his head in order to punish him. This causes a sharp reaction from his part and he starts to admit for a certain time that the psychiatrist is indeed a man. Leuret concludes: "Finally, after tormenting and threatening him with the shower, ... he ended up being afraid" (436).
9. "It is by force that the furies of a maniac are overcome; it is by opposing fear to anger that anger may be mastered. If the terror of punishment and public shame are associated in the mind during attacks of anger, one will not appear without the other;

in case he disobeys his psychiatrist, he is prone to a disproportionate punishment compared to the gravity of the offence[10]. Thus, Leuret wants to pull him out of his torpor, to stimulate his feeling of injustice, to induce the possibility of revolt and finally to provide him with the feeling of weakness towards his psychiatrist. Using these tactics, one can insure the obedience of the patient that paves the way to the acceptance of the normative order in which the doctor wants to make him function. Obedience works as a form of asymmetric recognition in which the patient accepts the authority of the psychiatrist and his commands. In short, fear is a useful affect which accompanies the cure from the beginning until the end. As we have noticed, fear has a triple function. First, fear is internalized within a therapy of pain. Second, fear works as punishment and as a means of dissuasion. And finally, fear seals the obedience of the insane towards the psychiatrist and the recognition of his authority.

My second point is to pursue the analysis of violence within asylum with a cure by Philippe Pinel, which will provide us a clear vision on the investment of terror in the therapeutic process of the insane. As Pinel relates, he accepted around 1810 under his supervision at the Bicêtre Asylum the case of a young religious affected by the "abolition of the catholic religion in France" (Pinel 1806, 61). The confused imagination of the young man "tormented with the dangers of the other world" found the hope for his salvation in the monastic practices of abstinence of the ancient anchorites. Consequently, he constantly refused nourishment and rudely rejected the efforts of the medical staff to persuade him of the contrary. Then, Pinel asks himself: "How was such a perverse train of ideas to be stemmed or counteracted?" (62). Terror as a therapeutic method emerged as the most appropriate solution to the young man's problem. I quote Pinel in length:

> The excitement of terror presented itself as the only recourse. For this purpose, Citizen Pussin [Pinel's Assistant] appeared one night at the door of his chamber, and, with fire darting from his eyes, and thunder in his voice, commanded a group of domestics, who were armed with strong and loudly clanking chains, to do their duty. But the ceremony was artfully suspended;-the soup was placed before the maniac, and strict orders were left him to eat it in the course of the night, on pains of the severest punishment. He was left to his own reflections. The night was spent (as he afterwards informed me) in a state of the most distressing hesitation, whether to incur the present punishment, or the distant but still more dreadful torments of the

---

the poison and the antidote are inseparable." (Crichton, Alexander, *On Mental Diseases*, cited in Regnault, Elias, 1830:188. See also, Foucault, 1988: 180).
10. "My injunction looks strange, unjust and ridiculous to him, but I am the strongest, and when I threaten him, he knows that I keep my word." (Leuret, 1840: 436).

world to come. After an internal struggle of many hours, the idea of the present evil gained the ascendancy, and he determined to take the soup. (62-63)

Now, let me make a few remarks on the articulation of terror in Pinel. First, as we can see, the therapy does not consist in establishing a diagnostic from a nosography. On the contrary, it seeks to define cure through the organization of a battlefield. As Foucault notes, the asylum is a space where a confrontation between two wills takes place (Foucault 2006, 7). The will of the psychiatrist elaborates strategies to submit the will of the patient[11] that Pinel and Leuret interpret as the product of his whims[12] or the effect of an error. The cure takes the form of an evacuation of evil through a fight between the psychiatrist will and the insane will[13]. It is a theatre where a confrontation of forces takes place and victory is awaited.

Second, Pinel uses terror with the purpose to act directly on the passions of the maniac. In order to activate the cure terror must thoroughly invade the patient's body. Terror is expected to produce an interior conflict which must overcome internal resistances and force the patient to recover sanity. By using terror, Pinel seeks to modify and convert his patient representations[14]. We have here the inscription of the insane in an economy of truth through the

---

11. According to Leuret, what prevents the insane from seeing the world is his "ego" (le Moi). "I never saw in Mr. Dupre, during his treatment, nor since, finer feelings, a generous or an elevated thought. His *ego* always had the first and often the most important part in his behavior." (Leuret, 1840: 459).
12. Leuret "refuses to believe that my will would break against that of a lunatic, that my spirit would remain powerless against his whims" (426).
13. In order to obtain the obedience of the insane, Leuret must yield and break his patient' will. In this respect, Leuret decides to force Mr. Dupré write the story of his life: "I use against him my best argument. I send him to the room with showers. I ask my assistants to strip him. I place him in a bath-tub and one throws two cold water buckets over his body. He promises to write, dries out, gets dressed, and says that he will not write. Four water buckets. He is stripped, receives them, promises to write but he does not. Eight water buckets. One brings them and when he sees them arranged in front of him, and is sure to receive all of them, he yields and devotes the rest of the day and the following day to write his story with great details." (444).
14. "One maniac had the habit of tearing her clothes and breaking any object that came into her hands; she was given showers, she was put into a straitjacket, she finally appeared "humiliated and dismayed"; but fearing that this shame might be transitory and this remorse too superficial, "the director, in order to impress a feeling of terror upon her, spoke to her with the most energetic firmness, but without anger, and announced to her that she would henceforth be treated with the greatest severity." The desired result was not long in coming: "Her repentance was announced by a torrent of tears which she shed for almost two hours." (Pinel, *Traité medico-philosophique sur l'aliénation mentale* (1801, Paris), p. 205, cited in Foucault, 1988: 267-268).

use of therapeutic ends. In other words, terror must produce a division within the representations of the maniac in order to distinguish clearly between the truthfulness of the medical practice and the error of its own representations. The process of cure through terror consists in a practice of the self and in an apprenticeship of an intellectual process. Moreover, terror must cause a sharp reaction from the patient in order to instil a doubt and a moral distress into his own convictions. Precisely, terror must shock the patient in order to instilling him a moral conflict by stimulating a sense of guilt which connects him to his psychiatrist. Terror is used as a powerful therapeutic instrument which modifies the patient relation to one self in order to sustain a durable cure.

## The 'Pitesti Experiment'

In the second part of this paper, I will outline a few constitutive elements of the Pitesti experiment, which took place in Romania between 1949 and 1952. The Pitesti experiment is a specially designed prison with the purpose to re-educate the so called "enemies of the people" formed of young people resistant to the new Communist regime. But the Pitesti experiment is not a singular institution of this type. Along with other prisons from Suceava, Gherla, Aiud which functioned during the 1950s and the 1960s, they constituted centers for the political reformation of individuals.

In the following, I will analyze the Pitesti experiment from three perspectives. First, I will focus on the political function of torture. Second, I will show the effect of terror over the individuals as a useful political affect. And in the end, I will discuss the double function of confession.

There are two types of groups which are functioning in the Pitesti prison: the group of overseers or reformers and the group of prisoners to be reformed. The overseers had been themselves political prisoners now converted to the new ideology. They are calling themselves New Men teaching others the way of self reformation. Here is the political innovation of the Pitesti laboratory: the prisoners must torture each other. (cf. Ierunca 1990, 18-19). The exercise of violence is not inflicted by a professional torturer, but instead it is a practice administrated by the prisoners themselves. Since there is no stable function of a torturer the political divisions suspend the organization of resistances. In other words, the victims cannot articulate forms of solidarity in their common fear.

Within the prison the re-education process has four stages. (cf. 32-34). 1) The *external unmasking* consists mainly to gather information[15] with the aim of

---

15. "The first phase carried to completion the secret police's earlier investigations through a torturing system whereby they sought to squeeze a man into the position of declaring all, but absolutely *all*, that he had done or intended to do prior to his arrest. He had to name and denounce all persons he had been in contact with, all who helped him with money or food, advice or moral encouragement; all who had

objectifying the self and others. 2) The *internal unmasking* seeks to unmask those who have helped the individual resist during the interrogation procedure—either someone from the administration of the penitentiary, either a friend. 3) The *public unmasking*. The prisoner must repudiate his values, beliefs and ultimately himself[16]. The aim of this tactic is the self-transformation of the individual precisely his subjectification. 4) Finally, in the last stage of the re-education process the prisoners must torture their best friend in order to seal their allegiance to the new normative order and the complete repudiation of their own past[17] (cf. Idem, 19).

The thesis that I would like to defend in this second part is that in the Pitesti laboratory torture seeks primarily the reformation of the individual, and not simply the production of truth, or the atonement of a crime. One does not torture in order to confess. One tortures in order to educate.

More precisely, the effect that torture has on individuals is to produce a prolonged state of terror as a means of education. Thus, torture becomes a reforming practice of words, behaviors and thoughts. Moreover, this pedagogy of violence works within the cure for it is formulated as an urgency to be saved from the "bourgeois" and the "religious" ideas alike. Violence is an encircling movement deployed as a reformation practice with pedagogical and therapeutic functions.

The exercise of violence must be continuous in its manifestations and not temporary in its deployment. In other words, another manner to think the individual pain and the terror effect emerges. The inflicted pain is a circu-

---

sheltered him; all who knew of his activities even if they did not participate in them; all who did not sympathize with the Communist regime; all whom he suspected of having infiltrated the Party or having joined it opportunistically; anybody who seemed likely later to engage in anti-Party activity; malingers of the Party; etc. Then he had to tell whether he had any ideological material books, documents, newspapers, circulars, etc. which he had not declared during earlier questioning; where they were hidden; who else knew of their existence; whether he possessed firearms; if so, where hidden. Particular emphasis was placed on firearms, especially those stored away by peasants as the German troops retreated in 1944; and on any individuals of the "people's army" who might later, through bribery or corruption, place at the disposal of the "enemies of the people" weapons or anything else that could be used against the Party." (Bacu, 1971: 39-40).

16. "the students were obliged to crush underfoot everything they held most sacred God, family, friends, love, wife, colleagues, memories, ideology everything which bound them to the past, anything that might give them inner support while in prison." (Bacu, 1971: 41).

17. "Hungry, tortured, humiliated for weeks and months on end; sleepless, terrified, terrorized, struck by him who but an hour earlier had been his friend and brother in chains; forced in his turn, [...], to become a torturer of others; without the slightest hope of escape; isolated from the world by a curtain of steel; brought to the edge of the grave but denied the privilege of dying of such was comprised the calendar of a student subjected to this experiment [...]". (Bacu, 1971: 56).

lar political affect and not simply a passing event which coerces the body to confess the truth. On the contrary, it constitutes its own purpose and it is virtually indefinite. In other words, modern torture is not a 'wild' practice as Foucault states in *Surveiller et punir* (1975), but that the reformation of bodies is elaborated through a therapy of pain. This way of investing the pain in modern torture has a consequence on its political objective. Torture is a political operator which seeks to constitute a political individual in a state of pure receptivity. What this individual must retain by all means is the memory of an incorporated pain. In other words, the distribution of pain in modern torture aims to produce a *bodily memory*. The effect of terror articulated through this excessive pain distributed over the body insures the permanence of torture as a political act[18].

From this, one can see that confession is not the final objective of torture, but rather a method of control in order to ensure the receptivity of the individuals to the new normative order. This receptivity provides the political objective of torture which is to use the confession as an efficient tool to transform the individuals into legible souls. Thus, the first meaning of confession is to objectify the individuals. The second meaning of the confession would be its investment in practices of resistance. The confession as a form of resistance emerges from the constitution of what I have called a bodily memory—which is the incorporation of terror as a political affect. Torture creates a body state and ensures the necessary background which incites the confession of the prisoners. The consequence would be that the confession works as the equivalent of a true political initiation (for example through the conversion of a resistant individual into a political informer[19]). But one should notice that resistance is located in this precise place. The question then is how the resistance practice works? The answer is: through a reinvestment of the confession. The confession is no longer an instrument of objectivation under the form of a knowledge extracted from the individual's discourses. The point of reactivation of resistance is when the terrorized individual starts to tell the story of a body in pain integrated into a political experience. A prisoner forced to become other and to maintain the secrecy of his becoming in the political order, now seeks to be delivered of his secrecy. He confesses, becomes a singular victim by eliminating his duplicity, and do-

---

18. "The resurrection of the values which had been superseded by re-education was not in itself too difficult a task, as frequently a simple stimulation sufficed to impel the person back to his former equilibrium. But one real obstacle, very hard to surmount, was the haunting fear, locked into every fiber of the unmasked victim, that any day the re-education terror might be resumed. Life inside the prison did nothing to dispel that fear." (Bacu: 1971, 122).

19. "But when the unmaskings were over, and the terror of 'reeducation' had lost much of its virulence, Teodoru switched to the other extreme, becoming one of the most dangerous denouncers, with not the slightest excuse for this change of attitude, this strange new viciousness." (58).

ing so introduces an element of liberation in his own politically codified existence. Confession is a practice which allows a transformation of the self that is operated by the self with the assistance of others and emerges as a form of subjection through a mechanism of liberation.

Like the fear and terror techniques in Leuret and Pinel, one can see in the Pitesti experiment a cleavage between a resistant individual and an obedient individual. Generated by an intense pain over the body, terror produces a politically useful and docile individual—a receptive body which can be manipulated and transformed. But this receptive body is in fact a body that incorporated the memory of an inflicted pain. This means that terror produces at the same time a docile body and a resistant individual through the investment of a bodily memory. As a political tool, terror forms an obedient individual and a resistant individual who keeps the memory of the pain and the memory of his injustice in the marks applied on his body[20].

## Conclusion

One should close this inquiry on the terror techniques in Pinel and Leuret asylum and in the Pitesti laboratory with a few general remarks on the political status terror. While terror has a therapeutic function in Pinel and Leuret, within the Pitesti experiment, terror works as an educational tool. However, as we have shown, these two political aims are not in contradiction. In Pinel and Leuret, extreme pain has the effect of tormenting and of dividing the individual representations. Terror works within the cure of the insane which elaborates the effect of an imperious necessity in order to modify his predispositions. It is a political operator which invests the individual's behaviors and it inscribes them into a new normative order.

The Pitesti prison is a laboratory of human behaviors where one innovates in the political field starting with systematic practices of violence which involve continuous torture, terror and confession. Here we have a school of political conduct, a factory of ideals which has a definite objective: to produce New Men from qualified resistant individuals. The penitentiary system

---

20. The subject of the Pitesti experiment maintains a double disposition: that of a torturer and that of a victim. "Escaping from the terror of their former milieu, from that closed-in hell in which they reciprocally tormented each other; seeing that the administration no longer supported those in charge of maintaining the atmosphere created at Pitesti; and finding that on the contrary they were looked upon with a significant 'lack of understanding,' the students gradually began to change their own attitude toward both their colleagues and the other prisoners. Little by little, where before even the thought was impossible, some began a process of self-examination, of critical analysis, or, as it was said back home, a digging out of the problems covered by the ashes of terror. Timidly at first, then with greater daring and in increasingly greater numbers, the students gradually began to see things through their own eyes and to draw logical conclusions without quailing in fear of being suspected of thinking other than as ordered." (97).

achieves this political objective by breaking their flesh in order to remake them again. Here is an unexpected form of power which is strengthened by the investment of individuals' resistances and which reinforces from its spectacular exercise. The rationality of abominable produces this laboratory of souls where the intolerable works as an ordeal for the formation of a new political thought. Terror is educational not in the sense that is attributed by a master of morality, but it is educational because it is "taught" by the prisoners themselves in order to divide themselves and their relation with others. Torture and terror are practices of government which inscribed in a rationality of excess capture the bodies and by breaking them, it raises to 'N' power the political reform of the individuals.

# References

Adansom, Kevin. 2007. "Discourses of violence and the ideological strategies of the Romanian Communist Party, 1944-1953." *East European Politics and Societies*, 21: 559.

Arendt, Hannah. 1973. *The Origins of Totalitarianism*. New York: Harcourt Trade.

Bacu, Dumitru. 1971. *The Anti-human: Student re-education in Romanian prisons*. Englewood, Colorado: Soldiers of the Cross.

Deletant, Dennis. 1999. *Communist terror in Romania: Gheorghiu-Dej and the police state*. New York: St. Martin's.

Foucault, Michel. 2006. *Psychiatric power: Lectures at the College de France 1973-1974*. New York: Palgrave Macmillan.

——— 1988. *Madness and civilization: A History of insanity in the Age of Reason*. New York: Vintage.

——— 1995. *Discipline and Punish: The Birth of the Prison*. New York: Vintage.

Hegel, G.W.F. 1977. "Spirit. Absolute freedom and terror" in *Phenomenology of Spirit*. Oxford: Clarendon Press.

Ierunca, Virgil. 1990. *Fenomenul Pitesti*. Bucuresti: Humanitas.

Leuret, François. 1840. *Du traitement moral de la folie*. Paris: Hachette.

——— 1834. *Fragments psychologiques sur la folie*. Paris: Crochard.

Pinel, Philippe. 1806. *A treatise on insanity*. London: Messers, Cadell and Davies, Strand.

Regnault, Elias. 1830. *Du degré de compétence des médecins dans les questions judiciaires relatives aux aliénations mentales et des théories physiologiques sur la monnaie*. Paris: JB. Baillière.

Schmidt, James. 1998. "Cabbage heads and gulps of water: Hegel on the terror." *Political Theory*, 26, no. 1: 4-32.

Tismaneanu, Vladimir. 2003. *Stalinism for all seasons: A political history of Romanian Communism*. Berkeley: Univ. of California Press.

Westphal, Merold. 1992. *Hegel, Freedom, and Modernity*. Albany: SUNY Press.

Wokler, Robert. 1998. "Contextualizing Hegel's phenomenology of the French Revolution and the Terror." *Political Theory*, 26, no. 1: 33-55.

# THE POSSIBILITY OF TERROR THROUGH THE STORY OF ANXIETY

*Melissa Abbey Strowger*

There is a fascination in our culture with a concept we simply call 'terror.' Somehow the utterance of this one, simple word, drums up all sorts of political, emotionally loaded discussions. Discussions that are emotionally loaded because, since '9/11', the idea of something or somebody being 'out to get us' is something that we all are aware of as a conversation in progress, even as many of us vehemently oppose the characterizations that have been and continue to be borne out of this notion of 'terror'. Whatever newspaper I pick up, whatever news show I am listening to, I notice that there seems to be a little something here about this commonplace idea of being 'terrorized,' and a little something there about an understanding of communities that are 'in panic' about being attacked. Terror has woven itself into the most subtle *and* overt conversations of our social fabric. From politics to literature, health news to fashion, classroom to pub, to one's own living room, this idea of 'terror' has become understood as a naturalized state.

Personally, I find that I cannot help but to also take notice of this cultural manifestation because truthfully, it is constantly in my face. So one day I decided to stop scoffing at terror's sensational presence. I resolved to not flip the channel, turn the page, nor change the subject. I wanted engagement with the meaning being made of and through our collective 'terror.' I wanted to violate terror with my own gaze as much as it was violating me. I wanted to find the opening that I could critique and panic the panicked about the seemingly 'normal' state of 'being terrorized.' I looked and then ...

I saw it ... me ... *gasp* ...

The story of anxiety—a narrative so central to my life by virtue of personally living it, as well as academically exploring it—had come to life in every piece I was reading about The War on Terror. A vivid connection became available to me that I had to pursue. It was the same connection I had made when I stopped ignoring my anxious body, because I had noticed that in my culture's desire to calm anxiety, there also lies a paradoxical desire to narrate our lives in ways that *require* anxiety to propel its sense of urgency. Thus, I could no longer listen to and read about stories of terror without also hearing anxiety's story. Like the ironic story I have just mentioned here of a cultural need to calm (erase) and yet narrate through (*require*) anxiety, anxiety appeared to me as yet another layer of terror's narrative, performing for us the meaning we *make* of terror. Whatever that possibility means, whatever our cultural need for these two stories to narrate one another, this paper is a brief retelling of *my* story of noticing what makes anxiety, and also in this case, terror, story-able at all.

In his book *The Truth About Stories*, Aboriginal author Thomas King says that, "The truth about stories is that that's all we are" (2003, 2). I would like to pause with this observation of King's because I think it has a lot to offer us in terms of thinking through the conceptual construction of this 'thing' we all know as terror. News headlines constantly bombard us with images of that which we are supposed to 'fear' or be in a state of 'panic' and 'crisis' about, and yet, in them, we cannot help but hear an ongoing story that we have all come to know—a story that we have all contributed toward and *reproduce* in the sheer act of this knowing. Terror is present in our culture because we have all put it there. Without coming to a halt in asking, "then why do we, or more specifically, certain groups, continue to tell such stories?" or "why create such alarm and hatred *at all?*" I feel there may be something more to examine in terms of how it is that we *need* to story concepts such as terror. Even more fascinating is how we need *other* stories, like anxiety, to fulfill this cultural need to make meaning for ourselves through these stories. Thus, I cannot help but be compelled to also ask: How is terror then, a story about who we are as a culture, and further, how does the story of anxiety serve terror? As a culture, what is it that we *need* such that these two stories (currently) exist together? And in terms of my own location—as anxious person attempting to observe and make my own meaning of how anxiety is being taken up in our culture—what is it about anxiety that propels the narration of The War on Terror? How is it that this one story (anxiety) makes this *other* story (terror) possible at all?

Disability Studies scholar David Mitchell tells us that (2002, 20):

> The very need for a story is called into being when something has gone amiss with the known world, and thus the language of a tale seeks to comprehend that which has stepped out of line. In this sense, stories compensate for an unknown or unnatural deviance that begs for an explanation.

The War on Terror is a story that tells us about moments of disruption. 9/11, London, Paris and Bali bombings, are just some examples of individual moments of disruption of the seemingly 'known' and 'normal' state of affairs in our world (as understood within a North American context). The War on Terror is therefore, a story about making sense of what Mitchell is referring to as "unknown" or "deviant." The War on Terror is our cultural way of giving explanation to that which seems *sense-less* in a moment when our normal state of being is somehow thwarted. Enter anxiety: Another story or *metaphor* that makes sense of 'being terrorized'. Let's listen to some of these stories:

A New York newspaper called *The National* tells us a story captured as the "Age of Anxiety" (2002). The article begins as such (Ibid.):

> ... recent terrorism events ... [have] pushed up the already elevated level of national anxiety. The *New York Times* reported that Gothamites are "more fearful" these days, even though the crime rate has dropped. "All across the political spectrum," says Fred Siegel, a history professor, "there is an uneasiness, a sense that something is happening, though people can't put their finger on it." Police Commissioner Raymond Kelly attributes the uneasiness to fear of terrorism.

Anxiety *makes sense* in this situation. As a culture, all this talk about terror has made it *known* that the very idea of terror makes us socially 'uneasy'. As a descriptor of this unease, anxiety acceptably lends terror the emotional impact it requires to make itself meaningful to readers. Anxiety normalizes the reader's reaction to the unsettled feeling associated with having been or potentially being terrorized by cueing one to feel panicked. Thus, the storying of terror *through* the story of anxiety paradoxically illustrates our social need for both; though anxiety about that which we are fearful of (being terrorized) is understood as problematic, it is also still required for our collective rationalizations as it serves to attempt to resolve the situation.

Anxiety is a perfect descriptor for terror because, like the fear and panic associated with these 'moments of social disruption', anxiety itself is something of a 'crisis' to be averted. Looking to a *New York Times* fashion article, we again can make sense of this though the journalist's comments about the "current mood" of "nervously" dressed political leaders being the result of the "age of anxiety" in which we now live—a climate which she as the writer describes as something like that of "the Cuban missile crisis 41 years ago" (2003). Like that of the 'Cuban missile crisis', anxiety brings us back to the 'known' that Mitchell describes; as a way to explain a crisis to us that *appears* to be new, unknown, and disruptive. Thus, as we live in a period where being 'senselessly violated' is not understandable in rational terms, when we classify it as a shared crisis of our time, it (terror) becomes something we have normalized.

Anxiety's story therefore serves in narrating terror by storying how we should collectively organize ourselves in relation to this (supposedly) unknown social experience. With book review articles that begin as such (Turrentine 2004):

> It's been 40 years since Richard Hofstadter diagnosed the "paranoid style" in American politics, conveniently handing fiction writers useful tools for making their [characters] ... From the Warren Report and Vietnam through Watergate and the war on terror, the cognitive

dissonance between what we suspect to be true and what we're told is true leads, predictably, to anxiety. And for candid snapshots of anxious people, there's no better place to look than the newest wave of short fiction to emerge in the post-9/11 era.

And Canadian opinion pieces suggesting post-9/11 America as "perplexed and anxious" (Simpson 2008, A21), it is pretty suggestive that what *is* known about terror is that if we orient ourselves toward it through our understanding of anxiety, terror *makes sense*. Through already knowing the one story (anxiety) and applying it to this new one (terror), it becomes possible to know *exactly* how to collectively, and thus, individually follow and respond to the story of terror. And yet ironically, we *need* both stories to make sense of who we have been, who we are now, and who we hope to be (in moving beyond these stories, particularly the story of terror).

Of that which I have described so far, anxiety is therefore something that makes terror a possible and known 'thing' in our collective because of anxiety's own cultural story of worry, fear and panic. Given then, that these are some of the commonsense traits 'known' about anxiety, how is it that anxiety *itself* is being taken-for-granted in terms of making sense of the story of terror? Put another way, how is it that we can so readily use anxiety as an embodied metaphor to collectively understand the 'crisis of terror'? Returning to Mitchell (2002), anxiety serves terror in the way that disability narratives alike serve the world's discourses over. In the lesson that Mitchell gives us about what he terms as a "narrative prosthesis", Mitchell describes the use of embodied metaphors as such (20):

> What calls stories into being, and what does disability have to do with this most basic preoccupation of narrative? Narrative prosthesis (or the dependency of literary narratives on disability) is the notion that all narratives operate out of a desire to compensate for a limitation or to reign in excessiveness. The narrative approach to difference identifies the literary object par excellence as that which has somehow become out of the ordinary—a deviation from a widely accepted cultural norm.

In other words, although anxiety seems to be the obvious descriptor for terror, it actually is Mitchell's "narrative prosthesis" for terror's story, in that, while being the seemingly obvious 'outcome' of the terror experience, it simultaneously is *unobvious* in the way that it narrates many of terror's stories without drawing attention to itself. Anxiety stories terror's story in such a sensible way that it makes sense of the senselessness that terror tells the story of. So what then happens to anxiety in all this? What of the quiet partner who simply tells the sensational story of terror without drawing attention to the *implicit* sensationalism being made of anxiety within each telling of terror's story? I cannot help but question how easily this embodied metaphor gets dismissed in terms of examining the detrimental work being done in the telling of terror's story. I cannot help but be in wonder when I hear anxiety being taken-up as the naturalized state of terror, like when I hear such cultural stories as this one taken-up by an American 'panic disorder' website:

> How to Stay Calm in a Changing World:
> Tips for coping with anxiety about war and terrorism
>
> The world has changed for many of us, and anxiety is a normal response. We hear about the war and terrorism everyday, and no one should be embarrassed about feeling fearful as a result. The problem is, we live in a changing world. We can become paralyzed by our anxiety or we can figure out how to live safely and fully. What follows are tips about taking control.

What follows are indeed tips about how to 'take control' of terror—that is, take control and *erase* the anxiety found in knowing the story of terror. Yet in this 'changing world' that this (hilariously problematic) website claims we are all living in, present is a story we *indeed* all know from times past, the story of terror. Terror is 'scary' and anxiety is a 'normal' reaction to it; it is something we know from our history with terror. What perhaps, might therefore be buried within the co-dependence of these stories, is that *within* the story that speaks of erasing the anxiety of terror, lies the other paradoxical story I spoke of before, that being the story of *requiring* anxiety and terror (good or bad), in order to tell *any* of our stories that call attention through the voice of alarm.

Ergo, what I notice happening—what I can personally make sense of in relation to everything I have discussed so far—is that anxiety *cannot* be erased by terror's stories, even though they all ask it to be. Anxiety itself cannot be overcome nor ever fully be averted because without anxiety *the crisis can never be storied.* Without anxiety, a major piece of the social would be lost, and thus, the very way that we make sense of our worries, stresses, and fears would not be possible. And likewise, in this moment of terror, there is an equally unsettling need for terror's story in order to come full circle and put a name to our anxieties. I am compelled to recognize this because, I think it is here that we may all learn from our need, or better, our *desire* to always story ourselves through our bodies. It is here that we might make sense of the *further* possibilities that might be borne out of recognizing what makes each story, story-able at all.

## References

Bellafante, Ginia. "In an age of anxiety, dodging adulthood." *The New York Times*, 12 February 2003. Available at: http://query.nytimes.com/gst/fullpage.html?res=9A0DE2DF163AF931A25751C0A9659C8B63 andsec=andspon=andpagewanted=print [retrieved 4 April 2008].

Henning Fenton, Cathleen. "How to stay calm in a changing world." *About.com*. Available at: http://panicdisorder.about.com/cs/ptsd/a/copingterrorism.htm [retrieved 26 March 2008].

King, Thomas. 2005. *The truth about stories: A native narrative*. Univ. of Minnesota Press.

Simpson, Jeffrey. "Can the U.S. get back its grip?" *The Globe and Mail*, 29 March 2008, A21.

Mitchell, David T. 2002. "Narrative prosthesis and the materiality of metaphor." In *Disability Studies. Enabling the Humanities*. Eds. Sharon L. Snyder, Brenda Jo Brueggmann, and Rosemarie Garland-Thomson, 15-30. The Modern Language Association of America: New York.

Turrentine, Jeff. "Chronicle: Short stories; Anxiety attacks." *The New York Times*, 5 September 2004. Available at: http://query.nytimes.com/gst/fullpage.html?res=9800E5D9113EF936A3575AC0A9629C8B63 [retrieved 4 April 2008].

Unknown author. "Age of Anxiety." *The Nation*, 21 November 2002. Available at: http://www.thenation.com/doc/20021209/editors [retrieved 26 March 2008].

# CONSTRUCTING THE ABORIGINAL TERRORIST: DEPICTIONS OF ABORIGINAL PROTESTORS, THE CALEDONIA RECLAMATION, AND CANADIAN NEOLIBERALIZATION

*Jennifer Adese*

The impetus for this project comes from eight months spent as a research assistant sifting through Aboriginal and non-Aboriginal print and online news articles, as well as pro- and anti-reclamation websites, concerning the reclamation of land used for the Douglas Creek Estates housing development project. The land has been classed by the municipal, provincial, and federal government as part of the town of Caledonia, Ontario, a classification that is being disputed by members of the bordering Haudenosaunee community of Six Nations. It is the central assertion of this paper that the image constructed in the media is that of a group of "renegade Natives": terrorist "others" who challenge the tenets of "secure" land ownership, and threaten the lawfulness and safety of Canadians and their society. The Haudenosaunee involved in the reclamation are described in blanket terms as "Native," and "Aboriginal," and are held accountable as representative of the terrorist inclinations of *all* Aboriginal peoples (inclusive of over roughly five hundred different nations/communities of indigenous peoples within the colonial territorial boundaries of the Canadian state).

To begin, I will provide an overview of "The Report of the Senate Special Committee on Terrorism and the Public Safety." Published in Ottawa in 1987, a convention of representatives of the federal government, the Royal Canadian Mounted Police (RCMP), the Department of the Solicitor General, and the media, met to discuss the climate of terrorism in Canada and to devise counter-terrorism measures. This Report will demonstrate how the federal government has defined domestic terrorism in recent decades (most notably since the passing of the July 1984 *Canadian Security Intelligence Service Act*, an *Act*, which the Committee feels is the defining moment in Canadian anti-terrorism measures and which made explicit the state's intent on preventive law enforcement aimed at limiting domestic terrorist reprisals). I will also discuss Canada's 2001 *Anti-Terrorism Act*, in particular sections that have raised concern among indigenous peoples for their potential to characterize indigenous resistance movements as terrorism.

I will discuss the media's function in informing and educating society and its influence on citizen perceptions of domestic terrorism in Canada, through reference to select articles from regional newspapers, most notably the Brantford Expositor (Brantford being an area adjacent to the Six Nations reserve), as well as articles picked up by and/or written by national newspapers, such as *The National Post*. It is important to note here that not every article published by these sources is overtly negative in their portrayals of the reclamation. There are balanced articles, and in that balance, some more balanced than other ones. However, it is my contention that it is not enough to write a few "middle of the road" articles (that are by no means free from slant or bias towards non-Aboriginal peoples), while the remaining articles tend towards the opposite extreme of depicting Aboriginal peoples as violent, lawless, and perpetrating an injustice against innocent "law-abiding" citizens and the "just" state.

## Aboriginal Peoples, Terrorism and Public Safety in Canada— Posing a Threat Since (at least) 1987

In 1987, a Senate Special Committee convened to discuss Terrorism and Public Safety in Canada. A select eighty-three witnesses testified on issues related to terrorism and public safety, while an additional seventy were interviewed in private. Chairman William M. Kelly identified in his preliminary statement that there had been an occurrence of several major terrorist incidents in Canada, or with the involvement of Canadians in years prior to the Committee meeting, which led to the decision to pull together this team of consultants (xi). A framework for mapping terrorism in Canada had become necessary.

The Committee members define terrorism by the words of Dr. David Charters:

> Terrorism is the threat or use of violent criminal techniques, in concert with political and psychological actions, by a clandestine or semi-clandestine armed political faction or group with the aim of creating a climate of fear and uncertainty, wherein the ultimate target (usually one or more governments) will be coerced or intimidated into conceding the terrorists their specific demands or some political advantage. (4)

The Senate Special Committee surmises that while Canada had not been the focus of *significant* terrorist threats or violence, the potential for terrorist action against Canada is increasing and there is a need to prepare effective responses for the protection of public safety. They speculate that this increased threat will come from two sources. First, the Committee believes that international terrorism will increase (1). The second source of threat comes from domestic terrorist actions—situations that occur in Canada, as a response to issues originating within Canada.

To this end, the Committee's Report refers to a study conducted by Jeffrey Ian Ross and Ted Robert Gurr titled "Domestic Groups Actually Responsible for Terrorist Actions in Canada, 1960-1985." The American Indian Movement (AIM), the Ojibway Warriors Society, and "Canadian Indians-various" constitute seven actions (just over 2%) of domestic terrorist acts over the course of nine years (from 1974-1983) (411):

> reawakened nationalism of native peoples. Native activists in both countries [referring to Canada and the U.S.] have voiced increasingly strident demands for autonomy and compensation and some have carried out disruptive protest. In Canada seven terrorist attacks were carried out between 1974 and 1983 in the name of indigenous peoples. In late 1981 some Indians warned the Canadian federal government of 'IRA-type strikes' if their demands were not met, and the following July a spokesman for the Assembly of First Nations threatened violence and revolution if indigenous needs continued to be ignored (423).

One current conflict which could lead to terrorism in either or both societies is the

## Canada's *Anti-Terrorism Act*—
## Recent Interventions, Enforcing the Frame

Passed in the aftermath of September 11, 2001, Canada's *Anti-Terrorism Act*, Bill C-36, aims at defining and legislating state-response to terrorism. The *Act* poses significant problems for Aboriginal peoples. Of particular concern, section 83.01 part 2 (1) (b) (II) (E) of the *Act*, which designates any action that causes the "disruption of essential services" a terrorist action (58). Alan Borovoy, head of the Canadian Civil Liberties Association, expresses concern that overly broad definitions of who can be defined as terrorist make Aboriginal resistance movements that take the form of highway blockades likely targets for classification as terrorist, under the new legislation (59).

The other clauses in this section categorize any action that intentionally causes death, serious bodily harm (by the use of violence), or any action that intentionally endangers a life, as terrorism. Additionally, an act of terrorism is defined as any act that causes a risk to the health or safety of the public, or which causes damage to public or private property, that subsequently results in a person's death, serious bodily harm, or the endangerment of a life. Part 2 (1) (b) identifies an act of terrorism as any that has a political, religious or ideological purpose, objective or cause, and that is intended to intimidate "the public, or a segment of the public, with regard to its security, including its economic security, or compelling a person, a government or a domestic or international organization to do or to refrain from doing any act."

Matthew Coon Come, former Grand Chief of the Assembly of First Nations (AFN) refers to the killing of protestor Dudley George of the Kettle and Stoney Point First Nation, by Kenneth Deane of the Ontario Provincial Police (OPP), during the Ipperwash reclamation of 1995. He states that the death of Dudley George, "demonstrate(s) the risk posed to First Nations. Legislation that gives heightened powers to police narrows the civil rights of those involved in legitimate dissent and protest activities and/or suspends the civil rights of those perceived by the government to be involved in 'terrorist' activities'" (59). Further, Coon Come cites the law-and-order response to a number of Kanien'keha peoples action to protect their community's burial grounds from the town of Oka's development plans in 1990, whereby the media, government, Quebec police, and the Canadian army characterized and treated the protestors of Kahnesatake as representative of a nation-wide problem of Native terrorism (60).

## What's Goin' On—
## Non-Aboriginal Media Coverage of the Six Nations Reclamation

On February 26, 2006, four months after former Six Nations Chief David General wrote to Henco Industries informing them of the ongoing claim for land in the Haldimand Tract, land where Henco continued to develop the Douglas Creek Estates subdivision, a number of residents from the Six Nations reserve moved onto the construction site. A few months later, the Ontario court system enacted a permanent injunction ordering protestors from the site. When the injunction failed to have the desired effect of scaring protestors from the site, the OPP conducted an early morning raid, arresting sixteen protesters. An immediate backlash led to the arrival of more protestors, to stand in solidarity with the original occupants of the site. Now past the two-year mark, the land reclamation has yet to be resolved, and despite numerous attempts by the residents of the town of Caledonia, the developer, courts, and government attempting to compel people to abandon the site, the resistance endures.

My interest is not in recounting systematically the events as they have unfolded from any of the possible perspectives, but instead to engage some of the images of the Haudenosaunee people involved, as presented by dominant news sources. In order to frame the reclamation at Six Nations as a terrorist action, and the people involved as terrorists, newspaper articles mobilize three dominant rhetorics. First people involved in the reclamation are configured largely as "aboriginals" or "natives" whose actions represent the interests of *all* indigenous peoples and who speak to the likelihood of *all* indigenous peoples to engage in similar modes of resistance. Second, people involved in the reclamation are depicted as violent, law-breaking, and militant, and third, as people who are constitutive of a "splinter group," a group of "rebels" against the backdrop of a normally peaceful co-existence of "Natives" and "Canadian citizens."

A vast number of references made to the reclamation workers characterize them as "aboriginals" or "natives" constructing "native blockades," when in fact the participants in the reclamation have included an array of Haudenosaunee —members of the Six Nations of Mohawk, Oneida, Seneca, Tuscarora, Onondaga, and Cayuga, who represent diverse groups, or nations, if you will, of people. When other peoples attend/have attended in support, it is in solidarity with, and out of appreciation for, the struggles faced when an "other" asserts land rights against the colonial Canadian state.

Bill McIntyre in the Canadian Free Press issues a statement cautioning against the continuance of the reclamation which reflects the aforementioned tendency toward pan-Aboriginalizing, "If this assault on property continues, and the courts back up the natives' assertion of authority and control over non-band lands with the subsequent loss of private ownership rights, the door will have been opened to an unprecedented backlash against the native community." Taiaiake Alfred writes, "In the long process of gaining control over indigenous nations, Canadian governments and other institutions of Canadian society have created false images of indigenous people to suit the imperatives of dominion—the Savage both vicious and noble, the Indian, and now the Aboriginal (Alfred 6). "The native community" is unilaterally configured, and as McIntyre points out, any outcome in favour of "the natives" that is not negotiated on the terms of those who hold "private ownership rights," will result in a "backlash."

Miller, in an analysis of articles/stories covering events at Ipperwash, determined that the media used its publications to characterize Aboriginal peoples as troublemakers, as social problems, and as those doing something illegal and violating the acceptable order of a just society (30). John Findlay writes in "Sacrificial lambs at the alter of Ipperwash":

> [A] flood of aboriginal protesters arrived to occupy the development site, most of whom were not form the local Six Nations reserve. Many of these protesters were blatantly militant, threatening people both off and on the reserve. Some had association with cigarette, weapon, and drug smuggling and other criminal activities. They flew Mohawk Warrior flags and espoused the Warrior Society philosophy that included the right to use whatever force was necessary 'to defend' native territory—their justification for violence (January 30, 2008).

Findlay also claims that "The Haudenosaunee do not acknowledge that they are subject to the Canadian legal system" (qtd. in Coutts). Bill McIntyre, writing for the Canadian Free Press on March 8, 2008, claims: "The often violent occupation in Caledonia by Six Nations warriors has prompted the natives to claim even more territory while the McGuinty Liberal government does nothing to protect the citizens of not only the community, but all of Haldimand Region." These depictions are not entirely fabrications of newspaper journalists themselves. Ontario Progressive Conservative leader John Tory spoke to the media, encouraging the liberal provincial government "to make a clear statement that there is one rule of law for everyone in Ontario, a policy that the government will not negotiate on the substance of any legal dispute with any person or group involved in an illegal occupation, a commitment to use the courts to ensure one rule of law and to not stand in the way of police enforcing the law" (qtd.in Wormington).

I would suggest that this frame—that of protestors as criminal, violent and lawless, has been renewed since 1995, becoming more insidious and re-energized by the events of September 11 and subsequent media coverage, as well as the passing of Canada's ant-terrorism legislation. Henry Giroux writes that the media and the culture it produces is the single most influential educational force(s) in society today (Stormy Weather 21). Canadians are influenced to a great extent by the cross-border flood of information from the American media addressing the "war against terror." The Report of the Senate Special Committee on Terrorism and the Public Safety recognized this, stating that the "average" Canadian's understanding of terrorism is formed largely via the American media's characterization of "the terrorist threat" (12). Kent Roach, in an analysis of Canada's *Anti-Terrorism Act* (2001) asserts that the American "war on terror" in the wake of September 11, 2001, has led to the conflation and expansion of the definition of terrorism (51). The result, in the eyes of the Senate Committee, is that Canadians greatly misunderstand the history of terrorist action in/against Canada, and misinterpret the most dangerous source of threat to their security, which has been posed, and will continue to be posed, by domestic groups taking action within the country (Ibid).

Canadian media, then, in times of indigenous resistance, uncritically cloak these movements in the rhetoric of domestic terrorism. With regard to the Six Nations reclamation, Findlay writes:

> They [Caledonia residents] have been disturbed by loud noise at all hours of the night, including gunfire, shouting, the noise of heavy machinery, music, fireworks and drum beating...Houses are pelted with rocks...The occupiers verbally assault the nearby residents with derogatory and racist comments, threatening them with physical harm. They appear in camouflage attire, with bandanas covering their faces and carry bats or large nail-studded clubs. (Findlay)

Findlay describes the protest in terms of its lawlessness, emphasizing the actions that violate the "safe" social order, and in terms of the climate of fear created by "gunfire," "noise," "verbal assault," and "threats of physical harm." Citing John Tory, Joe Wormington writes in the *Brantford Expositor* that "The people of Caledonia have had to deal with arson, extortion, barricades, and seizures, occupations, militant protests, harassment, intimidation, mob violence and threats to public safety" (February 23, 2008).

Similarly, Alison Hanes writes in the *National Post*, that residents of the town of Caledonia are calling for the government to "restore the rule of law" in a community where an "illegal occupation" inspired by a "native land claim has brought repeated experiences with arson, extortion, violence and intimidation"("Tory Condemns Caledonia 'lawlessness'" Alison Hanes, February

21, 2008). The Member of Provincial Parliament for the region, Toby Barrett, is quoted in the same paper as saying that, "Barricades, arson and violence surrounding the land claim dispute in Caledonia, Ont., have been accepted by police, who are enforcing a two-tiered justice system and condoning native lawlessness" (qtd. "Police ignoring native violence, MPP alleges" Matthew Coutts, February 13, 2008).

The parties directly engaged in the reclamation are also characterized as a "splinter group," or party of "rebels" who are engaging in illegal activity that is at odds with the desires of the main body of the community (Miller, 30):

> the real 'interlopers' that have caused the harm are the self-proclaimed native 'warriors' from Montreal and Cornwall—not to mention Toronto bureaucrats and politicians; and the out-of-town police...None of them have been able to distinguish between the criminals and the responsible members of the native community. (Findlay)

Findlay feels that this "splinter group" of "rowdy Indians" ultimately caused the so-called "problem." This depiction, of the protesters as "rebels," as a "rebel faction," which makes it easier for "white" society to comprehend the people involved in the reclamation as terrorist. While inspiring fear on one hand, depictions of the protestors as "rebels" anaesthetizes on the other, reassuring citizens that not *all* "Natives" are dangerous, that it is a select few, that when contained, will see peace and security return to the lives of Canadians.

Second, if it appears as though the body of the Six Nations community supports the protest, then a greater possibility exists, that Canadian citizens would read this as a legitimate claim. Any inkling that Aboriginal claims are legitimate jeopardizes carefully crafted boundaries between "settler" and "native," between "citizen" and "non-citizen," between "just" and "unjust," thereby making it more difficult for the state to continue subordinating indigenous peoples through the denial of sovereignty rights. In the words of Tai Alfred:

> Canadians accept and celebrate indigenous movements for cultural restoration; indigenous spirituality is acknowledged as an aspect of the healing process, etc. Why is it that reconnecting to land and asserting nationhood, which are just as much a part of recovering from colonization, are criminalized by the state and disdained by the Settler population? The obvious answer is that land and nationhood assertions have political and economic implications. Culture and spirituality and the arts are tolerated by Canadian society because for the most part they are depoliticized and integrated in to the social and

> economic institutions of Canadian society—they are non-threatening to the interests and identities of Canadians. (4-5)

As frustration mounts over the years at this "splinter group," and citizens increase their cries for law-and-order solutions, any actions taken by officials in the name of removing this threat to public safety, to private property and to public land ownership, will be viewed as legitimate.

Non-Aboriginal citizens so frustrated with the perceived lack of government inaction have openly supported more aggressive measures to remove the "warrior threat," no matter what the cost:

> With squatters going unpunished from assaults against non-native senior, news crews and even OPP officers, the whole area must seem like an anything-goes zone…On the second anniversary of the occupation, the rule of law is Caledonia's greatest casualty. Our elected officials must either strike a deal with the squatters, or evict them by force. (Caledonia, +2)

A great number of articles written by non-Aboriginal peoples do not present fair and balanced perspectives, but instead to are written in a manner so as to generate fear and panic, while reassuring citizens that if the "rule of law" is militarily or police enforced, that safety and security will be restored. As Giroux writes, patriotism marks the line between terrorist and non-terrorist, fueling a system of militarized control. Any act of resistance by indigenous peoples, therefore, which challenges state hegemony, is construed as unpatriotic and therefore terrorist.

## Concluding Thoughts

As previously expressed by the Senate Committee's Report, media coverage plays an important role in impeding and resolving incidences of terrorism. Miller reinforces this assertion:

> Media coverage plays a key role in determining how events are dealt with in a democratic society…How a crisis is reported, the sources that are used or ignored, and how those stories are 'framed' can impact the actions of governments, participants, police and onlookers, who frequently act according to how the media set the agenda…Accurate, comprehensive coverage can promote understanding and resolution, just as accurate, incomplete and myopic coverage can exacerbate stereotypes and prolong confrontations (13-14).

The media is a significant part of the social establishment, and in most cases, they blithely resist engagement with the voices of peoples who are marginalized, in any credible way (Augie Fleras qtd.15). Val Morrison writes that the construction of identities "as they often are, through popular cultural forms...particularly in moments of crisis involving the group, [are] at the mercy of the very media through which the identity is portrayed" (132).

The media's communication of terror, in combination with a tenuous history when covering issues related to indigenous peoples (specifically covering land reclamation issues), as well as the Canadian state's purposeful designation of various indigenous resistance movements as terrorist (prior to September 11), and the ambiguity of the *Anti-Terrorism Act* (post-September 11), create dangerous conditions for Haundenosaunee reclamation protesters. The state recognizes the importance of media in communicating terrorism, as acknowledged in the Senate Committee Report, and evidenced by government officials making statements to media regarding the reclamation. A great number of newspaper articles discussing the reclamation have vilified the protestors and all indigenous peoples unilaterally.

If resistance movements are classified by the state and depicted in the media as unpatriotic acts, and accordingly, as acts of terrorism, what does this say for the future of land claim protests? What does it say for the future of indigenous peoples in engaged in decolonization efforts? The picture is bleak. Take for example, June 27, 2005. David Dennis and James Sakej Ward were arrested following a legal firearms purchase for a youth cultural hunting program in Vancouver, British Columbia. This was not, however, your "typical" firearms arrest. As reported by George Young for the indigenous newspaper Windspeaker (also reported by "mainstream" media outlet CBC), the arrest was carried out by a team of tactical RCMP officers carrying submachine guns and blocking off the Burrard Street bridge. The RCMP Integrated National Security Enforcement Teams (INSET) orchestrated the arrest, INSET being the unit charged with investigating violations of Canada's *Anti-Terrorism Act*.

The climate for peoples trapped by Canadian domination is a difficult one. Like it or not, attitudes toward "national security" have been changing in Canada, and as definitions broaden regarding who can be classed as terrorist, the activities of each and every person classed as "Aboriginal" are placed under a microscopic lens. The Canadian media has actively crafted the image of indigenous peoples as *internal* terrorist threats, not only offering images that are seen as legitimating state action, but far too frequently *encouraging* it. The land claim actions of indigenous peoples consistently denied voice regarding ownership, usage, and preservation of their traditional lands, are essential and consistent targets. Trapped in an enduring struggle for sovereignty, Aboriginal peoples are depicted as the quintessential "homegrown terrorist," the internal threat to the Canadian state.

## References

Alfred, Taiaiake, and Lana Lowe. "Warrior Societies in Contemporary Indigenous Communities."

"Arrested First Nations activists allege intimidation." www.cbc.ca. 29 June 2005. Canadian Broadcasting Corporation. 21 Feb. 2008. www.cbc.ca/story/canada/national/2005/06/29/rifles050629.html.

Bill C-36 *Anti-Terrorism Act*. www2.parl.gc.ca. Government of Canada. http://www2.parl.gc.ca/HousePublications/Publication.aspx?DocId=2330951andLanguage=eandMode=1andFile=34

"Caledonia + 2." www.nationalpost.com. 4 Mar. 2008. *National Post*. 4 Mar. 2008. www.nationalpost.com/opinion/story.html?id=350837.

Coutts, Matthew. "Caledonia dispute; Illegal action 'appears to be tolerated.'" www.nationalpost.com. 13 Feb. 2008. *National Post*. 13 Feb. 2008. www.national post.com/news/canada/story.html?id=304103.

Elmer, Jon. "Counterinsurgency manual shows military's new face." www.ipsnews.net. 22 Mar 2007. Inter Press Services News Agency.21 Oct. 2007. <www.ipsnews.net/news.asp?idnews=37050>.

Findlay, John. "Sacrificial lambs at the altar of Ipperwash." www.national post.com. 30 Jan. 2008. *National Post*. www.nationalpost.com/opinion/story.html?id=272688.

Friere, Paolo. 2000. *Pedagogy of the oppressed*. New York: Continuum.

Gaudet, Kevin. "Two years of Caledonia thanks to McGuinty." www.canadafreepress.com. 21 Feb. 2008. *Canada Free Press*. 21 Feb. 2008. <www.canadafreepress.com/index.php/article/1971.

Giroux, Henry A. 2006. *Stormy weather: Katrina and the politics of disposability*. Colorado: Paradigm, 2006.

——— 2004. *The terror of neoliberalism: Authoritarianism and the eclipse of democracy*. Aurora: Garamond.

Hanes, Allison. "Tory condemns Caledonia 'lawlessness.'" www.national post.com. 21 Feb. 2008. *National Post*. 21 Feb. 2008. www.national post.com/news/canada/story.html?id=322487.

Hardt, Michael and Antonio Negri. 2004. *Multitude: War and democracy in the age of empire*. New York: Penguin.

"In Depth: Caledonia land claim: Historical Timeline." www.cbc.ca/news. 1 Nov. 2006. Canadian Broadcasting Corporation. 15 Oct. 2007. <http://www.cbc.ca/news/background/caledonia-landclaim/historical-timeline.html>.

Miller, John. "Ipperwash and the Media."

Morrison, Val. 1998. "Mediating identity: Kashtin, the media, and the Oka crisis." *Re-Situating identities*. ed. Vered Amit-Talai and Caroline Knowles. Peterborough: Broadview, 115-136.

Roach, Kent. 2003. *September 11: Consequences for Canada*. Montreal and Kingston: McGill-Queen's Univ. Press.

Rohrich, Klaus. "Ontario: Happy Family Day, suckers." 2008. *Canada Free Press.* 18 Feb. 2008. www.canadafreepress.com/index.php/article/1918.

Rourke, John T. and Mark A. Boyer. 2002. *World politics: International politics on the world stage, Brief Fourth Edition.* Guilford: McGraw-Hill/Dushkin.

The Senate Special Committee on Terrorism and the Public Safety. 1987. The report of the senate special committee on terrorism and the public safety." Ottawa: Minister of Supply Services Canada.

"Two wasted years in Caledonia." www.news.thercord.com. 4 Mar. 2008. The Record. 5 Mar. 2008. www.news.therecord.com/Opinions/article/317888.

Wormington, Joe. "McGuinty owes apology for a horrible wrong." www.brantfordexpositor.ca. 23 Feb. 2008. *Brantford Expositor.* 23 Feb. 2008. <www.brantfordexpositor.ca/ArticleDisplay.aspx?e=914347>.

Young, George. "Can warrior societies in a post-9/11 world?" www.accessmylibrary. 1 Sept. 2005. *Windspeaker.* 21 Feb. 2008. www.accessmylibrary.com/com/comsite5/bin

# Unresolved Issues:
# The Roots of the 1970 FLQ Crisis in the Rebellions of 1837-1838 in Lower Canada

*Marty Wood*

Referred to by the media and historians as the "October Crisis" or the "FLQ Crisis," Canada's most well-known terrorist uprising came to the public's attention on October 5, 1970. The British Trade Commissioner, James Richard Cross, was kidnapped from his Montreal home by two armed men. They later identified themselves in a communiqué (showing an outline of an 1837 *patriote* rebel in the background) as members of the Libération cell of the *Front de Libération du Québec* (FLQ). On October 10th provincial Cabinet Minister Jerome Choquette publicly announced the Quebec government's rejection of the communiqué's demands for the release of twenty-three FLQ "political prisoners" being held for terrorist bombings and robberies during the 1960s. At that time, provincial Labour Minister Pierre Laporte was across the street from his home throwing a football with his nephew. Moments later he was abducted by four terrorists wielding an automatic rifle and sawed-off shotgun. A message sent by the Chénier cell of the FLQ the next morning, again with a *patriote* outlined in the background, set deadlines for provincial authorities to meet their demands.

Significant roots of the FLQ Crisis can be found in the unresolved issues of the Rebellions of 1837-38 in Lower Canada, as Quebec was known at the time. Formerly the colony of New France, Quebec had become a British province in 1760, following General James Wolfe's earlier victory over the Marquis de Montcalm at the Battle of the Plains of Abraham. Although Quebec was under British administration, the population had remained almost entirely *Canadien*: French-speaking Roman Catholics who lived along the St. Lawrence River. With the arrival of United Empire Loyalists following the American Revolution, the British divided Quebec into English-speaking Upper Canada (later Ontario) and French-speaking Lower Canada (today's Quebec). Government structures set up by the Constitutional Act of 1791 favored an English-speaking merchant and military élite closely connected to the British governor of each province. In 1837 there were rebellions in both Upper and Lower Canada. In the latter, French Canadian rebels known as *patriotes* rose up in a bitter battle against British control. Like the rebels of Upper Canada, they sought to end political control by a small powerful oligarchy, but unlike the protestors of their fellow province, the *patriotes* had a far more fundamental racial battle to fight as well.

In the uprisings of both 1837-38 and 1970, French Canadian nationalists came up against the Anglo-imperialism of their age, seeking to liberate *Canadiens* from their "colonial masters." In 1837-38 these colonialist masters were English-speaking merchants and officials with close ties to the British governor; in 1970 they were the English-speaking "imperialists"—industrialists, financiers, and politicians with ties to big-business throughout Quebec, Canada, Britain, and above all, the United States. In both 1837-38 and 1970, French Canadians viewed themselves as being impoverished by a master-servant relationship that kept their English masters living in fine, luxurious style. In his rationale for the October kidnappings, Pierre Vallières, the key theorist and one of the founders of the FLQ, wrote:

> The failure of 1837-38 scarred us more deeply than did the first English conquest of 1760. In 1960, it no longer seemed possible to question the integration of Quebec society into the dominant Anglo-Saxon society, nor, consequently to challenge Canadian federalism and North American continentalism. It became clear what was really at stake: …political and social emancipation, independence for a nation that has been dominated and colonized ever since the Conquest of 1760, and doubly so since the defeat of 1837-38.[1]

Much of the imagery, ideology, and organizational style of the 1837-38 Rebellions re-surfaced in the terrorism of "Black October," 1970. In their October Manifesto, with its signature 1837 *patriote* line-sketch in the background, the FLQ identified itself as a "revolutionary movement of volunteers ready to die for the political and economic independence of Quebec."[2] They resolved to create a free Quebec liberated from the grips of Anglo-Canadian colonialism. FLQ members depicted themselves as a group of Quebec workers who had decided to use all necessary means, including arms and dynamite, to ensure that the people of Quebec take control of their own destiny—"to rid ourselves of these economic and political bosses who continue to oppress us."[3]

One of the original conditions set by the FLQ in October 1970 for the release of James Cross was the broadcast of their Manifesto by radio and television networks. This was one of only two demands to which the federal government agreed, along with the eventual safe conduct to Cuba of Cross's abductors, the Libération cell, after they had released him. Read on television on October 7th, the FLQ Manifesto was heavily-laced with Marxist rhetoric

---

1. Pierre Vallières, *Choose!* (Toronto: New Press, 1972), 4.
2. Translation of the FLQ Manifesto is taken from Malcolm Levine and Christine Sylvester, *Crisis in Quebec* (Toronto: Ontario Institute for Studies in Education, 1973), 91-96.
3. "The FLQ Manifesto," *Crisis in Quebec*, 94.

that identified English-speaking capitalists as the bourgeois enemy, and French Canadian nationalists as the oppressed proletariat. Relating back to the injustices of Lower Canada, the FLQ Manifesto proclaimed in 1970:

> We must fight, not one by one, but together.
> We must fight until victory is ours with all the means at our disposal as did the patriots of 1837-38....
> Our struggle can only be victorious. You cannot hold back an awakening people. Long live Free Quebec.
> Long live our comrades who are our political prisoners.
> Long live the Quebec revolution.
> Long live the *Front de Libération du Québec.*[4]

Symbolism and imagery that appeared during "Black October" frequently referred back to roots in the Lower Canada Rebellions of 1837-38. The choice of hostages, the use of a secret, independently-controlled cell structure for their organization, the *patriote* image on FLQ communiqués, as well as the language of imperial domination and oppression had strong ties to the emotions and experiences of the *patriotes* of 1837-38. The first hostage, James Cross, as British Trade Commissioner to Canada, was representative of domination by a powerful English-speaking business establishment in Quebec, particularly in the financial centre of Montreal. French Canadian business interests had been largely destroyed in Quebec following the British Conquest of 1760, with the arrival of British merchants and the Hudson's Bay Company. Sometimes referred to as the "decapitation thesis," British interests were seen as having destroyed the French Canadian merchant class and financial capabilities. Thus, the 1837-38 Rebellions had been targeted not only at gaining political independence from Britain but in solving economic domination, particularly of land ownership, viewed by the *patriotes* as the deliberate impoverishment of colonial French Canadians by their British imperial masters.

The reasoning behind the FLQ choice of its second hostage—Pierre Laporte, Minister of Labour and Immigration for Quebec's provincial government—was not as readily apparent as the choice of James Cross had been. As a high-profile French Canadian, part of a more nationalistic-oriented government emerging from "the Quiet Revolution" of the 1960s and making progress in modernizing education, public ownership of hydro, and language issues, Laporte might at first be seen as "one of their own." However, Laporte was seen by the FLQ as a "collaborator" with English-speaking business interests in the province. In the communiqué announcing his execution, Laporte was labelled as *ministre de chomage et de l'assimilation* ("Minister of Unemployment and Assimilation"—unemployment and underemployment for

---

4. "The FLQ Manifesto," *Crisis in Quebec*, 96.

French Canadians, and forced assimilation to earn employment of any value). Indeed, both victims were not the FLQ's first choice as hostage by the Libération and Chénier cells respectively. Captured documents later revealed that previous plans to kidnap the United States Consul-General and the Israeli trade consul in Montreal had been abandoned prior to October when authorities came too close to detecting these actions.[5] However, both Cross and Laporte were unguarded and had opportune addresses: Cross's Westmount address was symbolic for English power, and Laporte's home was near the Chénier cell hideout on Armstrong Street. The FLQ Manifesto targeted the "big shots who live in Westmount" and stated: "We will banish from our state all the professional robbers, the bankers, the businessmen, the judges and the sold-out politicians."[6]

As with the symbolism in choosing hostages, the FLQ's cell structure, containing individual units with separate leadership and plans that were unknown to other cells, had direct links to the Rebellions of 1837-38. Particularly in the second year of the rebellions in Lower Canada, raids were conducted by a secret organization, the *Frères Chasseurs*, (the hunters' brotherhood) divided into separate cells that had no direct knowledge of one another's members or planned raids. Similarly, in 1970 the Royal Canadian Mounted Police had some knowledge of a cell-based organizational structure within the FLQ from investigating the bombings that had started in the Montreal area in April 1963. The RCMP believed the membership to number approximately one hundred and thirty, organized into about twenty-two separate cells, and supported by a larger membership of at least two thousand.[7] Each cell had a special function: activist cells stole dynamite and planted bombs; intelligence cells collected information on targets, such as banks or armories, or on kidnap victims; and propaganda cells spread the ideology and recruited new members. The cells, each with three to six members, remained independent with minimal contact with other cells. Members used code names and did not keep written lists of contacts. While twenty-three FLQ members had been imprisoned for bombings or for robberies of banks or armories, the remaining members could not be identified and continued to promote their anti-English, capitalist ideology and strategies.

The targets of over two hundred FLQ bombings during the 1960s had been buildings, businesses, or symbols representative of English ownership, such as the Queen Elizabeth Hotel, Murray Hill transportation, and Westmount postal boxes. The intelligence-gathering process of the Royal Canadian Mounted Police was made more difficult by FLQ cell structure: those captured could not be forced to betray others, not knowing the names, locations, or plans of other cells. For example, the Libération cell, abductors of

---

5. George Bain, "The Making of a Crisis," *Canadian Forum* (January, 1971), 320.
6. "The FLQ Manifesto," *Crisis in Quebec*, 96.
7. Levine and Sylvester, *Crisis in Quebec*, 78.

James Cross, only learned that the Chénier cell had been involved in Laporte's kidnapping when the licence plate of a car that they knew to belong to Paul Rose was announced on the news. To that point they had believed the Chénier cell to be against the idea of hostage-taking.

## Unresolved Issues: 1837-38

The Chénier cell (Paul Rose, Jacques Rose, Francis Simard, and Bernard Lortie) of the FLQ was named after a rebel leader of 1837—a young doctor killed by the British Army at St-Eustache. Here more than sixty *patriotes* under the leadership of Dr Jean-Olivier Chénier were surrounded by British troops in the church that had served as their battle post. After British Governor Sir John Colborne ordered the church to be set on fire, Chénier leapt from a window and died fighting as he tried to escape through the churchyard. After the battle, his heart was cut out and displayed by the British in a tavern window for several days.[8] Reprisals by British troops following this battle were especially brutal, leaving bitter memories for generations of French Canadians to come. The outline drawing of an 1837 *patriote* on FLQ communiqués of 1970 is based on a sketch by artist Henri Julien and connects the imagery of both uprisings. A statue of the symbolic *patriote* is also found at the top of a monument at St-Denis commemorating the November 1837 battle.

Economic concerns arising from the recession of 1837 and resentment of English-speaking dominance of the province's finances further connect the 1837-38 Rebellions to the high unemployment rates among French Canadians in 1970. Economic problems had increased in the early 1830s, leading to a widespread dissatisfaction with the government of Lower Canada. Discrimination exacerbated the issue: a list of government employees in 1832, for example, noted that 20% of its positions were filled by people of French origin, even though they made up about 80% of the population.[9] Wealthy French Canadian seigneurs were viewed as collaborators with English wealth and ownership. The French Canadian middle class felt frustration with its inability to bring legal constitutional change. Unsympathetic British governors, backed by an unresponsive colonial ministry at Westminster, rejected *Patriote* Party leader Louis-Joseph Papineau's Ninety-two Resolutions in 1834. Papineau's demands would have increased the power of the francophone-dominated Legislative Assembly and reduced the economic and political stranglehold of the English speaking élite of the appointed Legislative Council, branded the *Chateau Clique* by the reformers. In the spring of 1837 the London Colonial Office, through the imposition of Lord Russell's Ten Resolutions, destroyed any hope of constitutional change. Thus by early 1837, al-

---

8. Greg Keilty, ed. *1837: Revolution in the Canadas* (Toronto: NC Press Limited, 1974), 165.

9. Jean-Paul Bernard, *The Rebellions of 1837 and 1838 in Lower Canada*, Canadian Historical Association Historical Booklet No. 55 (Ottawa, CHA, 1999), 22.

most a year before armed struggle erupted, Lower Canada was already embroiled in a serious political crisis. Legislative business had ground to a halt, owing to acute conflict between the elected and appointed elements of the legislature. The resulting conflict between "Tory" government supporters and the *Patriote* Party radiated outward from an epicentre around Montreal.[10]

The *patiote* aims in 1837-38 were initially to gain constitutional reform for Lower Canada. An increase in power for the elected Legislative Assembly would enable redistribution of land from the seigneurial system for the benefit of the *habitants* and reduce the *Chateau Clique*'s abuse of power through its control of the Legislative Council, appointed by the British-governor. Repeated denial of constitutional reform to be achieved through legal means led to a growth in demand for independence from Britain, replacing the existing government with American political structures. Support for rebellion increased with insurrection breaking out near Montreal on November 23, 1837. After an initial victory at St-Denis, however, the *patriotes* were defeated by British troops two days later at St-Charles. The end of the 1837 uprisings came at St-Eustache on December 14th with the defeat of Chénier's rebels. In 1838, the *patriotes* reorganized, forming the *Société des Frères Chasseurs*. They modelled their secret groups and rituals after Hunters' Lodges common in border states from New Hampshire to Michigan, and linked up with those radicals of the *patriote* movement who had avoided arrest. They were ready to risk their lives in the cause against British domination. In July of 1838, having more or less rejected Papineau's leadership after he fled to the USA during the battle at St-Denis, the *patriote* leaders established a new unanimity among themselves by forming the *Société des Frères Chasseurs*.

The members of the *Frères Chasseurs* took an oath based on an ideology that would sound familiar in 1970. They swore allegiance to republican institutions and ended by declaring that they would, "until death, attack, combat, and help to destroy, by all means that their superior officer should think proper, every power, or authority of Royal origin, upon this continent, and especially never to rest till all tyrants of Britain cease to have any dominion or footing whatever in North America."[11] "Collaborators"—those who worked for British colonial officials—were ferociously threatened and *charivaried* by rebel groups in Lower Canada, forcing the victims to give up their employment or trade with British administrators or officers.[12]

The *Frères Chasseurs* began as a coalescing of half a dozen secret and rebellious groups, particularly in the Richelieu and Montreal areas. British governmental policy, land and business ownership was seen as political domina-

---

10. Allan Greer, "1837-38: Rebellion Reconsidered," *Canadian Historical Review* LXXVI, no.1 (March, 1995): 11.
11. D. B. Read, *The Canadian Rebellion of 1837* (Toronto: C. Blackett Robinson, 1896), 353.
12. Allan Greer, "From Folklore to Revolution: Charivaris and the Lower Canadian Rebellion of 1837," *Social History* 15, no.1 (January, 1990), 30.

tion, economic subjugation, and religious and cultural assimilation.[13] *Chasseur* leaders, Dr Cyrille Côté, John Picoté de Belestre-MacDonnell and Lucien Gagnon, were joined by British-born Dr Robert Nelson who likewise fought for liberation from the British stranglehold over Lower Canada. In September 1838, lodges of the *Frères Chasseurs* existed in 35 communities in Lower Canada.[14]

The secret society appealed to new members with its oaths, ceremonies, and secret rites—"the handclasps, putting the fingers to nostrils, and trading mystic jargon that made them brothers."[15] Their symbol was a rifle crossed by a long dagger. Organized in grim secrecy and bound by anti-British oaths, all information about them was contradictory, confused, rumor-based, and almost useless. As with the FLQ, nicknames were used to prevent members from being able to betray one another, no matter how unintentional. The *castor* (beaver) commanded a company of ten platoons of ten men; *l'aigle* (eagle) was a divisional officer responsible for an entire district, and over him, passing from region to region, and rarely seen, was the shadowy super-authority—the *Grand Aigle*—Elisée Malihot. Commanders framed and reframed manifestos, and once the raids began, arrested leading *bureaucrats*—as they called the English-speaking population—holding them as prisoners at a camp near Chateauguay.

Along the Canadian-USA border in 1838 the economic situation became more desperate and the hatred toward English politicians and owners correspondingly stronger: everywhere, disgruntled men, often hungry and jobless, were easily recruited to rebel forces when work was not to be found.[16] Bitter battles broke out once again, as in Prescott, where 150 *patriotes* were killed at the Battle of the Windmill. The *Frères Chasseurs* were urged on by their leaders to continue the fight: "Soldiers! The time has arrived for calls to action—the blood of our slaughtered countrymen cries aloud for revenge…. The murdered heroes of Prescott lie in an unhallowed grave in the land of tyranny…. Let us march to victory or death!" [17] However, isolated, separate cells were not effective in battle, even though hatred ran deep. A lack of military leadership, organization, and the failure to arrive of promised weapons from the USA led to the ultimate defeat of the *patriote* cause. Only 800 of the 4000 insurgents of November 1838 had guns.[18] British rule was preserved through deployment of regular troops, the imposition of martial law, and widespread

---

13. Fernand Ouellet, *Lower Canada 1791-1841. Social Change and Nationalism* (Toronto: McClelland and Stewart, 1980), 324.
14. Jean-Paul Bernard, *The Rebellions of 1837 and 1838 in Lower Canada*, 11.
15. Joseph Schull, *Rebellion: The Rising in French Canada 1837* (Toronto: Macmillan Canada, 1971), 151.
16. Schull, *Rebellion*, 151.
17. Read, *The Canadian Rebellion of 1837*, 359.
18. Ouellet, *Lower Canada*, 320.

reprisals; however, the failure of the insurrection may be attributed more to the inefficacy of the businessmen and professionals who were the *patriote* leaders than to the power of the British army.[19]

The issues underlying the Lower Canada Rebellions of 1837-38 remained unresolved. There had been far greater repression and brutality than would be witnessed as radical separatist discontent re-surfaced in 1970. By 1838 over 300 lives had been lost in the *patriote* rebellions, with 1300 imprisoned (500 in 1837; 800 in 1838), 12 leaders publicly hanged, 66 transported to Bermuda or Australia, about 500 rebels fleeing to the USA, homes burned, and communities destroyed.[20] The colonial government succeeded in quelling the rebellions only through British military intervention and the armed organization of loyal elements of the population. Historian Fernand Ouellet says of the 1837-38 Rebellions: "This resounding failure, followed by severe repressive measures, was to have a profound influence upon the future course of the French Canadians."[21]

Following the defeat of the rebellions, the British Parliament's Act of Union of 1840 united Upper and Lower Canada into the "Province of Canada," with the express aim of assimilating French Canadians (the overwhelming majority in Lower Canada and overall majority in the new province) to progressive, British-business ways. Such assimilation was often considered as the "only" means of guaranteeing the loyalty of the French Canadian population and of ensuring, on what were considered to be British lands, a permanent "British" civilization.[22] However, the planned assimilation of the 1840 Act of Union did not occur as French Canadians increasingly learned to use their unified voting power to advantage. The introduction of Responsible government in 1849 gave a stronger voice to elected French-speaking representatives and reduced the power of the appointed English-speaking Executive and Legislative Councils. By 1867, a federal structure introduced at Confederation entrenched provincial powers over cultural concerns, ensuring *la survivance* of a distinct culture within the newly-created province of Quebec.

## Terrorism in Resistance to the State

In the uprisings of both 1837-38 and 1970, frustrations of French Canadians—who saw a legitimate route to the changes they sought as an impossibility—led to their choice to resist the government through force. The years between the two uprisings had brought many changes for French Canadians. Confederation created a provincial level of government with Section 92 of

---

19. Ouellet, *Lower Canada*, 309.
20. Bernard, *The Rebellions of 1837 and 1838 in Lower Canada*, 24.
21. Fernand Ouellet, "The Insurrections," in *Readings in Canadian History: Pre-Confederation*, edited by R. Douglas Francis and Donald B. Smith (Toronto: Nelson, 2002), 280.
22. Bernard, *The Rebellions of 1837 and 1838 in Lower Canada*, 23.

the British North America Act designed specifically to protect concerns of a "local" nature, such as French Canadian culture and religion. Section 93 left the control of education in the hands of each province, again specifically to protect the unique needs of the *Québécois*. However, even as the rights and education of French Canadians had increased, British colonial control of Lower Canada's politics, land, and wealth of the 1837-38 time period was eventually replaced by the domination of Quebec's economy and government by what many French-Canadians saw as an anglo-colonialism based on English power in Montreal, the rest of Canada, and the USA.

Many French Canadians of the 1960s felt their culture was disappearing before a rising tide of English imperialism: political, economic, and cultural. While many sought a new-found sense of nationalism in the growth of separatist parties throughout the 1960s, others found the pace too slow and turned to terrorist methods. The FLQ choice of bombings in the years following 1963 dramatically demonstrated their rejection of anglo-domination in Quebec. After gaining the attention of the media and public by kidnapping James Cross, the FLQ demanded heightened publicity for their Manifesto, the release of 23 "political prisoners" arrested during the 1960s, and $500,000 in gold bullion. The prisoners and gold were to be put aboard a chartered aircraft for passage to Cuba or Algeria in full view of television cameras.[23]

Most Canadians were horrified by FLQ bombings, but even more so by the kidnappings of Cross and Laporte. They wondered whether these were isolated acts or the beginning of a terrorist revolution:

> Was any public figure safe? Had all the arms and ammunition reported stolen over the past few years found their way into a secret cache of the FLQ? And was that organization, dedicated to social revolution and the forcible independence of Québec, now about to bring down the government? No one knew....[24]

In a speech to the House of Commons on the day the War Measures Act was invoked by Prime Minister Pierre E. Trudeau to enable swift arrest of suspected terrorist sympathizers, federal Cabinet Minister John Marchand declared that the FLQ was poised to destroy the country. He said that 3,000 members of the organization had infiltrated into key decision-making positions throughout Quebec and added: "If we had not acted, the separation of Quebec would have been a fact, a month or a year from today."[25] Marchand warned also of the explosives and armaments the FLQ had amassed during

---

23. Bain, "The Making of a Crisis," 321.
24. Susan Mann Trofimenkoff, *The Dream of Nation. A Social and Intellectual History of Quebec* (Toronto: Gage, 1983), 324.
25. Ottawa Bureau, *Globe and Mail*, "Trudeau Refuses to Elaborate on Need for War Measures Act," October 24, 1970, A1, A4.

robberies of the 1960s. While it was widely believed that there were thousands of FLQ supporters in 1970, due to the secret cell structure Canadian enforcement officials did not realize that there were only about 100 to 150 members at the time.[26]

The FLQ sought Quebec's separation from English-dominated Canada, socialist control of resources, business, and transportation. Government revenues were to be distributed for the benefit of French-Canadians: health care, education, and social services to restore equity to the rightful inhabitants of the province. Their frustration with the inability to bring change through democratic means was expressed through bombings and attempts to raise a terrorist army of liberation throughout the 1960s, but the provincial election results of 1970 drove them toward action that would grab the attention of the media, and all Canadians. Electoral riding distribution in Quebec favoured traditional parties, especially through a lack of representation for urban ridings, where separatist Parti Québécois (PQ) support was strongest. Thus, in the spring election of 1970 while the popular vote for René Lévesque's PQ was 24%, the party gained only 7 of 108 electoral seats. The provincial Liberals under Robert Bourassa had won a strong majority government. Certain that there would never be change through electoral means, the FLQ now turned to more desperate measures with the kidnappings of Cross and Laporte on the 5th and 10th of October.

In a widely-reported interview on October 13, 1970 with CBC reporter Tim Ralfe, Prime Minister Trudeau firmly presented the stance of the federal government. He disputed FLQ and media use of the term "political prisoners" to describe the twenty-three FLQ members being held in jail for terrorist crimes committed during the 1960s. Trudeau stated: "They're not political prisoners—they're outlaws. They're criminal prisoners, they're not political prisoners, and they're bandits. That's why they're in jail." Disturbed by the presence of armed guards in Ottawa, Ralfe asked just how far Trudeau would go to keep law and order. The Prime Minister replied, "Just watch me."[27] Trudeau rejected terrorist measures used to extort action from the State:

> I think society must take every means at its disposal to defend itself against the emergence of a parallel power which defies the elected power in this country and I think that goes to any distance. So long as there is a power in here which is challenging the elected representatives of the people I think that power must be stopped and I think

---

26. Bain, "The Making of a Crisis," 322.
27. John Burns, "Ottawa is Prepared to Go Any Distance to Stop FLQ, Trudeau Says," *Globe and Mail*, Metro Edition (Wednesday, October 14), A1, A8. The fear of an estimated number of 3,000 FLQ members is also stated in an article by the Quebec Bureau quoting Quebec Minister Jerome Choquette, *Globe and Mail*, November 26, 1970.

it's only, I repeat, weak-kneed bleeding hearts who are afraid to take these measures.[28]

The demands put forth by the October Manifesto, including the release of FLQ prisoners, were not met. With federal intervention invited by Quebec Premier Robert Bourassa, Prime Minister Trudeau declared the War Measures Act at 4:00 a.m. on October 16, 1970 to combat what the Act terms as "real or apprehended" insurrection. In an unprecedented peacetime suspension of civil rights, almost five hundred suspected FLQ sympathizers were arrested and detained. A Gallup Poll revealed that 87% of Canadians, including 86% among the French-speaking population, supported Trudeau's decision.[29] FLQ terrorist methods, however, had shown Canadians, including Quebecers, what they did not want—and that was the use of violent means to achieve political or societal goals.

Most of the detainees were released the next day but the response of the FLQ was swift. An anonymous phone call the following night led the police to Laporte's body in the trunk of a car. The "Dieppe cell" of the FLQ claimed responsibility. It was later learned that it was still the Chénier cell at work—perhaps designating themselves as yet another unknown group to increase public perception of greater strength. Much of the initial enthusiasm of hopeful separatists, such as that shown by five thousand cheering supporters at the Paul Sauvé arena on the night of 15 October, was lost when Pierre Laporte was assassinated (or "executed" in the words of an FLQ communiqué). Most Québécois were horrified by terrorism: "They were not prepared to sanction noisy revolution no matter what the bombers might be saying about the uneven distribution of power and wealth."[30]

By early December of 1970 the members of the Chénier cell who had killed Laporte had been captured and imprisoned. After holding James Cross hostage for sixty days, members of the Libération cell released him in exchange for a flight to Cuba. The group included Jacques Lanctôt, his wife and daughter, his sister Louise Cosette-Trudel and her husband Jacques Cossette-Trudel, Marc Carbonneau, and Pierre Seguin.

With the public rejection of terrorism and defeat of their socialist revolutionary dream, the FLQ had failed to achieve its goals through terrorist means. However, just as the aftermath of the rebellions of 1837-38 brought great reforms within a few years, leading to Responsible government in 1849,

---

28. John Saywell, *Quebec '70: A Documentary Narrative* (Toronto: University of Toronto Press), 74.
29. "Gallup Poll of Canada: 87% Approve the Invoking of the War Measures Act," *Toronto Star*, December 12, 1970. See also *Globe and Mail*, October 24, 1970, A4; Blair Kirby, "Extend War Measures Act Bill, Public Tells TV Pollsters, *Globe and Mail*, November 16, 1970, A3; and "Logic and Manipulation," November 20, A5.
30. Trofimenkoff, *The Dream of Nation*, 313.

Lévesque's PQ achieved victory in the 1976 provincial election. Lévesque now led a democratically-elected majority government dedicated to seeking out a route to separatism. His Sovereignty Association referendum of 1980, asking Quebecers if they were willing to give the PQ government the power to negotiate national sovereignty for Quebec, combined with a continued economic association with Canada, returned a vote of 60% *non*, 40% *oui*. Fifteen years later, the PQ tried again, with the 1995 referendum returning a precipitous 50.6% against, and 49.4% in favour of negotiating separation. To date, a slim democratic majority in Quebec has continued to choose a federal partnership above Quebec nationalism, most recently electing a government under the provincial Liberals led by Premier Jean Charest.

In the years leading up to the October Crisis, FLQ founder and logician Pierre Vallières wrote *Nègres blancs d'Amérique* (White Niggers of America) and captured the imagination of revolutionaries in Quebec and elsewhere. He wrote his call to action from jail, having been sentenced to thirty months for manslaughter in the death of Thérèse Morin during the FLQ bombing of a shoe factory, and later to seven months for contempt of court. Vallières condemned the growing control by American financial interests in Quebec, with 80% of the provincial economy under direct or indirect US control[31]

At the time he promoted the raising of a revolutionary army. He predicted the FLQ future to be:

> militarily effective; psychologically, intellectually and economically de-alienating; democratic; and, morally, founded on solidarity, equality, justice, and honesty. Such a revolution cannot be accomplished without war, without violence. For the established Order will try to the end to wipe it out in blood. Such a revolution, therefore, means the organization of an anti-capitalist, anti-imperialist, and anti-colonialist war that can end only with the victory or defeat of the working class.[32]

In the 1960s, while recruiting his hoped-for revolutionary army, Vallières told his separatist followers: "Even if violence is a phenomenon detestable in itself, it is nonetheless true that for exploited and colonized people like ourselves, freedom grows out of the barrel of a gun....It is in Quebec that I hope to overcome tyranny with my comrades, or else to die with them, weapons in hand."[33] However, in 1972, following the failure of the FLQ uprising, Vallières, wrote *Choose!*, a careful renunciation of the actions of October 1970 in which he denounced terrorism as an effective means of bringing about inde-

---

31. Pierre Vallières, *White Niggers of America* (Toronto: McClelland and Stewart, [1968] 1971, 47.
32. Vallières, *White Niggers of America*, 221-2.
33. Vallières, *White Niggers of America*, 269, 278.

pendence for Quebec. He believed that acts of terrorism would only play into the government's hands, giving it the needed excuse to impose repressive measures to destroy separatist leadership forever: "They face the possibility of having the fruits of their struggle stolen by a new class of swindlers, or of being annihilated as their ancestors were in 1837 by the weapons that the enemy seeks to use massively and pitilessly against them."[34] Taking into account present objective conditions, he stated, only a legitimate political party could unite the separatists. The principal strategic force for the liberation struggle "…is, and only can be, the Parti Québécois." [35]

Historian Fernand Ouellet has judged that for the Rebellions of 1837-38, some *patriotes*, including Chénier, were "bent on social revolution, not simply political independence, but for the time being this radical wing was content to postpone settlement of social goals and work for the common priority of independence." [36] Their unresolved issues, political, social, and economic, were echoed in 1970 by the FLQ as stated by Vallières:

> The independentist movement, which is also a movement of social liberation, clearly is a result of a collective will to structure a politically free Quebec State and a radically transformed Quebec economy….The independentists demand nothing less than the separation of Quebec from Canadian Confederation, the total liberation of Quebec from the domination that has oppressed it since 1760. [37]

While both uprisings in hindsight proved to be of little actual military threat, in the frightening, unknown situation of the time, the events of 1837-38 and 1970 each produced a fear that the government of the day could find itself in the position of not being able to control the action of the terrorists. Resistance to the state created by both the 1837-38 Rebellions and the October Crisis of 1970 posed a threat to the established government and power base. Both uprisings failed to attract the anticipated popular support. In 1837-38, middle class leaders believed working class discontent and support from neighbouring Americans who detested British rule would materialize in the form of fighters and weapons. Similarly, the FLQ in 1970 expected more support from the thousands of separatists who had cheered "*F-L-Q: nous vaincrons!*"—in a vow to conquer—at the Paul Sauvé arena. The *patriotes* had preached a republican ideology; the FLQ a separatist and socialist one. Both reflected the most radical thought of their day.

In 1970, the spirit, ideology, and symbols of the defeat of 1837-38 were present. The anger, sense of oppression and determination lived on from one

---

34. Vallières, *Choose!*, 105.
35. Vallières, *Choose!*, 87.
36. Ouellet, *Lower Canada*, 33.
37. Vallières, *Choose!*, 97-8.

revolt to the next. For some, the unresolved issues of 1837-38 remain even today—yet the existence of powerful federal (Bloc Québécois) and provincial (Parti Québécois) separatist parties builds a greater possibility for peaceful resolution of nationalist concerns in the future. Since 1960 the French-speaking people of Quebec have developed a strong, nationalistic *"Québécois"* identity as opposed to the federalist "French Canadian" identity encouraged by Confederation. The 1995 Referendum—with its mere support of 50.6% support for federalism—leaves Canadians to ponder our future. An awareness not only of the deep roots of *patriote* and FLQ discontent, but also of the strong bonds that unite *Québécois* today may contribute to greater understanding within our bicultural nation.

# TECHNOLOGIES OF RESISTANCE: THE ROLE OF PUBLIC AND COLLECTIVE MEMORY IN RESPONDING TO PAST AND PRESENT STATE-VIOLENCE IN ARGENTINA

*Ana Laura Pauchulo*

**Background and Statement of Problem**

On April 3rd 2008, during their weekly Thursday marches at Plaza de Mayo—the hub of political activity in Buenos Aires—Hebe de Bonafini, President of the human rights group 'Association of Mothers of Plaza de Mayo,' spoke to the crowd: "In this country, where so much blood has been shed…we have to work, we have to fight…to do it the way we deserve to have it done, but most of all, to do it the way our children deserve to have it done…we have to construct the country that our children dreamed of, like they were constructing it…" (Asociación Madres de Plaza de Mayo 2008a). In Hebe's speech the children are both the future generations and the 30,000 who were disappeared during the 1976-1983 Argentinean dictatorship. "The country that our children dreamed of" is a 'better Argentina' than the one that exists today in which state violence continues by way of police repression and mass unemployment and poverty. Hebe evokes the children of the future and the children of the past to remind us of the responsibility we have to those in the past and in the future—a responsibility to construct a 'better Argentina' and to 'do justice' for the Disappeared.

It is because of human rights groups, such as the Association of Mothers of Plaza de Mayo, who have for the last 31 years articulated demands of the state and of civil society for a 'better Argentina' that the transition to democracy in Argentina has been embedded within the memory of the Disappeared. While these groups have always been united in their understanding that remembrance of this past is necessary for a democratic future, they have also been divided in their individual struggles to legitimate particular remembrance practices as the most appropriate way to remember the Disappeared. Both the differences and the similarities between human rights groups are inherently linked to the ways in which these groups conceptualize memory and the work of 'doing justice' for the Disappeared. Drawing from interviews I conducted in 2007 in Argentina with human rights groups who constitute a social movement that grounds it's work in remembering the Disappeared, in this paper I examine the similarities and differences between how different groups work to construct a 'better Argentina' and voice their demands for a 'better Argentina' based on particular claims for 'memory, truth, and justice' in the name of the dead. This study of the differences and similarities is aimed at lending to a further understanding of what the politics of memory in Argentina can teach us about what it means to construct a democratic relationship that demands attentiveness to another's life—an other that is unknowable and whose experiences are incommensurable. Although I conducted 34 interviews with members of 23 different groups across three provinces, in this paper I focus on the work of the following three groups: The first two groups, Association of Mothers of Plaza de Mayo and the Mothers of Plaza de Mayo-Founding Line (two separate groups composed of mothers of Disappeared persons who from 1977 to 1986 organized under a single group, Mothers of Plaza de Mayo); and the third group, Grandmothers of Plaza de Mayo (composed of mothers of Disappeared persons whom at the time of their disappearance were pregnant with children who were kidnapped by the military at birth and are still considered to be alive and living unknowingly under a false identity).

## Constructing a 'Better Argentina': The Struggle over 'Memory, Truth, and Justice'

Conceptualizations of a 'better Argentina' and calls to construct a 'better Argentina' have throughout the years reflected the changing political context. While during the dictatorship demands for a better Argentina were demands for truth about the fate of the Disappeared, the return to democracy in 1983 opened new grounds on which human rights groups could demand for both truth and justice. However, although the 1985 trial of top military officials marked a moment in which the state attempted to rectify the injustices of the past, this moment was short lived, as two laws of impunity which halted all trials at convicting only 9 military officials entrenched the transition to democracy and demands for a 'better Argentina' in an unresolved past. As such, for the two decades following the trial human rights groups marked the country with an urgency to remember through events organized as public and collective rituals of remembrance which defied government attempts to "forgive and forget" and acted as the only avenue to work towards truth and justice. Recently, with the Kirchner governments' attempts to respond to the injustices of the past—by for example having the laws of impunity declared unconstitutional in 2003 thus securing the conditions necessary for the current federal trials of repressors of the dictatorship—there has been yet another shift in how groups have chosen to demand for 'memory, truth, and justice'. What remains the same is the understanding of Argentina as a country in transition to democracy, evidenced by the continuing state violence such as the recent disappearance of Juilo López—a witness in the 2006 trial of a former police agent who human rights groups maintain was disappeared by the Federal Argentine Police.

Today, human rights groups' work of remembering the Disappeared and resisting Argentina's continuing legacy of state violence and culture of impunity is implicated in many current political issues both directly and indirectly linked to the violence of the dictatorship. These groups consider their responses to current state violence and injustice a measure of the most appropriate way to remember the Disappeared. Although these groups continue to organize remembrance events that can be identified as contained performances of remembrance, the memory of the Disappeared is primarily conveyed through responses to current political issues. Human rights groups ground their responses to current political issues in a shared conception of the truth—that the period between 1976 and 1983 was a genocide of an entire generation who was working to transform the inequalities between the rich and the poor and that it is the responsibility of Argentinean's today to continue this work. They argue that the Disappeared were disappeared as part of a larger economic project implemented in the Southern Cone of Latin America with the support of the U.S. government and the elite class in the region which required the extermination of left-wing community activists, union workers, and student movements. This truth underpins the consensus amongst human rights groups that the most appropriate way to remember the Disappeared and to 'do justice' for the Disappeared is to continue the work that they began and for which they were disappeared—the work to construct, as Evel of the Association of the Mothers of Plaza de Mayo told me, "a society of solidarity with work and education for everyone" (Interview, July 20, 2007). Importantly, to 'do justice' for the Disappeared is a direct translation of the Spanish term *"hacer justicia"* whose meaning cannot be effectively expressed through terms such as "seeking justice" which conveys a process of looking for justice, or "administering justice" which is considered to be solely a function of the state. Instead, to 'do justice' means that the act of constructing a 'better Argentina' and thus continuing the work of the Disappeared results in justice for the Disappeared. Human rights groups communicate the responsibility of 'doing justice' for the Disappeared as being that of the state and of civil society. What is at issue between groups then, is *how* to continue the work of the Disappeared—in other words, what is the work that must be done in order to construct a 'better Argentina' and 'do justice' for the Disappeared and thus adequately carry their memory into the future?

Debates on *how* to continue the work of the Disappeared are linked to differing notions of memory and justice, which implicate the state and civil society in varying ways. Thus, decisions on how to remember the Disappeared are also decisions about to whom demands for 'a better' Argentina will be articulated. The Association of Mothers of Plaza de Mayo ground their work of memory and resistance in a distinct conceptualization of memory, which they refer to as *"memoria de acción"*—"memory of action." This is a memory that focuses on remembering the Disappeared's life and disavows their death because the culpable have never admitted to their murders. Although the women in the Association understand that their children are dead, they believe that if they represent the Disappeared as dead they are in effect killing them because no one has ever confirmed their death. It is this understanding of memory that fuels their decisions not to attend the current federal trials and to focus their energy on what they call "work for life," such as the cooperative housing building projects which they have organized across the country. Explicitly, the Association has said: "The Mother's have asked themselves, what is more important, to continue chasing the military or that one child have food to eat and one person have the opportunity to be happy? And we decided that what is more important is that one child have enough food to eat and that one person have the opportunity to be happy. The lawyers can keep chasing the military." (Asociación Madres de Plaza de Mayo, 2008b)

While Mothers of Plaza de Mayo-Founding Line and the Grandmothers of Plaza de Mayo do not align themselves with this conceptualization of memory, as Nora from Mothers-Founding Line told me, "we do memory work everyday when we fight for justice and punishment of the repressors [of the dictatorship] and when we take up our children's banners and protest with the Aboriginals who are reclaiming their land" (Nora Cortiñas, Interview, June 22, 2007). Thus, while these groups coincide with the Association's housing projects as a way to 'do justice' for the Disappeared, they have been present at all of the current federal trials, maintaining that these trials are crucial in positioning the state as accountable for attending to the past in the present and for ending the continuing culture of impunity and violence. These groups unremittingly insist that in a democracy the work of justice to publicize the truth, punish the guilty, and repair the damage is the responsibility of the state and that the Kirchner governments have not assumed this responsibility to their full capacity. They cite the state's initial argument that the case of the recently disappeared Julio Lopez was in fact a case of an elderly man who had gotten lost rather than a case of disappearance, as evidence of such and they understand part of their role as human rights activists as that of "keeping an eye on the state and the justice system" (Alba Lanzilotto, Grandmothers of Plaza de Mayo, Interview, July 23, 2007).

## Conclusions

In Argentina, the work of memory and the work of 'doing justice' is constantly being redefined and challenged both between and within groups, creating a politics of memory that is full of contradictions, tensions, and conflicts. That being said, although the Association of Mothers do not attend the current federal trials and have stated that "the enemy is no longer in the Government House" (Hebe de Bonafini, President of Asociación Madres, as cited in Keve 2006) last month they directed a list of demands to the state that they believe are necessary to speed up the current federal trials and assure that the state administer justice. In the same vein, while Mothers-Founding Line for example direct most of their demands to the state, this does not mean that they consider the state "the enemy"—as they recently demonstrated through their support for President Kristina Kirchner at a public assembly she held in response to the current political and economic conflict between farmers, landowners, and the state. Thus, unlike that of 1980s and 1990s Argentina in which the struggle was one against policies and practices of forgetting sanctioned by the state, within this messy politics of memory varying choices on how to voice demands for a 'better Argentina' and how to construct a 'better Argentina' are not simply about being with the state or against the state. They are choices made by groups of people in response to a particular political moment in Argentina—a moment marked by a government who calls itself the "government of human rights", a moment in which over half of the population lives in extreme poverty, a moment which is perceived by most to be moving closer towards democracy, a moment in which those who were direct victims of the military's policy of disappearance continue to be threatened physically, psychologically, and emotionally, and a moment which sits within the broader context of a country in which the social fabric is haunted by ghosts whose absence is forever present.

Argentina, like much of Latin America, is a country in which the absence of properly marked gravesites and the absence of bodies to mourn concurrently places these bodies in every corner of the country marking absence with presence. Thus, while the Disappeared may be inherently present in their absence, in the transition to democracy Argentineans have been left to grapple with the issue of weaving this present absence into the social imaginary. When human rights groups make demands of the state and of civil society to remember and to 'do justice' for the past in the present, they are asking others to be accountable for their memories and stories of historical violence and trauma. In other words, they are asking others to construct a 'better Argentina' in which the dead live with the living. Every time these groups debate about how to most adequately remember the disappeared they seek to construct a democratic Argentina that is rooted in the understanding of democracy that, as Roger Simon writes, is one of "making decisions regarding aspects of one's life with others…and being open to the realities of the incommensurable character of the experiences of others" (Simon 2005, 6)—others who are here and others who are gone. In her demand to "construct the country that our children dreamed of" Hebe de Bonafini is naming her audience heirs to her stories of loss, pain, and resistance and calling her heirs to witness the lives of those who are absent, explicitly including them in this 'better Argentina' despite their already intrinsic presence. The way in which human rights groups choose to construct a 'better Argentina', and in turn the way in which their heirs choose to construct a 'better Argentina', is not about how to best represent the Disappeared's work for a 'better Argentina' but rather a demonstration of how these people are taking these difficult memories into their lives and living "as though the lives of others matter" (Simon 2000, 9)—including the lives of those who are gone, but are still with us.

A common objective of public and collective remembrance of violence is to heal a perceived rupture in the community—people come together and work together to heal, based on a shared indescribable experience. However, it is the very indescribability of loss, which defines the experience of mass loss and violence as untranslatable and incommensurable that also often divides people at the same time that it unites them. The spaces in which we consider how public and collective memories can establish the conditions needed to work towards an alternative future than one which is dominated by violence necessitates and understanding that, as Judith Butler (2004) writes, "there is no 'I' without 'you'" (22).

In coming to bear witness to violence and in carrying these memories forward and passing them on 'I' live with 'your' memories of 'your' experiences with violence while remaining attentive to the untranslatability of these experiences and therefore the differences between 'us.' Thus, differences in how human rights groups in Argentina articulate their demands of the state and of civil society are inherently linked to differences in how these groups conceptualize memory and the work of 'doing justice' which is inextricably linked to how people attempt to live with experiences of violence, loss, and trauma—experiences which are at once unifying and dividing. And so, in the transition to democracy in Argentina, human rights groups' work to consolidate a democracy that includes the living and the dead is thus embedded not only in the memory of the Disappeared but also in questions of how to live with and alongside other's endlessly incommensurable experiences—questions that demand that we think about how our lives are intricately bridged and that foster a critique of how we live our lives with those who are gone and with those who are still here, with those whom we know and with those whom we will never know, enabling a learning *from* the past for a democratic present and future.

# References

Asociación Madres de Plaza de Mayo. 2008a. *Los pueblos siempre solucionamos los problemas en la Plaza* [The people always resolve their problems in the Plaza]. Retrieved April 03, 2008, from http://www.madres.org/asociacion/jueves/jueves.asp.

Asociación Madres de Plaza de Mayo. 2008b. *Las Madres firmaron un convenio con el Ministerio de Trabajo.* [The Mothers signed an agreement with the Ministry of Labour]. Retreived May 23, 2008, from http://www.madres.org/asociacion/novedades/novedades.asp.

Butler, J. 2004. Violence, mourning, politics. In *Precarious life: the powers of mourning and Violence* (19-49). New York: Verso.

Keve, C. 2006. "Las Madres nunca retrocedieron, las Madres van a estar siempre." [The Madres have never gone backwards, the Madres will be here forever]. *Página* 12: 1, 3.

Simon, R.I. 2005. *Touch of the past: Remembrance, learning, and ethics.* New York: Palgrave MacMillan.

――― (2000). "The paradoxical practice of Zakhor: Memories of 'what has never been my fault or my deed.'" In *Between hope and despair: pedagogy and the remembrance of historical trauma.* ed. R.I. Simon, S. Rosenberg, and C. Eppert. (9-26). Lanham: Rowman & Littlefield Publishers Inc.

# TERRORIZING (UN)CITIZENS:
# A GENEALOGY OF SECURITY CERTIFICATES

*Sarah Hamilton*

Although they form a key component of the post-9/11, US-led, "War On Terror" in Canada, and were only struck down as unconstitutional by the Supreme Court of Canada in February 2007 (with mandated changes in 2008), "security certificates" appear in Canadian legislation shortly after the "FLQ" or "October Crisis" of October 1970, and thus predate the precipitating events of the War On Terror by at least thirty-one years.[1,2] The main focus of this paper is not on the 2001 model of security certificates, nor on the slightly modified 2008 version, but on the 1970-71 security certificate and its origins in the suspension of civil liberties and citizen rights during the FLQ Crisis. To illustrate what might be at stake in a genealogy that spans the brief time period of thirty years, I will begin with a description of the 2001 model of security certificates.

In their 2001 post-9/11 incarnation, security certificates are the juridical mechanism within Sections 33 and 76-87 of the *Immigration and Refugee Protection Act*[3] that declare "permanent residents" and "foreign nationals" inadmissible to the state of Canada for reasons of "national security" (IRPA s. 77). Produced by the Canadian Security Intelligence Service (CSIS) and issued by the Minister of Citizenship and Immigration and the Solicitor General of

---

[1] The Public Safety Canada webpage on security certificates incompletely states that certificates have "been in place since 1978," without specifying a particular statute, possibly to detract attention from the use of security certificates on Canadian citizens during the FLQ Crisis. The site also states that "only" 27 people have been held on security certificates since 1991, omitting to note that major revisions to certificates occurred that year, concurrently with the Oka Crisis in Québec. (Public Safety Canada, "Security Certificates" (online), available: http://www.publicsafety.gc.ca/prg/ns/seccert-eng.aspx, 8 March 2008, 30 May 2008.) (Hereafter referred to as "PSC-SC.")

[2] Wikipedia makes notes of an article in the Calgary Herald on 13 June 2006 that I haven't been able to source, tracing the usage of security certificates back to the deportation of "an alleged Italian mob boss" in the 1960s. ("Security certificate," Wikipedia, The Free Encyclopedia, 25 Feb 2008, Wikimedia Foundation, Inc., 31 May 2008 <http://en.wikipedia.org/w/index.php?title=Security_certificate&oldid=193951567>.)

[3] "Immigration and Refugee Protection Act," in *Statutes of Canada 2001*, Chapter 27, Ottawa: Queen's Printer for Canada, 2001, Sections 76-87. (Hereafter referred to as "IRPA.")

Canada (currently the Minister of Public Safety and Emergency Preparedness), security certificates allow for the detention and/or deportation of the individual named.[4] Illuminatingly, on its introductory page on National Security, Public Safety Canada describes security certificates as "a rarely used mechanism for removing a person from the country" and "a way to ensure Canada's immigration laws are not misused by people who pose a threat."[5] This language immediately divides threats from non-threats and the entitled from the unentitled with cartoon-like efficiency, while identifying the state as a reasonable, and reasonably active, political actor who upholds the rule of Canadian law against the unentitled, threatening individuals who would abuse it, to the detriment of entitled, non-threatening "Canadians." The page on "Security Certificates" states that persons detained on security certificates are "non-Canadians" who "have no legal right to be here" and "pose a serious threat to Canada and Canadians"; the "objective" of the security certificate process is their "removal" (PSC-SC 2008).[6] In spite of this stated objective, Canada notoriously detained the "Secret Trial Five" on security certificates under indefinite circumstances until the intervention of the Supreme Court of Canada in February 2007. Of the five men detained on security certificates after

---

[4] *Charkaoui v. Canada (Citizenship and Immigration)*, [2007] 1 S.C.R. 350, 2007 SCC 9. (Hereafter referred to as "Charkaoui.")

[5] Public Safety Canada, "National Security: Security Certificates" (online), available: http://www.publicsafety.gc.ca/prg/ns/index-eng.aspx, 8 March 2008, 30 May 2008.

[6] In equivocal language, the site notes that "All individuals subject to a certificate have been deemed to be inadmissible for reasons of national security, violating human or international rights, or involvement in organized or serious crimes," using the symbolic-logic conjunction "or" to mean that at least one of these things is true in all cases, while two of them need not be true in any case. The connotations of the second and third clauses nevertheless give affective weight to the idea that individuals held on security certificates are "threats" who violate rights, while the Canadian government upholds public and moral order. This sense is compounded by the following odd paragraph, which: a) places blame for the undue length of detentions on the detainees themselves, or on the civil liberties safeguards they "choose to" exercise, b) implies that all of "the individuals" held are not entitled to remain in Canada by inserting "the" in this clause, without recognizing that some individuals may be held unjustly, nor that all individuals are entitled to the right of *habeas corpus*, and c) does not mention the possibility of an "expeditious" removal to torture:

> The length of time it takes to remove an inadmissible person is determined by a range of factors and is different from one case to another. In more straightforward cases, removal can occur very expeditiously. Individuals currently subject to security certificates have exercised their right to pursue appeals of removal decisions made against them. This has delayed removal in many cases. Due process must be followed and if obstacles to removal have been cleared, the government will act by removing the individuals who have no legal right to remain in Canada. (PSC-SC 2008)

9/11, two were arrested before that date: Mohammad Mahjoub in June 2000 and Mahmoud Jaballah in August 2001. Three arrests followed 9/11: Hassan Almrei in October 2001, Mohamed Harkat in December 2002, and Adil Charkaoui in May 2003.[7] With the construction of a $2.2 million facility in Kingston, Ontario to hold detainees,[8] opened on 24 April 2006,[9] the Government of Canada made good on its promise that it "takes its obligation to safeguard public safety and national security very seriously," notably at the expense of its "commitment" (not its obligation) to respect "individual rights under the *Canadian Charter of Rights and Freedoms*" as well as "international human rights obligations," which it takes "seriously" (but not "very seriously") (PSC-SC 2008). With the exception of Almrei, these men were released under house arrest or other strict conditions between February 2005 (Charkaoui) and March 2007 (Jaballah), but nevertheless remain the subjects of certificates and continue to face deportation, including possible deportation-to-torture like that experienced by Maher Arar. Almrei remains in detention at the Kingston Immigration Holding Centre, and has undergone several hunger strikes in protest.

With the *Charkaoui v. Canada* (2007) decision, the Supreme Court altered the Canadian security certificate system and adopted the British "special advocate" model. Why this model is not an unequivocal success for the "rule of law" is discussed in Dyzenhaus (2007),[10] and I will refer to the beginnings of this argument later in order to make my analysis of the 1970-71 model of security certificates. Before I return to Dyzenhaus, some historical details are needed about the FLQ Crisis and the legislation that emerged from it. Prior to Canada's shift to the "special advocates" model, the IRPA granted sole discretion to the broadly defined "judge" (appointed by the Solicitor General) to determine the length and circumstances of detention, and authorized *in camera* assessments of evidence which could be withheld from both the detainee and their legal counsel if the disclosure of this evidence might compromise national security; these assessments were not subject to judicial review. The problem with this system, of course, is that it is open to abuse: it is very difficult to assess whether disclosure of such information would actually compromise national security, or whether it is *ever* justified to withhold evidence, when checks on the legal authorities making these judgements, namely CSIS, the Minister of

---

[7] Security Certificates: Is This Canada?" *Homes Not Bombs*, http://www.homesnotbombs.ca/secrettrialprimer.htm, 3 May 2004, 30 May 2008.

[8] Sara Falconer, "Canada's Secret Trial Five: Guantanamo North," *Hour*, http://www.hour.ca/news/news.aspx?iIDArticle=9074, 4 May 2006, 30 May 2008.

[9] Canada Border Services Agency, "News Release: Kingston Immigration Holding Centre Opens," http://www.cbsa-asfc.gc.ca/media/release-communique/2006/0424ottawa-eng.html, 25 April 2006, 30 May 2008.

[10] David Dyzenhaus, "Cycles of Legality in Emergency Times," *Public Law Review* 18 (2007), 165-185, received from the author by email 22 Jan. 2008. (Hereafter referred to as "Dyzenhaus.")

Citizenship and Immigration, and the Solicitor General of Canada, are foreclosed by those same parties on the non-negotiable grounds of "threats to national security." Free of judicial checks, between 2001 and 2008 security certificates suspended the writ of *habeas corpus*, a writ requiring that detained prisoners be brought before court to ascertain whether they are being lawfully held, and which has existed in British law since the Middle Ages. The right to *habeas corpus* has been suspended at least three times in Canadian history: during the Internments of "enemy aliens" during World Wars I and II, and during the FLQ Crisis of October 1970. Suspension during wartime of *habeas corpus* and other enshrined civil liberties and human rights is certainly questionable and not necessarily morally or legally correct, but within European legal traditions this suspension is frequently viewed as a "necessary evil" that ultimately safeguards what it temporarily suspends, human liberty, which is suspended with the purported end of ensuring its continuation in peacetime. This "ideal" of the noble wartime exception may be underscored by racist and colonialist assumptions, but it is nevertheless given the weight of reason within a legal tradition that recognizes a necessity for "extraordinary" measures under "exceptional" circumstances, operating as what I will call, following Kent Roach, a successful "trade-off between security and rights."[11]

Suspension of *habeas corpus* during peacetime, however, contravenes this tradition and opens the way to a Schmittian "permanent state of exception." This third, purportedly temporary, suspension of *habeas corpus* during the FLQ Crisis is the focus of my current research. A pattern seems to emerge out of the time-limited peacetime suspension of civil liberties in October 1970, coincidently with the rise of legal positivism and an entrenchment of market capitalism during the three decades to follow, gradually creating the conditions of possibility for an ossification of "exceptional" suspensions of civil liberties and human rights between 2001 and 2008. What emerges in legislative statutes, House debates, and Cabinet meetings during 1970-71 seems to have this effect in spite of the very carefully placed safeguards that were deployed along with the "War Measures Act"[12] and the "Public Order (Temporary Measures) Act"[13] that replaced it. The shifts in language during this juncture, in legislative language and in daily language, and the shifts in attitude that they seem to reveal, are the subject of my current research, and of this paper.

---

[11] Kent Roach, "Must We Trade Rights for Security? The Choice Between Smart, Harsh, or Proportionate Security Strategies in Canada and Britain," revised version of the twenty-seventh Viscount Bennett lecture given at the University of New Brunswick Faculty of Law on 27 October 2005, received from David Dyzenhaus by email 22 January 2008.
[12] "War Measures Act," in *Revised Statutes of Canada 1970*, Chapter W-2, Ottawa: Queen's Printer, 1970. (Hereafter referred to as "WMA.")
[13] "Public Order (Temporary Measures) Act," in *Acts of the Parliament of Canada, 1971*, Chapter P-2, Ottawa: Queen's Printer, 1970. (Hereafter referred to as "POA.")

October 1970 and the months that follow: at 4 a.m. on 16 October 1970, under Prime Minister Pierre Elliott Trudeau and in response what it will refer to as the "October" or "FLQ Crisis," the Government of Canada invokes the WMA, effectively suspending all citizen and civil liberties in the state of Canada and giving the Executive the "necessary" powers, by the only legal means available, to apprehend any and all "terrorism suspects" associated with the FLQ. According to Cabinet documents, 495 people are arrested during the ensuing blitz of army deployment in Montréal and throughout Québec, of whom only 62 have been charged with a crime as of 8 April 1971.[14] The public and press and some parliamentarians, notably NDP leader Tommy Douglas, react with an outcry about the blanket suspension of civil liberties, and as the WMA comes to be universally acknowledged as too heavy-handed and too broad for addressing the FLQ Crisis, the government's response is to draft the POA.

It is within the POA that a "certificate stating that just cause exists for the detention of" a person who threatens the public order of Canada (POA s. 12.2b) is first deployed. By the time this "certificate" turns up in the IRPA (s. 77.1), it contains no explicit reference to "a person charged with an offence" or a "person... in custody," but refers instead to "a permanent resident or a foreign national" on every occasion in which mention is required of the subject of the certificate. There are two things to note about this transition: the figure of the presumed-criminal who threatens public order within the POA becomes the juridical inspiration for the "permanent resident or foreign national" of the IRPA security certificate; and the "subject-to" of this certificate, who is arguably already a subaltern subject in the POA, becomes an even emptier placeholder within the IRPA, rendered utterly generic and no longer "personned" or otherwise given identifying characteristics within the text of the act (presumably because such characterizations would become the grounds of contest within law—the less said about the subject of the certificate and the less said about the crime, the broader the reach of the certificate itself).

So what prepares the ground for this "fixing" or "determining" of the subaltern status of the subject of the IRPA security certificate? In attempting to sketch the beginnings of an answer this question, I will give some details about the historical transition from the WMA to the POA, and the push within Cabinet to enact permanent "emergency" legislation to supplant the POA after it expires in 1971.

Government officials James Cross and Pierre Laporte are kidnapped in early October 1970, and communiqués are subsequently issued by the Front de libération du Québec claiming responsibility for the kidnappings and call-

---

[14] Canada, Privy Council Office, "Emergency Legislation," in *Cabinet Conclusions 1971*, Library and Archives Canada: RG2, Series A-5-a, Volume 6381, 8 April 1971. (Hereafter referred to as "EM 8 April 1971.")

ing for the release of several people detained for "terrorist activities." Québec at this point has sole jurisdiction over its own security, but in mid-October, Québec Premier Robert Bourassa and Montréal Mayor Jean Drapeau are required by the Government of Canada to "formally request," in writing, the intervention of the Canadian army in the "aid of civil power" in order to grant Québec "emergency powers" to apprehend and detain terrorism suspects.[15] In response to receiving these letters of request, Trudeau's government invokes the WMA.

Created on the cusp of the First World War, the War Measures Act of 1914 gave powers to the government of Canada to detain "alien enemies" in internment camps, including but not limited to thousands of Germans; and history repeated itself during the Second World War, when every foreign national and citizen of Japanese descent within the state of Canada was incarcerated within internment camps for the duration of the war, in what was known as "the internment," and then subject to restricted mobility rights that forbade former residents of the West Coast of BC from returning to the West Coast for five years after the end of the war, in what was known as "the dispersal" (and within this number are included two of my grandparents, which motivates my interest in this subject). "War Measures Act" is the abbreviated title; the full title of the 1970 WMA reads: "An Act to confer certain powers upon the Governor in Council in the event of war, invasion, or insurrection" (WMA Full Title). The WMA states, in a section entitled "EVIDENCE OF WAR":

> The issue of a proclamation by Her Majesty, or under the authority of the Governor in Council shall be conclusive evidence that war, invasion, or insurrection, real or apprehended, *exists and has existed for any period of time therein stated*, and [shall be conclusive evidence] of its continuance, until by the issue of a further proclamation it is declared that the war, invasion or insurrection no longer exists. (WMA s. 2.0; my emphasis)

Again, two important notes: war, invasion, and insurrection are of equal gravity, and the latter two terms take on the weight of the former by virtue of their inclusion within the "*War* Measures Act"; the declaration of any of these three things by the Executive *constitutes the ontological existence of such a state* (e.g. a declaration of insurrection constitutes the ontological existence of a state of insurrection). Empirical signs of insurrection such as rioting, or someone other than Elizabeth II standing upon a wooden podium and declaring herself queen, or an organized group issuing communiqués with lists of demands, or the execu-

---

[15] I am using the old-fashioned phrase "terrorism suspects" here, meaning "people suspected of terrorism," instead of the more contemporary "terror suspects." In my view, the latter implies something entirely different and begins to collapse definitions of "the human" and "personhood" into empty consumerist placeholders.

tion of a kidnapped government official, are not necessary for constituting this state; although we assume, perhaps, that they will underlie such a declaration.

A notion of Executive absolutism is thus in evidence within the WMA, and to say that the act grants sweeping powers to the Executive is an understatement. It explicitly states that "[t]he Governor in Council" may authorize "by reason of the existence of real or apprehended war, invasion or insurrection" *anything* "he" "deem[s] necessary or advisable for the security, defence, peace, order and welfare of Canada" (WMA s. 3.1), and this power extends to censorship of media, "arrest, detention, exclusion and deportation" of people, and control over marine ports, control over the "transportation... of persons and things," and control over trade and private property (WMA s. 3.1a-f). In the event of deportation, or of being arrested or detained "as an alien enemy, or upon suspicion that [one] is an alien enemy, or to prevent [one's] departure from Canada," the WMA stipulates that the detainee cannot be "released upon bail or otherwise discharged or tried, without the consent of the Minister of Justice" (WMA s. 5.0). That is, the right to "innocence until proven guilty," as manifest in freedoms of movement and association, is inverted by the requirement of an explicit permission for the detainee's release. By virtue of being an element in a series of statutes that belong to Volume VII of the *Revised Statutes of Canada 1970*, and thus "Proclaimed and Published under the authority of chapter 48 of the Statutes of Canada, 1964-65" (Statutes cover), the powers granted to the Executive by the WMA are presumably applied throughout the geographical territory of what is commonly understood as Canada; yet mention of this territory is only made analogously, with reference to the security of Canada or the governmental apparatuses of the state, or through direct references to entries into and departures from its borders (WMA s. 3.1, 3.1c, 5.0). In spite of the dearth of direct references to the Act's jurisdiction over people, it was construed to apply to everyone within Canada's territorial borders upon its invocation during both World Wars. The power of the Act comes into effect not upon the signing of a certificate, but "only upon the issue of a proclamation of the Governor in Council declaring that war, invasion or insurrection, real or apprehended, exists" (WMA s. 6.1); the powers it grants to the Executive are conditional upon a declaration, rather than an explicit writ. The Act carefully stipulates in Section 6.5 that everything within its purview and every action undertaken in its name "shall be deemed not to be an abrogation, abridgement or infringement of any right or freedom recognized by the *Canadian Bill of Rights*. 1960, c. 44, s. 6" (WMA s. 6.5). No action of government undertaken with the force of the WMA can be construed as a violation of rights according to the *Canadian Bill of Rights*;[16] in other words, the WMA grants full impunity to Executive powers, "notwithstanding" the rights outlined in the BOR, suspending them for

---

[16] "Canadian Bill of Rights," in *Revised Statutes of Canada 1970*, Chapter B-44, Ottawa: Queen's Printer, 1970. (Hereafter referred to as "BOR.")

the duration of the WMA's invocation.[17] The language of the WMA Section 6.5 directly echoes that of the BOR Section 2; the latter states: "Every law of Canada shall, unless it is expressly declared by an Act of the Parliament of Canada that it shall operate notwithstanding the *Canadian Bill of Rights*, be so construed and applied as not to abrogate, abridge or infringe or to authorize the abrogation, abridgment or infringement of any of the rights or freedoms herein recognized and declared" (BOR s. 2.0), and then goes on to list specific rights, stating that "no law of Canada shall be construed or applied so as to" justify arbitrary detention, "cruel and unusual treatment," or to deprive a detained person of the right to *habeas corpus*, "counsel," and the right to "be informed promptly of the reason for his arrest or detention," etc. (BOR s. 2c.i-iii). Interestingly, the BOR ends with a definition of what counts as a "law of Canada" that includes any "Act of the Parliament of Canada enacted before *or after* the coming into force of this Act" as well as "any law in force in Canada or in any part of Canada at the commencement of this Act that is subject to be repealed, abolished or altered by the Parliament of Canada" (BOR s. 5.2; my emphasis)—this seems to contradict the "notwithstanding" element of Section 2, which may have been added later. The BOR could thus be construed as applying to both the WMA and the subsequent POA, except insofar as both documents exempt themselves from its purview. Finally, to highlight just exactly what is at stake during an act of war, the WMA ends with final comments about compensation for the seizure of property and restricts the mobility of, and gives the government the right to seizure of, any "ship or vessel" whose movements contravene the terms of the WMA; I will return to this regulation of mobility briefly below.

To return to the sequence of events that takes place from October 16th to October 18th, 1970: after Trudeau invokes the WMA on the 16th, he presents the reasons for his decision to Parliament later that day. On October 17th, 1970, one of the two kidnapped officials, Pierre Laporte, is executed, and the FLQ claims responsibility. On October 18th, René Lévesque, future Premier of Québec, calls the invocation of the WMA by Trudeau's government "panicky" and "excessive," suggesting that it overestimates the scope of the threat posed by FLQ. At question in Lévesque's statement is whether a state of "insurrection," and thus war, actually exists. The last invocation of the WMA had ended only twenty years previously, with the final days of the dispersal of Japanese-Canadians in 1950. The government now comes under fire both from the NDP and various agents of the press for its deployment of the

---

[17] The reference is interesting, because the *Canadian Bill of Rights* of the 10th of August, 1960, only goes up to Section 5—there is no Section 6—suggesting either that the numbers have carried over from some previous BOR enacted between 1914 and 1960, or that the notation refers to the WMA itself, which gives more force to the punctuation after "*Rights*" and suggests that the powers given to the Executive by the WMA override the whole of the BOR.

WMA, which grants the Executive the same powers it had recourse to during the Second World War, a time of perceived threat that seems to exceed that of the FLQ Crisis. The invocation of the WMA is also acclaimed by some within Parliament, and the protests of the NDP decried, notably by one Mr. Jean-R. Roy, MP for Timmins. He states:

> [The NDP] would now abandon [the people of Québec] and throw them to the extreme socialists; the anarchists, the Maoists, and the FLQ. No doubt chaos and disorder in Quebec would help the socialist cause. They thrive on that sort of adversity, but what a price for Canada to pay for the sake of cheap politics....
>
> [NDP] leaders and members are the ones who sow the seed that gives birth and strength to the anarchists, the terrorists, the Maoists and the murderers....their sinister politics would bring help for the terrorists, but Canadians want these terrorists eliminated....their bleeding hearts would bring anarchy and the termination of our freedoms, but Canadians want their liberty, with law and order.
>
> It is these extreme socialists, as I say, who condone violence as a sometimes necessary activity in labour disputes, who condone the destruction of property in the same disputes and then scream for justice having derided the laws. They may stop short of condoning sedition, they may stop short of condoning insurrection or treason, but there the terrorists start, continuing their work beyond the bounds of civilized society, beyond the intentions of these so-called reformers, but helped by their advance to the brink of disaster and social impropriety.[18]

In order to invoke the WMA, Trudeau declares on October 16th that a state of "armed insurrection" exists, but immediately undermines this claim when he takes pains to clarify that only the "absolutely necessary" measures of the WMA will be deployed.[19] He thus carefully skirts around the question of whether he has declared the country to be in a state of civil war; if it is not, the WMA should not be invoked; but if it is, then the scope of the WMA needn't be restricted. He is emphatic that *only the WMA* can grant the Executive the powers necessary for apprehending the kidnappers, or rather—the instigators of the insurrection. This is what spurs the subsequent creation of the POA, and underlies the push within Cabinet to enact oxymoronic "permanent" "emergency" legislation to supplant the POA when it expires on 30 April 1971. The

---

[18] All: Canada. Parliament. House of Commons. *Debates*, 28th Parliament, 3rd Session, 1970, vol. 2, 20 October 1970. Ottawa: Queen's Printer, 1970.
[19] Pierre Elliott Trudeau, "Notes for a National Broadcast," in *Canada's Prime Ministers, 1867-1994: Biographies and Anecdotes*, Ottawa: National Archives of Canada, 1994, 40 p., http://www.collectionscanada.gc.ca/primeministers/h4-3381-e.html, 23 April 2001, 8 April 2008.

Prime Minister and Solicitor General Jean-Pierre Goyer are strongly in favour, while Minister of Justice John Turner is strongly opposed. In Turner's opinion,

> ...the War Measures Act had been invoked in October, because the government did not have enough knowledge about the extent of the threat to public order posed by the F.L.Q. In retrospect it was evident that there had been 'substantial overkill' in its application.... In any future crisis he was confident that the police and governments had learned a great deal from their experience in October and it would probably not be necessary to invoke the War Measures Act on another such occasion. He himself now doubted that there had in fact been an 'apprehended insurrection' and believed that the Criminal Code was adequate for dealing with most aspects of civil disorder associated with terrorist activity. (EM 8 April 1971)

The POA passes in Parliament in December 1970. Its full title is "An Act to provide temporary emergency powers for the preservation of public order in Canada" (POA Intro). *Enter the security certificate*: upon the filing of a "certificate... stating that just cause exists for the detention of [a] person pending his trial" (POA s. 7.2a & s. 12.2b), the act grants the Executive powers to suspend civil liberties and restrict mobility. There is a critical difference from the WMA: powers applying to the citizenry of Canada under the WMA are individualized under the POA, and the POA is specifically addressed to the crimes of "the member[s] of the unlawful association," referring to the FLQ by name (POA s. 4a). Its measures are carefully tailored to suspend civil liberties in precise areas and through specified means that prepare the ground for the proper "management" of situations of real or suspected terrorism and insurrection. We have here entered the territory of Foucauldian governmentality and biopolitics. When Cabinet debates enacting permanent emergency legislation in April 1971, Turner asks a vital question:

> The Minister of Justice stated that the amendments being suggested in the draft bill to the Criminal Code [which is one half of the proposed legislation] raised a fundamental point of principle regarding the purpose of the Criminal Code. These amendments *would make it a crime under certain circumstances if there was reason to believe that an assembly if held would be unlawful*. It was being suggested therefore that the criminal code should be used *to anticipate and prevent* violence. Up to now, the criminal law had restricted itself to the actions of an individual at the time the crime was committed. (EM 8 April 1971; my emphasis)

With the creation of the POA, Trudeau's government rescinded its classification of the FLQ Crisis as a "civil war," which was necessarily entailed by the invocation of the *War Measures Act*. The POA limited the scope of this declaration of war, borrowed from the authority of Executive decree as it transcribed the medium from a "proclamation" to a "certificate," and created a new type of war: a tactical war of strategies aimed at managing, administering, and restricting the mobility of a specific class of people, not once a crime has been committed, but *before it starts*. If national security is at stake, the crime must be accurately anticipated no matter the cost: the terrorist must be spotted *before s/he becomes a terrorist*—unless one accepts the argument that a terrorist is a terrorist *before* s/he has committed an act of terrorism. A terrorist by nature? By race or by class? A theme develops, laden with "racist" undertones of the sort that Michel Foucault describes in *Society Must Be Defended*,[20] as one group restricts the mobility of another, in anticipation of a "potential" criminality. It is almost farcical that this theme, carrying through in the racialized application of security certificates in the present day, has its roots in a conflict between socialist Québec separatists and an absolutist declaration of perceived insurrection by the federal government. That the subaltern subject of security certificates has shifted from Québec sovereigntists to Canada's (usually Muslim) "foreign nationals" and "permanent residents" highlights the racialized effects of this biopower, which as Kim Rygiel argues stabilizes the nation as a fixed space of safety for a mobilized few,[21] while hampering mobility for "dangerous" others. The "terror-izing" of the (un)citizen is thus twofold: the direct subject of the security certificate is rendered a terrorist on suspicious grounds, by suspicion alone, deprived of *habeas corpus* in a permanent state of exception, without recourse to the rule of law. Indirect subjects related to these direct subjects by markers of culture, nationality, class, and especially gender (as Rygiel argues) are also "terror-ized," in an affective regime that promulgates guilt by association—not, here, association with "the members of the unlawful organization," but shadowy associations of commonality with the direct subjects of security certificates, by having such relational markers in common; by means of being *marked* within the national imaginary.

To return to Dyzenhaus: in "Cycles of Legality in Emergency Times, Dyzenhaus identifies a "compulsion of legality" within all three branches of law, namely the legislature, the Executive, and the judiciary, defined as "the compulsion to justify all acts of state as having a legal warrant: the authority of law" (Dyzenhaus 167). This compulsion can inaugurate two different "cycles of legality." In the first, "the institutions of legal order cooperate in devising controls on public actors which ensure that their decisions comply with the principle of legality, understood as a substantive conception of the rule of law" (Dyzenhaus 168), while in the second, "the content of legality is understood in an ever more formal or empty manner, resulting in the mere appearance or even... the pretence of legality" (Dyzenhaus

---

[20] Michel Foucault, *Society Must Be Defended: Lectures at the Collège de France 1975-76*, trans. David Macey, USA: Picador, 1997 & 2003.

[21] Kim Rygiel, "Protecting and Proving Identity: The Biopolitics of Waging War through Citizenship in the Post-9/11 Era," in *(En)Gendering the War on Terror: War Stories and Camouflaged Politics*, eds. Krista Hunt and Kim Rygiel, England: Ashgate, 2006, 145-67.

168). The first cycle of legality, that is, upholds the rule of law without allowing exceptions to be made by the Executive during times of emergency, while the second cycle allows for sweeping Executive powers even as it shows concern that the Executive not regard itself "as compelled openly to break free of the constraints of law" because this would enact "a kind of lip service to the compulsion of legality" (Dyzenhaus 168). I interpret Dyzenhaus's words to mean that the second cycle of legality occurs when the branches of law purport to uphold the rule of law without concern for its actual substance, thus trading in its affective benefits (e.g. public order) by means of a formal adherence that is ontologically (in times of emergency, if not always) without commitment to the rule of law. The security certificate of the 2001 and even the 2008 IRPA, as Dyzenhaus and others have argued, seems to inaugurate the second cycle of legality, veering uncomfortably close to the "thin veneer of legality"[22] usually associated with arbitrary Executive powers. I am arguing that the "thin veneer of legality" appertaining to present-day security certificates is facilitated and rendered possible by the affective apparatus surrounding their 1970 ancestors. With the creation of the 1970 certificate, a micro-civil war is instituted between the federal government and specific subaltern "threats" that it seeks to manage, purportedly ensuring "peace" and security for the "normal" citizenry of Canada by excising this subaltern threat from its midst. The terrorism suspect simply disappears from view, lacking access to proper counsel or to the evidence cited against him/her (especially pre-2008). No argument can be made against the chilling silence of arbitrary—or absolute—authority. Over the progressively more positivist decades following 1970, Executive powers seem to increasingly deploy this tactic as a strategy for policy. The individualization of a thinly legal war that cannot be viewed, perceived, responded to, or negotiated with prepares the ground for the ill-named, anxiety-producing, invisible yet ever-present War On Terror, as well as for the global networks that facilitate the "extraordinary rendition" of terrorism suspects to Guantanamo Bay, and the humiliation tactics at Abu Ghraib in Iraq. These tactics are purportedly applied to preformed terrorist individuals, but in fact produce and demarcate such subjects within a framework of intelligibility that only recognizes each iteration as confirmation of a preformed "terrorist" identity, rendering suspicious even the protest against typecasting. There is no possibility for this subaltern subject to speak in its own defence, and the logic here reminds me of medieval witch hunts: if a stone is tied to a suspected witch, and upon being thrown into a lake she *doesn't* drown, then we have confirmation that she is a witch. If she is not a witch, then this biopolitical "discovery" tactic renders her the ultimate, and ultimately silenced, subaltern subject.

In the meantime, deemed non-insurrectionists, namely the quotidian entitled, non-threatening citizens of Canada for whom security is promised through the excisive mechanisms of security certificates, seem to have no truck with this micro-civil war, and go about their quotidian lives as they "*norm*-ally" would.

---

[22] Dyzenhaus 168, citing *Secretary of State for the Home Department vs. MB* [2007] QB 415; [2006] EWHC 1000 (Admin) at 103.

# References

Canada Border Services Agency. "News Release: Kingston Immigration Holding Centre Opens." http://www.cbsa-asfc.gc.ca/media/release-communique/2006/0424ottawa-eng.html. 25 April 2006, 30 May 2008.

Canada. Parliament. 1070. "House of Commons." *Debates*, 28th Parliament, 3rd Session, 1970, vol. 2, 20 October 1970. Ottawa: Queen's Printer.

Canada, Privy Council Office, "Emergency Legislation," in *Cabinet Conclusions 1971*, Library and Archives Canada: RG2, Series A-5-a , Volume 6381, 8 April 1971.

"Canadian Bill of Rights." In *Revised Statutes of Canada 1970*, Chapter B-44. Ottawa: Queen's Printer, 1970.

*Charkaoui v. Canada (Citizenship and Immigration)*, [2007] 1 S.C.R. 350, 2007 SCC 9.

Dyzenhaus, David. 2007. "Cycles of legality in emergency times." *Public Law Review* 18:165-185. Received from author as a PDF, 22 Jan. 2008.

Falconer, Sara. "Canada's secret trial five: Guantanamo north." *Hour*. http://www.hour.ca/news/news.aspx?iIDArticle=9074. 4 May 2006, 30 May 2008.

Foucault, Michel. 1997 and 2003. *Society Must Be Defended: Lectures at the Collège de France 1975-76*. Trans. David Macey. USA: Picador.

"Immigration and Refugee Protection Act." In *Statutes of Canada 2001*, Chapter 27. Ottawa: Queen's Printer for Canada, 2001.

"Public Order (Temporary Measures) Act." In *Acts of the Parliament of Canada, 1971*, Chapter P-2. Ottawa: Queen's Printer, 1970.

Public Safety Canada, "National security: Security certificates" (online), available: http://www.publicsafety.gc.ca/prg/ns/index-eng.aspx, 8 March 2008, 30 May 2008.

———"Security Certificates" (online), available: http://www.publicsafety.gc.ca/prg/ns/seccert-eng.aspx, 8 March 2008, 30 May 2008.

Roach, Kent. "Must we trade rights for security? The choice between smart, harsh, or proportionate security strategies in Canada and Britain." Revised version of the twenty-seventh Viscount Bennett lecture given at the University of New Brunswick Faculty of Law on 27 October 2005. Received as a PDF from David Dyzenhaus, 22 Jan. 2008.

Rygiel, Kim. 2006. "Protecting and proving identity: The biopolitics of waging war through citizenship in the Post-9/11 era." In *(En)Gendering the war on terror: War stories and camouflaged politics*. Eds. Krista Hunt and Kim Rygiel. England: Ashgate, 145-67.

*Secretary of State for the Home Department vs. MB* [2007] QB 415; [2006] EWHC 1000 (Admin) at 103.

"Security certificate." *Wikipedia, The Free Encyclopedia*. 25 Feb 2008. Wikimedia Foundation, Inc. 31 May 2008. <http://en.wikipedia.org/w/index.php?title=Security_certificate&oldid=193951567>.

Trudeau, Pierre Elliott. 1994. "Notes for a national broadcast." In *Canada's Prime Ministers, 1867-1994: Biographies and Anecdotes*. Ottawa: National Archives of Canada, 40 p. http://www.collectionscanada.gc.caprimeministers/h4-3381-e.html, 23 April 2001, 8 April 2008.

"War Measures Act." In *Revised Statutes of Canada 1970*, Chapter W-2. Ottawa: Queen's Printer, 1970.

# CTOs:
# A NEW ORDER OF TERROR?

*Katie Aubrecht*

This paper charts the relations between psychiatric knowledge and the production of the modern subject through an examination of the recent addition of compulsory outpatient treatment in mental health legislation. Involuntary Community Treatment Orders (CTOs) represent a challenge to conventional notions of community and human rights. The progressive broadening of the criteria for commitment in the language of the laws and ambiguities surrounding the corresponding conditions for treatment orders make it difficult to challenge their enforcement. CTOs do not simply offer an alternative treatment option, "less restrictive" than commitment (Trueman, "Least Restrictive" 1). Rather, they represent the expansion of institutional forces of social control and the systematic coordination of a collective orientation to difference as a threat to the very values and belief systems to which notions of community are explicitly oriented.

My method involves a discursive analysis of the legislation and reviews of Bill C-68 or "Brian's Law" (2000) and its amendments to Ontario's *Mental Health Act* and the *Health Care Consent Act*. Named after Brian Smith, the Ottawa sportscaster who was shot to death by a man with schizophrenia, "Brian's Law" provides new grounds to the civil commitment criteria, authorizing involuntary examination, assessment and detention at an earlier stage in a person's illness than the existing criteria. It also ratifies the commonsense of the vague danger of mental illness and the call for its containment.

The emergence of CTOs in Ontario signifies what Nikolas Rose refers to as the *new biology of control*, which is grounded in "conceptions of crime control as public health" (*Politics of Life* 248-49). Concentrating on the recent amendments to Ontario's mental health legislation and reviews, my research charts the specific linkages between medical, psychological, and criminological knowledge structuring modern modes of social control. More specifically, I investigate the changing role of the state in mediating the relationship between the hospital and the social worlds beyond its walls. Should the recent legislative amendments be read as a sign that the role of the state is changing—that it heals rather than punishes social exclusion? How do perceptions of community as a self-evident good influence how we relate to state intervention in individual lives?

In the new social order, created under the auspices of a public health and safety initiative, citizenship is understood in terms of health. It is assumed everyone has and ought to have an interest in their health and the health of others, and that good health involves more than the absence of disease. It also assumed that good health can be measured by an individual and society's attempts to improve the health of all citizens. But, where are these cultural assumptions of the good of public health grounded? And who or what is public health good for: the individual, society, or the state? What happens to those who refuse treatment, and who are viewed as not having the "insight' to know what is good for them and society?

Richard O'Reilly defines a CTO as, "a legal provision by which a physician may require a person with mental illness who meets specific criteria to follow a course of treatment while living in the community" ("Why Are CTOs Controversial" 579). O'Reilly tells us that there are two kinds of CTOs—diversionary and preventive CTOs. The distinction is not specifically mentioned in the legislation and contributes to the ambiguity and controversies surrounding the use of CTOs. O'Reilly cites the existence of various other forms of mandatory outpatient treatment (MOT): court-ordered outpatient committal, conditional leave from the hospital, and guardianship legislation (579). According to O'Reilly, "The rationale for the use of CTOs rests primarily on the fact that deinstitutionalisation resulted in the discharge to the community of a cohort of individuals without the insight to recognize that they are ill or that they need treatment" (579-80). Those in favour of CTOs suggest that society has an obligation to provide care and treatment to individuals who are "at risk" of harming themselves or others, citing current research that supports the use of CTOs. Those who are against the use of CTOs perceive the legislation as coercive. They believe that CTOs have "negative unintended consequences" such as overuse, and challenge their use based on the existence of other available alternatives (O'Reilly 580).

What grounds the appearance of "at-risk" individuals and populations? To whom or what are they at risk of, and why? In debates surrounding the legislation of mandatory treatment, it becomes clear that individuals with a history of psychiatric treatment are at risk to themselves or others because of their lack of insight into their conditions. Refusing treatment is interpreted both as a refusal to participate in the construction of a new healthy order, and a refusal to support a mode of governance that aims at achieving objective improvements in the lives of ordinary citizens. Adherents of the need for a common health agenda orient to the consent to treatment as an indication of individuals' desire to improve their lives and life circumstances. Moreover, in the new medico-juridical order, psychiatrists, doctors, nurses, social workers, lawyers and families are all enlisted as part of a strategy to re-integrate alienated and excluded individuals through the promise of a return to normal life. The bureaucratic organization of social relations in service of public health is authorized in mental health legislation. Legislation like Brian's Law mandates both the preservation of the current order, and citizens' active participation in the evolution of this order.

The visibility of the "progress" of mentally ill individuals, to which their rights and freedom from constraint is bound, is evaluated in a manner similar to convicted offenders, using rates of "recidivism". Those who fail to demonstrate their internalization of the values of the new order, represented as the values of medicine and public safety, are considered threats to themselves and others. More importantly, such individuals represent a threat to the notions of social progress, which the mental health system and affiliated disciplinary regimes have claimed to advance. Recognizably "at-risk" individuals who do not show measurable improvement from when they entered the mental health system, but whose pre-determined period of confinement has reached its end and who can no longer be justifiably detained, pose a major problem for the legitimacy of the system and its efficacy. The persistence of socially unacceptable, inappropriate or offensive behaviors after treatment serves as a reminder of the history of the psychiatric profession's questionable status as an authoritative knowledge regime. It also calls into question all the other subsidiary authorities whose power and knowledge moves through channels this profession has helped shape; authorities most commonly associated with the clinic, the hospital, the pharmaceutical industry, the school and the university, the prisons and the courts. Involuntary community treatment represents a way to identify and control this dangerous population. Dangerous, in the sense of its potential to de-legitimate modern governance; characterized by its reliance on the more dispersed but highly coordinated proliferation of disciplinary knowledge and population governance.

In this context, we should think about how the interests of mentally ill individuals are made visible, and who has a say in *what* these interests are. Some advocates of mandatory treatment support the amendments in Brian's Law because of the new modalities it offers for ensuring consent against coercion. The Review and Appeal Boards and Rights Advice Boards are described as checks on the violations of the rights of vulnerable individuals. Proponents suggest that even in the absence of individuals' *insight* of their conditions, the amendments build in a guarantee that they will receive a socially acceptable level of institutional and communal support. The viability of CTOs is contingent on the visibility of the patient's consent to treatment.

In "Personal Responsibility Under Dictatorship" Hannah Arendt writes that, "An adult consents where a child obeys; if an adult is said to obey, he actually *supports* the organization or the authority of the law that claims 'obedience'" (46). The stated purposes of the amended *Health Care Consent Act* present a contradictory picture of the mental patient as a passive agent. There is no treatment without consent, but consent can be given by a "substitute decision-maker." The mentally ill individual is thus represented as one who supports the new social order, even if only implicitly through the support of someone else who has agreed to take responsibility for the individual's best interests. The Act states that "capacity", the ability to understand the information relevant to a treatment decision and foresee the consequences of that decision, can fluctuate, depending on treatment, time and the opinion of the health practitioner. Where capacity is understood as fluctuating, a space is created for the disqualification of the mentally ill individual's decisions, even as this individual is formally recognized as a responsible social actor.

At the final hearing of Brian's Law, Bob Muir, a representative of the Ontario Hospital Association (OHA), noted that CTOs would provide an increase in work for rights advisors working outside institutional settings. For that reason, work in rights counseling and advice should receive more funding. During the discussion, one party to the hearing raised the need to make a distinction between a rights advisor and a rights advocate. Even if the rights of individuals on CTOs are recognized, without an advocate, "those rights are unenforceable. It's rights without a remedy" (Legislative Assembly of Ontario Committee). Here, rights talk is represented as contributing to the problem. How can that be the case? Unlike those mentally ill accused who are processed through the criminal justice system, individuals under CTOs do not have access to a lawyer who can advocate on their behalf. If believed incapable of consenting to the treatment order, consent is provided by a substitute decision-maker. But, beyond consenting in the place of the mentally ill individual; who, in being deemed incompetent has been disenfranchised and disqualified from participating in the construction of an order to which he or she is to be subject, the substitute decision-maker has little to no say in the process; no legal authority or expertise.

Muir states that individuals under CTOs in the community should be afforded the same "rights and privileges" of those involuntarily confined in hospitals. This statement is very troubling, for it reveals an understanding of individuals with mental illness as requiring a different set of rights and responsibilities than those of the ordinary citizen. Furthermore, it models the rights of mentally ill individuals living in the community after notions of rights born out of an interest in involuntary confinement. Establishing a separate notion of rights for mentally ill individuals which mirrors those of the involuntarily confined should be terrifying for all Canadians, considering the fact that Health Canada's 2002 "A Report on Mental Illness in Canada" tells us that around 20% of Canadians will personally experience mental illness in their lifetime, about one in five Canadian adults will experience it each year, or that "mental illness indirectly affects all Canadians through illness in a family member, friend or colleague" (3). It is also terrifying because of the fact that individuals are placed under CTOs at the discretion of their doctors and psychiatrists and that, while an extensive psychiatric history is a good reason to initiate a CTO, no such history is required. In fact, CTOs can be used to build up a new psychiatric history where one was previously absent. CTOs may be initiated after a brief stay in hospital, after one is released from involuntary confinement, or even if one visits one's doctor and the doctor finds that such an order is necessary. Something that may be hard to imagine in more rural close knit communities, but which is certainly possible in cosmopolitan areas where patients do not necessarily have a strong rapport with doctors or who may only enter the hospital in emergency circumstances. Once under an order, the individual is subject to supervision by police, social workers, nurses, doctors, and psychiatrists, as well as regulated check-ins at local clinics. Once an individual receives a CTO, which tends to last about 6 months, the likelihood of receiving another is very high. The refusal of treatment or lack of successful outcomes after repeated hospitalization, which are some of the criteria for issuing CTOs also constitute signs that the CTO is not working; at which point the individual is returned to the hospital and a new CTO can be initiated. This adds more to the patient's record and psychiatric history, making this person more likely to qualify as an untreatable or incurable case.

Why is the "risk" in a refusal to community treatment, framed in the legislation as the product of a lack of insight, competence or capability, so problematic? In examining representations of mental illness that produce a common sense of an association between criminality and mental illness, Riley Olstead notices that mentally ill individuals are represented in terms of US versus Them, where "They are represented as having 'degrees' of difference that radiate from what is constituted as the core, 'normal'" ("Contesting the Text" 628). Through the Us/Them framework, the mentally ill are understood to have rejected common values, morality and life itself (Olstead 629). The risk that qualifies mentally ill individuals for community treatment is the risk of a deterioration in all that is self-evidently good in society—values, morals and life. It is not actually *what they do*, but *who they are* that constitutes them as an at-risk group. Their perceived distance from normal values and normal life renders them dangerous. The assumption of the social distance and negative social difference of mentally ill individuals also provides for the amendment of Canadian legislation excluding a need for the police to directly observe any offensive behaviors or activities before returning individuals under CTOs to hospital. Even if they are present in the communities, there is a collective sense that they should not be there and that they really belong somewhere else; and that they are responsible for the fact that they do not fit in.

Prior to the ascendance of Brian's Law Richard Pattern said that, "whereas the roots of the history of CTOs is a court-legal system, this is really a medical plan, albeit it does have some accountability and some teeth to it, But it is a medical plan, maximizing the opportunity for it to become consensual" (Legislative Assembly of Ontario Committee). What are the political implications of orienting to CTOs in terms of a right to medical treatment, and then using this right to identify at risk populations for involuntary committal? In "Personal Responsibility Under Dictatorship," Arendt writes of the "new order" in Nazi Germany and how people believed in it because it was "the law of the land" and "for no other reason than that was the way things were" (43). She remarks how, in the trial of Adolf Eichmann, Eichmann's lawyer had referred to the extermination camps as a "medical matter" (43). Without conflating what happened in Germany during the 1930s and 40s with what is happening today in Canada, it is important to remember how the mentally ill were one of the first groups targeted by the Nazis in the events leading up to the Holocaust. We would thus do well to think of the social and political consequences of framing social difference as a medical problem; or, of viewing the trend in Canadian legislation towards the re-confinement of individuals identified as mentally ill as a rational response to the "risks" they are presumed to pose.

## References

Arendt, Hannah. 2003. "Personal responsibility under dictatorship." *Responsibility and Judgment*. Ed. Jerome Kohn. New York: Schocken Books, 17-48.

Legislative Assembly of Ontario Committee. 2000. "Brian's Law: Mental health legislative reform." 29 March 2008 http://www.ontla.on.ca/committee-proceedings/transcripts/files_html/2000-05-29_G015.htm.

O'Reilly, Richard. 2004. "In review: Why are community treatment orders controversial?" *Canadian Journal of Psychiatry* 49: 579-584.

Olstead, Riley. 2004. "Contesting the text: Canadian media depictions of the conflation of mental illness and criminality." *Sociology of Health & Illness* 24, no. 5: 621-643.

Ontario. *Health Care Consent Act, 1996, S.O. 1996, Chapter 2, Schedule* A. 2007. 3 March 2008 <http://www.e-laws.gov.on.ca/html/statutes/english/elaws_statutes_96h02_e.htm>.

——— *Mental Health Act, 1990, R.S.O. 1990, Chapter M.7*. 2004. 3 March 2008 <http://www.e-laws.gov.on.ca/html/statutes/english/elaws_statutes_90m07_e.htm>.

Public Health Agency of Canada. *A Report on Mental Illness in Canada*. 2002. 29 March 2008 <http://www.phac-aspc.gc.ca/publicat/miic-mmac/chap_1_e.html>.

Rose, Nikolas. 2007. *The politics of life itself: Biomedicine, power, and subjectivity in the twenty-first century*. Princeton: Princeton Univ. Press.

Trueman, Shelley. 2003. "Community treatment orders and Nova Scotia— The least restrictive alternative?" *Health Law Journal* 11: 1-25.

# Taking Back Projections: The Despair and Hope in Projective Identification

*Karyne Messina*

Men and women are not inherently bad, but inherent in all of us are aggressive impulses and tendencies that are fraught with explosive possibilities. We can destroy our children, families, and our countries, not because we are bad or evil, but rather because we have not modulated, or had modulated for us, aspects of ourselves that are unknowable, aspects we cannot bear. Hence, we project these things outwardly ridding ourselves of unwanted feelings and ways of being that we do not or can not accept; the "not-me" parts of ourselves.

We see this phenomenon occurring on the current, world stage where all types of actions are directed towards others that are hard to comprehend, from vindictive, verbal attacks to horrendous acts of terror. *How* and *why* do these things occur? *Why* are such happenings so ubiquitous? Do we not know what we do to others? How does simple conflict escalate into attempts to annihilate individuals, groups of people, and entire countries?

In an attempt to better understand how these things happen, I will examine a few, key, psychoanalytic ideas that are particularly pertinent when trying to make sense of what we see in our world today; ideas developed by Melanie Klein and some of her followers that help explain the tendency to disavow and then attribute to others what we can not tolerate within.

The mechanism itself is called projective identification, which is primarily a primitive process: One wherein an unacceptable or even monstrous aspect of an individual's internal world must be expelled. Although Klein did not coin the term herself since it was used earlier by Edoardo Weiss to describe choice of sexual partners (Spillius 2007), the specific process to which *I* am referring was described by Klein in 1946 as she was developing her ideas about intrapsychic states of mind she called "positions." Simply put, she was talking about ways in which people experience and relate to each other. In what she called the paranoid-schizoid position, Klein talked about the need to mentally "get rid" of bad, threatening aspects of the self that are too much to bear. Other people are not experienced in one's mind as complete or whole with good and bad qualities in this position, but rather are experienced in a limited way, i.e., the entirety of one's being is not acknowledged. In this state, internal, unbearable feelings and thoughts are projected outwardly and thereafter are attributed to the other or others because they cannot be tolerated. In the paranoid-schizoid position wherein anxiety is intense, and mostly persecutory, people figuratively or literally, retaliate, seek revenge, hurt or otherwise "get-back-at" a person or people with no understanding of what is occurring: It is a time when raw aggression and aggressive tendencies are ever-present. In this state, thinking is distorted and action without thought predominates, i.e., action replaces thought.

When movement or growth occurs, however, when aggression and other unbearable feelings are modulated, modified or made tolerable in some manner, the way of experiencing the self and others shifts. In this second state or way of relating to the world, the position Klein called the depressive position (not to be confused with clinical depression), feelings are "taken back" or reclaimed. They no longer have to be projected but can be experienced as belonging to the self. Others are experienced as whole people, with various qualities and characteristics, some may be appreciated, and some not but good and bad qualities can co-exist within the same person, without one part having to be eradicated or disavowed. In this position, opportunities for mourning, repair, and learning from past experience become possible. Thinking also emerges or is restored in this state. This process of change occurs in the context of a relational world wherein one's initial, raw aggression is modified and made bearable with the help of another or others.

Although Klein's ideas were originally conceptualized as a way to describe how children develop intrapsychically, they were later woven into her understanding of adult patients. Today, they are used as they were originally conceived and have also been elaborated upon by various people to describe how groups of people interact, e.g., Bion, 1970. This includes infant and mother dyads, patient and therapist pairs as well as couples and families. Other theorists, for example Donald Meltzer (1973) and C. Fred Alford (1989), have incorporated these concepts to describe aspects of internal terror and social theory.

Since Kleinian concepts have evolved to include so many situations and now have such wide-ranging appeal in terms of describing the human condition, I believe their application should be considered when thinking about *all* interactions that are perceived to go awry, whether they be interpersonal exchanges, historical events of the past, recent political developments, or global issues of war. When communication breaks down, or has not occurred at all, between two people or among many, varying degrees of difficulty ranging from simple misunderstanding to horrendous acts of terror can result as individuals or groups of people rid themselves of negative feelings. They then project them onto others and proceed by navigating in the world as if the original feelings emanated from another or others in the first place. This then provides justification for the projector(s) to engage in violence against the perceived enemy or enemies whether in thoughts, words, or deeds. Hence, while many factors are involved in conflict of any type, I believe the mechanism of projective identification is a major component of the process. When any type of revenge or crime or heinous act of terror against another is committed either by one individual to another or by one group to another group, projection of some form of aggression that cannot be tolerated "rears it ugly head."

To further elaborate on the aggression and aggressive tendencies inherent in all of us, it is worth considering certain aspects of Newton's Laws of Thermodynamics and Einstein's later interpretation of them. Extrapolating from and incorporating the essence of the idea that energy can neither be created nor destroyed, but only modified (Newton's First Law of Thermodynamics), one might reasonably postulate that the same theory applies to aggression. Whether we are born with it, as many theorists believe, or whether it emerges as part of normal development as we encounter inevitable frustrations and disappointments in life, aggression is part of the human condition. It is within each of us as long as we are alive and does not simply disappear: For like energy or perhaps more aptly stated as a form of energy, it can not be destroyed but only modulated or modified in some way. Assuming then that raw aggression does exists within all of us, it must be converted, to a more palatable form to be experienced, contained, understood within, and then used productively. If this transformation does not happen, violence against the self or others can occur in a myriad of ways, including the infliction of pain and terror on people, since as is the case with energy, aggression does not simply disappear.

In order to illustrate the effects of unmodified, uncontained, or otherwise unconverted aggression or its derivatives and how it impinges upon us, I will now provide examples while contemplating the idea of its indestructibility.

When a young toddler feels unbearable feelings of jealousy and rage after the birth of a sibling, he or she projects this aggression outwardly often by kicking, screaming and sometimes biting the new arrival. He or she is filled with angry feelings that cannot be understood or tolerated. At this point in life, the new baby is bad and should be harmed or destroyed. The young child who is emotionally devastated, cannot process internal feeling of hatred, fear of abandonment or loss of love. The "badness" is external. In this case, without modification of aggression, the only answer is damage and destruction to the other, for it is felt by the toddler that he or she is being hurt, persecuted, or otherwise damaged because of the newly-arrived infant or perhaps because of the parents. This is an example of the paranoid-schizoid position.

Another example of projection of aggression can be seen in the following situation with one of my male patients. I will call him John. Many months ago John had a brief affair with the woman of his dreams who I will refer to as Alison; a woman with whom he had a long-standing friendship. Although married, John claimed to desperately want and need a "perfect" person like Alison, stating that his wife was an aggressive woman who only cared about her work. After a year-long email and phone relationship with this "ideal" woman who had been very flirtatious, provocative, and seductive, often stating that she longed to leave her husband for him, they met and shared one

romantic evening culminating in, "the most tender, best sexual experience either had ever had." After that night, they vowed to find a way to be together. Shortly thereafter, however, Alison wrote one short email saying that John had misunderstood her. She added that she did not wish to be in further contact with him ever again. My patient was devastated, briefly blamed himself, and initially stated that the entire incident had been his fault from the beginning. Alison, on the other hand, was exonerated from any culpability.
John steadfastly maintained her innocence claiming that she embodied goodness and personified, "the saintliness of an angel." As this perplexing picture continued to unfold, the focus of John's feelings about his participation in the events leading up to the affair began to shift as I became in his eyes, inept, not helpful, and generally of little use to him, i.e., I became the "bad" one. He said I was disingenuous and was only interested in payment of my fees. In spite of my many attempts to interpret and help him understand what had occurred with Alison and what was happening between the two of us, one month of subtle dissatisfaction with me turned into many months of more blatant denigration of my thoughts and ideas. At that point he started to talk about looking for another type of therapy. He said he needed something more "proactive" all-the-while maintaining Alison's goodness while highlighting my lack of understanding and uselessness. In this case, the patient could not deal with the aggression he felt towards Alison, projected it onto me, and planned to exit so he would not have to deal with all of the unbearable anger and hatred he felt towards her as well as the emotional pain he initially felt.

This is another example of the paranoid-schizoid position, wherein Alison could not be experienced as a whole person but rather was idealized and protected from my patient's wrath, disappointment, sadness, and pain. It is also an example of distorted thinking wherein without fully understanding what occurred, John wanted to take action by finding another therapist who would not remind him of his feelings. Unconsciously, I believe he also wanted me to feel what it was like to be abandoned; hence his wish to leave his analysis which had previously been important and helpful to him.

Similarly, projective identification can also be understood by studying transcripts of family therapy sessions wherein the reader sees how ... [an] identified family member carries and holds projected aggression for the group allowing others to freely romp in fields of caring and togetherness. Dare not *they*, the others in the family, be bothered with unpleasant feelings that plague the identified one, for he or she *surely* is the troubled one, the problem, and the issue (Messina 2008).

The tendency to disavow aspects of the self can be observed in many family interactions, where one can see multiple projections of unwanted parts of all members as they are attributed to the perceived bad or troubled person in the group, the *identified patient* the others want to "help." This type of situation often happens when families come to treatment after having identified an adolescent as having problems. When all goes well, it eventually comes to be understood that he or she is actually *holding* or *carrying* the problems of the others. For example, when parents cannot deal with aggressive feelings and rage they feel towards each other, they often criticize, belittle, or find fault with a child or children. Because they cannot tolerate their feelings towards one another or accept their own responsibility for a failing marriage, they project their rage and aggression onto their child or children. If their aggression is not modified within or towards their spouse, if the true source of the problem is not acknowledged or dealt with, chances are it will not be owned and will be projected.

To widen the scope of this phenomenon by looking at the world arena, I will examine several different situations; all of which involve prejudice, a form of aggression, as well as various aspects of terror whether they be the perceived potential for terror or actual acts of terror.

To begin with a more benign but nevertheless hurtful example, I will explore aspects of Senator Barack Obama's recent speech on race (2008), wherein he attempted to discuss issues that have lurked beneath the surface of American politics for decades: He dared to say openly what many people only say behind close doors or are afraid to say at all. He tried, as he said, to take the discussion of prejudice and race to a new level; to begin a dialogue in which we all might participate if we could be or would be honest, since we all harbor prejudice of one type or another. In his appeal for self-examination and understanding, he talked about his grandmother and his controversial pastor, Reverend Jeremiah Wright, and their feelings of prejudice, yet he also talked about their strengths: He talked about real people, whole people, who have good, admirable traits as well as negative, less admirable traits. This is an example of the depressive position wherein one navigates in the world and experiences real individuals who have many characteristics; those we think of as good and those we think of in a more negative way. For some, it was a brilliant speech that offered hope and optimism and a chance for developing a new, honest, and more authentic way of relating to and engaging with each other. For others, it conjured up images of paranoia and fear; fear that the majority would be swallowed up and overtaken by a radical, angry element in society that would wreak havoc on them. Operating from the paranoid-schizoid position, they criticized, belittled and generally devalued the speech, projected their own aggression and prejudice outwardly, while declaring themselves to be the true champions of freedom and the "American way." Some also called on the Senator to totally denounce Reverend Wright, to rid himself of this "evil force." From their paranoid-schizoid positions, the man had to be done away with, for he certainly represented that which is bad without possessing any redeemable or good qualities. Sometime after the speech was made, Reverend Wright made additional comments that caused even more problems for Senator Obama, yet he still did not totally belittle or renounce his former pastor. Instead, with sadness and disappointment, he talked about his disagreement with certain ideas while maintaining his earlier stance regarding the good things that the pastor had also done for so many. It would have been easier and perhaps more politically advantageous to totally devalue him, yet he did not go down that path. Instead, Senator Obama kept the whole person in mind, which again is an example of the depressive position.

To illustrate a much more blatant act of aggression and terror while examining the same mechanisms, we might consider the genocide in Rwanda that occurred over the last decade. How could such a thing happen today in our seemingly sophisticated world? Why did the Hutu and Tutsi people nearly wipe each other out? Was it about prejudice passed on from colonialists who occupied their country? Was unmetabolized aggression, greed, and the wish for power of these outsiders projected onto the people of Rwanda? Did they thereafter project what was originally European aggression onto each other causing the slaughter of hundreds of thousands of innocent people?

Using more historical examples, the events of World War II provide us with a plethora of situations wherein egregious acts were perpetrated against others. In this regard, it is difficult to comprehend how Hitler succeeded in amassing a group of followers who in turn criminally terrorized millions of people. Why did his projections resonate with so many? Why did he attempt to wipe out the Jewish people? What form of aggressive or other feelings could he not bear? Can Kleinian ideas help us deepen our understanding of Hitler's treatment of millions of people?

In the same timeframe, shortly after Germany surrendered to the United States ending the war in Europe on May 8, 1945, the bombing of Hiroshima and Nagasaki occurred; actions that should be considered when thinking about projective identification. Was the atomic bomb a justifiable means to end our struggle with Japan? What was so untenable and unbearable that led to this action? Were the newly-developed, scientific advances in weaponry used responsibly? It is true that the Japanese did attack America first and they did kill, maim and otherwise cripple thousands of soldiers, as well as many civilians, leading many top officials in the United States to conclude that dropping the bomb was the only way to end World War II. But was it the only way? Many scientists involved in developing this new atomic technology were against using it for destructive purposes. For example, Leo Szilard, chief physicist of the Manhattan Project, and 69 co-signers, sent a petition to President Truman urging him not to use this horrific weapon against the Japanese people, at least without demonstrating its power or warning them (Dannen, 1995-98). According to leading historians, Truman knew nothing about America's atomic capability when he took the oath of office a few months before he decided to drop the bomb (National Public Television, 2008). Hence, did action replace thought before our American political leaders understood the long-term implications of their decision? How can we better understand the events of history to help prevent horrific acts against others in the future? Was this an example of projective identification? Although complicated, I contend that it was, at least in part, a projection of intense aggression that was not metabolized. From a paranoid-schizoid position wherein anxiety was intense, I believe that the Japanese people could not be kept in mind as an entire group, but rather, the military, one part of the group, came to represent the entire society.

Of course all of the aforementioned situations are complex and no single factor led to or caused them. However, I think all such atrocities start with unbearable feelings that cannot be tolerated, feelings that must manifest themselves somehow or come into play in some way. In all of these examples, I believe acts of terror occurred because as is the case with energy, aggression can not be destroyed, only modified, contained, understood, or otherwise dealt with productively within an individual or within groups of people. When it is not, it is most often projected outwardly which affects others; sometimes mildly, sometimes moderately, and sometimes in most devastating and destructive ways.

Now that I have defined projective identification and outlined the despair that emanates from it, let me move on to hope, which involves modification of aggression and metaphorically speaking the "taking back" of projections as one moves from Klein's paranoid-schizoid position to the depressive position. The hope to which I refer occurs when raw aggression and aggressive tendencies are modified which happens in the context of another person or other people; a form of identification with the essence of the other. While different terms have been used by Klein and her followers to describe this process, most notable by Wilfred Bion (1962), who called it *"Containment"* and the *"Alpha Process,"* simply stated, what these theorists are describing is the way in which aggression, in all of its forms, is transformed, wherein it thereafter becomes a "new" *aspect* of the self.

One example of this process can be seen when observing exchanges between babies and mothers. For example, if the jealous toddler referred to earlier, is picked up, talked to, and held by a patient mother who soothes and comforts him or her as she continues to demonstrate feelings of love and inclusion, that which was unbearable becomes tolerable: The world becomes "ok" again. This shift can be observed by watching as the child settles down, stops crying, and reengages with his or her surroundings. Though we often do not know exactly what troubled the young child initially, we can ascertain by considering the intensity of the distress that the feelings involved in the episode were difficult, and more than the child could handle alone. Over time as distressing states of intense anxiety and projected aggression are handled in a similar way, the infant or toddler eventually "takes in" or identifies with the mother's attitude and makes it his or her own which leads to the formation of patience. In this case, the child also comes to know through experience, that the new baby will not totally replace him or her, that there is room for both, and that love from the mother is still available. He or she learns how to integrate another into his or her life by taking in transformed, raw aggression, and using it more productively.

Another example of the process to which I am referring can be seen in the case of the male patient described earlier. As I was able to mentally "take in" and bear this man's rage and emotional pain, and thereafter "give it back" to him in a more palatable form through interpretation and our experience together, he eventually came to understand how the feelings he was attributing to me were actually feelings *he* had that he could not tolerate. He also came to see that he wished to get rid of me because I reminded him of his painful experience with Alison that he could not bear and that getting rid of me in his fantasy was a way to get rid of her. Hence, he planned to leave me as she had left him so I would truly understand the intensity of his feelings. Eventually we came to understand together how he needed me to hold onto and tolerate the aggression he felt towards Alison because it frightened him so much. He was afraid of his anger, hatred, and rage towards her for betraying and then leaving him as well as other feelings he had about his affair with her. Once he began to recognize his own feelings, Alison became much more real to him. She became a person he had loved, even still loved but also someone who was not perfect. As he began taking responsibility for his contribution to the situation while dealing with the loss of his fantasy woman, he also began to see his wife as someone with whom he could have a real relationship. As he acknowledged the damage he had done to her and their marriage, he began to truly mourn what had been lost between them. He was thereafter able to feel grief and sadness because of his actions and was able to apologize for his affair allowing the process of reparation to occur. Through acknowledgement of his transgressions he was able to experience true sorrow, which led to repair.

As he moved from one position to another, knowledge and the capacity to think were restored to him as well. He also was able to know better his own pain and was able to bear it more easily. He metaphorically "took in" and made his own, the experience he learned from our work together as he mourned the loss of what could not be. As he began the process of repair with his wife as well as with me, both of us became whole people to him with negative and positive attributes.

With regards to work with families, when one manages to help break the cycle of denial, each member can eventually take hold of their own feelings. Perhaps by metabolizing the chaos and offering it back in a more palatable form, change occurs. In so doing, one helps families know, tolerate, and come to truly love one another in mature and healthy ways, sometimes for the first time wherein the identified patient no longer must be the repository for all unwanted or difficult-to-bear feelings.

Although it is possible to help an individual whether it be as a parent, friend, or therapist as described above, one might justifiably wonder how this type of change could ever be attempted when considering aspects of terror as it applies to Heads of State, large groups of people, or entire countries. Do the same mechanisms apply when thinking about terrorism between and among countries? Can we begin to *think* about terror without simply reacting to it? Can we better understand our world without having to immediately take action; action that has untenable and long-lasting effects? I believe we can by apply the principles inherent in projective identification and the paranoid-schizoid and depressive positions. If we can find a way to have aggression on a large scale metabolized, if we can own our aggression, mourn losses of what can not be while working towards repairing misunderstandings, as we accept the uniqueness of others, then I believe the possibility of hope can exist.

Having suggested that hope and change are possible when considering large groups of people, in order to maintain a Kleinian perspective in the depressive position, it is important to look at and think about the *difficulty* inherent in this endeavor. C. Fred Alford, in his book that integrates Kleinian thought with social theory (1989), illustrates this point. He says,

> If one is to take Klein seriously, one will not, however, be terribly optimistic about the emergence of a reparative morality [an aspect of the general reparative process I previously mentioned] among elite—or any other group—groups. Groups tend to stay stuck in the paranoid-schizoid stage. (84)

Yet through his further, in-depth analysis of social theory, as he integrates Kleinian thought with the Frankfurt Theory of Critical Thinking (an anti-capitalism philosophy initially developed by the Institute for Social Research in Frankfurt, Germany that is still incorporated into many college curricula today), he raises the possibly that Melanie Klein's thinking might provide what is needed to consider change on a larger scale. He elaborates on this possibility by saying:

> my goal has been to show that a Kleinian account can successfully address key problems raised, but not solved, by the Frankfurt School. In chapter 1 I called these problems the four R's: remembrance of those who suffered; reparation for their loss; reformation of reason; and reconciliation with nature. (170)

He goes on to say that the Frankfurt School's philosophy cannot deal adequately with the issues outlined in the 4 R's. Specifically, he suggests that this is due to its tenacious adherence to Freud's instinct theory, which focuses on the pleasure-seeking aspect of the individual, as opposed to suffering which is an essential part of Klein's thoughts about reparation.

Although Alford's analysis is complex, in part due to its comprehensive nature, what he is essentially saying is that because Klein focused on the "need" for suffering as she moved beyond Freud's pleasure-seeking ideas, she developed the possibility of hope, through understanding and tolerance of emotional pain. In other words, change is possible when considering these four R's, if one can hold in one's mind the suffering of others, past and present, and make amends in a thoughtful manner, which is an essential part of the depressive position, as one reconciles with all aspects of what it means to be human.

Alford adds another dimension when talking about Kleinian theory as it applies to groups as he describes "Reparative leadership" (89-90). He says,

> Responsible political leaders will recognize that the public is scared to death: of its own aggressive urges, as well as of the enemy. Responsible leaders will therefore not exaggerate the goodness of their own group and the badness of the other. Talk of the opposition as an 'evil empire' only encourages splitting and projection....Who is the reparative leader [Alford asks]? One for whom the opposition, no matter how intensely fought, remains part of a moral or ethical whole to which all people belong. As part of the whole, the opposition partakes of the good; it is not simply the evil other. Such a leader also recognizes that his own group's claim to goodness is incomplete. The reparative leader does not protect either his leadership or the unity of his group by demonizing others. Rather, his leadership is based upon the ability to interpret the group's moral tradition in such a way that it included the opponent, without utterly remaking the opponent and denying his otherness. The last clause is important [adds Alford] otherwise the leaders of the Crusades could be called reparative. Gandhi and Martin Luther King come to mind readily as genuine reparative leaders. (90)

In brief, what Alford is telling us is that reparative leaders exhibit behavior consistent with the depressive position as they metabolize aggression and anxiety for the people they govern. They hold in mind not only negative aspects of the enemy but also their positive attributes without demanding that opponents give up their identities. Instead, the opponent is encouraged to maintain their otherness.

To summarize, we all start with or develop very early, feelings of aggression in one form or another. As babies, we cannot metabolize or tolerate these feelings because they overwhelm us. We have no words. We need others to help make the world understandable and bearable. We are in the paranoid-schizoid position. If we are to optimally move forward and develop intrapsychically in a healthy way, we need someone, most often a parent, to help us make our inner worlds more palatable, less frightening, and more understandable so that we can own, take responsibility for, and tolerate aspects of life we initially project because we can not bear what is too frightening.

This same process occurs in adulthood with individuals and with large groups of people as we move from one position to another. When we are most vulnerable, we all have the potential to have paranoid-schizoid moments. However, when we reconstitute ourselves, because we have learned to do so from someone else at an earlier time, or because we have reparative leaders, we move to the more integrated, depressive position wherein we can experience all aspects of people. In this position we grapple with the human condition that includes suffering, pain, sadness and sorrow. These emotions help us become more authentic beings as we come to accept others; an acceptance that can ultimately lead to positive change.

Although I have talked about the theoretical aspect of change by considering Kleinian theory and have suggested that certain leaders can make a difference (as described by Alford 1989), a major question remains regarding an individual's or small group's ability to affect change. How can one person or how can small groups of people have any impact on a broad basis in our complex world? In that regard, I recently saw an interview with Al Gore on Global Warming (Gore 2008). When talking about how to change the mindset of many people, i.e., the number it would take to make a real difference in the effort to slow the effects of climate change, he talked about a campaign he is developing and will launch. While his plan is comprehensive, one part of what he is doing may be applicable to ameliorating aspects of terror in our world, i.e., he is personally talking to small groups of people in various settings throughout the world with the hope that those individuals will in turn talk to other small groups of people. It is his hope that this process will continue and become a type of movement wherein real change can occur. If this small group phenomenon helps the cause of global warming, is it possible, it could help the cause of global terror? Could individuals talk to small groups about aspects of aggression, how it is projected towards others if not converted into that which is understood, and how terrorist acts towards others can occur thereafter as a result of aggression that has not been metabolized? Perhaps this idea is grandiose and a bit optimistic but then again, maybe not. When passionate, interested people get together with the help of what Alford calls "reparative leadership," movements can emerge that lead to major and lasting change.

## References

Alford, C. Fred. 1989. *Melanie Klein & critical social theory*. Chelsea: Bookcrafters, Inc.

Bion, Wilfred. 1984. *Learning from Experience*. London: Heinemann; reprinted in paperback, Maresfield Reprints, London: H. Karnac Books.

——— 1970. *Attention and interpretation: A scientific approach to insight in psychoanalysis and groups*. New York: Basic Books.

Dannen, Gene. Transcript as an e-text, 1995-98. http://www.dannen.com/decision/45-07-17.html. Original in the public domain and located at the Nation Archives.

Gore, Al. Interview on *Sixty Minutes*, March 30, 2008.

Meltzer, Donald. 1973. *Sexual states of mind*. Perthshire: Clunie Press.

Messina, Karyne. "Projection, Projective Identification, and Containment." Closing remarks made at an International Conference on projective identification in Washington, D.C., February 15-17, 2008. "Taking Back Projections: The Despair and Hope in Projective Identification." Paper presented at the 2nd Annual International Conference on the Human Condition Series, Topic: Terror, Barrie, Ontario, May 2-3, 2008.

National Public Television, WETA. "The American Presidency: Truman (viewed on May 26, 2008).

Obama, Barack. "A more perfect Union." Speech broadcasted on National television in the United States (viewed on MSNBC, March, 18, 2008).

Spillus, Elizabeth. 2007. *Encounters with Melanie Klein*. New York: Routledge.

# LEARNING RULES AND ROLES

The following three inter-related papers are linked via the theoretical underpinnings of Linda Bain's (1990) hidden curriculum and Paulo Freire's (1987) application of his archeology of consciousness, housed within his politics and pedagogy of liberation.

The authors take up issues of power, fear and dread at all levels of education. Hidden curriculum (Bain 1990) refers to what is taught to students by the institutional regularities, by the routines and rituals of teachers' and students' lives. The dynamics of power or normative logics are not explicitly or didactically promoted by rather are lived as normal, familiar and unquestioned. Join us now, as we interrupt the normal, familiar, and unquestioned.

# LEARNING RULES AND ROLES

*Dianne D. Bergsma*

In *Macleans* magazine of March 3, 2008, in the section on Society, there is an article on education with the provocative title: "How To Fix Boys."[1] Our sixteen-year-old granddaughter, who has two older brothers, has no idea on how we can fix boys! But this article helped me to again evaluate my own theories and experiences on education, and reflect on the influences, both positive and negative, that help one to become an educated person.

Throughout history various philosophers have written about the best way to educate a person. Note that the emphasis is not on how to teach or learn a subject, but on education where the person *is* the subject. We are aware of the various learning methods in education, including the formal curriculum, where the focus is on the content of what is being taught, the classroom as curriculum, where the focus is on how that content is taught through pedagogical styles and socialization, and the invisible, also called the evaded or the hidden curriculum, the things that are not talked about but are learned nevertheless. It is in the invisible curriculum where both learning and terror are experienced.

Terror in this context is understood as fear, sufficiently great or intense fear to frighten or cause dread. This terror in often present in relations with power and experienced as power-over and powerlessness, and this terror may come from unknown and invisible or known and authoritative sources with its subtleties and undermining force. Its consequences are that it intimidates and subjugates, and influences the development of a person's identity and a healthy sense of self.

The article in *Macleans* is based on an interview with Leonard Sax, a family physician and research psychologist in Maryland, and author of the book *Boys Adrift*, where he writes about gender differences in learning, and how there is a "new buzz: there's a crisis among boys" in education. Our local newspaper featured a report that followed up on the *McLean's* article entitled "Profoundly different" of families who have been meeting together to discuss Sax's book. As an example of the difference between boys and girls one mother notes that her ten-year-old daughter has been choosing her own clothes since she was two. On school days she and her seven-year-old sister get up an hour earlier than their twelve-year-old brother and struggle to be on time. "They have, after all, important decisions to make. What to wear? What accessories go with what they're wearing?"[1] It is reported that their brother has "just one criteria when it comes to fashion. Does it fit? Yes? Then, deci-

345

sion made." Is a child taught what our culture determines as 'feminine' and 'masculine' or, as this mother believes, is it innate? Do we allow for what children are taught explicitly and implicitly by their parents? What about differences between girls and girls and between boys and boys? Some girls also love to ride their bicycles, and wear a t-shirt and jeans, and play sports. Some boys also like to draw and read. Psychological differences between boys and girls are emphasized with an Alpha Bias that argues for the differences between boys and girls. However, with a Beta Bias one could argue for the similarities between boys and girls.

In response to the very first question of the interviewer, Sax places himself in opposition to the Ontario Institute for Studies in Education (OISE), where, he asserts, we will "find people who will vigorously contest the assertion that there's any problem at all with boys." Sax then gives the "hard data" of percentages, and shows that "about 60 per cent of undergraduates are women," and he notes that this "is a stunning reversal" but perhaps more noteworthy is that, "women have better grades and test scores at university than the men have." I wonder if this is the moment where I take pride in women and say with the old Virginia Slim commercial, You've come a long way baby!

The history of education for girls and boys, and for men and women is distinctly different. Margaret L. King and Albert Rabil Jr. write of the exclusion and inequalities historically experienced by women, and some of the positive changes that have occurred in the twentieth century, including "curriculum revision with an eye to the inclusion of women." Although we may celebrate that these changes have occurred, their origin are not in the twentieth century. King and Rabil note that: "These recent achievements have their origins in things women (and some male supporters) said for the first time about six hundred years ago." They write of "The Old Voice and the Other Voice" and explain that a woman's voice is 'the 'other voice,' in contradistinction to the 'first voice,' the voice of the educated men who created Western culture." Women were largely excluded from education and the educated men had the power to create their culture and their laws. King and Rabil note that "The 'other voice' emerged against a backdrop of a three thousand year history of misogyny—the hatred of women- rooted in the civilizations related to Western culture: Hebrew, Greek, Roman, and Christian." They explain that, "Embedded in the philosophical and medical theories of the Ancient Greeks were perceptions of the female as inferior to the male in both mind and body."[1] We now know that our senses of self, our identities are inescapably rooted in our body, even as they exceed and go beyond the physical of our embodiment. How we see ourselves, how we think of ourselves, how and what the mind is taught from an early age, explicitly and implicitly, is crucial in the development of the self and in establishing our identity. Julia Kristeva explains that we do not live a static stage of being, but our identity and sense of self is always becoming, hence the importance of everything that influences us in this process.

Neil Peart, in *Snakes and Arrows*, writes that children are imprinted with faith and beliefs, "along with their other early blessings and scars. Most people simply receive it, (their faith/beliefs) with their mother's milk, language, and customs." What we put our faith in, what we believe, especially what we believe about ourselves, shapes the person we are becoming. However, as Peart notes, "people are also shaped by early abuse of one kind or another." These abuses can take many forms, and what terrorizes a child is not always understood by those who, knowingly or unknowingly, inflict the words and actions that create fear, dread, and even panic. Especially in elementary school, its power structure is everywhere in evidence. This may well be necessary for the smooth running of the school and for the safety and well-being of the students and the teachers, and is therefore not necessarily bad, but it all depends on how this power is exercised, and how it is perceived and experienced by the child. It becomes problematic when students feel they are at the mercy of their teachers, and there is no one to protect them or speak for them. These mental abuses, especially or perhaps because they are always experienced by the powerless in the face of power and the voice of authority, have lasting damaging effect. Peart tells about "rescued puppies, receiving unlimited love, care, and security, but if those puppies had been 'damaged' by their earlier treatment—made nervous, timid or worse, they would always remain that way, no matter how smooth the rest of their life might be—it seems the same for children." We are not talking about overt, explicit physical abuse *per se* here, but rather the covert, implicit mental abuses, the fear that is part of power plays and mind games. Peart claims that, "The abuses are enough to leave a thousand cuts."

We all know of children who do not want to go to school, who say that they do not like school, who even claim that they hate school. We know very few, if any children who do not like to learn. Placed in the right environment, taught in the right way, they enjoy learning and thrive in becoming an educated person. But how do we ascertain what is the right environment and the right way of teaching? Sax argues that a vital element in teaching a child to become an educated person is doing the right thing at the right time. He notes that, "Farmers understand this. You can have the best farmland in the world and the best feed corn in the world, but if you try to plant your crop in the middle of a January snowstorm, you will not be successful." Sax connects this to education that is not developmentally appropriate, for instance, he decries the changes in kindergarten curriculum where, instead of children "doing lots of different activities: singing, playing, dancing, finger painting" now "the primary activity is formal didactic education, with kids sitting still and the teacher instructing." Kindergarten should be a time when children learn to love school, where they learn to look forward to the learning processes that take place in school. However, today children in kindergarten have homework, and we see them trekking to school with heavy backpacks.

Ontario Education Minister Kathleen Wynne has suggested that "school boards in Ontario study their homework policies." Lee Bartel, author of a study done for OISE, posits that "Just because something is a good thing for university entrance doesn't mean it should be happening in kindergarten. There is more to life than schooling. There is more to learning that schooling." Wynne is reported as saying that, "Reducing the load for kindergarten students, not assigning homework over the holidays, and killing penalties for assignments for assignments turned in late seems like "reasonable suggestions." It is important to remember that we are discussing homework for kindergarten students here. Bartel notes that "Assigning homework to four-year-olds doesn't compare to a parent reading to their child and is actually "counterproductive. It turns kids off school."

In this system, and at a very early age, the mind of the child is being instructed while the body is being controlled. Here the child learns the roles and rules by which to live. The child learns the importance of sitting still, of obeying, and of being quiet, and the punishments for those who do not sit still, who talk, and who disobey. Most children do not know how to use their voice, especially in the presence of authority, and often respond to stressful situations by using their bodies, they fidget, they cannot sit still, they need a drink, they need to use the washroom, and anything else that they can think of that will release them from the confines of their chair, even if only for a moment. But on the whole, they are told to sit still and behave and concentrate on their work. The key element is that they must learn to obey the voice of authority and not disturb the mores and norms of the classroom, or face the consequences.

The teacher's disfavour may be the most terrifying. The child quickly learns the terror of what it feels like to be admonished in front of the class, to be embarrassed, to lose face. This will also affect whether a child will experience a sense of belonging to the class community or whether they feel like an outsider. Different children will react differently to classroom power dynamics, some will become quiet, subdued and learn to suppress the itching and twitching of their body, and the teacher might call them "good" because they cause no trouble. Others may become restless, unable to sit still when told, they scratch their itch and move their twitch, they rebel against the restrictions and the warnings, and begin to think of themselves as 'bad' because they know they behave differently than the 'good' kids do in class. The fear that is experienced in the suppression of unlawful movements of the body is an intimidation and the psychological imprinting of the mind, of what entails being good or bad, has long lasting consequences on the child's attitude towards education as it grows into adulthood.

The control of our bodies and the call to obedience in educational settings is basic in the invisible or evaded curriculum. However, this control has deep consequences, because the colonizing of the mind often happens through the controlling of our bodies, to trap us into rules and roles, with apparently insignificant but nevertheless life-sculpting events. We live in a 'rape culture,' that is, a culture that is permeated by rape understood as the doing of violence, to seize, or to violate. The terror that is experienced in violence and violation is often related to the physical rape of the body, but the rape of the mind and the spirit of a person is no less a crime.

Our academic discourses help us to understand the theories of power, of terror, fear and dread. It addresses how language, personality, and social context interact in education to form an educated person. Sax claims a gender distinction between the development and readiness of boys and girls for formal didactic education. He claims that girls are ready at an earlier age and "you may have a very bright boy, but if you're asking him to do things that are not developmentally appropriate, he won't be successful. And the danger is that he will develop negative attitudes toward school, and it will be very difficult to change them." But whether a child fearfully suppresses bodily movement or defies the fear and risks being punished for bodily movement, whether a child quickly understands what is being taught, or whether it takes some time for it all to sink in, and the child fears having to ask for clarification once again, or does not even know how to articulate the question, once a child has been imprinted with a dread and a dislike of school based on fear, it will affect his or her attitudes towards school, to the school community, and to their ability to learn and become a socially adept, comfortable and educated person.

There is no doubt that gender distinction in education is a highly debatable point. When women first obtained access to higher education, it was with the understanding that they entered a male domain, and that it was up to her to fit in. Even our language reflected a masculinest worldview and women had to carefully translate to know where the word 'man' meant all of humanity or only the male part of humanity. In order for a woman to become educated it was important for her to think like a man and to write like a man in order to make it in this man's world. There was no recognition as yet that the supposed objective way of teaching and learning was a presumption and that it was the subjective perspective of the men who wrote and taught the traditional masculinist way. Women worked in fear that they would not be able to live up to the educational expectations, and dreaded the educational politics that made every woman representative of all women, making their success or failure not only personal but also political. The use of inclusive language has helped pave the way for a more inclusive worldview, and a more inclusive curriculum in school. Some argue that the pendulum swing of our educational system has gone too far the other way and now speak of the feminization of education, and why it is difficult for boys to adapt to a new perspective on curricular activities and expected classroom behavior. However, an equality-valued perspective does not mean making boys and girls the same, similarly, it does not make women and men the same, for 'equal' is not 'the same as'. Our development as persons is not limited to our identity as female or a male, and our sense of self is not only nourished through our gender. The use of power-over is not only a male prerogative, and gender boundaries are invisible as terror, fear, and dread enter our minds, whether we are young or old.

Post-structural theory looks at gender and identity as a social construct, and focuses on the construction of gender identities rather than gender differences, with an analysis of the different understandings of power. Modernity values hegemony and hegemonic beliefs, that is, dominant ideological beliefs about our world and our selves that exist and are enforced in our subconscious, because they keep structural systems in place by functioning as the *status quo*. This becomes problematic when individuals or groups realize that the dominant ideologies of the *status quo* are not benefiting them, that in fact they are power-over strategies that are detrimental to their well-being. Postmodernity understands and conceptualizes power differently. Here is a call for anti-hegemonic understandings and practises that shake and shift the *status-quo* and its power. Here power is not focussed on maintaining the *status quo*, but it is multi-directional, and exercised through relations and not possessed or held by any one person. Here power is implemented not as power-over but as power-with, an empowering of the person. This discourse does not accept but disrupts the notion of a dominant discourse of cohesion and uniformity with its normative concepts and behaviors. It examines the wider social conditions that make possible alternative ways of adapting various economies of acquiring knowledge, of seeking meaning, and of gaining wisdom, through contestation and alteration, to change power relations from power-over to power-with.

In the psychological work of establishing an identity and a healthy sense of self, the mind is inscribed through all aspects of education. We see and are experiencing positive changes, challenges to the dominant discourse and relations of power-over. Anti-hegemonic practices are altering ideology, creating new meanings, and showing new possibilities, rejecting the notion that we are too power-less to do anything to change our world, but with a process of power-with encouraging us to make positive power-full choices, removing the dread, as we become full social and educated persons.

# NARRATIVE INTERLUDE: THE RULES AND THE GAME

*Beatrix Prinsen*

Here is a little background on our narrator.... A voice and a context for the story to follow :

married at 18, had 3 kids by age 24

bored by age 31 (well, bored from 18-31 as well), enrolled in Interior Design course. Did well (85+) but rather than consider that I was intellectually "smart," I instead assumed that the course of studies was not worthwhile pursuing (good old imposter syndrome) and so quit.

Part of the decision to quit was also that interior design did not fulfill the part of me that wants to "change the world," that interior design was (for me) a trite and useless way to spend my life—only served the privileged, those with money and did nothing to improve lives.

Still bored, friend suggested I enroll in University—I thought she was cracked, she said I was smart. I enrolled and no looking back.

During high school my daughter was a great one for questions:

Why did the boys get to play sports?

Why were only girls cheerleaders?

She hated baking and sewing—Why couldn't she take shop?

Why was she punished if she spoke without raising her hand?

Did she really need permission to go to the bathroom, or stay in during recess?

What was the point of learning math, or history?

Why did she need to smile when she felt grumpy?!

Teachers didn't like her questions. It unsettled their ideas of their institutionalized authority. We were told she was her own worst enemy—she needed to learn life would be easier if she learned to follow the "rules of the game." She needed to

stop questioning authority

conform

learn to do as she was told.

As parents, we knew that those who "bucked the system" have a more difficult time, yet we encouraged her

to keep asking questions

to keep examining authority

in order to overcome the dread of not following the rules of a game she had not yet learned to play.

We encouraged her to learn the rules, but to question the hegemonic game as it was being played so as to not place herself unreflectively in positions of acquiescence and submission—not to let the fear of consequences be used as an instrument of conformity.

Terrors, fear, and dread are often found safely hidden in labels and the concepts of terror, fear, and dread are also found in the labels of the "good" and "bad" student. These two labels work as a way of maintaining the "good" order of things. Whether one is a "good" or "bad" student generally depends on grades and classroom behavior. Those with higher grades are "good students"; those with lower grades are "bad students." Students who conform, who do as they are told are "good"; those that rebel, or just ask too many questions are "bad."

John Dewey posited that "anyone who has begun to think, places some portion of the world in jeopardy." By thinking about—critiquing and questioning the educational authoritarianism as it is found in the power relations between students and educators—we can interrogate the systematically embedded and institutionalized authority found within the educational system.

It is then that we can subvert—place in jeopardy—the power relations at play between the educators and students, particularly if these relations terrorize or instill fear, and so impact a student's learning experience. This is not restricted to grade school or high school. I am a TA—a teaching assistant in a University and am constantly confronted by the experience of power relations, as I am sandwiched between the professor and the student, where the friction of power is felt in a 'between' position that can be used and exploited by professors and students alike.

In this narrative I would like to address:

the links between educational authoritarianism and how students view their own intellectual abilities

the link between educational authoritarianism and systemic barriers that might prevent students from achieving their academic goals

Tom Nesbit (1998) argues that we must "Open the black box" of teaching and learning—that teaching and learning does not happen within a social vacuum; rather it occurs within situational, political, and social contexts. In other words, when teaching or facilitating a seminar discussion, I need to understand that I am not just teaching the subject matter, but also teaching the student. To explain this, I'd like to share an experience I had in Grade Four.

Until mid-way through Grade Four I was a A+ to B- student. That year, on New Year's Day my father unexpectedly died. When I got my report card at the end of the year, in June, I was shocked—most of my grades had dropped to between C and D minus. Thinking this must have been a mistake I went to talk to the teacher—with fear and dread– only to be shown the evidence of failed, or barely passed work in subjects such as spelling, math, geography. There it was—I was no longer a good student, and I had no idea what had happened. Apparently the rules of getting good grades had changed, but I didn't know what they were. There were definitely consequences to this report card filled with bad grades—for one, an angry mother.

The teacher—who must have noticed that there was a drastic change in my work—had never spoken to me about it. While that is mind-boggling and upsetting, given the times (the 1960s), it is to some extent understandable that no one put the failing pieces together. Today there is more understanding that life events impact one's in/ability to learn. Learning is not a single act but the result of a chain of responses that can be affected by factors such as emotion, motivation and interest as well as situational, institutional, and psychological barriers, or situations.

And so—albeit mysteriously—I was no longer a "good" student, but a "bad" one. If I was now a bad student, was I also now a bad person? Would the other kids still like me? Would the teacher still like me? The popular kids generally were the smarter kids.

I recall being baffled, and so I came to the conclusion that maybe I was never smart. Maybe all those perfect spelling and math scores were just luck, and my luck had run out. It never occurred to me that there was anything I could do to change this fate. This made sense to a 10-year-old. Why would I try to learn if the trying would not get me anywhere? I was a bit young to realize that this could be because of a depressed emotional state due to my grief at losing my Dad so unexpectedly at such a young age! I simply figured that I was now intellectually stupid (Schommer 1998). From that point on I did not respond to teaching because of my beliefs about my control over my own learning, which included:

inherited ability to learn
the speed of learning
how knowledge is organized
the stability of knowledge

So, what do I mean by all that?

Beliefs in speed of learning influence the amount of time one is willing to invest in studying and problem solving

Beliefs in understanding how knowledge is organized and the certainty of knowledge influence comprehension and problem solving

Believers in simple and certain knowledge search for single answers written in stone, that results in, as Marlene Schommer (1998) argues "simple-minded, inflexible, shallow thinkers."

Believers in complex and tentative knowledge are more likely to take on multiple perspectives, be willing to modify their thinking, withhold ultimate decisions until all the information is available, and to acknowledge the complex tentative nature of everyday issues (Schommer, 1998).

That learners may not respond to teaching may be the result.

I now know that my inability to learn was not only rooted in the mechanical acts of my individual learning processes but were also a result of the cultural attitudes and beliefs at the time. The culture at that time did not allow for a child to express sorrow at her Dad's dying. Neither the teacher nor my much older siblings had the cultural and emotional awareness of the impact of a parent's death on a child. As a ten year old I did not have the words, and the adults in my life could not help me explain why my grades would drop from an A to a D within six months. And so, my grades slipped, the die had been cast, and I accepted my fate, a fate that followed me right through the end of grade 12— I graduated high school with a 50%. The educational system had rules about how it defined a good student. I was filled with dread because while I knew the rules—good grades and good behavior—I had no idea how to go about that.

That experience significantly informs how I approach teaching or facilitating seminars today. As a Teaching Assistant, I long to be a "good" TA. And yet I am conflicted as to where my loyalties lie—to the institution or to the students? To myself, To all three? What are the rules here?

If loyal to the institution:
I am an agent for the status quo and teach in a way that reproduces, maintains, and perpetuates the "rules of the game." In other words, if I perform according to the rules, it means that I may become complicit in re-producing educational authoritarianism.

If loyal to my students:
I can be an agent of change; I can enable learners to critically think about the systems that may create conformity—or fear/ dread when one is unable to conform—and then to develop interventions to transform those oppressive learning systems and structures. I need to remember though that if I choose to be an agent of change, I place myself as an employee in jeopardy.

I prefer to be the latter—an agent of change. And so, rather than focusing only on the subject matter, I also think about the student.

Who is the learner?

What are the learners' beliefs about their ability to learn?

What is the connection between my position of power as a TA and the students' learning experiences?

In other words, if the student hasn't learned, is it that the fault necessarily lies with the student? Or, if certain segments of the population aren't learning, or the statistics show a higher rate of high school drop out in a particular geographic area, can we say for certain that it is based on individual meritocracy, or might we better look at what's going on in both the educational institution and in the cultural/social/political positions of the student?, and teacher?

A few examples:

Arguably, surprise quizzes can motivate students to do their readings; and yet, rather than motivate the students to learn, surprise quizzes act as a negative motivator if students only do the readings because they are fearful of the consequences. If a student fails the quiz can one say for certain it is because she or he is uncommitted and unprepared? The purpose of a surprise (be it quiz or party), the purpose is to catch people off guard.

Consider the dread of never knowing when this surprise will pop up. What if the student had childcare responsibilities; work conflicts; or the bus was late? University classes are generally set up for young singles who are not involved in the paid labour force. As a TA—I try to break down barriers—question the Professor about this—but what can I do if the prevailing rationale is that committed, sincere students put their studies first, did the readings, and came to class prepared?

And so once again I—and the student—hear the message—a low grade, or a non-conforming student equals a "bad" student.

Earlier I mentioned that there are always relations of power
Instructor and student
Instructor and TA
TA and student.
And so it's important to consider how this power is used.

If people don't come to class/ lectures we assign judgments, which are explanations to suit our purposes.

We might use words like lazy, uncommitted, unprepared—these are useful and powerful words when people do not perform, or conform the way we expect they should.

The power of the grade/evaluation.
How is the class/syllabus organized?
Power of the professor, in general, to set the 'standard' of the course, what is the 'standard'? Who benefits, who doesn't.
Does it allow for the older student?
Students with childcare responsibilities?
Students who also do paid work?

We're getting better at accommodating those who are confronted with certain barriers—such as identifiable learning disabilities, wheelchair users, or students for whom English is not a first language. But what about a single mother who is fully responsible for small children, has a job and now has a conflict with the exam schedule? Do we make accommodations or do we tell her it's her problem?

What makes learning possible for some, stressful for others, or nearly impossible for yet other people?

What makes the student dread coming to class? What makes the student excited and look forward to coming to class?

How can we as educational leaders make learning possible?

Are the students there for me, to receive my knowledge, or am I there for the students to help them learn?

My teaching is not synonymous with another's learning. I cannot say for certain that because I am teaching, others are learning. And so I live with the challenge of the tension of being both loyal to the student and to the university, and, to a certain extent, myself. Thinking back to Grade Four, my teacher was teaching the subject, not teaching me, the student.

Let's return to John Dewey—that "anyone who has begun to think, places some portion of the world in jeopardy." Another favourite quote of mine, again Dewey, is that "we only think when we are confronted with a problem." A friend told me that I have a subversive streak and to that I said "thanks, that's the nicest thing you've ever said about me!" As a TA I have an obligation to advocate for students who have barriers to their ability to learn. And so, when I perceive problems—these barriers or obstacles to learning, I try to remember

I may not have any choice

I may have a choice, and will make a choice

I may have a choice and do nothing, and so reproduce the status quo even when I am free not to do so

It is this last that I am most fearful of because education is never neutral, it either transforms political, social, economic, legal systems or reproduces them (Freire 1987).

When I am powerless, I try to bring the problems to the attention of those who have more power—generally the instructor of the course. But again, I need to do this within the confines of the rules. Not only do I not want to make things worse for the student, I also do not want to jeopardize my own job.

As an educator I believe I also have an obligation to ask my students to think—to teach students to challenge the assumptions—those things we consider normal, common sense, natural, the things we take for granted. In other words to make a problem in order to open the door to new viewpoints that hopefully lead to new and positive action (Brookfield 2000).

Reflecting on my experiences as both a student and a TA I see the how our human action (or inaction) can create our cultural world (Freire 1987). I often see an apparent lack of intellectual curiosity among students about the culture in which they live. Sometimes they see the barriers and power plays at work, but don't often think they can do anything about them; other times they don't see the barriers and power plays, either for themselves, or for others. They accept the culture—including educational authoritarianism—as natural, as an unchangeable mystical entity.

When they do encounter or perceive educational barriers, injustices, or inequalities, they response is often that "it's not fair and somebody should do something about that." Well, who are these elusive "some bodies?" My goal is to facilitate/teach in a way that allows students to understand how their perception of themselves and their perceptions of their culture affect themselves and their culture. In other words, to create an awareness that they themselves are either a perpetuator or creator of culture. In addition, my goal is to enable learners to critically think about the systems that oppress them and others, and then to develop interventions that transform them. To change the "oh well, nothing can be done", or "someone should do something about that" into the belief that somebody can do something, and that somebody is me and you!

# THE RULES DO NOT MAKE A GAME

*Maureen Connolly*

In this paper I will examine a variety of mundane and profane contexts within academic culture as sites for constructing and reproducing fear, dread and its consequences. To do so, I will consolidate the work of three important theorists in a helpful and disruptive convergence. I will describe the resonances across Bain's (1990) hidden curriculum, Cassier's (1946) technique of the modern political myth and Freire's (1987) superstitious consciousness in the service of interrupting particular disciplinary practices in academic culture.

My story begins in a mid-size Canadian University whose recent history includes a dramatic shift in its status from primarily undergraduate to research-intensive with increasing numbers of graduate programs. With some minority exceptions, faculty are in strong support of this shift and its concomitant emphasis on funding, grants, innovative knowledge economies, and other subtle and not so subtle signs of militarized corporatism.

Enter the protagonists: a small but vocal cohort of chalkboard defenders and a larger, more tactically sophisticated cohort of defenders of academic purity. Both cohorts have become increasingly vehement, some might say desperate, in their zealous affirmation of the righteousness of their respective causes. My analysis will interrogate the politics of increasingly urgent and intolerant academic contexts. I will begin with the previously cited examples as the mundane yet powerful ground of a semiotic, phenomenological exploration based on the work of Richard Lanigan (1988) and its integration with Bain, Cassirer and Freire. As the paper—and the stories within it—unfold, I will elaborate (applying Lanigan) on the normative logics within academic contexts, what behaviors count as signs and the larger sign systems, or codes, at work which reproduce and re-inscribe the desired currencies. I will also explore how Cassirer's notion of mythic consciousness, Freire's resonant conceptualization of superstitious consciousness and Bain's hidden curriculum support the ongoing sublimation of academic freedom from a critical politics of intellectual freedom to disciplinary practices of surveillance, regulation, exclusion and bullying.

## Theoretical Background: Bain

Bain's (1990) work in the hidden curriculum in physical education is highly applicable to other contexts, and resonates remarkably well with the aforementioned work of Lanigan, Cassirer and Freire. By "hidden curriculum"

Bain refers to what is taught to students by the institutional regularities, by the routines and rituals of teacher/student lives. The dynamics of power or normative logics are not explicitly or didactically promoted, but rather are lived as normal, familiar, and unquestioned. Three themes from Bain's work in hidden curriculum are meritocracy, techno- centric rationality, and construction of social relations. Meritocracy is the use of a standard to regulate goal directed behavior through the myth that hard work will get what it deserves, or, put another way, compliant behavior will be rewarded accordingly. The emphasis is actually more on order and control rather than achievements, and usually creates a two-tiered system of hard workers who believe they will be rewarded but who seldom get the resources or training they require in order to achieve at a higher level, and talented and/or clever individuals who get resources and continue to achieve regardless of how hard they work. Techno centric ideology constructs ends or goals as taken for granted and unexamined. Emphasis is then placed on the development of increasingly effective and efficient means of achieving these goals. In such an ideology, existing social arrangements tend to be reproduced rather than challenged and the body tends to become a commodity to be exchanged for admiration, security or economic gain (Bain 1990, 29). Construction of social relations is also a reproduction of power dynamics through unquestioned patterns of interaction, exemplifying a cavalier lack of awareness to diversity and implicitly perpetuating racist, classist, ablist, sexist, ageist, heterosexist, and healthist norms.

## Theoretical Background: Freire and Cassirer

In "Illiteracy and Alienation in American Colleges: Is Paulo Freire's Pedagogy Relevant?" Linda Shaw Finlay and Valerie Faith (1987) describe their efforts to improve the language skills of upper-middle-class American college students, based on the philosophy and methodology of Paulo Freire (63). Their students demonstrated weaknesses in and (on the surface, at least) apathy about reading, writing and intellectual curiosity. Finlay and Faith created a series of learning activities which moved students through Freire's "forms of consciousness"; they also drew on the work of the Russian cognitive psychologist Lev Vygotsky, whose work in the early half of the 20$^{th}$ century has an almost eerie cogency—much like Freire's—for early 21$^{st}$ century post secondary education, the context for my inquiry and my paper.

Both Freire and Vygotsky emphasize the importance of the interaction between persons and cultural elements in moving from inner speech to shared expression (i.e., from maximally compact inner speech to maximally elaborated written or outer speech). Freire also developed an archeology of consciousness wherein he explored the spontaneous, pre-reflective attitude that most accurately characterizes a person's consciousness of the world. He proposed these as naive, superstitious and critical forms of consciousness and further proposed—echoing Vygotsky—that language (and expressive) habits held clues to these forms of consciousness and hence could be viable sites for dignified and transformative pedagogic interventions.

In determining the form of consciousness, the question to be asked is: Do people recognize how human action and language create their world? or, in Freire's terms, do they distinguish between what is natural and what is cultural? (Finlay and Faith 1987, 65). Culture, being historically, materially and politically constructed or at the very least, conditioned, can, theoretically, be changed or acted upon by the humans inhabiting it. A failure to distinguish culture (the product of human action) from nature often impairs the ability to use language and other forms of expression critically, as well as the ability to act, and often contributes to feelings and lived experiences of alienation from culture, language and communication. In the archeology of consciousness, students and teachers focus on language use as the most accessible mirror of naïve, superstitious or critical consciousness (Finlay and Faith 1987, 65), i.e., language or expression is the mirror of the person's relation to culture.

The chief characteristic of naïve consciousness is an unreflecting acceptance of the absolute validity and unquestionability of the world as is and one's own views. Naïve thinkers cannot conceive of a basic perspective different from their own. Their thoughts and behaviors are connected insofar as those same thoughts (and values) are held unreflectively—i.e., there are no other alternatives to action but the ones governed by one's unreflectively examined thoughts and values. Superstitious consciousness is characterized by a recognition of cultural options but a concomitant sense of powerlessness to do anything about those options. Social institutions and practices are mysterious, endowed with almost magical status and are seen as monolithic entities outside of causes and control (e.g., "the media"). Critical consciousness recognizes that cultural institutions are created and sustained by human purpose and action and language both shapes and reflects people's perceptions of cultural institutions (Finlay and Faith 1987, 66). There is no innocent, separate "I" outside of or uninfluenced by culture; people shape and are shaped within culture; culture can be analyzed, deconstructed and, in principle, transformed by human action, language use being one of those actions.

It is important to realize that these forms of consciousness are not necessarily hierarchical—although in particular pedagogic contexts they can be seen as such. Certainly "critical thinking" has become ubiquitous to the point of tokenism in the academic planning discourse of most post-secondary institutions. I will suggest, however, that it is the superstitious consciousness that is most prevalent in these same institutions, regardless of the purported embrace of critical thinking as a valued learning outcome.

Finlay and Faith discovered—with and through their students—that "Freire's philosophy is not simply specialized to teaching Third World people how to read and write, but is also helpful for examining particular cultures" (83). Their early concerns with mechanical and technical skills lead them to re-imagine curriculum so that the study of language use was embedded in a consideration of the "nature of cultural institutions, the epistemological dimensions of language and the ethical dimensions of vocabulary, grammar, syntax and rhetoric" (83). Once their students achieved a "meta-awareness" of their own lived contradictions within a consumer culture, the skills of writing and reading unfolded in a relevant, meaningful and timely fashion. Finlay and Faith go on to propose that since the issues they encountered with their students are not isolated, that is, that students at many levels of intellectual and skills development have these same problems, that the roots are attitudinal and cultural rather than solely mechanical and individual (83).

The work of an earlier contemporary of Freire and Vygotsky, Ernst Cassirer, provides a helpful juxtapositioning of the concept of "mythic consciousness" and its strategic implementation in the technique of modern political myths. Like Freire and Vygotsky, Cassirer did his theorizing in the context of an oppressive totalitarian state (pre WWII Germany) and, while not exiled from his homeland, Cassirer was forced to take refuge in America at the height of his writing productivity. In his Myth of the State, Cassirer (1946) describes mythic consciousness as a necessary, but not sufficient developmental/liminal phase of emerging conscious awareness of the world of others and one's relations and responsibilities in that shared world. Mythic consciousness is that which unbinds humans from those features, themselves inherent in humanity, which are sources of constraint or fear.

> In mythical thought and imagination we do not meet with individual confessions. Myth is an objectification of man's [sic] social experience, not his individual experience... in myth man [sic] begins to learn a new and strange art; the art of expressing, and that means of organizing, his most deeply rooted instincts, his hopes and fears (47-48).

Simply put, and at its most insufficient, mythic consciousness is the construction of a world governed by fulfillment or avoidance of deeply rooted instincts (sex), hopes (I do what I want), and fears (death and lesser constraints).

Cassirer relates a return to or dependence on mythic consciousness as a premise for particular developments of totalitarian or colonial agendas, an undergirding for what bell hooks (2000) proposes as the paradox and premise of western political thought: the right of the superior to dominate the inferior. Cassirer's proposition is that myth does not disappear—it goes underground until people have to face unusual and dangerous situations; it appears if people are confronted with a task that seems to be far beyond their natural powers—when rationality and skill fail, there remains always the power of the miraculous and mysterious (1946, 279). Invariably accompanying this turn to the mythic and magical is the willingness—and necessity—to consolidate and personify this power in a hero-leader. The "technique" of the modern political myth is the active manipulation of this process. Cassirer lays out the process: 1) change in the function of language (i.e., new words; charged words; semantic and magical uses of words; old words used in a new sense); 2) supplement the magic word by the introduction of new rites and the flattening of personality and individual responsibility through repetition; (the "group" is the moral subject whose purpose is acquiescence: people no longer question their environment—they accept it as a matter of course); 3) remove the "burden" (dilemma) of freedom and with it relieve people from all personal responsibility; 4) use the hero-leader to re-affirm that what is unfolding is the "will of the gods" and the rightful enactment of manifest destiny (282-288).

Cassirer's mythic consciousness and its role in creating hegemonic structures is related to Freire's superstitious consciousness, and its role in reproducing internalized oppression. Interrupting mythic and superstitious consciousness is the challenge of this paper.

In "More Than the Basics: Teaching Critical Reading in High School" Nancy Zimmet (1987) states that "because my students' alienation and insecurities about school were at the heart of their learning difficulties, I decided to make schooling itself the object of study, to problematize, in Freire's words, the existential situation" (123). Like Finlay and Faith, Zimmet enacted Freire's approaches in her classroom with impressive results not only in improved language skills but in a marked improvement in critical thinking and application. She facilitated her students through a unit of readings about others' experiences in schools in an attempt, as Freire urges, to start objectifying situations in students' lives so they might be discussed. Zimmet also utilized Herber's (1978) three levels of reading in her application of Freire, these being

> literal, in which students simply determine what information is presented; interpretive, in which they look for relationships between statements and derived meanings; and applied, in which they question an author's premises, judge material in light of their own experience and formulate new ideas. (124)

In guiding her students through Herber's levels of reading, Zimmet also allowed her students to experience Freire's forms of consciousness, moving to a place of agency within and about their own experiences in school.

In his letter to the North American Teacher, Paulo Freire (1987) responds to editor Ira Shor's request to Freire for a reflective, epistolary commentary on the application of his pedagogic and political philosophy.

Paulo Freire's work in literacy education formed the template for educational work in the development of critical consciousness. Freire's work is remarkable for many reasons, not the least of which is its insistence on affirming the role of *oppressed* or *othered* groups in the construction of the discourse which shapes and describes their reality. Freire is adamant about the necessity for silenced and marginalized groups to refuse the definition of their identity and possibility by those assuming to be more powerful. In keeping with his commitment to education for social transformation, Freire (1987) also articulated some *rules of engagement* for teachers.

> Since education is by nature social, historical and political, there is no way we can talk about some universal, unchanging role for the teacher... a teacher must be fully cognizant of the political nature of his/her practice and assume responsibility for this rather than denying it. When the teacher is seen as a political person, then the political nature of education requires that the teacher either serve whoever is in power, or present options to those in power... Professional competence, command of a subject or discipline, is never understood by the progressive teacher as something neutral. There is no such thing as a category called "professional competence" all by itself. We must always ask ourselves: In favour of whom and of what do we use our technical competence? (211-214)

Linking education to a consciousness of the relationship between expressive bodies and the culture which shapes and is shaped by them, Freire engaged illiterate adults in dialogical situated pedagogy which allowed the learners to move from a näive to a critical consciousness of the culture and the dominant forces within it.

In Freire's archeology of consciousness, students who see themselves as makers of culture (i.e., as cultural agents) experience their relation to reality and their powers to change reality. This challenges their alienation. Their powers to change themselves and their reality are in their hands; this is not seen as an extraordinary act of human courage but rather as a basic act of human agency. Critical consciousness allows and enables this shift in responsibility. Superstitious consciousness, however, provides students with the desperation necessary to resort to the power of the magical and mysterious. A highly developed magic and connected with it a mythology always occurs if a pursuit is dangerous and its issues uncertain (Cassirer 1946, 279).

For Freire, people become "enconscientized" by oppression—that is, they internalize the doctrine of a superstitious consciousness to the extent that they can oppress themselves, whether a hero-leader is present or not. Cassirer also presents this acquiescence as a fundamental ingredient in the technique of the modern political myth. His description is unnerving:

> They have ceased to be free and personal agents. Performing the same prescribed rites they begin to feel, to think, and to speak in the same way. Their gestures are lively and violent; yet this is but an artificial, a sham life. In fact they are moved by an external force. They act like marionettes in a puppet show—and they do not even

know that the strings of this show and of man's [sic] whole individual and social life are henceforth pulled by the political leaders (1946, 286).

In Freire's model, alienation from forms of expression (especially language) leads to alienation from culture; for Cassirer, this alienation is also enacted in the disengagement from the burdensome trappings of freedom. For both, the results are a retreat from responsible, reflective engagement with the world of lived relation; and while this is achieved under the mantle of centralized power, it is the decentred "disciplinary practice" based power (á la Foucault), which makes its continuance possible. This active manipulation of instincts, hopes and fears, which culminates in the pursuit of the metaphysical shelter of myth and magic is not accidental or coincidental. It is alive and well in contemporary academic culture.

## Academic Culture—Applications and Examples

Faculty and students learn about relations of dominance and subordination through the subtleties of the hidden curriculum (Bain 1990) performed daily within the habitus of departmental and institutional politics (Bourdieu 1977). *Hidden curriculum* refers to what is taught and learned through institutionalized rituals, routines and habits. Typically, hidden curriculum has as much to do with the how, where, and who of the content as it does with the what of the curriculum, the agenda-ed character of the what notwithstanding (Brustad 1997). Freire (1987) insists that the act of teaching and the teaching of subject matter are inseparable. The teacher cannot present subject matter as if it were disconnected from an interpretive framework, yet the act of teaching also teaches learners about knowledge, values, and power distribution. How subject matter is taught affects not only what is learned, but also what is meaningful, i.e., what is worth knowing and doing.

Students at all levels encounter hierarchically organized subject matter and faculty members. Positivistic approaches to knowledge production tend to carry over into positivistic approaches to constructing teaching, learning, and supervisory contexts. Rigidity around contingency and diversity is usually performed and interpreted as rigorous standards.

The fragmentation of the curriculum, the lack of infused concepts across disciplinary areas, the core-elective designations, the numbers of courses in specific disciplines deemed necessary, who is assigned to teach what course, what content is evaluated and how, and how faculty members achieve progress through the ranks and institutional status are all signs of the norms and inscriptions of a productive academic institution. Ideology critique, if presented as a legitimate theoretical framework for undergraduates, is usually housed in elective courses, and is interpreted as tangential Here, Spivak's (1988) chilling conclusion that the subaltern cannot speak without risking their own eradication should serve as a reminder that privileged subject positions often exist without such risk and often at the expense of those who cannot, or dare not speak. Academic privilege without personal and political reflection will allow these conditions of unequal power distribution to continue and will model this as appropriate behaviors for students to emulate.

*Example 1: Promotion and Tenure*
The tension between agency and structure is certainly experienced in institutional rituals associated with promotion and tenure. Faculty members at various stages of career wrestle with paradoxes of creativity, innovation, authenticity and orthodoxy.

If we examine the technique of the modern political myth as proposed by Cassirer, we can see the strategic deployment of each step in the "progress through the ranks journey" of university professors. At my institution, the promotion and tenure process is governed by several articles in our Collective Agreement between our bargaining unit (the Faculty Association) and our administration.

In the Promotion and Tenure process, changes in language function are prevalent. Charged words such as "clear promise" and "achievement" are located within the rites of the disciplinary home world; candidates deemed insiders are socialized into the rites and rituals until the behavior and belief are seamless and the acquiescence is then performed as excellence. This connection of language and ritual also serves to normalize harassing behaviors as "standards". Since cultural participants neither owned nor created these standards, they cannot be held responsible for the price exacted by their deployment. These standards of disciplinary purity are then championed by an exemplar who confirms and reinforces the unquestioned appropriateness of the whole process.

*Example 2: Academic Freedom*
Again, drawing from my home institution, academic freedom has evolved from being a safeguard against censorship to being a tyranny of unregulated excess. Early efforts in academic freedom supported a professoriate's right to teach and research in knowledge areas that might be considered "outside the norm" or outside the paradigmatic constraints. Recently, professors have claimed that their academic freedom has been compromised because they do not have chalkboards in their classrooms or because they will be expected to demonstrate accountability for student learning, two sites of engagement previously less fraught with protest and hostility. A siege mentality established, ordinary means of negotiation and problem solving are abandoned as insufficient; when rationality and skill fail, there remains always the power of the miraculous and mysterious (Cassirer 1946, 279).

I have witnessed increasing incidence and intensity of academic freedom outrage (uber freedom, if you will) in the name of maintaining a ritual practice and avoiding accountability. Underlying manipulation of actual academic freedom quite possibly contributes to the overkill response in the teaching context. "Strategic grants" (language) are supported by application protocols and competition (rituals) accepted as not only legitimate practice but evidence of scholarship (acquiescence) and formally endorsed by recognition from key senior administrators. The sad reality that the context of choice (i.e., what I may research and how I may package it) is controlled by external agencies may be the fuel that is feeding the fires of academic freedom as "doing what I want" because I am the expert. The loss of agency in the choice of research contexts compels the urgency, which has "uber- freedom" as its (discharge) expression in the teaching context.

**Interrogations and Interruptions**
How might I interrupt these habit practices which fuel and reproduce fear and terror in mundane academic contexts? At the risk of putting forth a tokenistic checklist, I offer the following for consideration:

—problematizing romantic notions of unity, homogeneity and meritocracy
—resisting facile rationalizations based in monolithic and essentialist representations interrogating the "naturalization of progress" (Briskin 2004, 344); the common sense belief in a linear movement towards equality and that things will naturally get better, and of naturalism (Briskin 2004, 345); which implies an inevitability about social organization recognizing the importance of local, fluid and contextualized sets of meanings and practices; of negotiated and renegotiated historical circumstances acknowledging a self in production ... a subject in process/on trial (Kristeva 1984) building links cognizant of difference" "with local differences kept in focus and the gaze on difference refusing to construct exotic subject positions" (Briskin 2004, 352);
—accepting the ongoing tension between agency and structure (reminiscent of Marx: humans make history but not in circumstances of their choosing); realizing that some degree of agency is always possible and resistance reconfigures constraints.

In this next section will propose options for "reconfiguring constraints." In the interests of brevity I will address the strategies of forced dissonance and paradoxical juxta-positioning.

Forced dissonance is actually anticipating and creating a crisis, of sorts. Habit strategies (in students and professors) will not be abandoned or questioned or changed unless they do not work in ways that are undeniable. In my classroom I achieve this with in-class, open book, immediate feedback, pre-practiced assessments that nevertheless result in grade spreads from less than perfect to failing. This demonstrates how preparation is a skill as important as literal information retrieval. For many of my students it is a helpful encounter with failure or being less than perfect. The key is then unpacking the experience so the students see the constituent elements and do not resort to "mythic" or superstitious rationalizations; rather they see links between action and consequences. These insights can also be nurtured with group-based in-class assessment followed by analysis. Open-ended questions guiding the analysis are a significant component in the overall learning of both students and professor

Forcing the link between actions and consequences is also helpful in situations where faculty members—deliberately or otherwise—create situations where teaching assistants cannot ever perform at an acceptable standard. In these cases, it is often in the best interests of visibility to let a grading crisis unfold rather than scramble to camouflage an already untenable situation.

Paradoxical juxta-positioning is a somewhat perverse form of giving people what they say they want. Placing two (usually contradictory) elements side by side as if they could co-exist or be mutually supportive is one way of allowing a process to unfold which cannot reach a fulfilling resolution. The student or professor must then find ways to manage this tension (and, in the case of the student in my classes at least, analyze and report on it), or find an alternative. This allows for a self-located disruption of the belief that things will always work out for the best under forces outside of the student's or professor's control. It also encourages a more grounded consideration of what is theirs to control. I emphasize here that this exercise does not suggest control as a solution, but rather a consideration of the features where agency is possible, a recognition of the fluid and contextualized aspects of meaning and practices, and a commitment to negotiated and re-negotiated historical and actual circumstances.

Other "mundane" or everyday reconfigurings are also possible, for example, the creation of "new heroes" (echoing Cassirer) in the promotion and tenure process—scholars who are inter-disciplinary, who have diversified research portfolios, who disseminate across a spectrum of modalities; tenured full professors who are in a position to take risks—and interruptions of ritual processes with the right question at the right time or with the choice of what to say "yes" to, or the visible insistence of a "no" vote.

**Temporary Closure**

I have proposed that hidden curriculum and superstitious and mythic consciousness have power in academic contexts, are productive and effective forms of control and internalized oppression, and are active in contemporary academic culture. I remain convinced that Freire's, Cassirer's, and Bain's pedagogic and political theorizing have relevance for intergenerational, neo-colonial academic contexts and remain more committed than ever to taking seriously Freire's question—In favor of whom and of what do we use our professional competence?

# References

Bain, L. 1990. A critical analysis of the hidden curriculum in physical education. In *Physical education, curriculum and culture: Critical issues in the contemporary crisi*, ed. D. Kirk and R. Tinning, 23-42. Bristol, UK: The Falmer Press.

———— 1997. Transformation in the postmodern era: A new game plan. In *Critical postmodernism in human movement, physical education, and sport*, ed. J.M. Fernandez-Balboa, 183-196. Albany: SUNY Press.

Bourdieu, P. 1977. *Outline of a theory of practice.* Cambridge UK: Cambridge Univ. Press.

Briskin, L. 2004. Privileging agency and organizing: A new approach for Women's Studies. In *Feminisms and womanisms—a women's studies reader*, ed. A. Prince and S. Silva-Wayne, 343-358. Toronto: Women's Press.

Brookfield, S. D. 2000. Transformative learning as ideology critique. In *Learning as transformation: Critical perspectives on a theory in progress*, ed. J. Mezirow, 125-148. San Francisco: Jossey-Bass.

Brustad, R. 1997. A critical postmodern perspective on knowledge development in human movement. In *Critical postmodernism in human movement, physical education, and sport*, ed. J.M. Fernandez-Balboa, 87-98. Albany: SUNY Press.

Cassirer, E. 1946. *The myth of the state.* New Haven, CT: Yale Univ. Press.

Dunhill, Anne, ed. and tansl., Marinella, Lucrezia, d.1653, *The nobility and excellence of women and the defect and vices of men.* Chicago: The Univ. of Chicago Press, 1999.

Finlay, L. S. and Faith, V. 1987. *Illiteracy and alienation in American colleges: Is Paulo Freire's pedagogy relevant?* In *Freire for the classroom—A source book for liberatory pedagogy*, ed. I. Shor, 63-85. Portsmouth, NH: Boynton/Cook Publishers.

Freire, P. 1987. Letter to North American Teachers. In *Freire for the classroom*, ed. I. Shor, 211-214. Portsmouth, N.H.: Boynton-Cook.

———— 1973. *Education for critical consciousness.* New York: Seabury.

———— 1968. *Pedagogy of the oppressed.* New York: Continuum.

Herber, J. 1978. *Teaching reading in the context areas.* Englewood Cliffs, NJ: Prentice Hall.

hooks, b. 2000. *_Feminist theory from margin to center*, 2nd edition. Cambridge, MA: South End Press.

Kristeva, J. 1984. *Revolution in poetic language.* Trans. Leon S. Roudiez. New York: Columbia.

*Macleans* magazine, March 3, 2008, Editor-in-Chief Kenneth Whyte.

Nesbit, T. 1998. Teaching in adult education: Opening the black box. *Adult Education Quarterly*, 48 no. 3: 157-171.

Peart, Neil, *Snakes and Arrows*, © 2007 Anthem Entertainment, Colour Separations and Printing by Battlefield Graphics, Canada.

Schommer, M. 1998. The role of adults' beliefs about knowledge in school, work, and everyday life. In *Adult learning and development: Perspectives from educational psychology*, ed. M.C. Smith and T. Pourchot, 127-143. Mahwah, NJ: Lawrence Erlbaum Associates, Publishers.

Shor, I. (Ed.). 1987. *Friere for the classroom—A source book for liberatory pedagogy*. Portsmouth, NH: Boynton-Cook.

Spivak, G. 1988. Can the subaltern speak? In *Marxism and the interpretation of culture*, ed. C. Nelson and L. Grossberg, 271-313. Chicago: Univ. of Illinois Press.

*St.Catharines Standard*, February 19, 2008, B1, Publisher Paul McCuaig.

——— April 2, 2008, A2. Publisher Paul McCuaig.

"The Old Voice and the Other Voice" by Margaret L. King and Albert Rabil Jr., introduction to Marinella, Lucrezia, d.1653, *The Nobility and Excellence of Women and the Defects and Vices of Men*, ed., Dunhill, Anne, tansl., Chicago: The Univ. of Chicago Press, 1999.

Vygotsky, L. S. 1962. *Language and thought.* (originally published, 1934). Cambridge, MA: MIT Press.

——— (1978). *Mind in society: The development of higher psychological processes.* (M. Cole, V. John-Steinor, S. Scribner, and E. Souberman, Eds.) Cambridge, MA: Harvard Univ. Press.

Zimmet, N. (1987). More than basics: Teaching critical reading in high school. In *Freire for the classroom—A source book for liberatory pedagogy*, ed. I. Shor, 122-128. Portsmouth, NH: Boynton-Cook.

# YOUTH TERROR OR TERRORIZED YOUTH? YOUTH VIOLENCE IN NIGERIA: REDEFINING SPACES OF POLITICS AND BELONGING

*Andrea Kirschner*

**Introduction**

Young people in the countries of the South have increasingly become the focus of international debate and sociological research, not least because of demographic trends in these countries. The debates about the future role of "African youth" especially, oscillate between discourses of threat and victimhood: serving the stereotype of the unpredictable, violent African youth or drawing an oversimplified picture of the young victim. The high proportion of young men in the population as a whole is treated not only as a threat to the social order of the country in question but—in the context of a globalized security discourse—as a destabilizing factor for the global social order as a whole. Although nobody would dispute that young people in Africa—as in other parts of the world—play a large role in the "terrorization" of whole populations and even more frequently are themselves victims of political and social violence, this picture is in fact everything but complete and itself represents a kind of "epistemic terrorization" of young people whose role in such discourses is never more than that of objects to be organized, disciplined and controlled on the one hand, and protected on the other. In both cases they are denied agency to an equal degree. Thus constructed, "youth problem" contributes to a trivialization and criminalization of young people and is limiting in several respects, especially as it "implicitly sees youths as a coherent group where differences according to gender, class, ethnicity, and nationality or even by experience are secondary to a common identification of youthhood" (Ismail and Alao 2007, 5). Moreover, the "epistemic terrorization" of young people can legitimize physical terror, for instance in the form of brute force by government security agencies, and structural terror that leads to further political, social and economic marginalization.

The paper attempts to deconstruct this "youth problem" using the example of vigilante groups in Nigeria. This country has a complex landscape of violent youth organizations that permeates all regions and all segments of society. Most common in the south are ethnic militias and "area boys," best known among them the Bakassi Boys, who were active from 1998 to 2000, and the Oodua People's Congress (OPC) (Harnischfeger 2003, 2006; Nolte 2004; Adebanwi 2005; Gore and Pratten 2003; Pratten 2007; Reno 2005; Guichaoua 2006). Urban youth gangs are mainly concentrated in the major cities of the federal states of Lagos and Edo. In addition, the Niger Delta is a catchment area for numerous youth movements such as the Ijaw Youth Council, the Niger Delta Vigilante Group (NDVG) and the Niger Delta People's Volunteer Front (NDPVF), along with smaller street gangs and, again, ethnic militias such as the Egbesu Boys (Ukeje 2004; Ifeka 2006; Watts and Zalik 2006; Oruwari 2006; Ikelegbe 2006). In the predominantly Muslim north, the dominant form is groups of young vigilantes, *yan daba* and *yan hisba*, who use religious and regional identities to distinguish themselves from non-Muslim "outsiders" in other regions (Casey 2008; Last 2004). In addition there is a countrywide phenomenon of "campus cults," student fraternities that generally cut across ethnic and religious affiliations. In the Nigerian media, they are often blamed for downright "campus terrorism" (Rotimi 2005; Bastian 2001).

What these groups of organized youths have in common is that they regulate security as vigilantes and not infrequently use extreme violence against government security agencies, rival youth groups and sections of the general public. Against this background, Nigerian youths undoubtedly seem to be a social "problem"—"terrorizers" who frighten and terrify society. However, this paper argues that youth vigilantes in Nigeria play ambivalent and ambiguous roles as perpetrators who terrorize society on the one hand and as active shapers of society on the other. Their diverse practices go far beyond the mere spread of terror and use of "brute" force, and should be read not least as attempts by these young people to open up for themselves spaces for articulating alternative, localized ideas of authority and responsibility, and symbolic belonging.

The conditions of "hybrid" or "fragile" statehood form the youth vigilantes' "structural framework for action" (Siegelberg and Hensell 2006, 19). In the literature, opinions vary as to whether Nigeria should be considered a "fragile" or even a "failed" state. There is extensive agreement, however, that "the idea of Nigeria" is caught in a crisis of legitimation that is expressed in widespread rejection of, or at least pronounced scepticism towards, the present state structure in all ethnic groups, and in ever-increasing ethnic and religious polarization (Johnson 2001, 81; Lambach 2002, 92; Osaghae 1998). Against this backdrop of fragile national identity, young people in particular start to seek alternative regional, ethnic or religious identities. What is more, the instability of its norms, laws and institutions makes the Nigerian state a "privileged site for negotiation, bargaining and brokerage" (Gore and Pratten 2003, 214), one that youths are able to turn to their advantage in many ways by means of their fluid relationship with the state and changing coalitions with its elites and security agencies. In circumstances where a state is inefficient at guaranteeing security and its corruption and clientelism has for decades generated mistrust in broad sections of the population, it is not least youths who help take care of security in their respective communities. In return, they benefit from far-reaching social recognition and legitimacy.

In the next section I will start by discussing in greater detail the highly contentious and anything but conclusively explicable concepts "youth" and "terror." I will go on to outline several historical "stages" in the process whereby youths in Nigeria and elsewhere on the African continent came to be constructed as a problem. In the fourth chapter, current ways of representing African youths that are essentially based on three theses, the "troublemakers -thesis," the "instrumentalization thesis" and the "re-traditionalization thesis," will be reconstructed and the problems with them expounded using the example of Nigerian youth vigilantes. I will conclude with a summary of my findings.

## 1. "Terror" and "Youth"—Approaches to Two "Slippery" Concepts

"Terror" and "youth" are two highly ambiguous categories and "slippery" concepts. This makes an unambiguous, conclusive definition of them impossible and necessitates some consideration of how they are "rendered manageable," along with reflection on the multiplicity of their meanings and contexts.

### 1.1 The notion of "terror"—Violence, knowledge and order

> *"There are many ways to tell a story, and there are many ways to read a story. This is perhaps most true of tales of violence. Violence is essentially contested: everyone knows what it is, but no single agreed upon definition exists. What is reprehensible murder to some is a killing of honor for others; terrorism rests not in the acts of violence themselves, but in the subjective interpretation of the perceiver. Just wars are "just" only to the aggressors and the armed. On a more philosophical level, violence can be interpreted as inherently destructive because it tears at the very possibility of human existence. To others, it heralds the dawn of a new order, the proverbial phoenix rising from the ashes."* (Nordstrom and Giraldo 2002, 1-2)

The same applies to the concept of "terror" as to the concept of violence. What we should describe as terror is a highly contentious question and the answer can vary widely from society to society and in different cultural contexts. One reason is that the term "terror" incorporates, along with the perpetrators' intentions (which are usually imputed by others), the power relationships and emotions of both the perpetrators of violence and their victims.

Moreover, the understanding of terror, like the concept of violence, has been expanded continuously since it transpired that terror, like violence, need not necessarily emanate from persons but can also be discerned in structures and in forms of knowledge production. Serious objections may exist to such a broad understanding of the term, but in the final analysis its concrete use should be geared to the subject matter under investigation.[1] This paper is based on a broad understanding of terror that includes both physical and structural terror, i.e. social, political and economic structures that facilitate inequalities, oppression and exploitation, and also that which, following Foucault's conception of discourse and power (1974, 1981), I will call "epistemic terror." I take epistemic terror to mean a form of terror that lies in the production of a specific knowledge that is generated via discourse and therefore enables objects to be experienced in a particular way and constructs them only as what they are "meant to be" within that discourse. Simultaneously, the "knowledge" thus produced is used to legitimize certain practices such as, in extreme cases, extrajudicial killings of youth vigilantes represented as a "security threat," while other options for action are marginalized in discourse. Taking such a broad concept of terror as a basis is justifiable in that it enables one to consider the all too simplistic image of youths as "terrorizers" and to spotlight how youths themselves are "terrorized" by a certain form of knowledge production. In doing so, however, I must emphasize that I am not trying to justify physical terror by youths by interpreting it merely as necessary "counter-terror," for example. Thus the category "terror" is fundamentally ambivalent, in that it serves both as an instrument of the existing (knowledge) order and simultaneously as a means of questioning that order and challenging power relationships.

## 1.2 The notion of "youth"—Fluidity and power

*"Youth is just a word." (Bourdieu 1993)*

"Youth"—like the concept of "terror"—is a complex social category that can hardly be clearly and conclusively defined. International organizations such as the United Nations and the International Labor Organisation use the term to denote a chronological period from, typically, age 16 to 24, while historians and anthropologists tend to conceptualize "youth" as a contingent and socially constructed category, a stage in life that depends ultimately on the local micro-context and the respective historical period (Rodgers 2007, 439-440; Venkatesh and Kassimir 2007, 9; Evoy-Levy 2006). Definitions of youth vary according to geographical and cultural contexts and are subject to societal changes. It is a "position in movement," a position of social being and social becoming (Vigh 2006). This "fluidity" and dynamic of youth as a category is particularly evident in the phenomenon of "extended youth" that keeps youths in Nigeria and in other African countries, regardless of their actual age, "trapped" as it were in a state of youth and deters them from making the transition to adulthood. Due to economic and social circumstances, above all the reduction in public sector employment opportunities and an inadequate and underfunded education system, many youths find it increasingly difficult to become financially independent and thereby reach a position where they can marry and start a family of their own, which in the African context especially can be regarded as an essential criterion for making the transition to adulthood (cf. Gore and Pratten 2003, 216; Gavin 2007, 221). Moreover, "youth" is always defined in opposition to those who are established as adults and "elders" (Nolte 2004, 62; Last 2004). Thus it is a social category that is embedded in power relationships and simultaneously produces them. While traditional hierarchies in African societies rank "elders" above "youth," I show below that Nigerian youths are increasingly challenging these power relationships and that "youth" is not infrequently even a power resource used by political elites.

Rather than seeing youth as a "monolithic block" it is necessary to analyse the local, everyday and situational contexts in which the category youth, as described by youths themselves or others, is updated. These descriptions may vary, since the role assigned them by society need not necessarily tally with that which youths desire for themselves (Christiansen et al. 2006, 12). Only through this kind of examination will youth become more than just a word.

## 2. The Construction of the African "Youth Problem"— A Historical Perspective

> *"Looking to the past also reminds us that images of defiance have had their own generations of change." (Waller 2006, 91)*

In the following chapter I will outline briefly how youths in Africa came to be discursively constructed as a "problem," the continuities and changes that took place in this discourse, which produced a certain kind of knowledge about youths, and the practices for controlling and disciplining youths that were thereby made possible.

The need to keep young people "under control" and to channel their energies positively is widespread in most societies, since youths nearly everywhere are perceived as bearers of hope for the future on the one hand and a potential threat to the existing order on the other. This "youth as a problem or solution dichotomy" (Ismail and Alao 2007, 5) is a characteristic feature of African discourse on youth and in different historical epochs promoted different strategies, either for bringing the "youth problem" under control or for utilizing their "hope potential."

In pre-colonial African countries, for instance, initiation rites served as "modes of control" of youths. These ceremonies had the symbolic function of a rite of passage that enabled young men to acquire their gender-specific identity once and for all, and marked the attainment of a new social status. In addition, warrior bands, secret societies and militias composed of able-bodied young men from specific age groups played an important role as socialization bodies in many local communities and provided spaces for self-determination and proving of manhood (Waller 2006, 82; Sesay et al. 2003, 16). Not least, these groups, which in the case of Nigeria included the *hisba* in the Islamic cultures of the Hausa-Fulani in the north as well as the *Ekpo*, *Ekpe* and *Ekong* in different parts of the south, served for the maintenance of internal social order and public and external defence of the local community (Omeje 2005, 73). Groups like this were the predecessors, and more importantly the discursive reference point, of present-day vigilante groups in Nigeria. Their job was not just to ward off attacks from neighbouring communities and protect their community from witchcraft, but also to assist in law enforcement by punishing criminals and those who were more generally considered as threats to its unity (Sesay et al. 2003, 17; Nolte 2004, 65; Gore and Pratten 2003, 222-225). Thus youths played specific social roles that gave them orientation on the one hand and functioned as important sources of recognition on the other. Moreover, the usually unquestioned hierarchy of traditional African societies, which clearly subordinated youths to elders (Diouf 2003), formed a relatively stable social order that as a rule prevented inter-generational conflicts, because "if the future appeared to belong to the young, the past was the preserve of their elders, and it was from mastery of the past that authority sprang" (Waller 2006, 78). Consequently, in the pre-colonial era, thanks to appropriate social mechanisms and institutions, it was relatively easy to accomplish the goal of integrating young men into society in such a way that they not only posed no threat to the existing order, but stabilized it.

In contrast, "youth" as a unitary, inherently problematic category that needed to be disciplined and controlled emerged only during the colonial era, though the colonial view of young men was also ambivalent. The period of conquest and resistance was unquestionably "pre-eminently the time of young men, for it was they who, in and out of uniform on both sides, did the fighting" (Waller 2006, 78). Young men were extremely "valuable" to the colonial state not just as soldiers, but subsequently also as functionaries in the colonial bureaucracy. Yet the self-awareness that went hand in hand with this, their social and economic advancement, confronted the colonial regime with the problem of regaining control over these young men. However, the pre-colonial system of social organization and above all socialization spaces removed from its control were hardly compatible with colonial ideas of order and security and the ambition to establish a stable monopoly of violence. Instead, "security was systematically detached from society and its interrelated social structures, vested in the modern bureaucratic state and, consequently, the phenomenon became overly professionalized, secularised and militarised" (Omeje 2005, 73f). This was accompanied by increased efforts to proscribe warrior groups and militias, although many continued to operate, albeit mostly in secret (Sesay et al. 2003, 17; Casey 2008, 110). Thus the "antithetical colonial system" (Omeje 2005, 73-74) by no means completely obliterated or displaced the pre-colonial security order.

For "modern" modes of control and social integration mechanisms, the colonial state relied mainly on education and the labour process to turn youths into productive and responsible citizens. At the same time, education and vocational training enabled young men to understand how the colonial state functioned and potentially to participate in it, but also to challenge its authority and legitimacy. Especially since actual opportunities for upward social, political and economic mobility were extremely limited, not least due to racial domination, from the 1920s in particular the colonial state was more likely to spawn juvenile delinquents than responsible junior citizens (Waller 2006, 78-80; Fourchard 2006, 122).

Against this backdrop of "invention of juvenile delinquency," from the 1940s the problematization of youth took on a new quality. Now, youths were identified as an "urgent problem" to be dealt with by controlling their work and movements, because "their presence on the streets made urban public space, reserved for settled working families, dangerous and disordered in colonial eyes" (Waller 2006, 84). For these forms of surveillance and control, it was necessary to establish a legally defined age category of "juveniles" and, later, sub-categories of delinquents and juveniles "at risk" (cf. Waller 2006, 84-85), though very different behaviors were often subsumed into the same "delinquent category" (Fourchard 2006, 136). For example, living in the street, most often due to poverty, was not infrequently deemed sufficient cause to be classed as a delinquent (ibid.). Now, the colonial regime took over the "definition" of youth, responsibility for which until then been largely in the hands of parents, missionaries and employers, thereby providing an official focus for public concern (Waller 2006, 85). This simultaneously laid the foundation for governance, and epistemic terrorization, of young people on the basis of standardized categories. As Kelly (2000, 468) showed, "at-risk" discourses of this kind construct youth as making decisions, adopting behaviors and holding dispositions that may jeopardise certain preferred, "fundamentally normative" futures. In the process of trying to manage risk, new aspects of risk are created, thereby constituting further opportunities to regulate behavior and disposition. In its "invention of juvenile delinquency" the British colonial regime was largely guided by the same philosophy that had led to the invention of the notion of the "delinquent child" in early nineteenth-century Britain (Fourchard 2006, 116). According to this philosophy, it was necessary for the state to intervene in working-class family life in order to ensure that children were "properly educated, disciplined and given moral guidance." Now, to gain control of youth, the state extended its rule right into people's private lives.

At the same time, the process whereby youths were first systematically constructed as a uniform, problematic category was embedded in deeper worries and uncertainties both in government and among the populace. In the case of the British colonial regime, the concern about "delinquent youth" was simultaneously an expression of a far more fundamental worry about the future of empire, an "erosion scare" that swept the British Empire at that time. The negative images of "modern" youths that were widespread among the general public were a component of fundamental anxieties and uncertainties triggered by rapid social change (Waller 2006, 87). Youth, especially, seemed to reflect and magnify this change, thereby calling both the traditional and the colonial order into question. Against this background the African debate about maturation and authority and the colonial debate about control and criminality, despite divergent ideas of what "youth" should be, entered via their shared negative stereotypes of youths into a "discursive alliance" (Schwab-Trapp 2002, 59) that enabled both sides to legitimize stronger supervision, discipline and control practices and thereby stabilized existing power relationships.

After this one-sided problematization of youths during the colonial era, during the period of decolonization it is possible to identify a brief discursive discontinuity during which greater emphasis was placed on the representation of youths as a "solution" and as the main drivers of freedom and social progress. Nonetheless, the "nationalist project" had some continuities with the preceding youth discourse, for "youth achieved this status only because they were thought of as channelled and supervised by adults" (Diouf 2003). Thus even in the context of postcolonial construction of youths as bearers of hope, they were ultimately denied agency.

## 3. Ambiguous Roles of Nigerian Youth Vigilantes— Terrorizers, Guardians of Law and Order, Superheroes

As previously indicated, vigilante youth groups continued to exist in secret despite attempts to counter them, both in the colonial state and in the newly independent Nigerian nation state. Vigilante groups or "self-help organizations" became more visible again after the Nigerian civil war in the 1970s when there was a drastic increase in serious crimes of violence and robberies as a result of unemployment, demobilization and the proliferation of small arms (Oruwari 2006; Gore and Pratten 2003, 229). This development was intensified from the 1980s by an "extraordinary youth crisis" in the course of which economic crisis and the introduction of structural adjustment programs led to a collapse of the education system, huge public sector job cuts and extremely reduced employment opportunities on the formal labour market. During that period, youths were forced into the precarious informal sector (cf. Sesay et al. 2003, 20; Jega 2000). At the same time, there was an unprecedented degree of "identity politics," with youths in particular joining forces on the basis of shared ethnic, religious or regional identity to struggle for access to the state and the resources it controlled, or to demand basic rights and socio-economic provisioning and protest against exclusion and oppression (Jega 2000, 25). Against this backdrop, increasing numbers of urban youths, who due to the high rate of migration of young people, especially, to the cities were increasingly competing for economic opportunities, accommodation and land, joined forces as "area boys." By means of identification with a specific region of origin and us-and-them dichotomies between "indigenes" and "sons of the soil" versus "strangers," area boys produce a local form of collective identity that is simultaneously cited as a legitimation for regulating the flow of goods and services to their advantage (Gore and Pratten 2003, 226).

Vigilante youth groups received a further "boost" from Nigeria's formal return to democracy in 1999. Now, it was mainly "ethnic militias" formed on the basis of a shared ethnic identity and drawing legitimacy from complex and ambiguous conceptions of accountability that are played out in everyday politics within idioms of monitoring and surveillance, screening and vigilance who caused a stir (Gore and Pratten 2003, 214).

Although these vigilante groups emerged at different times and operated in different parts of the country, they share common tendencies. All emerged in the context of the above-mentioned "structural action framework" of fragile statehood and therefore constitute a reaction to perceived security and justice deficits in the Nigerian nation state. Moreover, all of these youth groups were set up to protect interests parochial to certain sections of the country that were perceived as being threatened by either developments at the regional level or at the federal centre (Sesay et al. 2003, 23) and they draw upon the above-mentioned pre-colonial discourses, in which youths were constructed as "moral guardians of the community" (Nolte 2004, 65) and "enforcers of community rights, morals and laws" (Gore and Pratten 2003, 223-224). Not least, the vigilante groups have in common, and this is the central focus of the following chapter, that they are described in the current ways in which African youths are represented while simultaneously calling these unambiguity-suggesting images very clearly into question. These incomplete images are reconstructed and problematized below on the basis of the "troublemakers thesis," the "instrumentalization thesis" and the "retraditionalization thesis."

## 3.1 The "troublemakers thesis"

Youths in Nigeria, as in other parts of Africa, are usually represented as "troublemakers" and a threat to security. However, we have demonstrated above that already in the pre-colonial era youths had an important function in *stabilizing* social order. In Nigeria, especially in view of the "crime waves" of the 1990s and the lack of confidence in the state's ability to offer security and to stabilize order, in many instances local communities "reactivated" youths as night watches and vigilante groups. Moreover, state governments did not just tolerate them as a complement to or substitute for regular police operations, but in some cases actively promoted them.[1] Consequently it is not surprising that youth vigilanteism does not project a revolutionary anti-state message (Gore and Pratten 2003, 232). As a rule, the state order is not fundamentally challenged. Rather, the state is still the principal addressee of demands for security and social welfare.

Yet youth vigilantes occupy an ambiguous position vis-à-vis the state and its security agencies. Despite a considerable degree of everyday cooperation between vigilantes and police, the former nevertheless occupy a precarious legal position (Pratten 2008, 189). Hence it could be argued with Lund (2007, 3) that vigilante youth groups are forms of "twilight institutions," that is organizations "that exercise legitimate public authority, but do not enjoy legal recognition as part of the state." This makes their relationship with the wider population similarly precarious. As will be outlined more detailed below, vigilante youths enjoy a high degree of social recognition and legitimacy on account of their frequently "magic" and supernaturally charged crime-fighting practices. However, this legitimacy is fragile and the population soon withdraws it if they fail to fight crime and establish security. If that happens, members of vigilante youth groups risk being drawn quickly towards the "other" criminal youths they are fighting, thereby becoming "alienated from the moral community to which they nominally belong" (Gore and Pratten 2003, 226).

It is scarcely possible for these young men to escape the dilemma that, on the one hand, they derive their legitimacy and self-image from local forms of moral accountability for the benefit of their community, while on the other, due to their marginalization and exclusion, they depend on utilizing the instrumental means of economic survival available in the patrimonial system, such as facilitated access to job or business places or rewards for services delivered to the population or political patrons (cf. ibid.: 228; Guichaoua 2006, 18). Against this background, since the late 1980s many vigilante groups have been successively criminalized as a result of their involvement in the drug trade and their use of violence in religious and ethnic riots and political protests (Gore and Pratten 2003, 223-224). This contradiction between their economic and social "survival" always makes the legitimacy and identity of vigilante youths seem fragile and thereby constantly in need of renewed self-legitimization.

Thus one must record that representing youths as "troublemakers," is inadequate insofar as youth vigilantes are concerned. Rather, by entering into fluid alliances they perform order-creating functions as a supplement to, and often even in direct cooperation with, the state. Or they articulate alternative ideas of order, though ultimately these, too, are presented as demands to the state. In contrast, representing them as "troublemakers" itself appears to be a discursive strategy that enables the "securitization" (Buzan and Waever 2003) of youths, that is their representation as a threat to security, and corresponding repressive practices. Thus, not infrequently the state was compelled to define vigilante youth groups as security threats, which enabled the state to carry out considerable military and police reprisals in the operational homelands of the stigmatized groups, leading to extrajudicial killings and devastation of defenceless local communities (Omeje 2005, 72).

### 3.2 The "instrumentalization thesis"

Against the backdrop described, the Nigerian state appears at once strong and weak (Nolte 2004, 84). On the one hand, the fact that youths perform state security functions indicates that the state is deficient in this area. At the same time, it is still first and foremost the state that controls economic and political resources, and this enables political office-holders to enter into fluid alliances with youths. In these circumstances it has become common to posit the thesis that youths are instrumentalized or coopted by dishonourable elites. Indeed, such tendencies towards "youth politics" can be observed in two ways. On the one hand, Nigerian politicians have appropriated the "youth" category, which in contemporary Nigerian parlance has almost become a synonym for "exclusion" and "political marginalization" and thus enjoys grassroots legitimacy, in order to identify with and mobilize youths. As Gore and Pratten (2003, 215-216) have shown, for instance, governors in the southern Edo and Ibom states have formed a "grouping as the self-promoted 'young' politicians" in order to form a common base for action to gain control over oil revenues and, thus, have "aligned themselves as part of the youth category in order to engage with and hold accountable the nation state." This again underscores the above-mentioned character of "youth" as a "fluid and rapidly shifting category that can be easily manipulated for one's own ends" (Twum-Danso 2005, 13). On the other hand, youth politics takes place in a much more direct way in that youths are used as "instruments of disorder." For instance, area boys in Lagos were recruited as political thugs in the Babanginda transition period or Hausa *Yandaba*—similar neighbourhood gangs in the North—have been used as henchmen by rival politicians during elections (Gore and Pratten 2003, 224; Babawale 2002, 3-5; Casey 2008, 114).

Still, youth groups do not constitute a resource that elites can manipulate in any way they want, but also pursue their own agendas. The fact that they make a point of not forming stable attachments to their respective political patrons, but enter into shifting personal alliances and loyalties, "continues to prevent the complete appropriation of youth by elite political strategies" (Nolte 2004, 85; cf. Baker 2002, 242). As discourses on political and economic marginalization, which are often furnished with additional ethnic, religious or regional framings, are incorporated into youths' self-description and identity formation, the thus "loaded" youth category becomes a resource for legitimization and mobilization in order to articulate perceived injustice and challenge existing power relations. The result is a seemingly paradox situation in which agency is exercised through "victimcy" (a word formed out of a combination of victim and agency), which is the "seemingly contradictory agency of presenting oneself as a powerless victim" (Utas 2003, 49). This form of youth politics, which from an outside viewpoint can hardly be distinguished from that of instrumentalization by elites, not least because the transitions in both directions are fluid, was already observed during decolonialization. "The anti-colonial movement was essentially led by men who were not necessary young biologically, but who identified themselves as "youth" in order to distinguish themselves from their elders, who were supposedly content either to be loyal colonial servants or placid rural chiefs and smallholders" (Twum-Danso 2005, 17f).

### 3.3 The "re-traditionalization thesis"
Finally, the third way of representing youths is based on the thesis that a clearly observable trend towards "re-traditionalization" is now visible in a resurgence of ethnicity and ritualized violence (Chabal and Daloz 1999). Since a proliferation of incidents of state failure in the 1980s, this argument goes, there has been a re-invention and comeback of traditionalism in all sectors of society, and consequently a "mystical re-traditionalization of security" as well (Omeje 2005, 71).

In fact, the widespread local support for youth vigilantes is often based on their use of magical forms of detection and protection that are believed to protect the "innocent" (Harnischfeger 2003, 30-35). For instance, the major defining characteristic of the Bakassi Boys was their possession of a peculiar type of occult power that, supposedly, made members impervious to bullets (Omeje 2005, 76; Harnischfeger 2006 and 2003). They employed two main types of charms: defensive charms, such as those that prevent harm from a bullet or machete, and revelatory charms that are used to extract confessions (Mc Call 2004). Similarly, the Egbesu Boys in the Niger Delta who are outmatched by the military power of their adversaries draw on the spiritual power of the ancient Egbesu deity in their homeland, a magical device that complements their limited firepower (Omeje 2005, 81). The members of "campus cults" are also believed to have a supernatural immunity to gunshot wounds and a magical ability to influence the minds of other people (Bastian 2001, 80).

However, one can hardly encapsulate these practices accurately in the concept of "re-traditionalization." Rather, they show how misleading this thesis is. The aforementioned continuity of vigilante youths operating in Nigeria, albeit in secret from time to time, speaks against re-traditionalization. Moreover, according to Foucault (1981, 33) the concept "tradition" "is intended to give a particular temporal status to a group of phenomena that are both successive and identical (or at least similar)." That is, present observations are placed in the direct continuity of a past interpreted in a specific way, thus isolating "the new against a background of permanence" (ibid.). This makes one lose sight of the fact that there are always different, parallel pasts and contradictory "traditions" and that one should therefore ask which of these pasts is updated for a contemporary narrative, by whom, and for what reasons. In drawing on "traditional" notions of accountability and "time-honored" occult belief systems, youth vigilantes do "not represent or memorize the past, they enact the past, bringing it back to life" (Pratten 2008, 199, following on from Bourdieu). Thus traditions become an "active political resource" which is used in order to balance or even invert power relations (cf. Adebanwi 2005, 341).

Moreover, the dichotomy of tradition and modernity behind the re-traditionalization thesis appears questionable even if one just looks at the use of a complex mix of "modern" and "traditional" technologies and recourse to apparently wholly opposing discourses. Rather, vigilante practices are "a hectic blend of tradition and modernity—magical charms and pump-action guns" (Ajibade 2006: 4). Some vigilante youths, via a style of dress that is geared to that of Los Angeles-based rappers (Casey 2008, 114), are embedded in a global youth culture. Some use the Nigerian movie industry to present themselves as mythic superheroes (Mc Call 2004; Ajibade 2006). Moreover, vigilantism draws on idioms of "traditional" accountability rooted in the supernatural as much as on "modern" ideals of democracy, development and progress (Smith 2004; Gore and Pratten 2003, 234). In every case Nigerian youth vigilantes cast doubt on a simple divide between modernity and tradition. Rather, they show that tradition such as "witchcraft is dynamic and engaged with the world and is, for this reason, eminently modern" (Moore and Sanders 2001, 10; see also Geschiere 1997). External rubrics of modernity are made recognizable and palatable to local people precisely *through* recourse to magic and spirituality (Bastian 2001, 90).

This again shows that present youth discourse stands in clear continuity with its historical precursors, although shifts in the elements of discourse are visible. As we have shown, whereas in the past it was the "modernity" of youths that triggered fear and insecurity in their elders and the colonial regime, the present production of fear is based mainly on representations of youths as "regressive" and "atavistic."

## 4. Conclusion

The representations of youth vigilantes in Nigeria connect in many ways to historical discourses about youths in Africa and draw simplistic pictures based on numerous dichotomies such as "problem-solution," "victim-threat," "order-chaos," "tradition-modernity," or "criminals-heroes." At the same time, the practices of these youths cast doubt on such dualistic ways of representation. They are troublemakers and terrorize the populace, yet at the same time contribute towards social order and security, albeit in a highly selective and in part commercialized form. They are instrumentalized by political elites for their own purposes, but via youth politics they pursue their own agendas and goals. Paradoxically, it is by invoking their status as victims that they develop agency. Their violence does not reflect re-traditionalization but complex, ambivalent discourses and practices, the elements of which are hardly possible to categorize meaningfully into "modern" and "traditional." Rather, they are used as "integrated" resources that are adjusted to particular local, present demands. The magical charging of their violent practices and the recourse to a specific pre-colonial past generate both fear and recognition. This same violence is sometimes described as "terror," thereby turning youths into outcasts and vandals, and sometimes as "protection," "security," or "self-defence," enabling youth vigilantes to be venerated as—supernatural—heroes. In both cases, violence supports processes of identity construction. In the former case, youths even move from the periphery to the centre through violence, while in the latter they become further marginalized:

> *"Excluded from the arenas of power, work, education, and leisure, young Africans construct places of socialization and new sociabilities whose function is to show their difference, either on the margins of society or at its heart, simultaneously as victims and active agents."* (Diouf 2003)

## References

Ajibade, Babson. 2006. Anti-bullet charms, lie-detectors and street justice: The Nigerian youth and the ambiguities of self-reaking. Paper presented at the International Conference Youth and the Global South, October 13-15, in Dakar, Senegal.

Babawale, Tunde. 2002. The rise of ethnic militias, de-legitimation of the state, and the threat to Nigerian federalism. *West Africa Review* 3, no. 1: 1-12.

Baker, Bruce. 2002. When the Bakassi boys came: Eastern Nigeria confronts vigilantism. In *Journal of Contemporary African Studies* 20, no. 2: 223-244.

Bastian, Misty L. 2001. Vulture men, campus cultists and teenaged witches. Modern magics in Nigerian popular media. In *Magical Interpretations, Material Realities: Modernity, Wichtcraft and the Occult in Postcolonial Africa*, ed. Henrietta L. Moore and Todd Sanders, 71-96. London, New York: Routledge.

Bourdieu, Pierre. 1993.Youth is just a word. *Sociology in question*, ed. Pierre Bourdieu, London: Sage.

Buzan, Barry, and Ole Waever. 2003. *Regions and powers: The structure of international security*, Cambridge: Univ. Press.

Casey, Conerly. 2008. Policing through violence: fear, vigilantism, and the politics of Islam in Northern Nigeria, *Global vigilantes*, ed. David Pratten and Atreyee Sen, 93-124. New York: Blackwell.

Christiansen, Catrine, Mats Utas, and Henrik E. Vigh. 2006. Navigating youth, generating adulthood, Introduction. *Navigating Youth, Generating Adulthood. Social Becoming in an African Context*, ed. Catrine Christiansen, Mats Utas, and Henrik E. Vigh, 9-28, Uppsala: Nordic Africa Institute.

Diouf, Mamadou. 2003. Engaging postcolonial cultures: African youth and public space. *African Studies Review*, Sept..

Foucault, Michel.1974. *Archäologie des Wissens*, Frankfurt am Main: Suhrkamp, 1981.

—— Die Ordnung des Diskurses. *Botschaften der Macht. Reader Diskurs und Medien*, Stuttgart: Deutsche Verlagsanstalt.

Fourchard, Laurent, 2006. Lagos and the invention of Juvenile Delinquency in Nigeria, 1920-60, *Journal of African History* 47: 115-137.

Galtung, Johan. 1975. *Strukturelle Gewalt. Beiträge zur Friedens- und Konfliktforschung*, Reinbek: Rororo.

Gavin, Michelle. 2007. Africa's restless youth, *Current History*, May: 220-226.

Geschiere, Peter.1997. *The modernity of witchcraft. Politics and the occult in postcolonial Africa*. Charlotteville: Univ. Press of Virginia.

Gore, Charles, and David Pratten. 2003. The politics of plunder: The Rhetorics of order and disorder in Southern Nigeria, *African Affairs* 102: 211-240.

Guichaoua, Yvan. 2006. The making of an ethnic militia: The Oodua People's Congress in Nigeria, CRISE Working Paper no. 26.

Harnischfeger, Johannes. 2006. State decline and the return of occult powers. The case of Prophet Eddy in Nigeria. *Magic, Ritual, and Witchcraft*, 1, no.1: 56-78.

―― 2003. The Bakassi Boys: Fighting crime in Nigeria. *Journal of Modern African Studies*, 41, no. 1: 23-49.

Ifeka, Caroline. 2006. Conflict, complicity & confusion: Unravelling empowerment struggles in Nigeria after the return to "democracy." *Review of African Political Economy* 27, no. 83: 115-123.

Ikelegbe, Augustine. 2006. Beyond the threshold of civil struggle: Youth militancy and the militia-ization of the resource conflicts in the Niger Delta region of Nigeria, *African Studies Monographs* 27, 3: 87-122.

Ismail, Olawale, Alao, Abiodun. 2007. Youths in the interface of development and security, *Conflict, Security and Development* 7, no.1: 3-25.

Jega, Attahiru. 2000. The state and identity transformation under structural adjustment in Nigeria. In. *Identity transformation and identity politics under structural adjustment in Nigeria*, ed. Attahiru Jega, 24-40. Uppsala: Nordic Africa Institute.

Johnson, Dominic. 2001. Staatszerfall in Westafrika, *Blätter für deutsche und internationale Politik*, 46, no.1: 77-85.

Kelly, Peter. 2000. The dangerousness of youth-at-risk: The possibilities of surveillance and intervention in uncertain times, *Journal of Adolescence*, 23: 463-476.

Lambach, Daniel. 2002. *Staatszerfall im postkolonialen Afrika*, Marburg: Tectum-Verlag.

Last, Murray. 2004. Towards a political history of youth in Muslim northern Nigeria. In. *Vanguard or vandals: youth, politics, and conflict in Africa*, ed. Jon Abbink, Ineke van Kessel, Seiten Leiden. Boston: Brill.

Lund, Christian. 2007. Twilight institutions: An introduction. In *Twilight institutions: Public authority and local politics in Africa*, ed. Christian Lund, 1-11. Malden (MA), Oxford, Victoria (Australia): Blackwell.

McCall, John C. 2004. Juju and justice at the movies: Vigilantes in Nigerian popular videos. *African Studies Review* Dec.

McEvoy-Levy, Shiobán. 2006. *Troublemakers or peacemakers? Youth and post-accord peace building.* Notre Dame, Indianapolis: Univ. Press.

Momoh, Abubakar. 2000. Youth culture and area boys in Lagos. In *Identity transformation and identity politics under structural adjustment in Nigeria*, ed. Jega, Attahiru, 181-203. Uppsala: Nordic Africa Institute.

Moore, Henrietta L., and Todd Sanders. 2001. Magical interpretations and material realities: An introduction, *Magical interpretations, Material realities. Modernity, Wichtcraft and the Occult in Postcolonial Africa*, ed. Henrietta L. Moore, and Todd Sanders, 1-27. London, New York: Routledge.

Nolte, Insa. 2004. Identity and violence: The politics of youth in Ijebu-Remo, Nigeria, *Journal of Modern African Studies*, 42, no.1: 61-89.

Nordstrom, Carolyn. 1999. Requiem for the rational war, Deadly Developments. In *Capitalism, states and war, War and society*, ed. S.P. Reyna and R.E. Downs, 153-175, Vol.5, Amsterdam: Gordon and Breach Publishers.
Omeje, Kenneth. 2005. The Egbesu and Bakassi Boys: African Spiritism and the mystical re-traditionalisation of security, In *Civil militias: Africa's intractable security menace?*, ed. D. J. Francis, 71-88. Aldershot: Ashgate.
Oruwari, Yomi. 2006. Youth in urban violence in Nigeria. A Case Study of Urban Gangs from Port Harcourt, Niger Delta Economies of Violence Working Papers No.14.
Osaghae, Eghosa E. 1998. *Crippled giant. Nigeria since independence*, Bloomington, Indianapolis: Indiana Univ. Press.
Pratten, David. 2007. Singing thieves: History and practice in Nigerian popular justice, In *Global vigilantes*, ed. Dabid Pratten, Atyree Sen, 175-205. London, New York: Hurst and Columbia Univ. Press.
Reno, William. 2005. The politics of violent opposition in collapsing states. *Government and Opposition*, 40, no. 2: 127-151.
Rodgers, Dennis. 2007. Researching youth and violence in Central America: Participatory methodologies, Introduction, *Bulletin of Latin American Research*, 26, no. 4: 439-443.
Rotimi, Adewale. 2005. Violence in the Citadel: Secret cults in the Nigerian universities, *Nordic Journal of African Studies* 14, no.1: 79-98.
Schwab-Trapp, Michael. 2002. *Kriegsdiskurse. Die politische Kultur des Krieges im Wandel 1991-1999*, Opladen: VS Verlag.
Sesay, Amadu, Charles Ukeje, Olabisi Aina, and Adetanwan Odebiyi. 2003. *Ethnic militias and the future of democracy in Nigeria*. Ile-Ife: Obafemi Awolowo Univ. Press.
Siegelberg, Jens, and Stefan Hensell. 2006. Rebellen, warlords und Milizen. Kritik der Kriegsforschung und Ansätze zu ihrer Neuorientierung. *Gewaltordnungen bewaffneter Gruppen. Ökonomie und Herrschaft nichtstaatlicher Akteure in den Kriegen der Gegenwart*, ed. Jutta Bakonyi, Stefan Hensell, and Jens Siegelberg, 9-37, Baden-Baden: Nomos.
Smith, Daniel Jordan. 2004. The Bakassi Boys: Vigilantism, violence, and political imagination in Nigeria. *Cultural Anthropology*, 19, no. 3: 429–455.
Spivak, Gayatri Chakarvorty. 1996. Can the Subaltern speak? In *The Post-Colonial Reader*, ed. Bill Ashcroft, Gareth Griffith, and Helen Tiffin, 24-28. London: Routledge.
Twum-Danso, Afua. 2005. The political child. In *Invisible stakeholders. Children and War in Africa*, ed. Angela McIntyre, Institute for Security Studies, Pretoria: BLDS.
Ukeje, Charles. 2004. From Aba to Ugborodo: Gender identity and alternative discourse of *social* protest among women in the oil delta of Nigeria, *Oxford Development Studies* 32, no. 4: 605-617.
Utas, Matts. 2003. *Sweet battlefields. Youth and the Liberian civil war*, Uppsala: Univ. Dissertations in Cultural Anthropology, no. 1.

Venkatesh, Sudhir Alladi, and Ronald Kassimir. 2007. Youth and legal institutions: Thinking globally and comparatively. In *Youth, globalization, and the law*, ed. Sudhir Alladi Venkatesh, and Ronald Kassimir, 3-16. Stanford: Univ. Press.

Vigh, Henrik E. 2006. Social death and violent life chances. In *Navigating youth, Generating adulthood. Social becoming in an African context*, ed. Catrine Christiansen, Mats Utas, and Henrik E. Vigh, 31-60. Uppsala: Nordic Africa Institute.

Waller, Richard. 2006: Rebellious youth in Colonial Africa. *Journal of African History* 47: 77-92.

Watts, Michael, Anna Zalik. Imperial oil. *Socialist Review*, April 2006, http://www.socialistreview.org.uk/article.php?articlenumber=9712, accessed January 12, 2008).

# HUMANIST TERRORISM IN THE POLITICAL THOUGHT OF ROBESPIERRE AND SARTRE

*Timothy Johnson*

The French Revolution was without doubt the defining event that linked the word "terror" to political, revolutionary struggle. While the actual French word, *terreur*, had been in use centuries before the Revolution began in 1789, it became a part of the modern revolutionary lexicon through what George Armstrong Kelly terms "the clearly unprecedented and unique nature of the Jacobin experiment and its break with the past."[1] The evolution of terror-talk from the premodern era to the French Revolution shows a steady addition of newer coinages and uses to older ones. While religious, metaphysical, and epistemological uses of the word were dominant in the sixteenth century, by the eighteenth century the word *terreur* came to be applied to the political realm. The generation of new uses of the word *terreur* that occurred during the Reign of Terror beginning in 1793 borrowed aspects of previous meanings and added to them the dimension of political manipulation. These changes marked what Steven Blakemore terms "a semantic revolution that aided and abetted the political one." The only difference in the entry *"terreur"* between the fourth (1762) and fifth (1798) editions of the *Dictionnaire de L'Académie française* was the addition of the example sentence, *"Faire régner la terreur"* ["to make terror rule"]; the words *"terrorisme,"* a "system or regime of terror," and *"terroriste,"* an "agent or supporter of the government under the [Reign of] Terror who took part in the abuses of revolutionary power" were first added in the 1798 edition.

If the Reign of Terror is the event where we mark the birth of terror talk, then Maximilien Robespierre is the situated voice of terrorist ideology that we hear the loudest and the most clearly. Robespierre was the man, who under the assumption of the revolutionary *vox populi*, the embodiment of the general will of the French people, spoke the words revolution and terror in the same breath as virtue and humanity.

One and three-quarter centuries later, the French-Algerian War brought the question of terrorist violence to the fore of post- World War French politics and was an important point in both France's history and the broader history of African decolonization. The Algerian quest for self-determination led to the loss of 400,000 lives and saw the employment of brutal tactics, from both French and Algerian sides, ranging from torture and assassination to guerilla warfare, terrorism, and counter-terrorism. For France, the war was another sign of France's pre- World War loss of international prestige and was, at the very least, an instrumental factor in precipitating a number of social and political changes, including the end of the Fourth Republic and Charles de Gaulle's return to political power. Before the war in Algeria, France had already lost its holdings in Morocco, essentially conceded defeat in Vietnam, and was close to brokering a deal guaranteeing Tunisia's independence. For Algeria, the war was a struggle to end the system of colonial repression that plagued it since the initial French imperial invasion in 1830.

Although many of the particulars of the French-Algerian War differ monumentally from France's first revolution, the association between terrorist methods and political-humanist goals remains the same. Just as Robespierre was the loudest voice of the Reign of Terror, French philosopher, author, and political activist, Jean-Paul Sartre was France's most prominent intellectual who clamored to the defense of the Algerian National Liberation Front [FLN], and their terrorist methods.

When we place Sartre's writings on terror during the French-Algerian War within his discourse of a revolutionary politics centered on human freedom—a discourse that began with Robespierre's revolutionary politics—we see that terror becomes part of the daily order of revolution. Furthermore, I believe our examinations of Robespierre and Sartre will show that on some level the motivations and rationales behind terror in our world of democratic justice and humanist rhetoric are born out of our desires for justice and humanism. It does not follow that the historic people Robespierre and Sartre are in any way 'fundamentally' the same. Robespierre's personal life and habits can perhaps best be described as monastic whereas during the Algerian War, Sartre used daily cocktails of stimulants and depressants along with large quantities of alcohol in order to write and publish as much as possible; his love affairs outside of his longstanding relationship with Simone de Beauvoir are also somewhat legendary. What anachronistically ties the two figures together so well is their commitment to the humanist ideals of their political philosophies and the extent to which Robespierre and Sartre felt that the use of terrorist methods are justified in order to attain those ideals.

## Robespierre and Virtue-Terror

Under the leadership of Saint-Just, Robespierre, and Danton, the Reign of Terror occurred from September of 1793 to July of 1794 and consisted of mass arrests and executions aimed at destroying the enemies of the Revolution, including royalist supporters, foreign armies, and Louis XVI who was executed 21 January 1793. Already in August of 1790, Marat was suggesting in *L'Ami du peuple* that the Revolution turn the aristocracy's practices of inducing terror against them. On September 22, 1792, in response to reports of famine riots in Orléans, Georges Danton of the National Convention stated that "the law must be terrible, in order that the people, assured of legal redress, shall be peaceful and humane."

Danton further stated, "Let us be terrible in order to dispense the people from being so," presumably as a measure designed to instate certain state injustices rather than to allow the populace to commit those injustices on a larger scale. May 8, 1793, Robespierre addressed his fellow Jacobins and said that a revolutionary army needs to be formed "to inspire all enemies with terror." On the first of August, 1793, Danton declared, "Very well, then, let us be terrible; let us make war like lions." On September 5, in response to bread shortages and the fear of Royalist oppression, the Convention heard Barère's famous proclamation establishing a revolutionary army and making terror "the order of the day." On December 25, 1793, Robespierre boasts that "The French Army is not only a terror to the tyrants, it is the glory of humanity and of the nation." On February 6, 1794, Robespierre affirmed that all of the virtuous aspects of the Revolution are impotent without terror to enforce them. In these instances, political terrors were no longer arbitrary measures employed by an equally arbitrary government, but were the representations of the strength and power of the Revolution's sovereign jurisdiction over the destiny of the French people.

Robespierre's convictions about the terrorist measures of the Committee of Public Safety are especially intriguing, since they were not born of a warmongering, evil genius, but rather out of the revolutionary ideals of a man for whom total commitment to the Revolution's goals was unwavering. As Slavoj Zizek reminds us, in matters of war between nations, Robespierre was an isolationist and pacifist, if only because "war *among* nations as a rule serves as the means to obfuscate revolutionary struggle *within* each nation." That revolutionary struggle for Robespierre is best outlined in his *Report on the Principles of Political Morality*. Here, Robespierre outlined the wishes of the Convention as being "That France, once illustrious among enslaved nations, may, by eclipsing the glory of all free countries that ever existed, become a model to nations, a terror to oppressors, a consolation to the oppressed ... I speak of public virtue." The point of the Revolution for Robespierre is to remodel the past greatness of the French nation that was built on the illegitimate and arbitrary monarchical governments on the virtuous system of a democracy where the general will outlined by Rousseau finds its proper sovereign expression. Furthermore, that Rousseau's and Robespierre's goals were a by-product of the Enlightenment's ideals of human rights and expanded suffrage is as obvious to us as it was to Robespierre: "Resistance to oppression is the consequence of the other rights of man and of the citizen."

However, while future virtues of democracy are the goal of the Revolution, France is still in the midst of overcoming its oppressive past; in this instance, virtue is not enough. Robespierre states that "In this situation, your first political maxim should be, that the people are guided by reason, the enemies of the people driven by terror alone." Because the enemies of the Republic are outside the scope of reason, mediation through discourse or concession is ruled out. The only means proper to deal with people blind to reason is through terror: "If virtue be the spring of a popular government at times of peace, the spring of that government during a revolution is virtue combined with terror: virtue without which terror is destructive; terror, without which virtue is impotent." Terror is the only means prepared to ensure the security of the Republic when confronted with its enemies. Without the foundation of terror to secure and protect the Republic's virtues, virtue becomes "impotent." It is precisely because of the fact the Revolution strives for virtue that the Revolution also requires terror. Moreover, the very degree to which the Revolutionary government sees the need to use terror is also a measure of the irreconcilable nature of the monarchical government. Robespierre comments that "The measure of [the revolutionary government's] strength is the stubbornness and perfidy of its enemies; the more cruelly it proceeds against its enemies, the closer is its intimacy with the republicans." The equation formed by Robespierre hinges upon a reflexive relationship between terror and resistance: the amount of terror that is needed to subdue the enemies of the Revolution is directly related to the perceived strength of the counterrevolution and the subsequent strength of the government. Without an irreconcilable enemy, terror has no justification; the more irreconcilable the enemy is, the more terrible the revolutionary must be.

Robespierre also critiques the desire for a more "moderate" stance on revolutionary policies that calls into question the need for terrorism by use of his own brand of identity politics. Roughly stated, if the enemies of the Revolution are in fact *reconcilable*, then terror is not justified. According to, "aristocracy and moderantism govern us ... by the dangerous maxims with which they have blinded us!" Robespierre calls moderates "feigned revolutionaries" in disguise and labels them as being in the pockets of the aristocracy who only wish to slow the progress of the Revolution and contradict its aims and actions under the guise of careful deliberation. The moderates "[Tell] the truth with sparingness" and there is really no difference between them and the counterrevolutionaries: "They are servants of the same master." No moderate stance may exist between the Republic and its enemies; you are either wholly for or wholly against the actions of the Republic.

The human renewal for which Robespierre yearned was based upon the political philosophy of Jean-Jacques Rousseau. The modern situation of Enlightenment-era France, according to Rousseau, is marked by a fall from natural grace where society has given privilege to an *amour propre*, or enslaving vanity characteristic of aristocratic societies, whereas people should instead be governed by an *amour de soi*, or correct love of oneself according to humanity's free state in nature. The way that humanity frees and reestablishes itself according to Rousseau is the *contrat social* that expresses the abstract general will of the people over the selfish will of all. Those who go against the general will "shall be forced to be free;" if detractors from the general will prove to be irreconcilable, then death becomes a viable option for "only those who cannot be kept alive without danger." The dangers that Rousseau discusses, of course, are dangers to the social contract and the stability of the general will.

Taking his cues from Rousseau, Robespierre explains that "For tyrants [the Republic] is a scandal, for most people it is a miracle. It must be explained to all, so that at least all good citizens may be rallied around the principles of the general weal." In addressing the Convention, Robespierre states that "We intreat, that no private interest or secret motive be permitted here to usurp the place of the general will of the assembly or the eternal power of reason," and Robespierre calls the Convention "the sanctuary of truth" where the "founders of the republic, the avengers of humanity, the destroyers of tyrants" are gathered. The goal of the revolution was the expression of this Rousseauan renewed humanity embodied in the general will of the French people, and, according to Robespierre, when confronted by instability and the threat of the Revolution's downfall from both outside and inside France, the Revolution's virtue can be kept in tact only through terror.

Finally, Robespierre sees the use of terror in the Revolution as an historical necessity. A program of terror was the means by which the Revolutionaries would "fulfill the intentions of nature and *the destiny of man*, realize the promise of philosophy, and acquit providence of a long reign of crime and tyranny," as Robespierre said. The "destiny of man" was "the dawn of the bright day of universal happiness" and the end toward which the Revolution worked. Thus, the Revolutionaries reset the calendar during the Revolution back to Year One as a commemoration of a rebirth and dawn of a new era. The founding of The Cult of the Supreme Being, a new religion with reason and autonomy as its highest principles, also evoked the feeling that something very new and historically unprecedented was being done. For the perpetrators of the Terror, however, the events were not merely unprecedented, but also historically *destined*. And this is a point at the center of all revelatory-revolutionary truths: that there is a better tomorrow that can be worked for; the very possibility of that tomorrow in fact and truth becomes a universalized obligation for all affected by the revolution. There can be no moderate stances, no hesitation—if you are with the revolution, then be prepared for virtue; if you are against the revolution, be prepared to be terrorized.

## Algeria and Sartre's *Fraternité-Terreur*

For Sartre, the French-Algerian War marks a turning point in both the focus of his political engagements and his philosophical views. When the Algerian War broke out in November of 1954, the French intellectual community was still in the process of dealing with the scandals in Eastern Europe and the USSR. Despite the apparent credit that the USSR had to its name after the victory of the Allied powers in the Second World War, which might have made internal purges and the dissolution of civil liberties excusable, the reoccurrence of totalitarian practices in Eastern Europe was not so easily over-looked; the Algerian War and other crises in the colonial world provided a relatively new arena for the French intellectual community to test out their hypotheses of social reform and liberation that left behind the political baggage of Soviet projects. After Sartre broke with the *Parti communiste français* [PCF] in 1947 over interpretations of the events in Hungary, revolution in the third world countries such as Algeria, Cuba, and Brazil came to the fore of his attention. Likewise, where Sartre's earlier philosophical mainstay, *L'être et néant* [*Being and Nothingness*, 1943], dealt mainly with issues of conflicting freedoms on an internal ontological level, his main work of the fifties and sixties, *Critique de la raison dialectique* [*Critique of Dialectical Reason*, 1960], deals with issues arising out of conflicting freedoms in a world of material scarcity and the forms of social interaction and social institutions that arise therein. A brief overview of the *Critique*'s themes will be useful in framing Sartre's more specific statements on terrorism in Algeria.

In contrast to Robespierre's vision, as well as the views of Hegel and Marx, of historically determined progress toward human liberation, Sartre held that history is an open-ended endeavor and it is impossible to be grasped in its totality. The goal of the *Critique*, was to lay bare the logic by which historical processes work. For Sartre, historical relations between people are based on a system of reciprocity over material goods that can be expressed in both positive and negative terms. Material goods are either shared between those recognized as part of a group, or denied to those outside of that group. The system of reciprocal relations in a world of scarcity, in turn, becomes the driving forces of history and politics. When reciprocity is expressed negatively, as refusal to cooperate or as oppression, humans are then seen in Manichaean terms, as good and evil, human and sub-/ "antihuman." This Manichaeism then becomes the basis for violent relations between people. In response to the violence and categorization of the "antihuman," people join together into groups to express their own humanity and unite under a common unifying force, what Sartre labels "the pledge" [*le serment*].

The humanist appeals of the past two centuries, for Sartre, have only been oppressive forms of "bourgeois humanism." The humanist appeals of the Enlightenment were solely reserved for the bourgeois European community; furthermore, this European group's identity was predicated upon an opposing nonhuman group, i.e. the peoples of colonized or third world nations. "Bourgeois humanism" is then a humanism that "is the counterpart of racism: it is [the] practice of exclusion." In Algeria, this process of racism and exclusion is manifest; the colonial situation is embodied in a Manichaeism that "makes the Muslim *other than man*." The war in Algeria is then to be seen as violence in reaction to the violence of colonial repression and in order to express the Algerian claim as human.

Under the status of the group's pledge, the measure used to insure the humanity of the group from both within and without is "Terror." According to Sartre, "Everyone recognizes violence in the other third party [the group's unifier or figurehead] as the agreed impossibility of turning back, of reverting to the statute of sub-humanity" and the Terror "is a terror *which unites* rather than a terror which separates." Terror then, becomes one of the necessary conditions for the operation and preservation of the group in history "And *all the internal behavior of common individuals* (fraternity, love, friendship, as well as anger and lynching) derives its terrible power from Terror itself." The massacres at Mélouza as well as urban terrorism in Algiers or Paris are thus, under this model, to be viewed as a means for preserving the solidarity of the FLN's resistance to French colonialism, and the only actions viable to reverse the violence inherent in France's colonial practices.

Sartre's first written statement on the war in Algeria and the legitimacy of the FLN's use of terrorism occurred on January 27, 1956 in a speech entitled *"Le colonialisme est un système"* ["Colonialism is a System"], addressed to the *Comité d'action contre la poursuite de la guerre en Afrique du Nord* [Committee for the Action Against the War in North Africa]. Following the argument laid by Sartre's colleagues Francis and Collette Jeanson in *L'algérie hors la loi* [*Outlaw Algeria*, 1955], Sartre denounces what he labels the "neo-colonialist mystification" that seeks to situate the problems in Algeria in either economic, social, or psychological terms but refuses to acknowledge the situation as fundamentally political. Sartre categorized the colonial system as fundamentally dualist, portraying the colonizers as good and human while portraying the colonized as evil and "sub human," and therefore deserving of exploitation. The Manichaean nature of the colonial world also does not allow for moderation between extremes. There is no such thing as a good or a bad colonizer, just as there is no such thing as the "semi-violent repression" of which the moderate political theorist and contemporary of Sartre, Raymond Aron, spoke. Note here the similarity in Sartre and Robespierre's stances on political moderation. According to Sartre, the only thing for the Algerian people to do was to "First of all overcome resistance, smash the framework, subdue, terrorize."

Already, Sartre had come to the conclusion that the French colonialist system was antithetical to the Algerian identity and action other than violent action such as terrorism would only prolong colonial exploitation under new guises. Sartre stated that "Algerian nationalism is not simply a revival of ancient traditions, old attachments; it is the only way for the Algerians to put an end to their exploitation." The FLN has therefore taken from the violence of the colonial system, turned it back upon France, and "have shown the hesitant that no solution was possible other than force."

In the introduction to Albert Memmi's book *Portrait du colonizé précedé par portrait du colonisateur* [*Portrait of the Colonized, Preceded by Portrait of the Colonizer*], published in July of 1957, Sartre further elaborates on the necessity of violence and terrorism. Sartre explained that the French "Conquest [of Algeria] was achieved by violence; over-exploitation and oppression demand the maintenance of violence" in the colonial system and it is only by violence that the Algerians can escape the colonial system. Furthermore, Sartre transported the familiar Marxist interpretation of class struggle to the colonial context by labeling the Algerian people "the agricultural sub-proletariat," asserting that "the secret of the proletariat, Marx once said, is that it carries within itself the destruction of bourgeois society. We must be thankful to [Albert] Memmi for reminding us that the colonized also have their secret, and that we are witnessing the awful death throes of colonialism."

Sartre's Preface to *The Wretched of the Earth* took the analyses of the *Critique* and applied them to the specific conclusions about colonialism developed by the Martinician psychologist Frantz Fanon. While the French colonial system and its neocolonial apologists want their "humanism to be universal," the racist structure of not only the colonial system and its constituent humanism differentiates colonizer from colonized. The bourgeois humanism of colonial Algeria at once demands and denies the human condition of the Muslim population and this "explosive contradiction" fosters an atmosphere where "Europeans are massacred at sight." Furthermore, because "it is not first of all *their* [Algerian] violence, it is ours [French]," the violent reaction on the side of the Algerians is the only way to reconcile the violence of the colonial system. According to Sartre, "the truth [is] that no indulgence can erase the marks of violence: violence alone can eliminate them." Political, social, or economic reforms do not have the power to right the wrongs of the colonial system; violence alone has the ability to do so.

In the annihilation of the colonial violence comes the reassertion of the human identity of the colonized. Sartre believed that Fanon "shows clearly that this irrepressible violence [...] is man reconstructing himself." Since the Algerian militant is the "offspring of violence, he draws every moment of his humanity from it: we were man at his expense, he becomes man at ours." The assertion of Algerian humanity through violence shows that "the power struggle has been reversed, decolonization is in progress; all our mercenaries can try and do is delay its completion." Moreover, this "striptease" of European humanism—revealing it for what it really is—represents another stage in "The history of man." According to Sartre, the "rural masses" are the embodiment of the anti-colonial struggle and are "the true reservoir for the national and revolutionary army." Fanon's work shows the rural Algerians as the true motivation or "midwife" behind the progress of history just as Marx, Engels, and Sorel similarly showed the proletariat as the class of historical destiny.

Recently, Marguerite la Caze made the case that "Sartre's stance seems to articulate the logic of terrorism rather than to approve of it." La Caze believes that Sartre wanted his audiences to "understand" terrorist violence, without ever condoning it and that Sartre's "words simply accept violence as the result of oppression." This line of reasoning, however, leaves the following question unanswered: 'What recourse do the oppressed have at their disposal to regain their humanity?' On this point Sartre is clear during the period of the Algerian War—violence, including terrorist violence, "is man reconstructing himself." Sartre's approval of the FLN's use of terrorism shows not only a close commitment to ending the oppressive French-colonial system in Algeria but also the belief that the terror imbued by bombs hurled into crowded cafes was a necessary and creative force used in the assertion of Algerian human dignity. The sub human becomes humanized; the disparate Muslims, Berbers, Kabyles, and Arabs become the Algerian people.

## Conclusions

The contemporary philosopher Jean-François Lyotard recently pondered whether Saint-Just, Robespierre's right hand man in the Reign of Terror, knew "that terror would be the lot of a world devoted to freedom?" The main political imperatives of both Robespierre's and Sartre's *milieux* in many ways were the same. Robespierre was determined to see the birth of a French Republic that upheld the rights and human dignity of all its citizens. As Albert Soboul reminds us, the Terror was not just a program of violence, but also the name given to the political, cultural and economic reforms that were to rid France of political corruption and ties to the old regime. Sartre viewed the plight of colonized Algeria as the new stage upon which the logic of history would unfold. The systematic dehumanization and exploitation of Algeria was to give way to a newly minted conception of Algerian humanity, one not predicated upon the wealth and dominance of Europe. Both men also saw the instrumental use of violence designed to evoke fear and terror into the enemies of the revolutionary goals they supported was a necessary and justified means to achieve their political goals.

The Reign of Terror, of course, did not last forever—the "White Terror" that followed Robespierre's red one was in many ways just as brutal as its predecessor and the glorious buttress of universal truths and human equality that Robespierre envisioned for the France of the future played back seat to numerous coups and revolutions, themselves dedicated to renew and rebuild France in its 'proper' image.

The legacies of the French-Algerian War in the recent history of both France and Algeria since the signing of the Evian Accords that ended it have kept alive questions about French humanist ideals. The student protests of 1968 in France and the subsequent "generation of '68" received Sartre's calls for colonial liberation with open arms. Today, however, political dialogue in France centers more on Enlightenment ideals of universal human rights, freedom, and Western individualism. In response, the same past critiques of colonialism have reemerged in the present post-colonial political context. Goux and Wood ask, "Is, for example, a Western universalism that subordinates local cultures to the increasingly constrictive imperatives of the global capitalist market simply a more pacific, insidious form of imperialism than its colonial predecessor, or is it instead a ferment of planetary liberation, as our political masters would have us believe?"

Although the war was technically a success for Algeria from the professed goals of the FLN, the political system established after war went into disarray in 1988 at the hands of politically charged Islamist movements. The movements of the Islamists and their promises of Messianic renewal and purging of harmful western values mirrored statements made by FLN supporters during the French-Algerian War. In essence, argues Benjamin Stora, Algeria has "entered a second—and identical—Algerian war" where even those who fought against the French are labeled as the "new *pieds noirs*," or colonizers themselves.

Furthermore, Robespierre and Sartre's political goals continue to foreground the political discourse of the modern world. With human rights, political freedom, and economic equity at the head of world policy, we find terrorism behind every corner. The France and Algeria of today, as they were in the past, continue to be confronted with this set of alternatives to viewing the ethics of human interaction that were born in the Enlightenment and post-Enlightenment. Both alternatives have been assigned blame for either the existence of or the need for terrifying action. The question remains open as to whether neither option presented is fundamentally right, or whether the right option has merely not been either properly conceived or practiced.

If Sartre's indictment of "bourgeois humanism" was ultimately on the right track—dispensing of the damaging paradigm human/sub- antihuman—but merely did not go far enough to dispense of humanism in any and all incarnations, then Slavoj Žižeck's question, "does the (often deplorable) actuality of the revolutionary terror compel us to reject the very idea of Terror, or is there a way to *repeat* it in today's different historical constellation, to redeem its virtual content from its actualization?" For Žižeck's part, he believes that "It can and *should* be done, and the most concise formula of repeating the event designated by the name 'Robespierre' is: to pass from (Robespierre's) [and I would argue Sartre's, as well] humanist terror to antihumanist (or, rather, inhuman) terror."

**References**

Blakemore, Steven. "Revolution in Language." In *Representing the French Revolution: literature historiography and art*. Edited by James A.W. Hefferman, 3-22. Hanover; London: University Press of New England, 1992.

Danton, Georges Jacques. *Speeches of Georges Jacques Danton*. Translated by André Fribourg. New York: International Publishers, 1928.

*Dictionnaire de L'Académie française*, 4th ed., s.v. "terreur."

*Dictionnaire de L'Académie française*, 5th ed., s.v. "terreur."

*Dictionnaire de L'Académie française*, 5th ed., s.v "terrorisme."

*Dictionnaire de L'Académie française*, 5th ed., s.v "terroriste."

Goux, Jean-Joseph, Philip R. Wood. "Introduction." In *Terror and Consensus: Vicissitudes of French Thought*. Edited by Jean-Joseph Goux and Philip R. Wood, 1-13. Stanford: Stanford University Press, 1998.

Kelley, George Armstrong. "Conceptual Sources of the Terror." *Eighteenth-Century Studies* 14, no. 1 (Autumn, 1980): 18-36.

La Caze, Marguerite. "Sartre Integrating Ethics and Politics: The Case of Terrorism." *Parrhesia* 3 (2007): 43. [journal online]. Available from http://www.parrhesia.org; Internet. Accessed 28 March, 2008.

Lyotard, Jean-François. "Terror on the Run." Translated by Philip R. Wood and Graham Harris. In *Terror and Consensus: Vicissitudes of French Thought*. Edited by Jean-Joseph Goux and Philip R. Wood, 25-36. Stanford: Stanford University Press, 1998.

Ozouf, Mona. "Danton." In *Critical Dictionary of the French Revolution*. Edited by François Furet and Mona Ozouf, 213-223. Translated by Arthur Goldhammer. Cambridge, Mass: Harvard University Press, 1989.

Robespierre, Maximilien. *Draft Declaration of the Rights of Man*. In *Slavoj Žižeck Presents Robespierre, Virtue and Terror*. Translated by John Howe, 66-72. London; New York: Verso, 2007.

—— *In Favor of an Armed People, of a War Against the Vendée*. In *Speeches of Maximilien Robespierre*. New York: International Publishers, 1927.

—— *Report on the Principles of a Revolutionary Government*. In *Speeches of Maximilien Robespierre*. New York: International Publishers, 1927.

—— *Report Upon the Principles of Political Morality*. Translated from a copy printed by order of the Convention. Philadelphia: M.DCC.XCIV [1794].

—— *The Social Contract*. Translated by Susan Dunn. In The Social Contract and The First and Second Discourses. Edited by Susan Dunn, 149-254. New Haven; London: Yale University Press, 2002.

Sartre, Jean-Paul. "Colonialism is a System." In *Colonialism and Neocolonialism*. Translated by Azzedine Haddour, Steve Brewer, and Terry McWilliams, 30-47. London; New York: Routledge, 2001.

—— *Critique of Dialectical Reason*. Vol. I. Translated by Alan Sheridan-Smith. London; New York: Verso, 1991.

———. "Preface." *The Wretched of the Earth*. Translated by Richard Philcox. New York: Grove Press, 2004.

Smith, Tony. "Idealism and People's War: Sartre on Algeria." *Political Theory* 1, no. 4 (Nov., 1973): 426-449.

Soboul, Albert. *A Short History of the French Revolution: 1789-1799*. Translated by Geoffrey Symcox. Berkeley; Los Angeles; London: University of California Press, 1965.

Stora, Benjamin. *Algeria 1830-200: A Short Introduction*. Translated by Jane Marie Todd. Ithaca: Cornell University Press, 2001.

Taine, Hippolyte. *The Origins of Contemporary France*, ed. and Translated by Edward T. Gargan. Chicago: University of Chicago Press, 1974.

Žižeck, Slavoj. "Robespierre, or, the 'Divine Violence' of Terror." In *Slavoj Žižeck Presents Robespierre, Virtue and Terror*. Translated by John Howe, VII-XXXIX. London; New York: Verso, 2007.

# THE IMPORTANCE OF PROPAGANDA FOR GERMANY'S FASCIST REGIME: A COMPARISON OF TWO ACADEMIC ACCOUNTS

*Beatrice Marry*

The Nazi regime relied heavily on propaganda as a tool for promoting its political ideology, thereby creating a new sense of German identity and political reality. This usage of propaganda as a means of redefining reality has had a lasting impact on creating a sense of communal identity in modern societies. In the context of this paper, ideology is defined as a set of political ideas that construct a belief system, while propaganda is specified as the spread of information to promote such ideological belief systems so as to influence the actions or ideas of people. The two terms are closely interlinked, which warrants an examination of propaganda as a vehicle for German fascist ideology. This paper intends to examine the importance of Nazi propaganda by discussing two academic accounts: 'The Primacy of Politics' by Sheri Berman and 'Stalinism and Nazism: Dictatorships in Comparison' edited and co-authored by Ian Kershaw and Moshe Lewin.

Berman and Kershaw and Lewin provide excellent historical chronicles; however their main focus differs in important ways. Kershaw and Lewin focus on Stalinism and Nazism with the goal of comparing their dictatorships. Berman, on the other hand, wants to account for the rise of social democracy in Europe by emphasizing the importance of ideology as expressed in party politics. In spite of these different emphases, both accounts are comparable, because they share a similar methodological approach in the form of historical process tracing and because both include insightful and complementary passages on German fascism.

In Berman's view, ideologies "exist at the juncture between theory and practice" (Berman 2006, 10), with parties as their de facto 'carriers'. Consequently, Berman does not distinguish between ideology and propaganda, but regards ideology as a concept that encompasses both terms. Kershaw and Lewin similarly fail to define propaganda other than mentioning that it delineates a form of "ideological abuse" (Kershaw and Lewin 1997, 4). This paper attempts to show that both accounts would have benefited from making a distinction between ideology as a political belief system and propaganda as the means of promoting that belief system.

Berman argues that European fascism had its roots in socialist ideas, but that fascism also distanced itself from other forms of socialism, for example by emphasizing the importance of private property (Berman 2006, 125, 140). According to Berman, fascist ideology utilized the rise of nationalism by providing the public with a new sense of communal identity tied closely to the nation-state. Furthermore, what made German fascism popular with the masses was its ability to create political support by appropriating the political platform of the incapacitated social-democratic German opposition party (SPD), thereby seemingly consolidating the interests of the bourgeoisie with those of the working classes (Berman 2006, 141). Berman's account of ideology greatly contributes to understanding why both left-leaning academic elites and politicians shifted over to the fascist right, because she does not only focus on the nationalist components of fascism, but also on its common socialist roots (Berman 2006, 17). However, Berman's approach to the rise of German fascism lacks precision because it fails to recognize propaganda as a crucial tool with the help of which German fascism re-appropriated key cultural and political ideas.

For instance, the Nazis redefined German identity by appropriating the concept of the *Volk* and tying it to an ethnic understanding of 'Germanness' in the form of the 'Aryan race'. There are two competing ideas of the Volk: one universalistic, the other tied to Prussian militarism during the 'Second Reich' (Vick 2003). The universalistic understanding of the Volk was outlined by the famous writers of the German romanticist movement, most prominently Novalis, Kleist, Hegel, Schelling, Schiller and Goethe. Goethe, the most important writer of the Romantic Movement, understood himself to be a 'Weltbuerger' or a citizen of the world. The Romanticists' understanding of the Volk, while tied to the nation-state, was not meant to be exclusionary. Rather, it was based on a universalistic approach to humanity and a form of nature mysticism that emphasized the spiritual ties between all human beings and nature (Vick 2003).

The Nazi regime aligned itself with this tradition of 'German mysticism' by mixing the cultural understanding of the Volk as 'a united community of Germans' with its contrasting military and exclusivist conception. The latter was used by the Prussian regime to delineate German 'virtues', such as work ethic, organization, obedience and diligence. The Nazi regime tied the two contradictory understandings of the 'Volk' to ethnicity and nationality, resulting in the fascist concept of 'Germanness'. An analysis of this appropriation of culture in the form of language is crucial, because it shows how the Nazis redefined and politicized notions of German identity.

Propaganda, in the form of posters and movies, served to promote this new ideological belief system that relied on the conception of the German *Volk* as essentially fascist. While Kershaw's account mentions political speeches as a form of promoting Hitler's 'grand vision' (Kershaw and Lewin 1997,105), Kershaw disregards the ways in which Hitler and his belief system were iconicized in the form of propagandist movies. Those propaganda movies provided a canvas for Nazi ideology via the means of heroic imagery and grand scale productions worthy of any Hollywood film. The image was therefore closely tied to the fascist belief system: Nazi propaganda dictated that to be German was to be fascist and to believe in the value of the German Volk was to exclude and ultimately eradicate those that were not of pure blood. Consequently, the success of the political ideas of the Nazis not only resulted from the utilization of their opponents' political ideology, as Berman suggests; it was also an outcome of the regime's intricate propaganda machine.

Although Berman recognizes that the Nazi's distinction between 'raffendes/ rapacious' and 'schaffendes/creative' capital enabled them to formulate an ideological "cross-class approach" (Berman 2006, 141), she does not explicitly mention the usage of language as a propagandist tool. Berman also fails to comprehend the significance of propaganda as a bridging mechanism that not only existed in the political arena, but that also permeated the 'apolitical' cultural and visual realm of German society. Just as the rise of fascism cannot be understood without examining the socialist roots of fascist ideology, the rise of German fascism cannot be understood without examining the ways in which it used propagandist means of self-promotion that established the Nazi's belief system outside of the traditional political arena and anchored it in Germany's communal psyche.

Omar Bartov, a co-author of Lewin and Kershaw, recognizes Nazi propaganda as a tool that tied the Nazis' political goals to the new sense of 'Germanness.' More specifically, Bartov interprets the *Blitzkrieg* as a large-scale industrial approach to killing that was justified by the Nazis as a means of preserving the "Volksgemeinschaft" community of the fascist German nation (Kershaw and Lewin 1997, 177). Thus, Bartov contends that the Blitzkrieg not only constituted "a new manner of deploying and employing forces" (Kershaw and Lewin 1997, 171), but that it also used propaganda in new ways. The *Volksgemeinschaft* was therefore both a "propagandistic myth," and "a social reality" (Kershaw and Lewin 1997, 172). Bartov hints at the fact that the term of the Volk was utilized to create other Nazi catchphrases, such as the term 'Volkssturm' that described a "mobilization campaign" (Kershaw and Lewin 1997, 85) intended to create a reserve army composed of the "true 'people's community" (Kershaw and Lewin 1997, 85). The concept of the Volkssturm exemplifies the disjuncture between the Nazi's egalitarian rhetoric and the reality of the Nazi regime: while the officers of the Volkssturm were selected from the ranks of the Nazi's political party, Germany's young and elderly men were sacrificed in a last attempt of defending the 'Reich.' Again, this disjuncture that Bartov mentions, was bridged and consolidated by Nazi propaganda, thereby delineating a new form of 'reality' that was fed to the German public.

Bartov raises the question of the relationship between the modern state and war by arguing that "Marxist-oriented" (Kershaw and Lewin 1997, 172) interpretations of the Blitzkrieg underestimate its significance for understanding the German fascists' usage of propaganda and the continued significance of propaganda in the context of modernity. According to Bartov, the Blitzkrieg's depiction of "modern warfare as fast, heroic and glamorous"

(Kershaw and Lewin 1997, 15) had a lasting impact on the portrayal of war by modern mass communication and can still be found in the news coverage of the 21st century (Kershaw and Lewin 1997, 15).

Bartov also shows that after the 1940s, the fascists were no longer in unison with the industrialized forces of modernity, but rather conceptualized the war as "a struggle between the German spirit and the cold, inhuman technology of the enemy" (Kershaw and Lewin 1997, 179), which shows that Nazi propaganda was not static, but dynamic in the sense that it managed to constantly alter itself. This re-conceptualization left Germans in an ambiguous state based on "two competing images of their war" (Kershaw and Lewin 1997, 180). Following Bartov's argument, these two images are perhaps similar to the two competing definitions of the Volk, which likewise continue to haunt Germany's sense of identity. The long-lasting confusion that Bartov mentions serves as a testament to the power of the Nazi propaganda machine.

Due to these two competing images of the Blitzkrieg, Bartov suggests that the Blitzkrieg needs to be understood as both a form of strategic reality and the means of representing that reality in the form of the image of the war (Kershaw and Lewin 1997, 181). This distinction explains the continued fascination with modern forms of warfare in spite of their gruesome results, suggests Bartov. It also allocates greater significance to the overall impact of propaganda in the Nazi regime and can explain the continued existence of propaganda as a way of utilizing the masses, defining subjects of the state and delineating forms of allegiance. Similarly, Mommsen (another co-author of Kershaw and Lewin) postulates that Nazi propaganda reflected the "increasingly fictitious world" that Hitler created and that mirrored his "mounting loss of any sense of reality" (Kershaw and Lewin 1997, 85). Mommsen shows that the fascist propaganda machine constituted an aspect of reality creation that has since come to be recognized as an essential part of modernity.

In sum, Berman interprets the rise of fascism from a purely ideological perspective that locates fascism in the past and firmly ties ideology to the political realm in the form of party politics, while Lewin and his co-authors examine the future implications of ideology by analyzing the ways in which fascist propaganda and imagery have permeated modern political 'popular culture' and communal identity. Although they do not always explicitly discuss the concept of propaganda, Bartov and Mommsen show that the strength of Nazi propaganda lies in its simultaneous versatility and widespread applicability, allowing it to function as a tool outside of the political realm in areas traditionally dubbed as 'apolitical' and therefore insignificant. Arguably, the Nazis managed to penetrate this apolitical realm in the form of seemingly simple and yet powerful statements, both visual and linguistic. Even though Hitler has generally been portrayed as a non-academic brute, he seems to have understood the basic need for a renewed pride in what it meant to be German and he managed to address that need through his usage of propaganda. The Nazis' strength resulted from the fact that they had a comprehensive approach to politics that allowed them to anchor fascist ideas outside of the political realm in the foundations of German culture, restoring a battered sense of German nationhood. By defining catch phrases for complex political processes that could easily be understood by the masses and that were constantly repeated in the form of propaganda (i.e. 'Volkssturm'), the Nazis permeated the German psyche and influenced German identity for years to come. Consequently, the Nazi regime not only mass fabricated weaponry and death camps, but ideas and belief systems as well—those ideas were accepted by the German public and came to delineate reflections of reality rather than political constructs. Herein lies the perverted genius of Nazi propaganda.

Leni Riefenstahl, the close friend of Hitler and filmmaker that produced the Nazi propaganda movies was arrested but never convicted for her role in perpetuating the war crimes of the Nazi regime. In spite of her close political association with the Nazis and the subject matter she depicted, critics hailed her on the grounds of her artistic talents. Arguably, this shows the continued disregard for the role of political propaganda in gaining mass support and committing crimes against humanity.

The mass fabrication of ideas in the form of propaganda continues to be found in many aspects of modern society and can equally be observed in modern advertising and political campaigns. Politicians of today also continue to appeal to a sense of national community. Some have even resorted to popular culture as an alternative to the political realm, while others began their careers in the movies and then transitioned into politics. The realm of popular culture has already proven itself to be equally effective if not more so than the political realm, because it transcends the widespread political apathy that seems to have become a defining characteristic of modern 'western' societies.

The accounts of Berman, as well as Kershaw, Lewin and their co-authors would have benefited from explicitly including the concept of propaganda in their respective analyses so as to distinguish between the workings of theoretical/ideological and social/ propagandist constructs. Such an approach would have allowed for a more nuanced interpretation of fascist regimes and for the examination of political ideology outside of the 'traditional' political realm (i.e. in the realm of culture). Finally, perhaps the greatest strength of propaganda in both the fascist and the modern contexts lies in its ability to bridge the cultural and the political while remaining virtually unnoticed at the same time serving as a lasting testament to the Nazi's propaganda machine.

## References

Berman, Sheri. 2006. *The primacy of politics: Social democracy and the making of Europe's twentieth century.* Cambridge Univ. Press.

Kershaw, Ian and Moshe Lewin, eds. 1997. *Stalinism and Nazism: Dictatorships in comparison.* Cambridge Univ. Press.

Vick, Brian. 2003. "The origins of the German Volk: Cultural purity and national identity in nineteenth-century Germany." *German Studies Review*, 26, no. 2: 241-256.

# The Man with the Hissing Bomb: Anarchism and Terror in the North American Imagination

*Richard JF Day*

## Introduction

This paper deals with the construction of anarchists as terrorist subjects within popular North American discourse throughout the nineteenth, twentieth, and twenty-first centuries. Although it is certainly true that anarchists, from Alexander Berkman to Ann Hansen, have from time-to-time taken part in violent direct action, it is easy to show that the vast majority of their theory and practice has been oriented not to taking or destroying state and corporate institutions, but to resisting and peacefully constructing alternatives to them.

It is also easy to show that, more often than not, anarchists who are accused of violence are being singled out not for what they have done, but for who they are. The most famous example is, of course, the US state's response to the so-called 'Haymarket riot'. "Not because you caused the Haymarket bomb," the judge intoned, "but because you are Anarchists, you are on trial."[1] What is it about anarchists that allows them to be jailed and killed just for existing, without ever a peep of protest from mainstream liberal citizens who would be outraged if anyone else were treated that way? Why do they inspire such terror in the heart of the state, or more precisely, in the hearts of those whose daily lives reproduce the relationships necessary to the maintenance of the state form? Why are there such strong links between anarchism and racialized modes of Othering? These and related questions will be explored from a historical / Lacanian psychoanalytic perspective.

## The Anarchist Other—Today

Although anarchism always runs like an underground stream hidden beneath the surface of the corporate mass media, it does occasionally erupt into view. In North America this happened most recently, and most spectacularly, after the protests against the World Trade Organization in Seattle in 1999. Figure 1. shows an 'anarchist' 'patronizing' Starbucks. One might well ask who is patronizing whom here.

---

1. Cited in Goldman, E. 'The Psychology of Political Violence' in *Anarchism and Other Essays*. New York: Dover, 1969, p. 55.

Engaging Terror

> **COFFEE TO GO** An anarchist patronizes a Seattle Starbucks
>
> ment with the sort of self-sufficient, egalitarian collective now aborning at 918 Virginia Street, a largely vacant building on the edge of downtown Seattle. The "squat" popped up two weeks ago as a protesters' crash pad. About 100 people a night sleep there. There's no power or water, but organizers have set up a kitchen

**Figure 1.** *Time Magazine*
'How Organized Anarchists Led Seattle into Chaos'
By MICHAEL KRANTZ; Steven Frank/Seattle and Margot Hornblower/
Los Angeles Monday, Dec. 13, 1999

There is absolutely nothing about this person that identifies him or her as an anarchist—no circle A patches, no black leather, not even a full facial ski mask. It does appear that the subject in question is wearing a bandana, but that was standard equipment for everyone (and their dogs) during the early 00's era of mass protests.

All we know for sure is that this is someone who is happy to grab a free pound or two of Starbuck's coffee if given a chance. The identification with anarchism comes from a network of discursive regularities upon which the caption writer is relying: this person is not only going through the window, he probably broke it, too; there has been violence against property and violence against property is something only anarchists do; therefore, this person is an anarchist.

The Starbucks example is from the USA, but we can see the same effect in Canadian mass media. The image in Figure 2 is from the Quebec City protest against the Summit of the Americas in 2001. Again, the caption is an important part of the working up of the image: 'police clash with anarchists known as the Black Bloc'. And again, there is absolutely nothing about any of these people that tells us what their political commitments or identifications might be. They could be skinheads, trotskyists, ecofeminists, or Christians who are fighting to save their separate (but still public) school boards from NAFTA intervention. However, they are fighting with police, so they must be anarchists.

RICHARD JF DAY

# Summit protest turns violent

Police clash with anarchists known as the Black Bloc at the perimeter fence surrounding meeting venues of the Summit of the Americas in Quebec City, Friday.

## Undercover police arrest B.C. protest leader amid clash

By KATE JAIMET, PATRICIA BAILEY, [...]

**Figure 2.** *Vancouver Sun* p. A1, Saturday April 21, 2001

But if we really want to know how anarchists figure in the popular North American imagination, we must turn to Hollywood. *The Anarchist Cookbook* (Dir. Jordan Susman, 2002) follows a group of nice, white, harmless, middle class suburban kids who are seduced into a vortex of drugs, sex, and violence by 'Johnny Black', a self-professed 'nihilist' (Nietzsche's ears surely get sore every time he hears this guy talk) and anarchist ecoterrorist. Like the man with the hissing bomb before him, Black 'believes in nothing' and blows stuff up mostly for the fun of it.

By being associated so strongly with senseless violence, anarchists are cast as radically other to the dominant societies in which they reside, which are presented as liberal, democratic, and peace-loving. But this is not the only way this distancing is effectuated. An equally potent and long-lived method is the racialization of anarchist activists and activism.

Here we see two people of colour representing anarchism, one of whom is noted to be a 'refugee' from Mexico in the caption. In the body of the article, the reporter finds it necessary to mention that the other person's parents 'came to Canada from India before he was born'. Because Jaggi Singh was

# Engaging Terror

Figure 3. *Vancouver Sun* p. A14, Saturday June 3, 2000

born in Canada, is a Canadian citizen, and has lived here most of his life, extra effort is needed to find a way to cast him as a foreigner.

If we look at the broader context of the racialization of dissent in the Canadian mass media, we can perhaps see why this sort of effort is necessary.

Figure 4 is a page rife with found poetry, which just happens to contain the photo of 'black bloc anarchists' fighting with the police at Quebec City to which I have already referred. It connects then-NDP premier of BC, Ujal Dosanjh, with a hidden past as part of 'radical Sikh groups' in India. It is, of course, Sikh militants who have been blamed for the famous attack on an Air India flight out of Vancouver, and several Sikh nationalist organizations in Canada appear on the official terrorism list. At the time, Dosanjh was seen as some sort of 'leftist', from the point of view of the rabidly neoliberal *Vancouver Sun*, so it made sense to associate him with his even crazier brethren.

Just to be sure that no one thinks this the Vancouver Sun is a racist hate-paper, the composers of this page have provided evidence that *some* people who come to Canada from India are peaceful and nice—like Deepak Chopra, for example, the 'popular spiritualist guru'. The links are subtle, for a mass-market newspaper, but also very clear, even though they are logically incoherent (now it's Aristotle who is pissed): Ujal Dosanjh as a Sikh radical, is clearly a terrorist. The anarchist Jaggi Singh, whose name reveals that he also comes from a Sikh background, must also be a terrorist.

RICHARD JF DAY

**Figure 4.** *Vancouver Sun* p. A1, Saturday April 21, 2001

It's important to note that all of this ideological work is done just with headlines and photographs—who knows better than newspapers that very few people can be bothered to read these days? However, for those who do venture into the perilous territory of sentences and even perhaps ... paragraphs ... there are rewards to be had, further and more detailed proof of the links between anarchism, terror, and violence. The 'New Anarchists' article mentioned above, in the discussion of Figure 3, provides many excellent examples.

> For much of the past 60 years, the currents of anarchism crackled softly in the relative obscurity of coffee houses and university campuses. That changed suddenly in May 1995, when the New York Times and Washington Post published the 35,000-word political manifesto of a mysterious domestic terrorist known only as the Unabomber. Its publication would lead to the arrest of mathematics professor Ted Kaczynski ... and provide inspiration to radical anarchists worldwide.

The writer of the article seems not to know, or not to care, that the social anarchists associated with the anti-globalization movement would almost

409

unanimously disavow any sort of connection with lone-wolf libertarians such as Kaczynski. He is, rather, the hero of the Michigan Militia and other related right-wing capitalist formations. Yet somehow he appears in this article as an 'anarchist icon' who has inspired us all to wreak 'havoc', 'mayhem' and 'destruction' on a benign and apparently defenseless society.

This fear is echoed in a Canadian Department of Justice report on the Anti-Terrorism Act, written by one of my colleagues at Queen's University, Robert Martyn. He notes that 'the decline in marxism as a viable political theory' has led to an accompanying decline in 'visible marxist terrorist groups'. Others, however, have stepped up to the plate:

> ... Canada remains inherently vulnerable ... we are threatened by the same disenfranchised terrorists that despise the US.... Anarchist and nihilist groups pose a great threat, in that countering their irregular strategy and often absence of political demands cause security forces to rely almost exclusively on luck.[2]

This rhetorical line is particularly humorous to anyone who knows anything about the radical political landscape in North America, or anywhere else in the global North for that matter. Nihilist factions blowing things up? Nihlilism has become rather more passive and mainstream than that, and is more likely to be found in the Shell boardroom or an advertising agency than in an anarchist affinity group.

It is interesting to note, though, how a tactic that we might call 'threat-borrowing' is being deployed in the Canadian mass media. Nothing much in the way of spectacular destructive poetry a la 911 has ever happened in Canada, but this doesn't prevent Professor Martyn from warning that it could happen here. Indeed, he argues, 'our multicultural society provides a potential recruiting ground for supporters of various militant causes'. Thus we loop back, again, to the racialization of dissent, the fear of the Other who comes from outside yet resides among us, waiting to strike should we, for only the briefest of moments, be so foolish as to let down our guard and start to enjoy our brief time on this earth.

## The Anarchist Other—Yesterday

While these representations arise from current events, they rely upon constructs that have been around for at least a century. It has long been standard practice, for example, that anytime anything blows up, the authorities go looking for some anarchists to blame. This was the case with the Haymarket

---

2. Martyn, Robert (2004) *The Views Of Canadian Scholars On The Impact Of The Anti-Terrorism Act. Appendix A.* Available at http://www.justice.gc.ca/eng/pi/rs/rep-rap/2005/rro5_1/a_04.html. Last accessed 15 January, 2009.

Massacre, as already mentioned, in which a peaceful strike meeting was broken up by a violent police attack. The judge who convicted six people, four of whom were hanged, simply didn't care that what he did, what the police did, what the executioner did, was entirely illegal and would never have happened to anyone else (except of course to indigenous people, but that's another, related, story).

A similar response was elicited in 1901when an obscure young fellow whom no one had ever heard of, including all of the prominent anarchist activists of the day, decided to kill President McKinley. Emma Goldman was arrested for this one, but she had only met the killer, Leon Csolgosz, once, and brushed him off because she found him more than a little unstable. She was released due to lack of evidence.[3] Despite various modes of torture used in his interrogation, to the end Csolgosz maintained that he had acted alone. This didn't stop good American citizens from going on violent rampages against anyone they thought might be an anarchist, while police turned a blind eye. Law is vengeance; vengeance is law.

DRAW AND STRIKE
—*Chicago Inter-Ocean*

TIME TO STOP ACTING AS A SEWER F
FOR THE WORLD—*St. Paul Globe*

**Figure 5:** *Public Opinion* Vol. xxxi, No. 12, Thursday Sept. 19, 1901, p. 359

In the cartoons above we can see that the racialization of anarchist others is also a long-standing trope. In the right-hand pane, the sword of 'military law' is cutting down a Bakunin-headed serpent, while on the left Uncle Sam displays his chagrin with the pollution of the American population by southern and eastern European immigrants who practice 'anarchy, nihilism, and

---

3. Goldman, Emma (1970). *Living My Life* New York: Courier Dover Publications, pp. 315-317.

mafia'. Indeed, it was commonly believed, as the New York Times stated in an editorial in 1893, that 'there are no native American anarchists.'[4]

Obviously, some people who identify as anarchists have carried out destruction of property in the territories claimed by the Canadian and US states, and some have killed, or attempted to kill, major capitalist and government figures. But so have many people who do *not* identify as anarchists, such as anti-abortion activists. For some reason, while all anarchists are thought to be violent, irrational monsters, the same assumptions are not applied to Christians. Why might this be the case? Perhaps it is because, while Christians also do a large number of 'nice' things a lot of the time, anarchists do not?

I have to admit that, if it were the case that anarchists just hid out most of the time, only occasionally popping up to destroy someone or something, I would not identify with the tradition at all. The reason I do call myself an anarchist, in fact, is precisely because this is a ridiculous caricature of a broad, deep, and long-lived tradition, whose focus has in fact been quite different. As pointed out by theorist-activist Gustav Landauer, a significant portion of anarchists have always held that a radical transformation of state-capitalist societies cannot be achieved by either instantaneous revolution or slow reform. Rather, they have acted on the assumption that that new institutions will have to be created *alongside* the currently dominant society. 'Let us destroy,' Landauer suggested, 'mainly by means of the gentle, permanent, and binding reality that we build.'[5]

## The Other Anarchists—Then and Now

These 'other anarchists' can and should be considered alongside the 'anarchist other,' to give a different perspective on the relation between anarchism and terror. They can help us, perhaps, to understand precisely what it is that mainstream citizens, and their rulers and exploiters, are so afraid of. Why *does* anarchism strike such terror into their hearts?

Although most people think first of the assassination of McKinley and the glory years of Goldman and Berkman in the early 1900s, the history of anarchism in North America actually began in the 1820s. This was the beginning of a major and very important phase of Utopian community-building that lasted for about 30 years. Many of these communities were religiously oriented - Quakers, Shakers, Hutterites, and so on. But many were explicitly guided by the ideas of anarchist writers such as Charles Fourier, Francisco Ferrer, and Robert Owen. There were forty 'phalanxes', attempting to implement Fourier's design for an ideal rural community, spread out from New Jersey to the Midwest, including the famous Brook Farm. Robert Owen

---

4. Jensen, Richard B. (2001) 'The United States, International Policing, and the War against Anarchist Terrorism 1900–1914' in *Terrorism and Political Violence*, Vol. 13, No. 1 (Spring 2001), p. 17.
5. Gustav Landauer, *For Socialism*, St. Louis: Telos Press, 1978, p. 83.

helped to found New Harmony, and there were several other Owenite communities.[6] The modern school movement gave rise to dozens of urban and rural schools and communities, oriented to providing alternatives to coercive state education. Some lasted only a few years, other several decades.[7] Other communities were started by US anarchists, such as Josiah Warren. All of these experiments shared a commitment to creating sustainable alternatives to the dominant order, using peaceful and constructive means. A vastly greater amount of energy was put into them than was ever devoted to propaganda by the deed.

Although the early 1800s did represent a golden age for this kind of activity, it has not stopped by any means. In the 60s, as is commonly known, there were many anarchist and anarchistic communities, which cut across lines of race and class, occurred in both urban and rural settings, and influenced the ideas and practices of an entire generation. Oz, Morningstar Ranch, the Hog Farm, Tolstoy Farm, are just a few of the better-known of these thousands of experiments.

Today, anarchist intentional communities are self-consciously engaging with the history of construction of alternatives in North America, taking into account the successes and failures of the past. They understand the need for organization, commitment, care in admitting members, and maintaining good relations with neighbours. They are both rural and urban, and include communities that cross over with other traditions. Examples include: Dragonfly, near Kitchener ON, 25 years old and still going; AKA Autonomous Social Centre, in Kingston Ontario; Jesus Anarchists, started in US, with sites in UK, Australia, Kenya; Struggle Mountain, started in 1976, Palo Alto Hills; Collective A Go-Go, Worcester Mass.[8] There are also many urban social centres scattered throughout the continent. And of course anarchists are often involved in Food Not Bombs, Independent Media Centres, and other related tactics.[9]

Given that anarchists have been devoting their energy to this kind of activity for almost 200 years, one must ask why they are known for mindless destruction, rather than for loving creation? I think it is important, here, to remember that the dominant order is itself founded on violence; as conservative sociologist Max Weber pointed out long ago, the state is that entity which claims a legitimate monopoly on the use of force in a given territory.

---

6. See Halloway, Mark. *Heavens on Earth: Utopian Communities in America, 1680–1880.* New York: Dover, 1961.
7. See Paul Avrich, 2005. *The Modern School Movement: Anarchism And Education In The United States.* Edinburgh: AK Press.
8. For further discussion of these examples, and much more on this topic, see www.affinityproject.org.
9. See Richard J.F. Day (2005) *Gramsci Is Dead: Anarchist Currents in the Newest Social Movements* London: Pluto Press.

And capitalism is obviously founded on the violence of exploitation and alienation, of classes, races, genders, sexes, abilities, ages and regions, and of nature by all human beings. So that it does not appear deficient, this order must propagate the idea that those who oppose it, and especially those who create alternatives to it, must also share this dirty secret. 'They' must be no better than 'us'; no more free than us; no less exploited or alienated. It must inculcate in good citizens a fear of living differently; what we might call a *terror* of freedom and empowerment. This terror must be visceral, intuitive, unthinking, and deep. The mass media are of course very good at creating this sort of affect, and once it gets going, it's very hard to shift, or even to detect as such. What right-thinking person would even go near an anarchist, never mind become one? The distance creates distance, in a positive feedback loop.

I want to suggest that this relationship between the good citizen and the anarchist other is 'imaginary' in the Lacanian sense, that is, it constitutes a duality that deeply structures how subjects relate to each other. It is also a fantasy, again in the Lacanian sense, in that this dualistic, imaginary relationship is necessary, productive, and functional. It helps to keep the system going by clearly defining what 'we' are and what 'we' are not. Certainly, this phantasmatic structuring of mainstream western societies is not likely to change anytime soon. So, if we are going to make any headway, it is up to anarchists to traverse the fantasy of terror, by overcoming our own fantasy of being radically other than the dominant. This does not mean to become dominant, nor even to become like the dominant, but rather to break the mirror that separates the dominant from the alternative.

We need to go out and meet people, talk to them in their own languages, about the things they care about. Say, for example, terror ... in the academy ... as I have tried to do here, in this chapter.

# ENDORSEMENTS FOR *ENGAGING TERROR*

"This collection is a timely and original interdisciplinary approach that examines the links between the current problem of international terrorism and the forms of terror too often ignored in the twin tasks of nation-building and international relations."

—Abdelkérim Ousman
Associate Professor of International Relations,
War Studies and Comparative Politics
Royal Military College of Canada

"The Human Condition Series' conference on terror was an exciting and very useful antidote to the ideological war on terror being waged around us. The proceedings of this conference collected here provide very useful methods of disrupting and resisting the ways that the war on terror is being used against people fighting for liberation here and around the world."

—Gary Kinsman
Associate Professor of Sociology at Laurentian University
Editor of *Whose National Security?* and *Sociology for Changing the World*,
Co-author of *Canadian War on Queers: National Security as Sexual Regulation*

"The analyses in this volume are outstanding. Recent analyses of terrorism have become 'routine' in that they are ritual condemnations of violence and calls for enhanced security measures. By exploring political violence and its consequences from a wide variety of perspectives, this excellent volume avoids easy answers and prescription. The collection covers a range of subjects that includes media, technology, outlaws, postcolonialsm, language and discourse, health, history and the narratives of security. The volume will stimulate reflection on what has become a central, if widely misunderstood, trope in the contemporary global scene."

—Michael Dartnell
Author of *Action Directe: Ultra-left Terrorism in France, 1979-1987* and
*Insurgency Online: Web Activism and Global Conflict*,
Member of Laurentian University's Political Science Department